THE 24 SOLAR TERMS

Mythology, Folkways, and Poetry
of the Chinese Nature Almanac

James W. Murphy

CAVERN
BIRD
PRESS

Paperback ISBN: 978-1-963613-10-0
E-book ISBN: 978-1-963613-06-3

Illustrations and book cover design by James W. Murphy

First paperback edition 2025 published by Cavern Bird Press
An imprint of Cavern Bird LLC
Portland, Oregon
www.cavernbird.com

Dedicated

to my mother

for giving me life,

and

to my wife

for sustaining it.

Table of Contents

Preface

For a book about changes in the natural world and the traditions of an ancient culture, it is strange that I first thought of writing it in a busy back-alley of a modern city bursting with five million people.

It happened while my wife and I were walking back to a horticultural therapy class we were taking in the crumbling remains of a now-shuttered vocational campus in the east of Taipei. The course -- eight hours a day, five days a week for two months -- covered a lot of ground. At one point in a presentation on agricultural cycles, buried in a slide deck of punishing density, flashed a perfunctory mention of the 24 solar terms of the ancient Chinese calendar.

I was intrigued. I had heard of the 24 solar terms, and saw them appear occasionally in our farmer's almanac, which my wife frequently consulted to see if it is a good day to get a haircut, visit the doctor, or sign a contract. But there was little information about the solar terms other than brief mentions of seasonal produce.

After class I went searching for English language books on the subject, but came up empty-handed. Or at least nothing with the detail I wanted. I was, however, able to get some Chinese books from the library.

Yet even those were not easy to locate. The 24 solar terms as a publishing genre has been cornered by the Chinese wellness industry. Most of the books cover seasonally-inspired ways of eating and exercising, but talk little of the actual lore of the terms, or the seasonal observances, or the rich mythology that lay behind these times of the year.

After some searching I was eventually able to locate some decent books on the subject in Chinese, and slowly made my way through them. Each chapter sent me off in new directions of research, trying to learn about the many stories or personages or deities mentioned in passing by the authors. Many of the references alluded to a body of common knowledge to which I did not have access having not grown up in the culture.

With one of the books in my hand, my wife and I were walking back to the aforementioned horticultural therapy class one day after lunch, dodging scooters and the occasional delivery truck in the narrow alley. I mentioned my difficulty to her: how each chapter, sometimes each paragraph, opened new avenues of inquiry that were exhausting to track down. I mentioned it would be convenient to have a book in English that explained the significance of each terms as well as some of the related historical and cultural aspects.

She responded that if there wasn't a book in English, maybe I could translate one. The idea rolled around in my head briefly before I rejected it. Existing works couldn't really be translated directly. There is too much inside cultural knowledge required by the reader. Either the translation would make no sense or would require a comical level of footnotes and parenthetical asides.

I explained all this to my wife, who then suggested that I just write a new one in English. I had my doubts. I wondered if a book in English for a Western audience on a seasonal calendar so culturally and geographically specific made any sense.

But then I considered there might be people like me out there, who would like to learn more about another culture and another calendar. And the 24 solar terms, as much as they are spokes in the wheel of year of natural changes and seasonal practices, are far more than just a way of experiencing a year. This solar calendar's dance with lunar calendar traditions radiate out into myriad aspects of Chinese cultures and other cultures such as Japan, Korea, and Vietnam. So much so that this ancient calendrical system is a good jumping off point from which to discuss many disparate aspects of the culture and can provide an overview of a rich tapestry of folklore, foodways, rituals, deities, poetry and proverbs.

The above line of thinking coalesced into three main reasons to write this book. The first reason was to fill the aforementioned gap of books covering the solar terms. The second was more personal: to rediscover the ancient culture which triggered my initial interest in studying the language so many years ago. The third reason was more universal in scope: to examine these traditions in order to see how they might enhance modern life.

As for the first reason, I had hoped to help others like me: readers who had an interest in the solar terms would finally have a comprehensive book to reference. The solar terms are also an ideal way to introduce many disparate aspects of Chinese culture to a general readership, since the calendar provides a natural structure for exploration. For those who already have a more intimate understanding of the culture, there should be plenty of new knowledge. Despite my over thirty years studying the Chinese language and living in the culture, there was much information that was totally new to me.

This brings me to my second reason, which is to look at the culture with a fresh pair of eyes. Having spent most of my life in either Taipei or Beijing, and being a voracious consumer of news in both languages, it becomes easy to perceive the culture through a very modern lens. And for others with a long relationship with China, whether involved with China through education, employment, business, family, or other interests, or even through a curiosity about China's ancient culture, modern notions tend to color perceptions of China's past. These perceptions run the gamut: from progressivist narratives about China's moving from weakness of the past to strength in the present to arguments over the benefits of certain political systems over others. As exciting as these discussions are, I was interested in looking beyond modern political struggle, and more closely at the innate beauty of a traditional folk culture apart from modern distractions. At the same time my hope was that by side-stepping sensational news cycles I could shine a light on unique cultural gifts that hold value for the world.

The third reason for writing this book is that these older traditions provide an instructive contrast to the common habits of modern life, and suggest ways in which to enhance our relationship with the world around us. A journey through the lore and practices of the 24 solar terms reveals a deep engagement with the natural world. Ancient manuscripts advise a careful balance between activities of society and the landscape. Centuries of poets and painters pause by rivers and mountain passes to pay tribute to their beauty. The 72 pentads, which split the year into 72 sets of five days, and the 24 solar terms themselves point to natural phenomena emblematic of a world bubbling with constant change that demands our attention. Then there is the colorful and busy schedule of festivals of ancient China, a number of which carry on into today.

By comparison, both in the West and to some extent most of urbanized East, the annual calendar we have inherited in our industrialized societies seems rather drab. The year is punctuated with a few state holidays and other observances that perhaps once had meaning but have now been transmogrified into commercial extravaganzas. Celebrations might take on the character of the season, like Halloween with its pumpkins or Christmas with its chemically snow-flocked trees, but they are more celebrations *during* the season than celebrations *of* the season.

My hope with this book is that these ancient ways of engaging with the world might inspire the reader's own thoughts about how to meaningfully pass the year and interact with their local landscape. The 24 solar terms imply a close awareness of the changes of nature, and while some aspects introduced are culturally specific and perhaps not always applicable to other cultures, they do provide an example of passing the year in a way that raises one's awareness on many levels.

One level is a regular, high frequency attention to the earth's path as it spins around the sun, and how that reflects our own journey during the year and in life. A second level is comprised of the changes of the earth itself as expressed in the natural world around us, drawing our focus beyond ourselves and our frustrations and anxieties. And a third level is the great scope of richness that is possible in seasonal celebrations, some of which can be inspired by one's own local cultures and ecologies and fashioned anew.

* * *

The writing of this book turned out to be a bigger project than I had expected. What I thought would be a year or so of focused effort turned into many years and required a lot of help. I would to thank my wife, Monica, who has been incredibly supportive in this multi-year project, and who was eager to spend a huge amount of her time reviewing my work, catching my errors, and verifying my sources. Despite her efforts, it is likely other errors winnowed their way into the text over the subsequent revisions, so any errors found are my own. Thanks also to Mom for her encouragement and interest throughout the writing process.

24 Solar Terms

Mythology, Folkways, and Poetry
of the Chinese Nature Almanac

THE 24 SOLAR TERMS

INTRODUCTION

Target Readership

The 24 solar terms contain themes far beyond their status as a rich cultural asset, and there are many avenues from which to explore this unique calendar. In consideration of the many possible topics raised by this calendar system, this book is written with three types of readers in mind.

The first type of reader is one with a general interest in Chinese culture. This would include those who wish to enhance their cultural literacy, improve their language skills, and gain a deeper understanding of Chinese history, philosophy, and literature. The 24 solar terms, like the annual wheel it comprises, spins into nearly every aspect of culture. It provides an ideal framework for students of Chinese topics, non-Chinese residents in Chinese-speaking countries, or anybody with a connection to China through family or friends.

A second group are people curious about mythology and folklore, and who wish to explore the rich motifs of Chinese folktales, both unique and shared with other mythological traditions. By studying these tales a deep connection emerges, uniting humanity regardless of time or geography. These motifs point the way to surprising synchronistic patterns as well as profound cosmic mysteries.

A third group are those inspired by the natural world and its cycles; those who desire to strengthen that connection with ideas for holiday observance, ritual, or direct experience with the natural world. As modern lifestyles encroach on our time with nature, our time with family, and even time with our own thoughts, the 24 solar terms provide a viable example for reconnecting with one's own home cultural traditions, or creating new possibilities.

Structure of the Book

This book does not necessarily need to be read from cover to cover. If the reader is interested in a certain time of year, they should feel free to just jump to its related solar term. That said, this book generally builds on concepts introduced earlier on, and are not re-explained to avoid repetition. However, in these cases the previous explanation is noted to so that the reader can refer back to it.

If the reader is completely unfamiliar with the 24 solar terms, then "The Basics of the 24 Solar Terms" in the next chapter is a helpful starting point. Following an introduction to the basics is a more in-depth discussion about the broader implications of the 24 solar terms in regards to our own lives. The rhythms and philosophical underpinnings offered by the 24 solar terms are grander than its status as a simple grid over the course of the year, so some time is spent examining those possibilities.

The book then moves into each of the 24 solar terms proper, starting with Spring Begins. Each chapter covers an aspect of the solar terms, which includes weather, the pentads, agriculture, health, ancient traditions, customs both old and modern, festivals, and folklore. A poem related to the solar term kicks off each chapter, and other aspects of literature and art are sprinkled throughout. The approach to these sections is described in more detail below.

WEATHER

As noted previously, whether systems vary greatly across China, so that each solar term carries different meaning from place to place. In light of this, discussion of the weather is brief, simply to give a sense of the general character of the term.

PENTADS

There are 72 pentads throughout the solar year, so named because each pentad represents a five-day period. Each section will discuss the three pentads of each term and their broader nature symbolism in Chinese culture.

AGRICULTURE

The 24 solar terms are dripping with agricultural symbolism, necessitating some discussion of the farming activities from which the names of the 24 solar terms were born. However, understanding most of the world -- and even most of China -- have vastly divergent agricultural cycles, these sections are brief and intended to give a sense of flavor. The weather on the first day of the term was thought to portend the success of crop and livestock yields. These are summarized in Appendix C: Weather Portents.

HEALTH

Like the yin-yang and five phases that interweave the terms and the pentads, there is a rich history of traditional medicine related to the seasons. In more modern times, a whole genre has surfaced in the Chinese publishing world covering health practices in alignment with the 24 solar terms or 72 pentads, covering everything from fitness to foodways. Given the breadth of the topic it would not be possible to do it justice in this volume, but the general health issues brought about by each of the terms are discussed briefly as they are a part of solar term lore. These sections are not intended as medical advice, and any health practices are best pursued after consultation with a certified health practitioner. The advice given would seem natural to someone born in a Chinese community, but could be perplexing to a Western audience unfamiliar with the tradition. The author makes no claims regarding the efficacy of the advice, and it has been included to understand common practice.

ANCIENT TRADITIONS

The *Yueling* (月令) section of the *Book of Rites* (禮記) details many ancient imperial rituals that followed the change of seasons. These are listed by certain months which correspond to the solar terms. Translating them literally and in their original sequence can be confusing, so they are rearranged thematically and their symbolism explained. These themes cover the seasonal rituals performed by the emperor and his court, followed by orders cascaded down to govern humanity's interaction with the natural world and with each other. This is always concluded with warnings about not performing the wrong ritual during the wrong season, and all the bad things that happen if that is done. This sections adds additional background in order to make sense of what exactly is happening with these practices.

First is understanding the role of the emperor. As much as modern Chinese dramas depict past emperors as living lives of great leisure -- when they aren't killing imagined rivals or the occasional eunuch for sport -- the *Book of Rites* depicts a different expectation. While the existence of hedonistic, paranoid emperors are a historical fact, the *Book of Rites* presents an ideal, where the emperor is more of a supreme priest or even a magician. "Son of Heaven" was not just a fancy title, but believed to be an accurate descriptor of the Emperor's divine power. No doubt the title was politically advantageous, but during certain dynasties this status demanded more of the person in the emperor's seat than managing palace intrigue or waging military campaigns. His personal engagement in ritual was believed to have a direct effect on the fate of his empire and his subjects. With the movement of the seasons standing as the most clear example of the powers of Heaven and Earth, the palace put on grand rituals where every detail was in sync with the time of year: the colors worn, the direction of procession, the sacrifices given, and the activities and prohibitions. Performing them incorrectly or enacting the wrong seasonal ritual during the wrong season invited natural calamity.

To the modern observer this appears like the pinnacle of fearful superstition or simply just some form of innate religious impulse. But the point of the *Yueling* section of the *Book of Rites* is much deeper, providing an analogy that behavior must be aligned with the larger processes of nature. The sequence of rituals demonstrate a keen sensitivity toward the movement of the year with their correspondences, but also show a tremendous respect for the natural world, treating it as an entity deserving of reverence and reserve. The *Yueling* encourages the seasonal practice of certain agricultural forms at certain times of year -- often with the emperor and key officials doing some of the work themselves -- and strict prohibitions at other times, such as decrees against tree cutting or animal hunting, acknowledging that nature is not some grand store to be mercilessly plundered, but a limited resource requiring occasional rest and careful stewardship. These ancient rights will be covered in their corresponding solar term, giving a sense of the character of the term from an ancient point of view, while also revealing an ancient wisdom when it comes to humanity's interaction with the world

CUSTOMS

While the emperor had his concerns and practices around the solar terms, the wider populace had theirs. One could say that in modern Chinese society, the 24 solar terms play a much more diminished role. Sure, the 24 solar terms decorate the wallpaper of modern Chinese culture, but are not necessarily a constant presence. Most study the terms sometime in grade school, but the terms are generally are not dwelled upon aside from occasional mentions during the weather forecast.

Perhaps the arrival a solar term will be noticed by those with an interest in the older ways, as they thumb through a modern Chinese almanac to determine if it is an auspicious day to move the bed or for newborns to get their first haircut. Most likely, as they scan over the crowded almanac page, the current term will be briefly noted and then rapidly forgotten. Occasionally someone might post a reminder of the term in their social media feed, along with a pretty picture, which is then quickly clicked away along with all the other random social detritus occupying their screens.

The customs described in these sections are mainly older observances, many of which have fallen out of practice or have been eclipsed by the larger lunar-based festivals described in the next section. Those practices that are still around are perhaps more vestigial, and are mainly concerned with foodways or other small observances. Some regions and cultures, however, have retained them, or have spun off their own variation. These are described where they are still practiced, and in cases where they have not been absorbed by other festivals.

FESTIVALS

No discussion of the Chinese calendar would be complete without a discussion of its many festivals. Some of these are related to the solar terms, and over time have been assigned to days of the lunar calendar. Others are associated more directly to the lunar calendar, but have a long-standing connection to the time of year bracketed by the solar terms. Most of all, these festivals are born out of colorful tales from Chinese mythology, which links the broader culture back to the turn of the seasons and humanity's place in the cosmos.

MYTHOLOGY AND FOLKTALES

Like all mythologies there are many competing versions, and the tales presented here are not meant to be a full compendium of all tales, but will cover the most commonly-known along with a few alternatives where available.

China's myths are a great cultural asset and deserve preservation and transmission, but for those who are not ethnically Chinese or who do not have any particular interest in myths, their inclusion might provoke a "so what" quality. Those thinking along these lines might claim myths are at best an odd cultural curiosity or at worst the fantastic imaginings from the muddied pools of ignorance and superstition -- the only pitiable method our naive forebears possessed to fashion some vague understanding of the universe.

The antidote to this sort of thinking is to realize that myth is not just a practice of the past. We are surrounded by myth. As Sallust put in the 4th century CE, and later paraphrased by Joseph Campbell, myths are: "things which never happened, but always are."[1]

This is the true dynamism of myth. As poet Marwenna Donnelly has said in response to W.B. Yeats' use of Irish mythology, "myth is unsatisfactory when it is used recollectively, the sole emphasis on its aesthetic content. Unless one can interpret the meaning behind myth, it merely becomes a historical curiosity -- an outworn vehicle of expression."[2] This is where myth holds more power than simple stories passed down through the ages.

The myths presented in this book have tremendous cultural value, but they are certainly more than that. As much as they have to say about one of the world's great cultures, they have even more to say about humanity and about our individual selves. Particularly in cases of seasonal myth: the stories that have been with us from every culture's earliest beginnings. As poet Ross Nichols put it, "myth appears as the essential shape of the cosmos of man, both externally in the turning year and interiorly as the process whereby he assimilates the particular events of his life in his own pattern."[3] Myths and folktales, especially when they are connected to seasonal events, reflect not only the world around us, but our interaction with it, as well as the trajectory of humanity's future.

CHINESE DYNASTIES

Historical information is referenced to its appropriate dynasty rather than a range of years. Years for each dynasty can be found in Appendix D: Chinese Dynasties, and the "Dynasties" section of the index at the back of the book contains page numbers where each dynasty is touched upon.

POETRY

The solar terms, just like the four seasons in the West, have been fertile ground for the inspiration of other projects, both old and new. One of the richest of all these projects is the tradition of poetry from China's most loved poets. Wang Wei, Li Bai, Du Fu, and many others had their ink brushes all over the 24 solar terms. A selection of these poems are included in their appropriate section. All have been translated by the author unless otherwise indicated.

Translation of Chinese poetry presents many challenges. Classical Chinese is a ferociously economic language, using few words, and often contain multiple intended meanings with each word. Poems are typically arranged with exacting meter and rhyme that is difficult to replicate in any other language.

This gives the translator a choice. One is translating only meaning, and omitting the parallelism and rhyme. This often results in a finger-snapping, daddy-o, beatnik-style free-verse. The other choice is to create a poem matching the rhythms of the original. The result is often doggerel: maddeningly repetitive, faucet-drip rhyme schemes that drown out meaning. Or twisted Yoda-like grammar and nonsensical word choice imposed by the need to maintain the rhyme.

Some poetic savants may have the ability to strike a happy balance between the two extremes, but this author is not one of them. The former option using free verse -- whatever its stylistic issues -- is often the better choice, allowing the translator to focus on accuracy of meaning, so that is the option chosen for poems in this book.

ARTWORK

Placed at the head of each chapter are paper cuttings by the author depicting seasonal changes in the landscape and the plants and animals symbolizing the 72 pentads. Also sprinkled throughout the text are re-creations of classic paintings in a papercut medium, using $15cm^2$ origami paper

China is known to be home to the longest-living tradition of papercutting art in the world, with the oldest surviving piece dating the Six Dynasties period[4]. It continues to be a lively art form, helped not only by a long-standing tradition but also its approachability and low cost. Often passed from parents to children, it is an art form practiced at all ages for different purposes, whether for interior decor, seasonal festivals, life ceremonies, spiritual talismans, or just for the joy of it. The papercuttings in this book have been done by the author, and although it is difficult to approach the technique and artistry of the output of this rich tradition, they are included to add flavor and as a homage to his popular folk art.

* * *

Following the chapters describing each solar term, the book concludes with summaries which attempt to encapsulate the key lessons of each term, particularly drawing from folklore, festivals and customs. The book ends with final notes about what the 24 solar terms have to say about living in the modern world, regardless of nationality or ethnicity.

Thorny Issues

With the endless stream of news and social media the fault lines of political, social, and cultural disagreement seem to have invaded every aspect of life. One would think this book about an ancient calendar tracking seasonal change in the natural world could steer clear of these disagreements, but that sentiment would likely inspire the most post-modern of sneers among those whose business it is to concern themselves with such exciting dramas and conflicts. And so there is some necessity in dealing with an ancient culture to briefly acknowledge the different conceptions of race, gender, and other general attitudes.

CHINESE DIVERSITY

China, like many countries in the world, is a multi-ethnic nation, but like many other countries, the dominant ethnicity comes to represent the nation. For example, ask any Chinese person what an American looks like and they will describe a white Anglo-Saxon Protestant, even though the composition of America is much more varied. Similarly, when the West thinks of Chinese people they picture the Han majority, and not the several dozen ethnicities that make up what the world calls "China". This is exacerbated by Han Chinese Nationalism, which is often used to glorify the uniqueness and supremacy of the Han, typically to the exclusion of other ethnic groups. Even Mao Zedong would later draw attention to the problem, coining the term "Han chauvinism." [5]

At the heart of this issue is the confusion between national identity and ethnicity. Although common knowledge in the Sinosphere, what is "Chinese" is not as monolithic as is typically understood outside the culture. This is in part the usual culprit: simple unfamiliarity, just as most people in the world have no idea of the ethnic makeup of most countries in the world. The confusion between national identity and ethnicity is further driven by other factors such as cultural pride and state propaganda. But these factors often sadly ignore the many ways other ethnicities have contributed to what is now known broadly as "China." Many of the 24 solar terms, although recorded and passed on among the Han majority, also contain influences from other minority cultures, particularly many of the festivals. It is important to acknowledge that the history and cultural traditions of China are much more colorful and complicated than what is often understood or presented. The influence of minority cultures will be noted where it occurs.

Similarly, the Han ethnicity -- or at least those who identify as Han itself -- encompasses a number of varied languages and cultural practices. There will be occasions where in one location, rain on the first day of a solar term is a bad omen, and others where it portends abundance. These differences will be discussed as they come up through the solar terms.

It is also important to note that the solar terms have been part of the culture of nearby countries for centuries, and the Japanese, Koreans, and Vietnamese all have claim to their own versions of this cultural asset. The names in those solar terms in their languages have also been included at the top of each chapter to emphasize this point: the 24 solar terms have wide applicability. An example of Japanese pentads are included in Appendix A: Chinese and Japanese Pentads.

CHINESE WRITING

For the benefit of those who are literate in Chinese this book includes liberal amounts of Chinese text to avoid ambiguity. One of the major frustrations when doing research for this book was coming across romanized Chinese words in an English source with no reference to the original characters. This required hours of reading through pages of Chinese source texts, using context to try to identify the original word. While including the original language has little utility for a non-Chinese speaker, in-text translations efficiently clarify the ideas and concepts for those who have access to the language.

For reasons of space, one system of writing was chosen -- Traditional Chinese -- namely because the concepts in this book are taken from ancient texts which used this system.

MODERN TENSIONS

As this book is being written, sentiment between China and much of the Western world is at its lowest ebb in decades. It would be exhausting to hash out the many disagreements, and as much as they merit discussion, the project of this book is to describe a rich array of cultural assets worthy of understanding by other cultures. The world's current disagreements should not result in some sort of retroactive anger that gets in the way of appreciating another country's ancient history, folklore, and literature.

Similarly, there are many practices in China's past that are unpalatable to those who view them through the modern lens of gender equality. There is a time and a place to assess older ways with a chronocentric view, but that is beyond the scope of this book.

Finally, as much as this project derives from an admiration and respect of the practices of an ancient culture, it is not intended to inordinately glorify it or presume any sort of cultural supremacy over other cultures or practices. Nor is this book an attempt to exotify a culture, or bask in some sort of Victorian, monocle-popping orientalism.

THE AUTHOR'S BACKGROUND

This previous point brings up one last issue to cover before moving on. This author was not born in a Chinese culture and does not presume to be speak for all Chinese people with this book, or to act as the final word on Chinese culture or this topic. It is an effort to understand and distill a complex subject based on a mixture of both English and original Chinese-language sources, combined with over two decades living and working in the region as a teacher, translator, publisher, executive, and as a spouse of someone native to the culture.

In ideal circumstances, I could translate an existing Chinese book, allowing a English-speaking audiences to come as close as possible to hearing a native Chinese voice. In fact, books on the 24 solar terms comprise their own lively genre of the Chinese-language publishing industry, so there are books that could be translated. Yet direct translation is difficult due to assumed cultural context woven throughout the original writing. For anybody who has not grown up in China, much of the underlying significance of certain themes would be totally opaque.

The next best option I saw was to use my past experience as a student of Chinese language and literature, as well as my experience a translator, and compile a book stretching across many different sources and ideas. But it was important that these ideas were not just squeezed out from the vacuum of my own head, and so the help of people native to the culture was sought to improve the accuracy of the book.

One of the fears of writing this type of book, particularly one which at times tries to interpret cultural myth, is getting overly fanciful with the interpretations, or even getting it totally wrong. With any interpretations of myth and folklore I have worked to augment them with explorations of other possibilities, rather than distort the original. But no doubt, some of my own biases will shine through. Of course, some might say that book without biases is not worth writing.

SOURCES

While there is a mountain of scholarship on many aspects of Chinese culture, there is not much on the solar terms themselves. For that I turned to Chinese language books, which in turn referred me to primary ancient sources. These ancient sources have been cited using the resources at ctext.org. Although ctext.org is not intended as a platform for formal reference, I have included their line numbers to make it easier for any readers to check the original text.

Where possible, I have cited English-language works, but given the lack of translated information, Chinese sources comprise the bulk. As can happen with many aspects of folk-practices and belief, they are not necessarily recorded in published books or journals, but fortunately this is where the Internet excels in preserving and disseminating cultural minutiae.

But that creates is own set of problems. There were many times where citations had to be pulled from ad-riddled content farms. Still, they present information I knew to be true from other sources and experience, and so they had to used. In as sense, whatever these sources lack in terms of academic formality, they make up for with a certain realness of a living and active culture.

* * *

With those thorny and potentially controversial issues out of the way, I would like to reiterate my hope that this book is of help to the reader in gaining an understanding of a rarely-translated aspects of Chinese culture. I also hope that this rich tradition can help us examine how we can live in the world today, and inspire us to think of new ways to best meet our future.

But before we can get to that, it is necessary to first explain the basics of the 24 solar terms.

OVERVIEW:
AN ANCIENT AND LIVING ALMANAC

"Look up to witness the stars,
stoop down to observe the earth,
and know the causes of the hidden and the visible."

The I Ching (易經), The Great Treatise I, Chapter 4

仰以觀於天文，俯以察於地理，是故知幽明之故。- 周易, 系辞上

Why the 24 Solar Terms?

Like most of the world's ancient cultures, early Chinese looked up and observed the movements of the sun, moon, and stars. They also looked to the earth, and noted the changes of nature, and its repeating rhythms as the heavenly bodies danced across the heavens above. As the sun rose in the east and set in the west, time split into day and night. And the moon, changing as it did from full and bright, to crescent, to obscured, and back again, gave rise to months. The revolutions of the sun and moon birthed times of cold and warmth throughout a year, dotted with the exciting forces of thunder and lightning, and the fertilizing influences of wind and rain.

And like other early cultures, the ancient Chinese worked to produce calendars to track the various movements of the heavens and the passage of time. From the earliest times in Chinese recorded history, during the Shang dynasty, people observed the four most pivotal quarters of the solar year: the Spring Equinox, the Summer Solstice, the Autumnal Equinox, and the Winter Solstice. By the time of the Warring States period, the 24 solar terms were established[1]. Sage kings and scholars devised many different calendrical systems over the centuries, but one of the most enduring is the 24 solar terms.

This calendar is a permanent fixture in modern Chinese almanacs and common cultural knowledge, not just within Chinese communities but also throughout Asia in countries like Japan, Korea, and Viet Nam.[2] Yet the 24 solar terms are relatively unknown in the West. Most Westerners know of China's lunar calendar, or at least the some of the zodiac animals of the 12-year cycle: the monkey, the tiger, the dragon, and so forth. But despite its cultural richness and some degree of applicability to other climates in the northern hemisphere, the 24 solar terms never made the same jump to the Western world as have so many other aspects of Chinese culture, such as Taoism, Zen (Chan) Buddhism, Feng Shui, and Traditional Medicine.

The 24 solar terms are akin to a farmer's almanac, although a very ancient one thousands of years old. The majority of China's festivals are linked to the lunar calendar, and generally lunations serve as the primary cycle around which regular rituals are practiced. But as an intensely agrarian society, China's farmers needed a solar calendar tied to earth's regular annual cycles.

Although the changing of the four basic seasons have been etched in the collective mind of humanity long before farming, the time between seasons is long, and the demarcation between them unclear. Often the season is only known when it has already arrived. For communities whose survival depended on farming, waiting for the climate to announce a change of season threatened either disastrously early or fatally late plantings and harvests. And a lunar calendar, with its changing cycles from year to year, requires burdensome calculations every year to map on to the seasons. (Though conversely, planting by phases of the moon are a key feature of Western almanacs.) Hence the 24 solar terms were devised to signal optimal times for agricultural activities, although they grew to encompass much more, including foodways, health practices, festivals, and China's rich folklore and mythology.

Definition of "Solar Term"

The phrase "solar term" is the usual translation of the Chinese word *jieqi*. The first word, *jie*, could be translated as "festival" or "holiday," but in the word in this case most likely derives from one of the other uses of the word, which is akin to "node," "joint," or "segment," or possibly "term,"[3] indicating a series of discrete periods linking one to another.

The word *qi* is the same one in common use in the Western world, more often spelled as "ch'i," meaning an unseen vital force, sometimes referred to as "ether," or otherwise in more mundane terms as "air" or "weather." [4] Thus another translation could be "Etheric Term," reflecting the word's use a descriptor not only for weather patterns and natural phenomena, but for larger, unseen forces governing the universe. This sense of mystery is a recurring theme that will emerge when exploring each of the terms.

The 24 solar terms divide the year into quadrants each comprising 15 degrees of the earth's orbit around the sun, or roughly fifteen days. On the Western Gregorian calendar, the terms typically start on a day between the 4th through the 8th of the month and between the 19th to the 23rd.

Those starting earlier in the month are called *jieqi* (節氣) -- the same Chinese word as "solar term," while those in the latter part of the month are called *zhongqi* (中氣) or "middle term."[5] *Jieqi* is in a sense the beginning, and *zhongqi* is the peak; otherwise, they describe the alternating character of terms throughout the year, from *jieqi* to *zhongqi* to *jieqi* again. The sequence starts with *jieqi* "Spring Begins," then the *zhongqi* Rain Water, then the *jieqi* Insects Awaken, and so on. However, somewhat confusingly all 24 are more generally referred to in Chinese as simply "*jieqi.*"

The full list of the solar terms and their approximate dates are on the next page. The actual date upon which the first day of the term falls can differ, by one day before or after. Online or published calendars need to be consulted every year because the determining the exact date requires astronomical software.

English Name	Chinese name	Approximate Start Date[6]	Sun's ecliptic longitude
Spring Begins	立春 lìchūn	Feb 3~4	315°
Rain Water	雨水 yǔshuǐ	Feb 18~19	330°
Insects Awaken	驚蟄(惊蛰) jīngzhé	Mar 5~6	345°
Spring Equinox	春分 chūnfēn	Mar 20~21	0°
Clear Bright	清明 qīngmíng	Apr 4~5	15°
Grain Rain	穀雨(谷雨) gǔyǔ	Apr 19~20	30°
Summer Begins	立夏 lìxià	May 5	45°
Little Fullness	小滿(小满) xiǎomǎn	May 20~21	60°
Grain in Ear	芒種(芒种) mángzhòng	Jun 5~6	75°
Summer Solstice	夏至 xiàzhì	Jun 20~21	90°
Little Heat	小暑 xiǎoshǔ	Jul 6~7	105°
Great Heat	大暑 dàshǔ	Jul 22~23	120°
Autumn Begins	立秋 lìqiū	Aug 7	135°
Heat Departs	處暑(处暑) chǔshǔ	Aug 22~23	150°
White Dew	白露 báilù	Sep 7~8	165°
Autumnal Equinox	秋分 qiūfēn	Sep 22~23	180°
Cold Dew	寒露 hánlù	Oct 7~8	195°
Frostfall	霜降 shuāngjiàng	Oct 22~23	210°
Winter Begins	立冬 lìdōng	Nov 8~9	225°
Light Snow	小雪 xiǎoxuě	Nov 21~22	240°
Heavy Snow	大雪 dàxuě	Dec 6~7	255°
Winter Solstice	冬至 dōngzhì	Dec 21~22	270°
Little Cold	小寒 xiǎohán	Jan 5~6	285°
Great Cold	大寒 dàhán	Jan 19~20	300°

The names of the different solar terms are derived from their connection to various natural phenomena. The 24 can be sorted into six major groupings[7]:

- Seasonal initiations: Spring Begins, Summer Begins, Autumn Begins, Winter Begins
- Astronomical events: Spring Equinox, Summer Solstice, Autumnal Equinox, Winter Solstice
- Phenological changes: Insects Awaken, Clear Bright, Little Fullness, Grain Ripens
- Precipitate types: Rain Water, Grain Rain, Little Snow, Heavy Snow
- Temperature extremes: Little Heat, Great Heat, Heat Departs, Little Cold, Great Cold
- Character of water vapor: White Dew, Cold Dew, Frostfall

The phenomena are mostly balanced among the groupings, with four to each one with the exception of the three for the water vapor which collects during the relatively short transition from autumn to winter, and the longer-lasting temperature extremes of winter and summer, which contain five.

Philosophical Foundations

Early on, before the tools available through modern science, the Chinese tried to answer the why and hows of the seasons. Whether we call it philosophy, religion, or metaphysics, ancient thinkers outlined very specific processes for how the seasons come into being, and the foundations of this thought are fundamental to understanding the 24 solar terms system. Moreover, ancient Chinese philosophy is a living tradition, permeating modern Chinese language and thought, and even inhabiting certain corners of the Western world. It is not possible to adequately cover the richness of Chinese philosophy in a few paragraphs, but a brief overview is necessary given the frequency which these themes emerge in the solar terms and their pentads.

YIN AND YANG

The most fundamental concept of cosmology is that of yin and yang. The universe was said to have formed out of a chaos of energy, and material existence[8] (and the not-so-material) exists in a constant state of flux between yin and yang. This material existence is often referred to as the "myriad things," one possible translation of the term *wanwu* (萬物).

The most common metaphors to explain the concept are plucked from nature, like a hill with a shady side (yin) and a side basking in the sun's rays (yang). Dark and light are the primary descriptors of yin and yang respectively, as are white-black, passive-active, negative-positive, female-male, contracting-expanding, earth-heaven, and night-day.

This notion of dualism inspires exhaustive treatises and meditations on ideas around the conflicting and complementary nature of the two, such as light not existing without dark -- one opposite defining the other. But for the purposes of the 24 solar terms, the turning of the year is set in motion by these forces and is a constant reflection of the advance of one and retreat of another. The Winter Solstice is the high peak of yin, after which yin begins to retreat and yang advances up until the Summer Solstice, then yang once again yields to yin. Balance is achieved at the Spring and Autumnal Equinoxes.

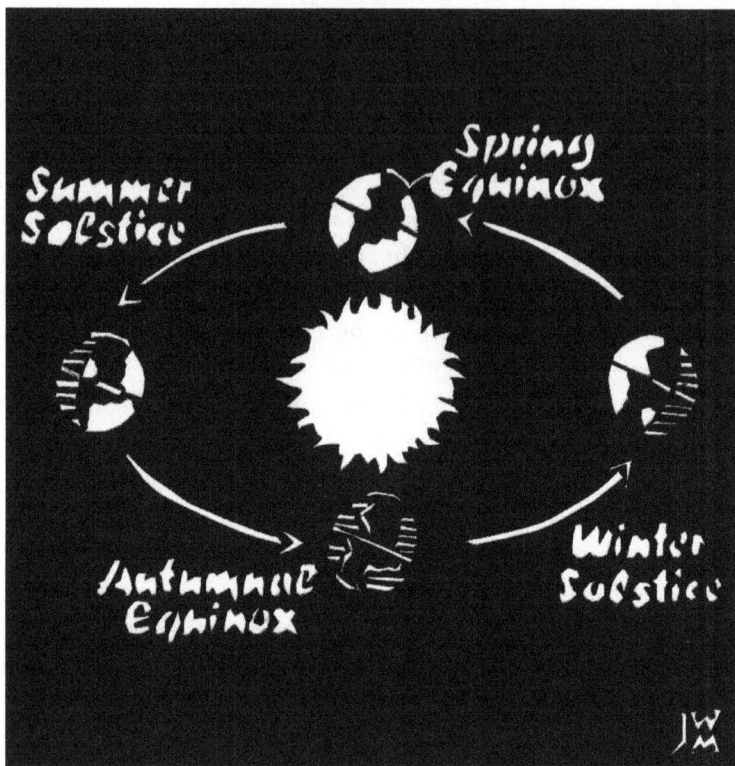

This movement, moving to one extreme and then to another -- a constant progression of returns -- is noted in an ancient commentary to one of the earliest Chinese texts, the *I Ching*, which states, "In returning we see the mind of Heaven and Earth" (復其見天地之心乎)[9] and in the *Tao Te Ching* (道德經) "Reversal is the movement of the Tao." (反者道之動).[10] This gives rise to a cyclical understanding of life and circumstance, giving hope in the midst of suffering and caution during times of prosperity. [11]

THE FIVE PHASES

Yin and yang further split into five phases or movements (*wuxing* 五行). These are the lesser yang of wood, the greater yang of fire, the center of earth, the lesser yin of metal, and the greater yin of water. The lesser and greater are also indicative of degree, literally in the sense that

22

they map onto the temperatures of seasons. Wood is spring, fire is summer, metal is autumn, and water is winter. [12] Earth in some systems stands for the center, and in some conceptions, very late summer -- a transitional point just before and during the harvest.[13]

The five phases have often been mistranslated as the "five elements," borrowing from the four elements of air, fire, water, and earth in Western traditions. This can lead to some confusion. Elements in the Western tradition were originally used to describe material phenomena. They of course have their other conceptual correspondences, like air-east-spring, fire-south-summer, water-west-autumn and earth-north-winter, and were very often related to nonmaterial phenomena, but they are in general assigned to -- for lack of a better word -- a "thing."

The five phases, however, are processes or aspects of change. Confusion easily occurs because they are often referred to in Feng Shui or Chinese Medicine in ways that make them sound like "things," with advice like "your house needs some pool of water in the northwest corner," but the philosophical underpinnings are about flow and interdependent movement.

To describe the five phases it is best to go back to their earliest definition in the original Chinese in the *Book of Han* (漢書):

- Wood bends and extends (木曲直)
- Fire inflames and rises (火炎上)
- Earth sows and harvests (土爰稼穡)
- Metal clears and changes (金從革)
- Water moistens and descends (水潤下)[14]

Note that all these have physical qualities but they are mainly descriptive of activity and movement – movement which mirrors the natural processes or themes of the season to which they are aligned. Wood of spring is the twisting, outward growth of new plant life. The summer is a time of rising heat but also when plants and trees stretch upward toward the sky. Earth is either the harvesting and collecting at the end of summer, or the more general activity of sowing and harvesting of plant life or the breeding and hunting of animal life -- all activities which are central for survival. Autumn is when cooling weather forces the clearing away of life -- or less diplomatically, death -- and a change-state between activity to rest. Water is the descent of activity into stillness, but the moistening quality of the phase hints at a growing fertility that will later explode outward and upward again in the phases of wood and fire.

This cyclical quality hints at their interdependence. Wood creates fire just as spring leads into summer, fire creates earth, just as summer hits a mid-year transition point before autumn. Earth creates metal, just as that mid-year runs into autumn. Then metal creates water, which is autumn transitioning into winter. Finally, water creates wood, once again winter rolling into spring.

There are also controlling aspects where one phase subdues another. This creates a sort of balance in the system as a whole, but is less applicable to the turn of the seasons.

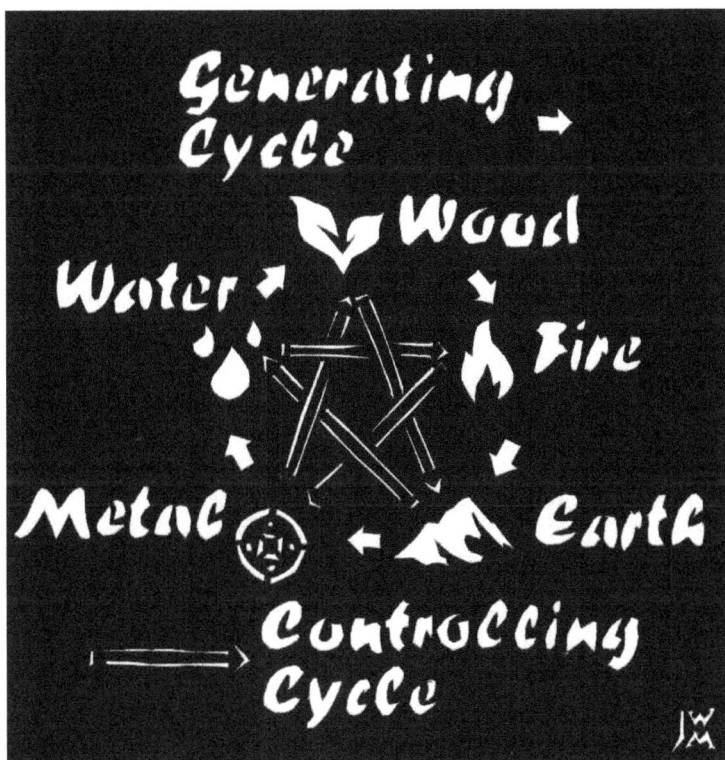

WATCHING THE ETHERS

The interplay of yin and yang and their effect on qi is deeply connected to the 24 solar terms. As early as the Western Han dynasty (206 B.C.E. to 8 CE.), court officials developed a practice called "Watching the Ethers" or "Watching the Qi" (候氣)[15]. Twelve pitch-pipes of different lengths, each capable of playing a half-note on the untempered chromatic scale -- the same scale as used by Pythagoras -- were placed in a circle, starting with the highest note in the north, then descending half-notes clockwise until reaching the lowest note in the northwest. Fine ashes were poured into each pipe, and during each middle term of the 24 solar terms (*zhongqi*) , ash would pop out of the pipe -- and only that one pipe -- for the corresponding term. In this way the circle of pipes would track the progress of the yin and yang over the course of the year: yin forces blow through the pipes from the Summer to the Winter Solstice, and the yang forces blow from the Winter and Summer Solstice.

Later scholars were unable to replicate this phenomenon, and the practice remains controversial, some calling it a centuries-long hoax[16], and others saying the correct procedures were lost to time. But the practice lived a long life, thanks to its importance in confirming to the emperor that yin and yang, and therefore earth and heaven, were in balance. Given imperial tempers, whether or not the ethers cooperated, administrators made sure the pipes played at their appointed time.

The 72 Pentads

Nested within the 24 solar terms are what are referred to as the 72 *hou* (候), or pentads, so named because they describe natural phenomena occurring at a more granular five-day periods. There are three pentads for each solar term, and they are a way to keep track of what is happening in the natural world at the beginning, middle and end of the term.

The pentads carry strong symbolic flavor, whether due to the symbolism of the animals or plants as harbingers of the season, or due to their relationship to the overriding philosophy of yin and yang. The yin and yang relationships can range from an animal's character, such as doves representing yang or voles representing yin, or involve what would appear to be the supernatural transformation of one into another, like hawks transforming into doves. These changes often referred to the advance of the population of one species over another as temperatures change.

To give a sense of flavor of the pentads, the middle pentad of the Summer Solstice states "cicadas begin to chirp." Japan has a different description based on its own ecology such as "sweet flag flourishes." Looking at almanacs for North America, a similar pentad at the same point of the year could be "young robins take flight." In the UK, it could be something like "bream tread still streams." There is a whole set of symbolism and yin and yang forces connected to this description which will be described in its appropriate chapter, but it is also a description of the natural phenomena of the seasons.

The pentads present a more complex view of the year than the solar terms themselves. For example, in the dripping heat of the summer, before even the summer solstice and yet higher temperatures, the actions of praying mantises show that the forces of yin are already on the rise. So it is not a matter of some sort of "yang-switch" getting flipped on right at the summer solstice. Rather, the movements of nature are much more subtle and mysterious, as if only giving the human observer a peak through small cracks into the grand forces shaping the world, and even contrary to our immediate experience of it.

The Challenge of Geography

The 24 solar terms were born in the political, economic, and cultural center of early China, the Yellow River valley,[17] an area of distinct seasons blessed with rich soil perfect for farming. The richness of this fertile land and the weather systems around it wove their ways in the foundation of the 24 solar terms and the 72 pentads, although the system was also enriched by other neighboring ethnicities over the course of time.

Given the size of China, it would be natural to wonder how accurate the 24 solar terms are for the rest of the country. The answer: not very. One might even argue the timing of certain terms, like "Great Snow" do not even match the weather calendar of the Yellow River Valley itself. Still, the terms are used as they were originally set out regardless of geography or climate. The cultural and cosmological value of China's almanac override its value as an precise descriptor of the natural world at any given time of the year.

Even in its original conception, a certain thematic symmetry of the cycle was more important than meteorological accuracy. For example, Great Snow was placed across its thematic antithesis, Grain in Ear, even though most people in the Yellow River Valley would be shocked to see large snowdrifts outside their door in December.[18] The reasons for this concern around symmetry are two-fold. One was to reflect the naturally-occurring balanced character the major solar terms, such as the solstices and equinoxes, which stand at near-perfect opposite across from each other. The other reasons goes back to yin-yang philosophy which treasures notions of balance.

One might then question the value of an almanac that is at times divorced from the realities of nature, even in the region in which it was devised. The answer is that almanacs -- in fact all calendrical systems -- are humanity's attempt to impose a sense of order on the passage of time and the cycles of the natural world. As such they will always be blunt instruments amid a finely nuanced, constantly changing reality. For the 24 solar terms in particular, its value is not in presenting a perfect, predicable mirror of the cosmos, but to keep its followers abreast of the great, slow, unseen forces taking their own time to appear in the world. Its value is not one of reportage and measurement, but of awareness and even prediction of the natural world around us.

And it is the system's slight divorce from concerns of climatic accuracy that gives it an enduring value that is more universal. While the foodways, customs, sayings, festivals, folktales, and deities woven around the 24 solar terms are part of the fabric of Chinese history and culture, the system expresses seasonal change applicable to most of the northern hemisphere, and provides a helpful gauge with which to track the passing of the year among people of the West as much as those in the East.

The 24 Solar Terms and the Lunar Calendar

Although most of the Lunar holidays are not synchronized with the solar terms, there is a certain recognized if unwritten seasonal match between certain solar terms and certain lunar months due to their proximity. The major holidays, and the solar term to which they generally correspond, are as below, keeping in mind the lunar dates can fall on different terms from year to year. "Beginning" here refers to the first of the month at the new moon, and "middle" the 15th during the full moon.

English Name	Chinese name	Appoximate Start Date	Lunar Month
Spring Begins	立春 lìchūn	Feb 3~4	1st beginning
Rain Water	雨水 yǔshuǐ	Feb 18~19	1st middle
Insects Awaken	驚蟄(惊蛰) jīngzhé	Mar 5~6	2nd beginning
Spring Equinox	春分 chūnfēn	Mar 20~21	2nd middle
Clear Bright	清明 qīngmíng	Apr 4~5	3rd beginning
Grain Rain	穀雨(谷雨) gǔyǔ	Apr 19~20	3rd middle
Summer Begins	立夏 lìxià	May 5	4th beginning
Little Fullness	小滿(小满) xiǎomǎn	May 20~21	4th middle
Grain in Ear	芒種(芒种) mángzhòng	Jun 5~6	5th beginning
Summer Solstice	夏至 xiàzhì	Jun 20~21	5th middle
Little Heat	小暑 xiǎoshǔ	Jul 6~7	6th beginning
Great Heat	大暑 dàshǔ	Jul 22~23	6th middle
Autumn Begins	立秋 lìqiū	Aug 7	7th beginning
Heat Departs	處暑(处暑) chǔshǔ	Aug 22~23	7th middle
White Dew	白露 báilù	Sep 7~8	8th beginning
Autumnal Equinox	秋分 qiūfēn	Sep 22~23	8th middle
Cold Dew	寒露 hánlù	Oct 7~8	9th beginning
Frostfall	霜降 shuāngjiàng	Oct 22~23	9th middle
Winter Begins	立冬 lìdōng	Nov 6~9	10th beginning
Light Snow	小雪 xiǎoxuě	Nov 21~22	10th middle
Heavy Snow	大雪 dàxuě	Dec 6~7	11th beginning
Winter Solstice	冬至 dōngzhì	Dec 21~22	11th middle
Little Cold	小寒 xiǎohán	Jan 5~6	12th beginning
Great Cold	大寒 dàhán	Jan 19~20	12th middle

Most of China's festivals are timed according to the lunar calendar; for example, Lunar New Year, the Dragon Boat Festival, and the Mid-Autumn Festival. The dates of the lunar calendar can be confusing since they change from year to year. To start, the first lunar month is determined by the first full moon of closest proximity to the solar term, Spring Begins (立春). Rarely, when the solar term was right in the middle of two moon cycles as was the case in 1985 and 2015, other adjustments were made, but this is the general rule.

The first lunar month always falls between January 21 and February 21, and from one year to the next it will fall 11 days earlier, because there are only 354 days in the lunar year as opposed to the solar year's 365 days. For example, if the Lunar New Year falls in mid-to-late February, you can count on it falling to early February the next year, and then late January the year after that. However, in years when it falls into late January, a leap month is inserted later in the year to get everything back on track. After that, the Lunar New year happens again in late February, and the cycle continues. [19]

In addition to these festivals, many Chinese communities also observe a more regular cycle on the first (初一) and fifteenth (十五) of every month. This is said to derive from ancient mercantilist practices[20], where trade occurred on these two days of the lunar month. Rituals were practiced to ensure the safety of the traveling ships and wagons, as well as future prosperity. This routine spread among the general populace, where it was practiced by families to venerate their ancestors and appeal to the gods for protection and fortune. These tend to be smaller, simpler household affairs.

* * *

In earliest times the Chinese calendar, like many of the ancient practices in other parts of the world, was a simpler annual system observing the summer and winter solstices and the spring and autumnal equinoxes. Over time, the calendar was extended to eight segments by adding the beginning of the four seasons. From there, the annual observances took on increasing complexity and evolved over thousands of years to comprise a very busy lunisolar calendar of today, packed with festivals and moon-cycle observances, not to mention numerous other calendar systems added and removed between then and now.

The Chinese have inherited a rich tradition of calendrical observance. And while the traditions contain great value as a cultural asset, they also contain universal wisdom for those living in other cultures as well as a very different modern world from when these seasonal celebrations were originally conceived.

Wisdom Ancient and Modern

The Appeal of the Seasons

The use of astrology, almanacs, and careful observation and recording of seasonal changes for so many millennia provokes certain questions: what exactly is the appeal of the seasons? Why is it, regardless of time or geography, the seasons are ubiquitous in the art, literature, and religions of all cultures?

Of course the seasons act as a way to track time, yet they promise more than just a demarcation of the year. They capture the imagination in ways that go beyond the mundane, like muses beckoning on the distant edges of the human imagination. What is it about the seasons that give them so much appeal?

The first, most obvious would be the pragmatic reasons: awareness of the moods of nature has been critical for human survival. Foragers needed to know times of plenty, farmers when to sow and reap, and seafarers when seas are calm or rough. Faced with the life-and-death demands of sustenance, migration, and war, the margin for error was slim. Tracking the changes in nature within one's immediate environment -- to the extent it was predictable -- meant failure or success for one's family, tribe, or kingdom.

A second motivation is that seasonal observances and celebrations are emotionally satisfying. They brighten the dreary corners of the annual routine. They are also a fitting allegory for the individual life-cycle and nearly any other transient aspect of existence. This is why the seasonal allegories are so often deployed in art and literature in ways spanning the most inspirationally poignant to the most exasperatingly clichéd. And they appear so regularly in art and literature because the seasons reflect a fundamental aspect of the human condition: the preciousness of our limited time.

A third major motivation has been to demystify and understand the wonders of the natural world and the greater cosmos. The earliest myths, the majority of active and defunct religions, and all the natural sciences owe a tremendous debt to humanity's never-ending struggle to explain the hows and whys of the seasons. Most metaphysical frameworks are wedded to the seasonal cycle, whether the four elements of air, fire, water and earth in the West, or the five phases of wood, fire, earth, metal and water in the East. The Greek gods are for the most part personifications of nature. Christianity, whether inheriting the habit from the pagan traditions it supplanted or through the common conceptions of the natural world at the time, maintains a clear connection to the rebirth of spring. The fundamental concepts of Chinese philosophy -- yin and yang and the five phases -- are all expressed within the seasonal cycle. Throughout the ages, people have turned to the seasons or their tangential concepts for reassurance in a world marked by unpredictability and disorderly flux.

Still, nature will always deny humanity's attempt to sort the timing of nature's workings into a clear, predictable grid. At any one time the forces of nature are engaged in a frenzied dance, and yet reveal themselves in their own time. Humanity's work to understand and predict the changes of the world we inhabit only begets more mystery. So by creating a model by which to grasp the universe, humanity only creates more questions. But the questions must be asked, and it is often the questions and mystery -- the ambiguous gaps between certainty and uncertainty -- which draw humanity closer to true understanding.

Shared Conceptions: East and West

Conceptions of the seasons between China and what is referred to collectively as "the West" are not vastly different since both cultures are rooted in the northern hemisphere along a similar latitude. In ancient times both cultures marked the solstices, and eventually came to demarcate the year by four seasons.

There are slight differences in agricultural and natural iconography. In the West, the autumn is associated with ripening fruit.[1]

China, with its longer fruiting periods throughout the year, tends to associate the fall with certain types of flowers, like the chrysanthemum.

Other than this minor difference, conceptions are strikingly similar. Both China and the West share a fascination with autumn foliage. Both also have traditions of nature observation that spring up from changes in the seasons. Both have a certain centuries-long concern about humankind's growing distance from the seasons as more people move out of the countryside and into towns and cities.

In fact it is this last aspect that both East and West have the most in common, and could be described less as an urban-rural divide and more as a general disconnect with what we typically identify "the natural realm." The use of the word "nature" here is an easy shorthand to refer to anything other than human-made systems, even if that word is flawed since humans and their creations are technically also "nature". But because "nature" is generally conceived as something wild and distinct from humanity, this is how the term will be used in this book.

There has been a long-standing dichotomy associating the countryside with simplicity and purity, and the town with complexity and corruption. [2] One might extend this association to align the countryside with nature and the city with human society, commonly conceiving highly-populated centers of civilization as a form of "non-nature."

This view is anything but new. In 29 BCE Virgil exhorted readers to get back to the country life[3] in his book of seasonal poetry, *The Georgics*. The trope was just as prevalent in ancient Chinese culture, and generations of scholars and poets describing life in the wilderness with romantic tones, appreciating the world far away from the political sniping of the imperial bureaucracy or the busy thrum of the villages.[4]

But this distance from nature has perhaps become more urgent in our modern circumstances. In *A Time for Every Purpose: The Four Seasons in American Culture*, Michael Kammen speaks of a "flattening"[5] of the seasons, where the character of each season takes on less significance and relevance to life amid the typical modern lifestyle with its refrigeration and global logistics. A sort of de-seasonalization has occurred, where seasons lose their meaning when you can get any fruit at any time of the year, while heating and air-conditioning keep environments within a thin range of comfortable temperatures.

This de-seasonalization is one symptom of a larger issue of humankind's degraded relationship with the natural world, as well as one of many factors perpetuating that degradation. An aspect of this degraded relationship was hinted at above, noting the common habit of conceiving human systems as separate from nature. This sense of de-seasonalization and sense of separation is endemic not just in West, but in pretty much every large population center across the globe.

This drives to the heart of the benefits of the calendars like the 24 solar terms, or any calendar that moves our attention toward the turn of the seasons. As this book moves through the year, three major ideas emerge which will be explored in more detail later in the book. The first is a peek into a world where the ancients used a calendrical system to fashion a working understanding of nature's great power and mystery, and with that understanding, an acceptance of the massive natural forces operating outside of their control. Second is the cultivation of ritual, both as an strategy to deal with uncertainty, but also as a way of aligning personal and societal actions with nature's moods. Third is a sense of careful observation -- a thrum of alertness tuned to the movements of the cosmos and the world beyond human society.

These ideas will be picked up later. Whatever the prevalence of these three themes, the 24 solar terms are yet far more complex and vast in scope. There are many abstractions that can be pulled from the 24 solar terms with which to view our world, but at base and in their original manifestation, the solar terms deal chiefly with practical matters. With that, let us move into the solar terms proper to see how they work in practice. We will start the solar term that kicks off the lunisolar calendar: Spring Begins.

CHAPTER 1: SPRING BEGINS 立春

立春 / 입춘/립춘 / りつしゅん / Lập xuân
Pinyin: lìchūn
Literal Meaning: "establishes spring"
Alternative names: Spring Commences
Period: February 4 ~ February 18 or 19
Sun's Ecliptic Longitude: 315°

The Day of Spring Begins
Lu You
Song Dynasty

Rising sun and gentle wind stir me from my hangover,
*   mountain families make merry in their remaining years.*
Three blankets of twelfth-month snow bring annual abundance,
*   the warming ground of spring in the outskirts is all turning green.*
Delicate greens and floral bouquets are ideal for making crepes,
*   the fragrance and foam of wine spills from tall bottles.*
The scenery of the mountain village defies poetic verse,
*   so I beg a noble family to have it painted on a screen.*

立春日 | 宋 | 陸游
日出風和宿醉醒, 山家樂事滿餘齡。
年豐臘雪經三白, 地暖春郊已遍青。
菜細簇花宜薄餅, 酒香浮蜡瀉長瓶。
湖村好景吟難盡, 乞與侯家作畫屏。

    Associated with the cacophony of birdsong and fragrant flowers, spring is a time when the earth wakes up and puts on a fresh set of clothes for the coming year. For much of the world the solar term of "Spring Begins" occurs while the ground is still covered in snow and frost. The sky is gray and horizons are dotted by the withered branches of dormant trees. In southern Chinese climates -- the south of the Yangtze River -- early signs of spring may begin to appear: budding willows and tiny green blades of grass reach out from the cold mud, impatient for the life-giving winds of spring (春風吹又生).

Pentads

First five days: East winds thaw the earth (東風解凍)
Middle five days: Hibernating insects stir (蟄蟲始振)
Last five days: Fish meander through receding ice (魚陟負冰)

The pentads of the first solar term describe the initial stirring of air, earth, and water as the fires of the sun advance. In the five phases system the eastern quarter is associated with spring; hence, the blow of wind from that direction. This is also in part due to the weather systems of some places in China. The natural world is still very much wrapped up in heavy blankets of winter, but beneath the surface insects get ready to wake up and the fish bob their way into areas of water once dominated by ice.

Agriculture

In Chinese farming communities the seasons are condensed to four short phrases: planting for spring, growing for summer, harvesting for fall, and storing for winter. (春種 , 夏長 , 秋收 , 冬藏[1]). Regardless of what is happening on the ground the term is named for the sun's position, and a signal to the farming community that the time for planting is drawing near. The cold, drab landscape will inevitably wake up and bring forth greenery and bountiful harvests. It is the time when farms prepare themselves for ramping up, and a common saying states "when Spring Begins and Rain Water arrive, late to bed, early to rise." (立春雨水到, 早起晚睡覺[2]).

Health

According to Chinese medicine the arriving spring, with it's changing temperatures, creates a number of conditions that require care. As temperatures increase the body loosens up, which lets the cold more easily penetrate the body. Some people, ecstatic at the approach of some warmth, cast off their heavier clothes too early. It's particularly a danger to the more frail and elderly.

In the five-phase system, spring is the phase of wood, which corresponds to the liver and the regulation of temper. Steps will need to be taken to manage the anger and depression that can erupt from liver issues. As yang kicks up in the spring, metabolism increases; however, it is also the season of epidemic meningitis, measles, pneumonia.

In terms of food intake, it is best to avoid sour foods, and eat foods traditionally associated as "sweet" in Chinese medicine: garlic chives, dates, peanuts, spring bamboo shoots, all of which are rich sources of vitamin B. Fresh fruit, vegetables and protein like milk, eggs, fish, shrimp, chicken, duck, beef, also boost immunity. Spicy and oily foods should be avoided since they burden the liver. As the liver is most active during this period, spring is the ideal time to treat liver diseases[3].

Ancient Traditions

In ancient times there were many practices during the time of Spring Begins, although most activity was supplanted by the main event of the season, the Spring Festival, covered later in this chapter.

In and around the imperial palace this was a busy time. The Grand Recorder (大史, 太史) would announce the arrival of the energies of wood, which correspond to the east. A retinue of nobility -- clad in azure -- would accompany the emperor to the eastern suburbs to welcome spring and pay their respects to the God of Spring, otherwise known as the Wood God (句芒). Numbers of ministers would be selected in groups that were numerologically significant, such as three ducal ministers and nine high ministers (三公九卿). Three represented the three main spheres of heaven, earth, and humanity, and nine was both the imperial number and a homonym with the word "longevity" (久).

The imperial court would harmonize government orders, disseminate lessons of virtue to the people, and bestow favors upon them. The Grand Recorder would send out orders to guard statutes and laws, especially when it came to the observation of the sun and moon. This was a key time for astronomical calculations, ensuring there were no errors and any failure to record calculations was not permitted.

The emperor prayed for a good year, and during some dynasties rulers would follow the recommendation of the *Book of Rites*, personally descending into the fields with their ministers to till the earth, and then return to the palace to toast them for their toil. Further instructions were issued for field inspectors to live in the countryside to manage the soil and instruct and lead people in planting and raising livestock.

In preparation for that year's rituals, the Chief Director of Music would enter the College of Music and lead his pupils in the practice of ritualistic dance. Other than the eastern procession by the emperor, it was important to make sacrifices to the forests, streams and marshes, demonstrating the importance which early dynasties placed on the powers of the natural world. Prohibitions were issued on the felling of trees, destruction of nests, or the killing of any form of immature life, whether insect, mammal, or bird, along with any form of egg. A certain stillness was promoted: crowds were discouraged and walls were fortified. Signifiers of death were to be avoided, and any exposed bones or bodies needed to be covered or buried. The *Book of Rites* recommended no change in the ways of heaven or extinction of the principles of earth, nor confounding the bonds of men. As such, any warlike operations at this time of year would invite calamity from heaven.

The *Book of Rites* was also very explicit about doing the correct ritual at the proper time. Summer rituals done at this time would invite unseasonable rain, premature death and decay of plants and trees, and wrap the empire in a state of continual fear. Autumn rituals brought pestilence, violent winds, torrential rains, and growth of undesirable weeds. Winter rituals done at this time of year would create destructive pools of water, injurious snows and frosts, and seeds hesitant to sprout from the ground. [4]

The common folk would affix to their person silhouettes of sparrows cut from colored silk to both signify and invoke the return of the flocks in spring. They also pasted the words "Proper Spring" (宜春) to their doors, a practice that evolved into many other Spring Festival traditions.

But by far the most important ritual among the people, only rarely practiced nowadays, was "Hitting Spring" (打春)[5], which involved the symbolic abuse of a bull made of earth. The earthen bull was taken to the eastern side of the city where the highest local official would crack a green and red whip against the bull three times, then passing the whip to other villagers. Each taking their turn, the bull would eventually be whipped to fragments, revealing a small dirt calf in the center.

Once given the go-ahead, the villagers would compete for the shattered pieces[6]. The head was considered the luckiest: horns would be placed in the field for a good harvest and the eyes mixed with medicine to cure illnesses. Parts of the body were placed in the home to ensure a good silk harvest. In other traditions, the pieces were placed in the pen of the family ox to promote more offspring.

The purpose of the ritual was to signal the start of spring planting. Hitting the earthen bull was said to awake actual bulls from their long winter break, ensuring they would shake off their torpor and gain the motivation to engage in the required plow work. The practice was first mentioned in the *Book of Sui* (隋書)[7], and was practiced up to the Ming and Qing dynasties. To this day the ox is associated with spring, and the image can be found in many farmer's almanacs (See Goumang under the folklore section of this chapter).

In certain localities "Hitting Spring" (打春) comprised a different set of rituals. People in Hangzhou would go to the east of the city to pray to the Spring God and then to a mountain temple, carrying a pair of red candles with which to exchange with strangers in a ritual termed "Losing Ingots" (掉元寶)[8]. Whether the candles received were long or short or elegant or cheap did not matter; as the intention was to circulate the family's luck with the greater populace. Even good luck is believed to grow stagnant, and the ritual ensures the arrival of fresh and auspicious influences.

Other areas practiced rituals to announce the arrival of Spring Begins, many requiring the participation of brothel staff. In Hubei (湖北), male servants in brothels dressed up, clad in a red costume resembling a deified spring official (春官). They would proceed to the local government office, where the official would ask him the date of Spring Begins, and the actor would answer[9]. Other than brothels having obvious connections to the fecund themes of spring, these men were chosen due to their job title: Brothel Turtles (妓院龜奴) . In Chinese the word for turtle (guī 龜) is a homonym for the term return (guī 歸),

indicating the return of spring (春歸) as the world cycled once again through the seasons.

In Jiangsu (江蘇), the day before Spring Begins the local official would order the brothels to hold a procession, including a Spring Fire Auntie (社火春婆), two "Spring Sisters" (春姐), a minor Spring Clerk (春吏), two yamen runners (皂隸), and one Spring Official (春官).[10] Participation of the brothels ceased when they were closed during the Qing dynasty under reign of Kangxi (康熙) and the festivities turned over to the general populace. Roles were thereafter portrayed by male professional performers, and the procession was called Spring Turtles (春龜，春歸) for the same reasons given above. Scores of merchants filled the streets selling Spring Bull Paintings and farmers' almanacs.

In the north, sellers lined the streets selling radishes, as a popular practice was biting into them raw, called "Biting Spring" (咬春)[11]. The action was auspicious and welcomed the new year. Also popular were plates containing five spices (五辛盤) for their presumed bacterial killing properties: green onions, garlic, pepper, ginger, and mustard (蔥、蒜、椒、薑、芥) as well as eating spring crepes (春餅) during the period of "hitting spring" (打春吃春餅)[12].

Customs

The customs of the Spring Festival are myriad, and would require a whole book to catalog the complete practices and foodways, along with their origin and meaning. Below are the primary, most common observances of the Spring Festival.

Festivals

SPRING FESTIVAL

The Spring Festival (Lunar New Year) is sometimes confused with Spring Begins, but they are currently different observances, the latter is simply the start of the cycle of solar terms, and the former is the most important holiday of the Chinese and other ethnicities in East Asia and their diaspora. As the Spring Festival follows a lunar calendar, it sometimes falls before Spring Begins, sometimes after, and very rarely on the same date.

Spring Begins and the Spring Festival were not always separate occasions, however. The Spring Festival was celebrated on Spring Begins since the Spring and Autumn period right up until the Han dynasty. It wasn't until 1913, when the newly founded Chinese Nationalist Government was realigning the national calendar, that observance of the Spring Festival was moved to the first day of the first lunar month[13]. Spring Begins then reverted to a simple marker in the annual farming calendars.

Sweeping and Cleaning

Like the spring cleaning habit maintained across cultures through the ages, the spring is a time to cast out the old and clean up the debris and dust of the torpid winter. In Chinese culture, this goes well beyond the pragmatics of sanitation and order: the practice clears away any bad luck accumulated during the previous year, and opens the home for the accumulation of fresh, auspicious influences.

Decorations

Paper with the words "Spring" (春) or "Prosperity" (福) or some derivative thereof are posted on the door and around the home, in some families serving a purely decorative purpose and a matter of cultural habit, but in most acting in essentially a talismanic fashion to call forth good luck. Annual paintings (年畫) and spring couplets (春聯) containing similar themes serve the same aim. Some families paste door guardians (門神) above on the door, which keep malign forces at bay.

New Year's Eve

The first character in the word for New Year's Eve in Chinese, chú (除) of chúxì (除夕), is synonymous with the ancient word yì (易), the word for change most commonly known for that venerable divination text, the *I Ching* (易經). New Year's Eve is more than just a marker in the calendar, but a observance of the importance of change, one of the core concepts of Chinese philosophy for its life-giving properties and its role as a force of healthy balance.

On the evening before the Lunar New Year, families gather for heavy banqueting, tables laden in orgiastic splendor as multiple day's worth of food is prepared, since using knives for cutting food is prohibited for a few days of the Lunar New Year. Concerns about harming one's luck has generated a long list of innumerable prohibitions during the following few days. Most of these revolve around the use of cutting implements (knives, scissors, shavers) or most types of cleaning (laundry, sweeping, mopping, sometimes showering) which are said to cut away or wash away one's luck for the following year.

Families come together for merriment and revisiting, exchanging red envelopes of cash between the generations. It is also an evening of paying respects to the ancestors.

Fireworks are typically lit, although the enthusiasm differs from place to place. The air of the countryside is typically filled with sparks and smoke, while urban centers can be far more sedate, either due to legal restrictions, the reduction of population as city folk head back to families in the countryside, or general disinterest. Occasionally lonely fizzles and pops can be heard ringing out into the quiet urban night, but most people in the cities choose other means of celebration, although those that live in closely packed apartments will recognize the celebrations are not necessarily quieter with the constant sound of clacking mah jong tiles echoing out of nearby windows.

With all this activity people stay up late into the night. Going to bed too early is said to invite sickness, as if expressing to the heavens an eagerness to spend the year in languishing in bed. In some traditions staying up late ensures the longevity of one's parents, and in nearly all traditions it is simply important to be awake and observant as one "passes the year" (過年) and ensures good fortune in the next. After midnight, many people hit the markets to spend their red envelopes, watch fireworks, and wish a happy new year to neighbors.

The next day, it is good luck to get up early and head outdoors, ideally decked out in new clothes, hopefully with some red on one's person. Temples are a popular destination, providing the opportunity to proclaim ones hopes for the new year and express gratitude. Second to this aim, and just as important, is converging on places where there are crowds. The agoraphobic or misanthropic might find the idea horrifying, diving into packed crowds of people, bodies well-greased and heavy with banqueting. But this is a key step in the process of changing one's luck (轉運), washing and cleansing one's energy in the auras of hundreds of other celebrants. Here, the emphasis is not on who has good luck or bad luck, or concerning oneself with catching the equivalent of bad-luck cooties; rather, the central idea is one of flow and change, keeping the energies of change moving and transforming into new forms of opportunity and growth.

Folklore

The use of fireworks and the general preference for a high degree of activity and noise derives from the practice of scaring away a mythological beast called the *Nian* (年 nián), which is the word for "year." *Nian* is a mysterious mythological animal, and no written record with any clear description exists, but oral tales of the beast have been passed down for millennia. It is said to look something like a large lion, or a thick-set bull. It spends most of the year hiding in the sea, but when spring arrives it emerges from the depths to terrorize humanity, ravaging people and their livestock.

People discovered that the red flames produced by exploding bamboo scared it off, and that it was generally frightened by any sort of flame or the color red. Wielding flame and red colors caused the Nian to pass by (in Chinese, 過年). It was eventually subdued by the Ancestor of Great Balance and Primordial Nature (鴻鈞老祖) [14], the teacher of the Three Pure Ones (三清) in Taoist mythology, and eventually serving as his mount.

Some contend that the beast is simply the product of cultural imagination, while other claim that the origin is more rooted in the natural world. *The Classic of Mountains and Seas* (山海經) describes the human-like mountain demons[15] that were later described as fearful

46

of fireworks in the *Book of Gods and Strange Things* (神異經) [16]. The description of these demons are now assumed to be the mandrill (山魈). The other theory is that the Nian Beast is a representation of pestilence, pointing to the early origins of the Spring Festival as a noise-making ritual to drive off disease[17].

THE SPRING GOD

The Spring God was an object of veneration in ancient times, and was one of the most important given its connection to birth and life since the deity was originally female [18]. Mythology has taken the image of the Spring God in many different directions with many different names, like Goumang (句芒), Gou Dragon (句龍), Wood Emperor (木帝), Wood God (木神), Azure Emperor (青帝), and the Blue Emperor (蒼帝).

GOUMANG

Goumang (句芒) is the most well-known and ancient of all the Spring God deities, and goes by other names as well, such as the Wood Emperor (木帝), also named the Wood God (木神), since spring was associated with the wood phase. The characters used in the name Goumang are less concerned with meaning and more visually evocative of the plant world. The character gōu (句) -- pronounced jù in modern Mandarin Chinese -- looks like a new sprout, just emerging from the soil[19]. *Máng* (芒) looks like the velvet coating a young plant. Many Chinese characters have a sense of internal balance and symmetry -- at least in their traditional form -- while these two characters are chosen for their unevenness, giving a sense of outward, bending, crooked growth – much like the definition of the phase of wood – mirroring the appearance of plant growth in the natural world and evoking a sense of young life.

Goumang was said to be a descendant of the Yellow Emperor, and advisor to the folk hero Fuxi, described in a later chapter. He was responsible for the growth of trees, and more generally the God of Life in *The Mozi* (墨子) [20]. According to the *Classic of Mountains and Seas*, the deity resided in the east, had a human face with an avian body, and rode two dragons[21, 22]. The deity's gender was ambiguous, but later was personified as a male heavenly official, a few feathers in his crown the only remaining vestige of his earlier avian appearance. He is said to be the subordinate of another Spring God, Taihao (太皞), who is often combined or confused with Fuxi[23], described in a later chapter.

Some believe, however, that the boy who appears in the "Spring Ox Paintings" (春牛圖), with his willow crop and hair in a bun, is Goumang[24]. This association could be connected with the "Hitting Spring" ritual, where Goumang was asked to wake up a sleeping bull for spring planting. Loath to hurt the bull, he made a bull made of mud and whipped it, scaring the actual bull and motivating it to work without having to hurt it. This aspect of the Spring God is thus not just associated with growth of the plant world, but also with benevolence and mercy.

THE AZURE GOD

The Azure God (青帝) is one of the five directional emperors (五方上帝), responsible for the eastern quarter corresponding to spring. The deity was a fixture in temples during ancient times. He is also called the Blue Emperor (蒼帝) or the Wood Emperor (木帝), similar to Goumang. The color azure is associated with the wood phase, and carries all the associations of that phase, including birth, the spread of life, and the flowering of the myriad things[25].

Before continuing, a momentary pause is necessary to explain the color *qing* (青), as it occurs with incredible frequency in Chinese culture yet it is a color that is maddeningly ambiguous. The other four colors associated with the five phases are straightforward: red is the color of fire and the south, white the color of metal and the west, black the color of water and the north, and yellow the color of earth and the center. *Qīng*, however, is described in various contexts as green, blue, blue-green, cyan[26], azure, or even black[27]. Given the variability of definitions, the more unique yet inadequate term "azure" is used to differentiate this mysterious and powerful color throughout this book.

The color is considered green due to its connection to plants and growing things which begin in Spring. The word for "birth" in Chinese is shēng (生), which is related to the character *qīng* (青). In this sense, it is the color lǜ (綠), the Western "green" that is the dominant color of the plant world.

The word *qīng* (青) is blue when describing the sky, but is also said to be the blue of the dye that comes from Chinese indigo (蓼藍)[28]. When describing black hair (青絲) or black eyes (青眼), the word *qīng* (青) means black and describes a luxurious, living brightness that a dull dark black cannot capture.

For those who crave specificity and concrete definitions, the wide range of different shades combined with the high frequency of the color's mention in Chinese culture can be frustrating. But it is exactly this enigmatic, unpinnable quality that gives the color its poetry. And as will become evident later in this book, the color is often associated with Taoist philosopher Laozi, who had much to say (or not say) about the limits of language and human perception in knowing the mysteries of the universe. Perhaps this curious color, which has so long resisted human attempts to define it, has something much more significant to say about the mystery of the spark of the life and the undefinable nature of the cosmos.

A Dynasty Born of a Dark Bird

Jiandi (簡狄) was the second wife of Emperor Ku (帝嚳). Two years after their marriage, she still had not given birth to any children. Concerned, her mother took her to a Temple dedicated to Nüwa (女媧), the mother goddess who molded people out of yellow earth, gave them life, and gifted them the ability to bear children. Lighting incense to the goddess, Jiandi's mother prayed for her daughter to get pregnant.

One day, the young woman was walking through a valley when she saw a beautiful pool. She was unable to pass up the opportunity to enjoy it, and with nobody around, she disrobed and went into the pond to enjoy its cool waters. As she played, a dark swallow (馹, 燕) landed on a stone bordering the pool, laid an egg, and then flew off. Intrigued, she swam over and picked up the egg, noticing that it was sparkled with many different colors.

She wanted to take it home, but with no pockets available, naked as she was, she put the egg in her mouth. Swimming a few strokes back toward the other bank, she mistakenly swallowed the egg, and as it descended into her belly she felt wave of heat penetrating her body.

A few months later, she gave birth to Emperor Xie (契), ancestor of the Kings of the Shang dynasty, the earliest known dynasty in Chinese history. Impregnated by the "dark bird" (玄鳥) and initiating the dynastic cycle that would continue for millennia, Jiandi became a fertility deity, and is viewed as a spring goddess.[29] [30]

***

This short tale contains many motifs seen throughout mythologies of nearly all cultures, most notably a virgin birth. In this particular case impregnation occurs by inadvertently swallowing an egg of a dark bird. The word "dark" here (玄) is less about a shade of color than another meaning of the word which is closer to "mysterious" or even "occult" -- occult in its original sense of something obscured, defined as "shut off from view or exposure." The Chinese word, like the English word occult, is connected to aspects of the inexplicable and spiritual. Like many myths it shrouds humanity's origins in mystery, yet hinting at a fantastic spark that began its genesis. And in all of the world's cultures, spring is just that: the beginning of new life and the start of growth.

CHAPTER 2: RAIN WATER 雨水

雨水 / 우수 / うすい / Vũ thủy
Pinyin: yǔshuǐ
Literal Meaning: "rain water"
Alternative names: More Rain Than Snow,
Spring Showers, Spring Rain
Period: February 18 or 19 ~ March 5 or 6
Sun's Ecliptic Longitude: 330°

Respectful Greeting to the Official of Waterworks in Early Spring
Han Yu
Tang Dynasty

A light drizzle coats the capital like butter,
  green grass blurs together from afar yet is sparse up close.
This time is the most beautiful of the year,
  victorious over a city dense with willows at the end of spring.
Do not speak of urgent official business while you get old,
  having lost the youthful heart to chase spring.
You should steal away to the riverbank for a look,
  and see whether the green of the willows has darkened.

早春呈水部張十八員外二首 | 唐 | 韓愈
天街小雨潤如酥，草色遙看近卻無。
最是一年春好處，絕勝煙柳滿皇都。
莫道官忙身老大，即無年少逐春心。
憑君先到江頭看，柳色如今深未深。

The time of Rain Water is when the land first begins to thrive. Snows start to melt as temperatures begin to rise. The increase in water flowing from the higher elevations combined with rain causes rising moisture and humidity.

The change to spring was famously captured by the poet Dufu (杜甫) describing the fall of rain and the arrival of moister weather:

Rainy Spring Night
Du Fu
Tang Dynasty
The rain chooses the right time,
  when all things sprout and grow in spring.
The rain sneaks into the night with the wind,
  moistening all things silently.
The wild trails and clouds are all dark,
  only the boats on the river are brightly lit.

At dawn, see where the red flowers are wet,
*   as flowers bloom in Chengdu City.*

春夜喜雨 | 唐 | 杜甫
好雨知時節，當春乃發生。
隨風潛入夜，潤物細無聲。
野徑雲俱黑，江船火獨明。
曉看紅溼處，花重錦官城

With the transition to spring, severe winter weather departs, but weather is highly unpredictable. Temperature ranges increase, bringing nightly freezes and warmer temperatures during the day. Arid climates may experience strong winds which can exacerbate forest fires, and other areas might get the occasional snow storm.

Pentads

Otters sacrifice fish (獺祭鱼)
Wild geese head north (候雁北)
Grass and trees bud (草木萌動)

The first pentad refers the otters that catch fish as the fish become active, swimming to the surface in search of food. Otters catch the fish and neatly line them up on the river bank, in a way that looks like an offering to the gods.

Texts refer to the *Yueling Guangyi* (月令廣義), describing that if the otters do not make offerings of fish to the gods, the nation will be overrun with bandits. In other words, if the otters are not catching fish, rivers and lakes are still frozen over. This means fewer crops available for the harvest. Less food means mass famine, and the lands will be plagued by roving bands of starving bandits[1, 2].

The second pentad describes wild geese heading north (候雁北) coming back north from the south where they wintered. The third indicates the time has come for plowing and sowing crops.

Agriculture

Soft yet constant rains foretell a good harvest, and farmers get started with weeding, fertilizing, and clearing up irrigation channels to avoid floods. Crops requiring ample water like rapeseed and winter wheat are typically grown during this time. It is also the time to graft fruit trees and plant saplings in certain climates. This is the time when peach and plum flowers start to bud, and cherry blossoms bloom. [3] [4]

Health

Taking care of one's health is particularly important as the erratic weather compromises the immune system, making the body an inviting playground for all the bacteria and viruses which run rampant during this period.

According to traditional medicine, the loosening up of the body by occasional warmth makes it easier for cold drafts to open the body to illness. The erratic weather also creates unstable moods, resulting in higher risk of high blood pressure, heart attacks, and asthma. Tradition advises increased exercise and the protection of the stomach and spleen, which are key to longevity and are the root of most illnesses if weak. It is also advised to work on maintaining a stable mood during this time, and avoid losing one's temper. The practice of remaining calm helps conserve and even generate vital energy. [5] [6]

Customs

Other than the widespread activities surrounding the Lantern Festival, customs connected to Rain Water are more regional, and mostly concern family relations. In some areas the first day of the term is Receiving Longevity (接壽), a time for daughters and sons-in-law to give a red string of a certain length to their parents. The string is typically tied to an arm of a chair, and is said to give health and long life. Sichuan has a practice called "Drawing in Protection" (拉保保) [7] [8], where the spirits are prayed to and divinations are performed to see if it is appropriate for a child to take on a godfather, which is said to bring protection and fortune. It is also another chance for married women to return to their families of origin for a visit. In farming communities, there is a tradition of popping glutinous rice like popcorn: the more popped rice, the greater the future harvest.

Festivals

LANTERN FESTIVAL

Other than farmers looking up to the sky and hoping for rain on the first day of Rain Water, the Lantern Festival is the major holiday which typically occurs during this solar term, on the 15th day of the first lunar month. It goes by many names: Yuanxiao Festival (元宵節), Shangyuan Festival (上元節), and First Night (元夜).There are different origin myths for the holiday, but in general it is a time when the populace expresses wishes for the future.

It also likely derives from old fire festivals meant to drive away malign forces. During the Han dynasty, farmers would go out into the fields, carrying torches to drive away pests and protect the harvest, a practice that is seen at other times of the year. Such activity was recorded in Sima Qian's *Records of the Grand Historian* (史記)[9], and is believed to be the basis for the modern holiday[10]. With the influence of Indian Buddhism in the Eastern Han, it was transformed into an evening of lamp-lighting in veneration of the Buddha[11]. Some areas worship the Fire God on this day, given the holiday's clear association with fire.

The holiday is celebrated differently depending on the location, and has been celebrated in a variety of ways over time. During Han dynasty, it was one day. In the Tang and Song Dynasties it was extended to three to five days, when all sorts of trees, pillars, and wheels of lanterns were erected. In the Ming dynasty, it was extended yet further to ten days, and this was when the holiday became more closely connected to the New Year -- a culmination of New Year festivities. During the Qing dynasty, it was cut back down to five days, although this did little to dampen on the atmosphere of merriment, with stilt-walking, folk dancing, and more complex lantern shapes in the form of dragons, tigers or rabbits.[12]

Traditionally, family members might play a game of guessing lantern riddles (猜燈謎). The answer is usually an idiom (成語) on topics covering anything from word forms, place names, Chinese medicine, lyrics, famous people, or animals. It was also a time of romance, when young men and women would have a chance to mingle with one another while the town was busy celebrating.

Nowadays, school children, companies, and those generally adept at handicrafts fashion lanterns out of paper, which take all sorts of creative forms: anything from a small zodiac animal hanging from a stick to giant parade floats. Fireworks are set off, depending on local enthusiasm and local regulations. The general din of constant explosions in many places can resemble something like a war zone.

In Taiwan, the Yanshui Beehive Fireworks Festival (鹽水蜂炮) is a prime -- and perhaps extreme -- example of Lantern Festival celebration. Participants don full-body rain gear and motorcycle helmets, covering any openings with duct tape or pieces of wet fabric, and join what is called a "baptism of fireworks." A towering "gun wall" bristling with bottle rockets is shot into the air, with sparks and errant rockets raining into the crowd. Worshipers dance from foot to foot in rhythm with the palanquin carrying Guan Gong, the God of War. The noxious smoke, explosions, sparks, flames, and inevitable burns, are said to bring good fortune for the year[13].

The major food of the holiday is *yuanxiao* (元宵), also referred to as *tangyuan* (湯圓). Strictly speaking, yuanxiao and tangyuan are prepared differently: yuanxiao are rolled into balls with a large sieve, but tangyuan are rolled by hand. And tangyuan were traditionally eaten at the winter solstice, not yuanxiao. But nowadays tangyuan are typically used during Yuanxiao Festival since they are more convenient to make or buy.

Tangyuan are spheres formed out of glutinous rice flour. They are either a natural white color or dyed with artificial or natural ingredients. Some are filled with meat and placed in savory soup. Some are filled with red bean, sesame, or peanut paste and served in a sweet soup. Some have no filling, and are deep fried. Tangyuan available at grocery stores offer a whole new level of variety, with fillings like strawberry, mango, and green tea. A more recent innovation is to serve them hot on a cold mound of ice cream.

SKY MENDING FESTIVAL

The first holiday occurring after the Lantern Festival is Sky Mending Day (天穿日), also called the Sky Mending Festival (天穿節, 補天節), which pays tribute to the benevolent actions of the primal goddess, Nüwa (女媧). It is usually held on the 20th of the first lunar month.

* * *

According to mythology the four pillars holding up the heavens crumbled, causing all sorts of misfortune to befall the world. Forest fires raged, animals turned vicious, attacking each other and humanity. Water burst from the earth, flooding the lands.

Moved by the horrible suffering, Nüwa worked quickly to repair the falling heavens. She took five stones from a riverbed - red, yellow, blue, black, and white -- melted them down, and used the molten rock to patch the sky.

She then killed a giant tortoise, chopped off its legs, and installed them as pillars to keep the sky in place. The four legs, however, were not of the same length, resulting in a tilted sky that survives to this day.

Having addressed the sky, she turned her attention to Earth. She pacified the vicious animals, extinguished the fires, and controlled the flood with the ashes of burning reeds. The world was once again at peace[14].

* * *

The *Yudingyuanjian Leihan* (御定淵鑒類函) mentions that the holiday appears in the *Record of Heretofore Works* (拾遺記)[15]. Observance took place on the 20th day of the first lunar month during the Eastern Jin dynasty, and later between the 19th to the 23rd. Traditionally, women would hang red cakes from the roof of their home with red string, praising Nüwa by matching her actions of "mending the heavens." The ritual was said to result in more favorable weather and prevent a leaky roof -- a serious omen of financial loss in Chinese culture. Concern with the mood of the sky clearly connects the ritual with the "Rain Water" solar term, when moderate rains are ideal for early spring planting. In ancient times, villagers would go to the outskirts and shoot arrows, displaying martial feats to win the continued favor of Nüwa[16].

Sky Mending festivities were widely abandoned after the Song dynasty, although there are records of celebrations occurring in Shanxi, Henan, and Shaanxi up until Qing dynasty. This is a shame given it is one of the few festivals in China's ancient patrilineal society where women played the main role. Most modern people are unaware of these older customs, although shadows of it remain among Hakka (客家) and Hoklo (閩南) communities[17].

Folklore

A HEAVENLY PRINCESS SAVES THE EARTH

The Jade Emperor's daughter was walking through the heavenly palace on her way to court when she was startled to hear her father's angry voice booming out from throne room. The whole palace shook with his fury. She froze, pausing to listen before she dared enter the room. Her father continued to complain at length, cursing the people of earth for killing one of his favorite heavenly birds. He concluded his tirade by ordering his heavenly guard to burn everything on earth, killing every living thing on the fifteenth of the first lunar month, in retribution for his murdered bird.

The princess spirited down to earth to investigate. She learned the people of the world had been preyed upon mercilessly by blood-thirsty beasts that had multiplied throughout the world. Exhausted by losing their loved ones and constantly living in a state of fear, they sent out a hunting party to kill the vicious beasts inhabiting the wild. During the course of the hunt, a giant bird burst out of the bushes, startling them, and causing one of the party to kill it. Listening to the story, the princess surmised that the heavenly bird had gotten lost, and must have made its way to earth, only to be killed in ignorance by a few scared hunters.

The princess knew what her father had in store for them, and thought the punishment was excessive. Risking her life and going against his direct orders, she told the people of earth and of her father's intent so that they could protect themselves. She then quickly ascended back to the heavenly palace before her absence was discovered.

The people wailed in sorrow, unsure of how to survive the fire and destruction from a furious god. The more clearheaded, however, gathered together and devised a plan. Over the course of three days, from the fourteenth to the sixteenth of the first lunar month, every household would hang lanterns, light fireworks, and set off firecrackers, fooling the Jade Emperor into believing the world was already on fire so that he would stay his hand.

On the evening of the fifteenth, the Jade Emperor looked down upon the earth, looking forward to watching the world burn. What he saw was a world aflame, shuddering with the din of explosions. Pleased, he went back to his throne, and thereafter dropped the matter. From that time onward, the people would make lanterns and light fireworks on the fifteenth of every first lunar month, staving off calamity for another year[18] [19] [20].

* * *

One of the major themes explored in this tale is humanity's fear of the natural world, and how that fear if left unchecked can result in catastrophe. The instinctual fear of being eaten alive drives people to eliminate animals that pose such a threat. This often creates even bigger problems. Apex predators play a key role in keeping ecological systems in balance, and their absence can reverberate throughout the wider ecology, resulting in mass die-offs of other organisms, including humans, eventually.

While the above myth on the surface concerns an angry god exacting revenge for the killing of his favorite pet, the myth contains a lesson on the consequences emanating from the larger natural world when ecological systems are carelessly or wantonly thrown off balance. This is just one interpretation, and the theme of divine retribution that springs up everywhere in the world's mythologies and religions provide an endless tapestry for interpretation on how to live in the world.

THE JESTER EXTRAORDINARY REUNITES A FAMILY

The Court Jester to Emperor Wu of the Han dynasty was walking through the palace gardens during a heavy snow, looking to pick some fresh plum flowers for the emperor. As he scanned the garden, the landscape silent and clothed in white, he noticed movement over by the well. He squinted, and saw a palace maid, face wet with tears, climbing up onto a high stone and working up the nerve to throw herself into the well. He overcame his shock, bolted over as fast as he could through the snow and slippery ice, and grabbed young woman, pulling her away just in time.

As the woman heaved and cried, working to compose herself, the jester realized she was one of the kitchen maids, who went by the name of Yuanxiao. Once the woman had settled down, he asked what afflicted her.

She answered that she missed her dearly loved family, particularly her younger sister. She had been away from them for a long time, closed off in the palace as she was, and had not seen them since she was inducted into service. Every New Year, typically the time spent with family, her heartbreak was especially acute.

The Jester expressed his deepest sympathies, and promised the maid that he would rectify the situation. Either genuinely consoled by his words, or simply careful not to express skepticism to a high-ranking court official, Yuanxiao thanked him profusely and vowed that she would not try to commit suicide again. He watched as the maid walked back through the snowy garden toward the court kitchen, flakes of snow landing on her slumped shoulders.

A few days later, making sure it was an auspicious day by the lunar calendar, the Jester set out into the town streets. He set up fortune-telling table, and waited for customers to come to him for advice. Impressed by his scholarly bearing, scores of townspeople lined up to ask their fortunes. To each person he gave the exact some message: "You shall find yourself engulfed in flames on the sixteenth of the first lunar month."

The dozens of querents, terrified of the answer they received, told scores of others. The macabre message passed from person to person, until the whole town was in a panic. The next day, the townspeople came to the Jester, some asking to explain the inauspicious divination, some asking how to avoid the horrible fate he cast for them. He remained silent until a large crowd of panicked townspeople assembled before him, screaming and pleading. As he stood up on his table to address them, the crowd went silent.

He looked over the crowd, his expression grave, telling them that on the thirteenth of the first lunar month, the Fire God would send a red fairy on a black horse to burn the town, and that when they see her, they should beg for mercy. With that he jumped down, took his table, and ran off down an alley. The townspeople looked at each other helplessly, faces white with terror.

On the night of the thirteenth, Yuanxiao, on the Jester's instructions, covered herself from head to toe in red silk and tore into town on a galloping black horse, and with the help of fireworks, fire and smoke streamed behind her. The townspeople got on their knees, begging for mercy. Once she reached the middle of town, she pulled hard on the reins as the Jester had instructed. The black horse reared up and the townspeople screamed in unison at the frightening sight. Yuanxiao, her face painted red, bared her teeth, growled, and threw an official-looking edict onto the ground. With that, she turned around and galloped out of town.

The Jester stepped out of the crowd and advised the edict be taken to the emperor. A lowly official scuttled over, picked up the edict with trembling hands, and made his way toward the palace.

The emperor was terrified when he read the edict. He issued a summons to all his advisors. The Jester hurried back, and feigned shock as the emperor had the edict read aloud. The edict stated that the capital city would be destroyed, and the imperial palace would be incinerated by fifteen days of fire.

Frightened, the emperor asked his advisors what should be done. The Jester waited while some of the more senior officials gave sage-sounding advice, much of it useless. Stepping forward, he assumed an innocent air, and said that he knew the Fire God's favorite food was tangyuan. And given that the palace maid, Yuanxiao, was well known in the palace for making delicious tangyuan, perhaps on the night of the fifteenth she should make a large batch, and go out into the town and offer them to the populace and to the god. At the same time, he advised, it would be prudent to have all subjects to come into the town to raise lanterns and light fireworks. With the town filled with light and sound, the fire god would then think his work was already done, and avoid setting fire to the town.

The Jester focused his gaze on the desperate emperor, appearing wise and calm and ignoring the shocked, disbelieving stares of the other officials. The emperor accepted his plan, and issued orders to make preparations according to the Jester's advice.

On the night of the fifteenth, the town raged with celebration. Firecrackers blasted the streets, rockets exploded in the air, lanterns lit the cloudy sky for miles around. Attracted by the lights and noise, Yuanxiao's family came into town. As they made their way through the gates, they were surprised to see Yuanxiao manning a large vat of boiling tangyuan. They rushed to be with her, and Yuanxiao rejoiced to see her parents and sister again.

As the revelry carried on through the night, the emperor grew pleased to see the town and palace saved from destruction. Thereafter, the tradition was continued every year on the fifteenth of the first lunar month[21] [22] [23].

***

The court jester referenced above is Dongfang Shuo (東方朔), a scholar-official to Emperor Wu of the Han dynasty. Dongfang Shuo was known for his witticisms, and was hence given the nickname "buffoon," (滑稽)[24] often acting as court jester. His recruitment to Emperor Wu's court occurred on the back of a self-recommendation letter he wrote, unabashedly praising his own memorization skills, the beauty of his eyes, and the health of his teeth[25]. Entertained by his antics and impressive learning, Emperor Wu took him on, and eventually promoted Dongfang Shuo to Superior Grand Master of the Palace (太中大夫). Due to drunkenness and urination in the palace, he was eventually demoted to Gentleman-in-Attendance (侍郎). Considering most scholar-officials faced decapitation for such offenses, his demotion demonstrates how much he was liked by the emperor.

Hemmed in by the lower title yet trapped in court -- an official couldn't just quit while serving at the pleasure of the emperor -- Shuo made light of the situation, famously saying, "People like me are known as those who escape the world by taking it easy at court.[26]" It is unclear whether he was just making a joke, or invoking Zhuangzi 's teachings: that a true sage hides among the people. In other words: hermitage as a state of mind.

Those who have found themselves in the modern world, stuck in a job or other situation that feels more like an exercise in tolerance than the fulfillment of a dream, will perhaps sympathize with Dongfang Shuo's situation. And like today, he had no other choice than to tolerate the disappointments of the civilized world, and escape into a hermitage of the mind. Even in 160 B.C.E., he notes escaping from civilization is not a realistic option from his "modern" perspective, saying "for only to the ancients was it given to take refuge from the world deep in the mountains[27]."

Dongfang Shuo is also associated with occult lore. He was said to be a *fangshi* (方士 or "master of esoterica"), and appears in the *Inner Biography of Emperor Wu* (漢武帝內傳) as an initiated adept, excelling in the esoteric arts. When the Queen Mother of the West (西王母) visits the court, she recognizes Dongfang Shuo as an immortal, the embodiment of the star Jupiter, previously sent down to earth as punishment for stealing her peaches of immortality. Other works say he is a reincarnation of Laozi, [28].

Whatever his pedigree, in the myth above he displays both mercy and humorous cunning. Various tales differ as to the position of the palace maiden, Yuanxiao: in some she is a concubine; others, a kitchen maid. But the message of benevolence is clear, as is a certain sense of wry joy as he enacts his complicated schemes. Once can easily imagine him on the palace walls, watching his handiwork unfold below: fireworks, thousands of lanterns lighting smiling faces, and a family reunited.

★ ★ ★

These Lantern Festival tales display many common themes. The first is one of mercy and kindness, with gods or people of exceptional ability going beyond just sympathy and taking action, using their talents to aid the world.

On the opposite end is a theme of trickery, in one case hoodwinking a supreme being: the Jade Emperor. In the other, manipulating a secular emperor, who effectively has just as much power as deity in matters of life and death to those he rules. It is a surprising inversion of Confucian ideals – tricking those of higher station – but likely a necessary pressure valve when bound by rigid hierarchies. It reflects a clichéd Chinese phrase uttered frequently in modern times: For every measure from above, there are countermeasures from below. (上有政策,下有對策).

Lastly, both tales feature giving the sufferer participation in their own salvation. For example, the Jade Emperor's daughter simply informs the people of the world of the forthcoming disaster, leaving the solution to them. Dongfang Shuo requires the palace maid to participate in frightening the townspeople. Like so many lessons of the world's religions, there is a clear message that success comes not from cloying dependence on divine intervention, but for assuming responsibility for one's fate.

CHAPTER 3: INSECTS AWAKEN 驚蟄

驚蟄 / 惊蛰 / 경칩 / けいちつ / Kinh trập
Pinyin: jīngzhé
Literal Meaning: "startle hibernation"
Alternative names: Hibernating Insects Awaken
Period: March 5 or 6 ~ March 20 or 21
Sun's Ecliptic Longitude: 345°

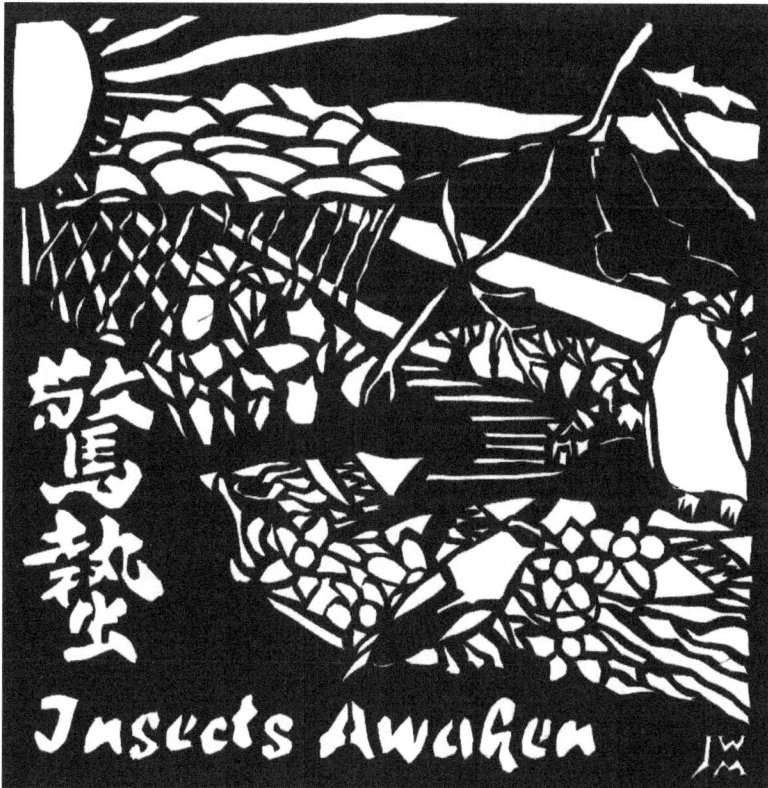

Thunder on Insects Awaken
Qiu Yuan
Yuan Dynasty

At midnight a peal of thunder roars across the land,
*   insect burrows and flower buds already open by dawn.*
Fields are vast and the fierce wind blows out candles,
*   lightning-lit rain impatiently smacks the window pane.*
Grass and wood blaze with vitality,
*   from here cold and warm hasten the change of weather.*
Only the stone tortoise and the wooden goose,
*   sit unmoving as spring returns to the land.*

驚蟄日雷 | 元 | 仇遠
坤宮半夜一聲雷，蟄戶花房曉已開。
野闊風高吹燭滅，電明雨急打窗來。
頓然草木精神別，自是寒暄氣候催。
惟有石龜並木雁，守株不動任春回。

    Insects Awaken is named after the thunder of spring, which is said to wake the insects from their hibernation. While modern biology attributes their arrival to the accelerating rise of temperatures during this time, the old lore is that the insects drink rain's nectar during the 10th lunar month in autumn, and then go dormant[1]. As Insects Awaken approaches, earth and sky come into closer contact with the rising of yang, resulting in lightning and thunder (天地陰陽氣接觸頻繁、大地激盪、產生閃電、雷聲隆隆).[2] Startled awake, the insects burrow out of the ground or wriggle out of dead wood to welcome the spring and to be baptized by rain. The land continues to show the stronger presence of spring: the sky brightens between rain showers, peach flowers turn red, and the trees are filled with a growing cacophony of chirping birds.

    This solar term displays strong aspects of nature and animal worship of the Chinese ancients, who often thought of themselves as descendants of powerful animals like lions or tigers. (The now popular idea of Chinese being descended from the dragon is a modern invention, rooted in a 1980s pop song. In the past, only emperors were allowed this distinction[3].) But in addition to top predators, meeker animals were also taken as representing the spirit realm, especially ones that appeared to die and were reborn. Snakes, bears, bats, frogs, squirrels, hedgehogs, all enter a state of hibernation, not moving and some not even perceptibly breathing -- for all appearances dead -- only to rise as if reborn as the energy of heaven and earth collide[4].

Pentads

Peach trees begin to blossom (桃始華)

Orioles sing (倉庚鳴)

Hawks are transformed into doves (鷹化為鳩)

While the first two pentads – blossoming peach trees and singing oriels – are straightforward heralds of spring, the last one would appear somewhat enigmatic to those unfamiliar with yin and yang symbolism. Hawks turning into doves essentially describes the severe death aspect of autumn yielding to the rebirth aspect of spring, or in other words, the retreat of yin and the advance of yang.

Agriculture

Insects Awaken marks a time of continued intensive farm work. Fruit trees are fertilized, tea bushes are pruned, and rapidly encroaching weeds need to be pulled. Traditionally, the strike of lightning and thunder on the day of Insects Awaken foretells plenty of rain and a good harvest[5]. A lack of thunder invites concern, depending on the location.

Health

The Chinese Medicine classic *Esoteric Scripture of the Yellow Emperor* (黃帝內經) states the third month of spring is the time when the myriad things are reborn, and as such recommends early bedtimes and wake-up times, as well as slow strolls[6] [7]. It is good to stay mindful of weather forecasts as cold snaps can make the body vulnerable to colds and other seasonal ailments.

Ancient Traditions

The *Yueling* of the *Book of Rites* encourages a number of rituals in the second month of the lunar calendar[8]. On an auspicious day sacrifices are made to spirit of the land, also known as *shè* (社), an earlier form of the Land God. The emperor was to perform the sacrifices in person with the empress and nine ladies of honor. Arrows – a symbol of male offspring[9] – would be given to each of the participants.

Yet another ceremony calls for the emperor to offer lamb to the gods as part of the auspicious procedures involved in opening the icehouses. The Chief Director of Music puts on an exhibition of civil dances and offers vegetables to the Inventor of Music (possibly Ling Lun 伶倫), while the emperor watches with his retinue. For smaller ceremonies during this time of year, the *Book of Rites* suggests silk as well as jade in square and round forms be used instead of animals. This would ensure that death aspects would be avoided during this critical time of year.

It is also for this reason the *Book of Rites* encouraged a number conservation practices in the natural and agricultural realms. No young plant buds were to be disturbed during this time because they nourish young animals. Farmers were to engage in only minor labors, like tending to living quarters and temples. Fishermen were advised against draining water from dams and ponds or draining rivers in order to catch fish. Hunters were prohibited from setting fires in the hills.

In the human realm, special care needed to be taken to look after orphans, matching the need to foster vulnerable young life in the natural world. Leniency toward criminals was also expected: officers were to examine conditions of prisons, remove handcuffs and fetters, and pause criminal litigation and punishments such as foot whipping. Finally, as trade activity was ramping up after the winter, it was a time for adjusting weights and measures.

The *Yueling* offers the usual warnings about performing rituals improper for the season. Autumn rituals would bring floods, constant cold air, and plundering from bandits. Winter rituals would call forth warm, genial winds, which despite their comfort would ensure that wheat wouldn't ripen, and stimulate raids and strife among the people. Summer rituals would invite droughts, prematurely hot winds, and an overabundance of caterpillars and other insects which would consume all the grain.

This time of year was expected to have the character of nurturing growth, taking a gentle hand with the natural world, and applying leniency to the human realm.

Customs

Among the general populace, particularly in northern climates where bathing was not as convenient, people would take out their clothes and shake them during the first thunder of the season, hoping to scare out any lice or fleas for the rest of the year[10]. Some poured lime along the door to deter insects during this time. Others placed wormwood into all corners of the house to scare off rats, snakes, ants, and other unwanted insects or malign forces[11].

Another tradition was to make offerings to the White Tiger, the Guardian of the West. By rubbing pig's blood or pork directly on the mouth of a paper effigy of the White Tiger is said to ward against evil and prevent harm from petty individuals who might cross one's path[12].

Festivals

DRAGON HEAD-RAISING FESTIVAL

Taking place on the second day of the second lunar month, the Dragon Head-Raising Festival (龍抬頭), literally called the "Dragon Raises its Head" and also known as the Azure Dragon Festival (青龍節), takes place during Rain Water or Insects Awaken depending on timing of the lunar calendar. The festival is said to have started in the time of Fuxi -- the mythological inventor of hunting, fishing, domestication, cooking, and the I Ching. In honor of Fuxi and to pray for the rain the dragon typically brings, high officials in many dynasties were required to go down into the fields, and personally plow roughly 3,000 square meters of soil[13] .

The "Dragon Raises its Head" (龍抬頭) comes from Chinese astrology, where "Twenty Eight Mansions" (二十八宿) are used to ascertain weather. The mansions are split into four quadrants (四象) and symbolized by mythological animals: the Azure Dragon of the East (東青龍), the White Tiger of the West (西白虎), the Vermilion Bird of the South (南朱雀), and the Black Tortoise of the North (北玄武)[14]. Once spring plowing is underway, the stars of the Azure Dragon mansions gradually come into view, first the dragon's head, then the constellation continues to ascend the sky until its full body is visible.

Another protective ritual during this time is called "Painting the Granary" (畫倉子). A box is filled with ash from the house furnace, and scattered onto the edges of the courtyard[15], symbolizing a closed perimeter of protection and storage. Some grain is then thrown into the middle, which is said to keep birds and animals from eating all the family grain.

The celebration of the Dragon Head-Raising Festival is more common in North China, especially given the fickleness of rain in more arid climates. In the hot and humid south, celebrations have transformed into Community Day (社日), which honors the Land God (土地神/土地公) during the Spring Equinox[16].

FLOWER FESTIVAL

The Flower Festival (花朝節), also known as the Flower Goddess Festival (花神節) or the Hundred Flowers Festival (百花節), is celebrated in different ways and at different times: the second, twelfth, or fifteenth of the second lunar month[17]. In Northeast, East, North, and South-Central China, families would head outdoors, watch lion dances, and release flower lanterns at night. One popular tradition was to place paper cuttings with the colors of the five phases to the branches of flowering plants[18].

Folklore

The flower festival is connected to three personages, all famous for their love of flowers: The Flower Goddess, Wu Zetian (武則天), and Cui Xuanwei (崔玄微).

THE FLOWER GODDESS

Nüyi (女夷) was a female disciple of Wei Huacun (魏華存), founder of the Shangqing (上清) sect of Taoism. Shangqing (上清), also called Supreme Clarity, is a mystical form of Taoism that moved away from physiological cultivation through herbs to internal alchemy by meditation and visualization of deities in the body, regarding the body as a microcosm of universal energies[19]. Nüyi was known to be good at planting and taking care of flowers -- so much that upon her death she ascended the heavens as an immortal, turning into the Flower Goddess responsible for all the flowers on earth[20]. Celebration of the Flower Festival are sometimes dedicated to her[21].

THE EMPRESS REGNANT

Wu Zetian (武則天) was Empress regnant of the Tang dynasty. It is said she established the Flower Festival[22], and would have her ladies in attendance gather white flowers. They would mix the petals with rice, and make all sorts of delicacies for her to enjoy.

THE FLOWER-LOVING HERMIT

Cui Xuanwei (崔玄微) spent a year away from home, deep in the mountains, hunting for herbs and mushrooms. Upon his return home late one moonlit night, he happened upon a young maiden walking through his overgrown garden. Before he could even ask what she was doing there, she asked whether could use his garden to hold a banquet.

Hesitant to refuse, he granted her request, and before long his garden was filled with beautiful young women. As he dined with them, he was amused to find that each one had a nickname belonging to a well-known flower, such as willow, plum, and peach.

During the course of the banquet Lady Gale stood up from the table and abruptly left, clearly offended in some way. The maidens, shaking with fear, turned to Cui and asked for his protection. Surprised, Cui realized that these women were flower fairies, and Lady Gale was the Goddess of Wind.

A few days later, a strong wind picked up, and the women instructed him to hang Taoist sigils on the branches to protect the flowers. He did as he was asked, and the next morning he found that all the flowers in his garden were untouched, while everything outside his garden had been blown away.

From then on, people would wrap the branches of flowers in colored paper to protect them from the wind and allow them to stay on the branch long enough to welcome the arrival of spring[23] [24] [25] .

***

In Chinese culture flowers are a vibrant expression of the divine in nature. As described at an earlier point in this book, each flower carries it own rich symbolism and has its own patron god or goddess. In addition to their beauty, flowers capture the transience of life: the solar terms of spring are the only terms assigned a set of representative flowers. By summer, the majority recede, so it is in this solar term of Insects Awaken, which is characterized by rebirth, when flowers are celebrated.

THE GOD OF MUSIC

This was the time of year during the more ancient dynasties that the highest music official would pay respects to the God of Music, also known as *Linglun* (伶倫). Ordered by the Yellow Emperor to establish a form of music, he set out into the world and came back with 12 pitch pipes – the same 12 pitches used in the "Watching the Ethers" system of tracking the solar terms mentioned earlier. These formed the base of the five notes of the ancient Chinese five-tone scale (五音) - gong (宮), shang (商), jue (角), zhi (徵), yu (羽), which is equivalent to do, re, mi, sol, la in Western music.[26] He also invented eight instruments (八音): 1) the xun (壎,塤) -- similar to the ocarina, 2) the drum (鼓), 3) the bamboo pipe (笛,蕭), 4) the sheng (笙) -- a wind instrument made from a gourd, 5) the zither (古琴), 6) the bianqing (編磬) -- a chime with many hanging pieces of stone or jade, 7) the bianzhong (編鐘) -- bronze chime bells, and 8) the zhu (柷)-- a percussion instrument made from a wooden box.

THE GOD OF THUNDER

The Thunder God (雷神) has been worshiped since very ancient times, peaking in the Tang and Song dynasties. Within the hierarchy of gods, he sits above the Rain Master (雨師) , the Earl of Wind (風伯), Madame Wind (風婆婆), and the Cloud Child (雲童), and is depicted as one of the main executors of the Jade Emperor's orders[27]. Carrying out the will of the heavens, he differentiates between good and evil and punishes grievous wrongdoing. He is therefore primarily a god of justice, although there are other, more benevolent aspects of the deity explored in various myths.

The god is male, as thunder is considered yang. Lightning is believed to come from Earth, and is therefore yin and female, the phenomena of thunder and lightning created by the friction of heavenly yang and earthly yin forces. Reflecting this dynamic, the Thunder God is accompanied by the Mother of Lightning (電母). Attired in blue, green, red, and white robes, she carries a mirror which brightens the flash of lightning[28]. Originally a dutiful earthly woman, she was hastily killed by the Thunder God when she was throwing out an uneaten bowl of rice. Realizing his overreaction, he transformed her into an immortal to accompany him in the heavens[29]. Given the numerous famines that have sprung up throughout China's history, both the Thunder God and the Mother of Lightning (電母) do not take kindly to wasted food.

The Thunder God is often portrayed in a variety of ways, human and bestial. Sometimes his image is vaguely simian or porcine, but the most common depiction is beak-faced and bat-winged, with giant claws, blue skin, and an otherwise human body. He carries a chisel or a hammer, which he uses to bang the drums to produce the sound of thunder. This fearsome image reflects the mystery and power of nature alongside the mortal terror that comes with unyielding justice[30]. Yet there are many tales of the Thunder God which show a more nurturing side.

PROTECTOR OF THE FIRST HUMANS

A peasant was out hunting, desperate for food as the land had long been barren. As he made his way through the forest he came across a sleeping creature with a dragon-like body. He managed to capture it with his net, brought it home, and threw it in a cage.

Before setting out to gather firewood with which to cook the strange creature, he told his son and daughter that under no circumstances should they give the animal water. With that, he set out, leaving the children alone with the beast.

Soon the beast was moaning, begging the children to give it water. Overcome with sympathy, they decided to give it a small amount in a tiny bowl. The dragon-beast lapped it up and with a loud bang the cage burst open. He leapt out of the cage and thanked the children, explaining he was the God of Thunder. He gave them one of his fangs, and told them to plant it.

The two children went outside and planted the fang into the ground, and returned to the house just as their father returned. He turned white upon seeing the broken cage, and ran outside and immediately began building an iron boat. He knew the Thunder God's punishment would take the form of an earth-destroying flood.

Meanwhile, the children watched as the tooth they planted quickly grew out of the soil, forming a large vine. Soon a calabash gourd grew out of the end of the vine, increasing in size until it was bigger than the both of them.

Their father was getting close to finishing his boat when a torrential rain started. While their father continued to work furiously on completing the craft, water began to rise. The children cut the calabash open, only to see it was filled with teeth. They ripped out the teeth, and took refuge inside just as a giant wave carried them all away.

The father was fortunate enough to have finished his craft, and the calabash and iron boat floated on top of the rising ocean until the height of the water scraped against heaven. Floating toward the gates of heaven, the father began banging on the doors, demanding entry.

Furious at the peasant's impropriety, the Water God, Gong Gong (龔工/共工/康回), forced the flood to retreat, causing the boats to fall to earth. The peasant's iron boat shattered when it hit the ground, killing him. The children, ensconced safely in the soft calabash, hit the ground without incident. The last two humans on earth, the two grew up together and repopulated the earth[31].

***

The above origin myth portrays the Thunder God as a protector of the progenitors of the human race, repaying the sympathy showed him by the two children. As with other tales, there are notes of reciprocity for good deeds, and punishment for those -- like the father -- who demonstrate a certain presumption or lack of propriety in dealing the gods.

The iron boat is a curious feature. Wood would seem more practical choice. The use of these materials could be related to the five phases of Chinese cosmology. The use of iron represents the metal phase, distinguishing it from the calabash, which stands for wood. In the five phases system, metal creates water. The peasant's choice of using metal for his craft points to his initiation of the water element, which destroys the world and himself. This is supported by metal's seasonal representation, corresponding for autumn and the start of decline, then moving toward the winter and repose of the water phase. On the other hand, water generates wood, represented by the calabash, and wood correlates to spring and rebirth -- in this case the rebirth of humanity.

The calabash is a potent symbol in Chinese culture. It represents health, longevity, and fertility, in part because it was used by Chinese doctors in ancient times to carry their medicinal herbs. Due to its hourglass shape -- fat on either end and narrow in the middle -- it is said to symbolize the integration of Heaven, Earth, and Man, and this unique shape is said to capture and hold harmful energies. The dried gourd is placed in bedrooms, both to absorb malign influences and to promote fertility or health. In variations of the myth, the seeds or the cut up flesh of the calabash are used to repopulate the earth with humanity.

The calabash is also the characteristic implement of one of the eight Taoist immortals, Li Tieguai (李鐵拐), who was able to leave his body and visit heaven, mirroring the gourd's symbolism as a link between heaven, earth and man. Similar to the Thunder God, this immortal was known for both his short temper and eagerness to aid the disadvantaged. He was also symbolized by a column of smoke, and an interesting synchronicity shows up in the frontispiece of alchemical treatise *Symbola Aureae Mensae* (1617) which shows twin pumpkins represented by two amphorae (a kind of thin-necked pot), connected by a column of smoke.

The Water God, Gong Gong (龔工), makes an appearance in this tale. He is associated with a number of flood myths, and is always shown as destructive. He is said to be responsible for the tipping of the sky, which required Nüwa's repairs as detailed in the previous chapter [32]. In other accounts, he quarrels with Zhurong (祝融), bumping into a mountain results in the recurring theme of jerking the sky askew, forming mountains and seas while at the same time causing all sorts of calamity for humanity [33]. He also battled with Yu the Great [34] (大禹), the dragon-son of a white heavenly horse [35] who defeated the Water God. The God of Water is depicted with a human face and the body of snake [36].

FATHER OF FUXI

Long ago there was an earthly paradise called Huaxu (華胥). There was no ruler, people lived without need and without fear, and could walk the invisible paths of the sky. Trees never dropped their leaves, and the land was filled with wonderful and diverse animals and plants.

One day a young maiden happened upon a giant footprint left in the ground by the God of Thunder. Curious, she stepped inside the print to examine it and soon after found that she was pregnant. She gave birth to a Son, and named him Fuxi

In the middle of this earthly paradise stood the Builderwood, the tree growing at the center of the world, connecting heaven and earth. No mortal being could climb it, owing to its smooth, soft bark. The lower section was a mass of tangled roots, and the trunk grew straight upward into the sky, with a proliferation of branches at the top, extending into heaven.

When Fuxi grew older, he easily traveled up and down the tree, making many visits into heaven, where he learned the skills of the gods. When returning to earth, he taught mortals how to create fire and cook. Inspired by what he learned in heaven combined with the ingenuity and beauty of the spider's web, he invented nets for fishing, and taught how to fashion bone and wood into weapons for hunting. He also showed the people of earth how to make and play musical instruments, instituted marriage, demonstrated the first offerings to the gods, and created the I Ching.

It was thus owing to the gift of the Thunder God, by begetting Fuxi, that humanity gained the means to satisfy earthly needs, enjoy the sounds of music, propagate the next generation, give thanks to the gods, and divine the future[37] [38].

***

The Builderwood (建木) mentioned here is the Chinese World Tree, which never casts a shadow as it is situated at the center of the world. It has a purple trunk, green leaves, black flowers, and yellow fruit. The tree is characterized by the number nine, the number representing the divine. The tree has nine twinning roots in the ground, drawing from the Nine Springs (九泉), and nine tangled branches supporting the Nine Heavens (九天).[39] [40] [41] The trunk of the tree links both ends, standing as the world axis and serving as a channel between ascending terrestrial and descending celestial energies and influences.

There is an enigmatic quality to this tale, where the people of the world live in an paradise, presumably where there is no pressing need that must be satisfied. Yet Fuxi brings back an array of skills that would assume a gap in the lives of humanity, while there is no indication in this myth that some cataclysm might have happened and humanity would require these skills. One possibility is that the Builderwood points more broadly to the rewards of educational or spiritual attainment.

GIFTS OF RAIN AND HEALING

A young woodcutter was making his way through a mountain forest, looking for wood and healing herbs. Dark clouds rolled in and the air erupted with the roar of thunder and the flash of lightning. He scurried under a large tree, and waited there for the storm to subside.

Hearing lightning strike the tree he was under, he quickly crouched on the ground, covering his head from any falling branches. But to his surprise, the sound of the thunder and flashes of lightening suddenly ceased, and everything was quiet.

He looked up to see a frightening blue creature stuck in the split tree. It had the face of a bird and tremendous claws. It turned its head toward the woodcutter and announced he was the God of Thunder, but had accidentally got stuck in the tree when he tried to split it. The God of Thunder asked to be freed, promising a reward to the woodcutter if he helped.

The woodcutter agreed, and helped free the beast, which immediately disappeared. Unsure what happened to his reward, the woodcutter simply shrugged and returned home.

A few days later, the Thunder God reappeared, this time with a book. He gave the book to the woodcutter, explaining it contained spells for making rain, curing illnesses, and assuaging sorrow. He explained that he was one of five brothers, and any of his brothers could be called upon to produce rain, and that the Thunder God himself should only be called upon in the direst circumstances, since he had a bad character tending toward destruction.

The woodcutter over time used the book to aid the populace. He became famous for his good deeds. One evening he got drunk, and while carousing in the streets was arrested by the magistrate. The woodcutter called upon the Thunder God, who came down to Earth and destroyed most of the houses of the village. The magistrate, terrified, let the woodcutter go.

From then on, the woodcutter was careful not to call upon the help of the Thunder God and used the powers contained in the book to save many regions from drought, famine, and illness.[42] [43]

***

Woodcutters were traditionally one of the four revered professions. The others were fishermen, farmers, and scholars[44]. It is clear that one of these is not like the others: the profession of scholar is an obvious outlier. But this highlights an equal footing of those that pursue the Taoist ideal of harmony with nature, comparable in importance with the learned scholars and officials that run the affairs of the empire. In fact in many tales the hermit professions are seen as more exalted, telling of top scholars recruited from among their ranks instead of from within the imperial bureaucracy. In other stories -- men living with nature, apart from the affairs of the world -- serves as a retirement profession of high-ranking scholars seeking the next stage of growth in their pursuit of Taoist ideals. This viewpoint is held up in Zen Buddhism as well. The *Platform Sutra* (六祖壇經) tells of a simple woodcutter discovering the truth for himself, and he is therefore preferable to a scholar of the scriptures.[45]

Within the tale above, the woodcutter, by the sake of helping the Thunder God but also living more closely to nature, is worthy of the gift he receives. Mirroring the recurring theme of those that return to society after a time in nature, he sets about addressing the ills of the human world.

The tale ends with what appears as the woodcutter's misuse of power: calling upon the Thunder God to escape the consequences of a drunken bender, with the homeowners of the village paying the price. Perhaps there is an aspect of forgiveness, or karmic debt that he addresses by continuing to help the populace. Perhaps it is to illustrate the sheer power of the Thunder God, and to serve as a warning for those that would call upon his power.

Although many of myths above show the deity's nurturing side, within all of them is an air of destructive power. During the time of Insects Awaken, the sound of thunder signals rebirth of spring and the animals coming out of hibernation, and the Thunder God reminds us that the process rebirth often carry aspects of destruction

CHAPTER 4: SPRING EQUINOX 春分

春分 / 춘분 / しゅんぶん / Xuân phân
Pinyin: chūnfēn
Literal Meaning: "spring center"
Alternative names: Vernal Equinox
Period: March 20 or 21 ~ April 4 or 5
Sun's Ecliptic Longitude: 0°

A Farming Family on a Spring Day

Song Wan
Qing Dynasty

As siskin birds flock together in wild fields,
   an old mountain villager passes near speaking of old times.
He feeds the cow at night and wakes his wife,
   talking of the next morning plans to plant trees at Spring Equinox.

春日田家 | 清 | 宋琬
野田黃雀自為羣，山叟相過話舊聞。
夜半飯牛呼婦起，明朝種樹是春分。

As the literal translation "spring center" implies, the Spring Equinox is the middle of the spring season. Temperatures continue their climb, although not as dramatically as the Rain Water and Insects Awaken solar terms. Flower buds open, and more birds are seen soaring in the air or flitting from tree to tree.

The defining feature of the equinox is the equal division between day and night. This balance is a celestial reflection of the symmetry that pervades so many of aspects of nature: flowers, plants, birds, beasts, cells, molecules, and DNA. It is said on this day the forces of yang in the east reach parity with the forces of yin in the west. Yin and yang, the key concepts from the *I Ching* (易經), form the basic structure of the universe, and a state too far one way or the other results in chaos[1]. Hence the prevalence of symmetrical designs in Chinese architecture, and the importance of balance in the design principles of Feng Shui. More broadly, the equinox is a time to remind us of the importance of balance in our lives, just as the world has reached a state of balance between the solstices.

Pentads

Swallows arrive. (玄鳥至；燕來也)
Thunder utters its voice (雷乃發聲)

Lightning begins (始電)

As indicated in the rituals outlined in the *Book of Rites*, the second month of the lunar year is a time when the swallows arrive, signaling the arrival of spring. Rising yang collides with and separates from declining yin with even more intensity, carrying forward the sounds of thunder and lightning[2] that started in Insects Awake.

Agriculture

For farmers it is the time for rice and corn planting. Sometimes plants will need extra protection, as there is often one last cold snap before severe cold departs for good until the winter, which can depress pollination, cause rot in seedlings, and retard maturation of fruit. With spring far enough along, it's typically a time to eat the first vegetables of spring and to brew spirits. A wind blowing from the east is a good omen; it indicates warm and wet weather, and thus a good harvest. A wind from the west was a sign of early heat, warning the harvest prospects for the year are poor[3] [4].

Health

Just as the day and night reach a point of balance, within traditional medicine it is important to maintain a balance of yin and yang within the body. One must harmonize the supply and demand of the "inner movements" -- organs, the blood, and the vital essences -- and the "outer movements" -- brain and bodily activity. Just as the natural world is reaching upward in a state of growth, human blood is said be similarly vigorous, which can cause all sorts of maladies like high blood pressure, irregular menstrual cycles, and hemorrhoids. Foods at the extreme ends of the "hot" and "cold" spectrums need to be avoided. An example of "hot" food include anything deep fried or certain fruits like durian. Examples of "cold" are iced beverages and shellfish. As usual, regular exercise, sleep, and moderate eating are advised.[5] [6] [7]

Customs

The Spring Equinox gave rise to a number of customs, many of which are no longer practiced, or if so very rarely. One was to plant cactus or stonecrop succulents on the roof[8], which was said to prevent fire for the rest of the year. Another was to get up early -- before the rooster's first crow -- and head down into the fields[9]. Once the first call of swallows was heard, they would offer sacrifices of lamb, pork, and beef to *Gao Mei* (高禖) -- a deity which will be discussed in the Grain Rain chapter.

According to Taoist alchemy, drinking the dew that forms on the morning of Spring Equinox improves longevity, so practitioners would go out to collect dew water for use in various elixirs[10]. Taoist practitioners would also look into the northwest sky at night to see if three-colored clouds of black, azure, and yellow would appear, signaling the arrival of the Taoist god, the Heavenly Thearch of Grand Tenuity (太微天帝)[11].

Festivals

SPRING CELEBRATION FOR THE LAND GOD

The Spring Land God Celebration (春社 chūnshè) is a very ancient festival, referenced in oracle bones in 2,000 B.C.E., and was very important up until the Yuan dynasty. Dates were at first decided by divination, then after the Tang dynasty the date was placed 41 to 50 days after the first solar term of Spring Begins (立春). Nowadays, it falls before or after the Spring Equinox (春分), in the second lunar month on the 2nd, 8th, 12th, or the 25th, depending on local customs. [12]

The modern meaning of the word *shè* (社) relates to some sort of organized social system, such as a community, a society, or an organization. But in ancient times it referred to the Land God (土地神)[13], as made clear by the construction of the character itself: a spirit radical (礻) alongside the character for earth (土).

The transformation from a hunter-gather society to one based on farming brought with it worship of the earth, eventually personified as the Lord (or God) of Soil and Ground (土地公 / 土地神). Celebration of the Land God usually took place at temples dedicated to the deity, with offerings of meat, wine, rice, and cakes, which the worshipers then enjoy together at a banquet. [14] [15] The wine was said to be a cure for deafness and imbibing it ensured the health of offspring. As part of the celebrations gongs would be struck, and the Land God was set on a palanquin and paraded through the town[16].

In some places, such as the Northern China, the Chunshe festival was combined with the Dragon Head-Raising festival (龍抬頭), and observed on the second day of the second lunar month, while the south preserved separate observances. They are in essence different holidays: Chunshe is for fertile soil, while the Dragon Head-Raising festival is observed to bring rain. Chunshe is still celebrated among the Hakka. [17]

There are a number of origin myths concerning the Land God, each portraying the god in varying degrees of eminence. In one, he is said to be the son of the Water God. His heritage gave him power to control rivers and flatten the soil, clearing it of snakes and fierce beasts and rendering the earth capable of bearing agriculture. [18] What is interesting is that the offspring of the god of water is the god of soil, matching five-phase cosmology where earth overcomes water.

In another myth, he is more of a labor hero, subduing the wild overgrowth and reclaiming infertile wasteland for farm production. There are also tales portraying the god as much less exalted -- more of a low-level official in charge of a small area. In this role he enjoys no particular sacrificial offerings, and his statue is the play-thing of children: he sometimes must endure the urination of misbehaving boys, who seem to suffer no repercussions. [19]

Within all these tales there is a certain closeness of the god to the people -- a familiarity that is not the case with the wider pantheon. Small temples to the deity are the most common, and likely make up the largest share of temples by number. They are typically highly respected and well-tended, but modest compared to the temples dedicated to other deities, reflecting a certain commonness and intimacy.

Whereas the male Land God is one of the most familiar gods, there is another land deity typically embodied as female: Queen of the Earth or Houtu (后土). She is depicted as far more powerful and mysterious than her male counterpart. Although both are considered expressions of earth in ancient times, they have evolved into very separate deities. In one legend she is the consort of the Land God, promoted by the Jade Emperor after being wrongly executed, and installed to ensure the Land God is not overly generous with the bounty of the earth.[20] In other tales she is described as a kind, wise, and powerful goddess, answering prayers for harvest, rain, children, health, wealth, and safety, or helping the mythological Yu the Great channel the Great Floods into the sea and battling turtle ogres. [21]

She was regarded as a female deity after the Sui dynasty. Prior to that the deity's gender was ambiguous. In one myth the god is the descendant of the Flame Emperor (炎帝) and the son of the Water God, similar to the Land God mentioned above. In others, Houtu holds the cords to the central part of the world and reigns alongside the Yellow Emperor. Houtu is also regarded as the ruler of the netherworld, called the "Dark Capital" (幽都), with a terrible assistant named Tubo (土伯) guarding the gates. [22]

So in addition to aspects of the Earth's surface, such as fertility and wealth, the Queen of the Earth is a chthonic deity of the deep earth. Given her shrouded origins, her role as a check and balance on the bounty of the Land God, her connection to the underworld, and general air of mystery and power, she is worshiped less widely than the Land god, but when worshiped, done so with great care and respect.

Folklore

THE LYCHEE GROVE

Long ago, in the town of Huazhou, a man and a woman were riding down the street, each on a white horse. The woman wore a crown, large earrings, a silver necklace, a bracelet of red jade, and a dress made of silver ringlets. She carried a fish basket filled with crabs they had caught at the shore, and were bringing them back to share with their family.

The horse unexpectedly stopped, and looked up to a group of old lychee trees. Despite the season, the old trees had no flowers and had an odd air about them. The woman led her horse around one of the trees, examining it. For no obvious reason, the horse was spooked. It kicked wildly, scratching wide gashes in the trunks of the trees and snapping a number of branches. Amid the chaos, the woman's basket of crabs fell to the ground, scattering the creatures all over.

The man and woman were mortified. They dismounted and knelt on the ground in front of the trees, and offered the crabs as compensation for the damage the horse had caused. The woman chanted something under her breath.

Once finished, the man and woman rode on. Ten days later the trees grew full with bunches of delicious lychees, and did so ever after. Ever since, during the spring equinox people have recited the lychee poem in commemoration of the event, and to ensure a good harvest. [23] [24]

***

The woman referred to above is Lady Xian (冼夫人), also known as Lady of Qiao Guo (譙國夫人), a chieftainess of the Li people (俚人) in what is now Guangdong province during the Liang, Chen, and Sui dynasties. Known for her martial as well as diplomatic prowess, she was later deified as "Saintly Mother of Lingnan" (嶺南聖母). Her history is one of both homeland defense and peace-making, defending her tribe from enemies while pacifying the internecine warfare between factions in her own tribe.

Her brother was said to be consumed with wealth and privilege, and would regularly rob the surrounding counties. She was able to convince him to stop, which earned the respect of the nearby groups. She was also key in stopping human trafficking common on the southern coast at the time. She married a Chinese general, and aided him in his affairs, often acting as a fair judge in lawsuits. Over the course of her life she served the emperors of three dynasties, earning numerous titles and a degree of renown rare in what was a highly patriarchal society.

Carrying on the tradition begun by Lady Xian in the above tale, people will make offerings of candles, ingots, and crabs to the lychee grove. The spring equinox is typically a time when growing lychees are hitting their stride, and the practice is a way of giving thanks to the trees and to hope for continued bearing of fruit in future years. Candles are used as they are in any religious or ritualistic setting: as a conduit to the spirit realm. Ingots represent wealth and a plentiful harvest. Crabs represent peace, as the word for crab, xiè (蟹), is a homonym with the word for harmony, xié (協).

The horse's damaging of the lychee trees could be an origin myth for the use of girdling with lychee trees, where bark is carved away to encourage fruit trees to bear larger, sweeter fruit.

THE SUN AND MOON GODDESSES

Di Jun (帝俊), also known as the Sun-Moon God, was said to have two wives, Xihe (羲和) the Sun Goddess, who lived in the eastern ocean and gave birth to 10 suns,[25] and Changxi (常義) the Moon Goddess, who lived in the western wilderness and birthed the 12 moons[26]. The emperor split his time between his two consorts, accompanying one during half of the year, and then the other during the next half[27].

The warming weather emerging in spring is the Sun Goddess getting excited at the approach of the emperor, who she meets on the Spring Equinox. She is so eager that she uses her privilege as first wife to shorten the month of February by two days to ensure she sees him sooner. In September, at the Autumnal Equinox, it is the Moon Goddess's turn, which is why the harvest moon blazes so brightly in the autumn sky. Meanwhile, the days thereafter shorten as the Sun Goddess grows sad and listless in the absence of her husband, coming out less and less until the next equinox[28].

Di Jun is a somewhat mysterious god, appearing only in the *Classic of Mountains and Seas*, and sits apart from the usual pantheon of early Chinese mythology. He is generally believed to be an ancestral god of the eastern Chinese Shang dynasty, also historically known as the Yin dynasty (殷代), who was replaced by the Yellow Emperor in myth when the Yin dynasty collapsed[29].

Di Jun was said to have befriended the five-colored birds of earth[30], sometimes interpreted as a kind of phoenix. They are his representatives on earth, and guard his two alters, they themselves becoming objects of worship or totems for the emperor. Birds figure largely in the Di Jun myth. The Sun Goddess's sun-children are carried across the sky by black ravens, and placed in the Fusang (扶桑) mulberry tree of life before being returned to the eastern sea to be lovingly bathed by their mother. The story of Hou Yi describes his shooting down the nine suns, and the trials he suffers under the furious Di Jun[31].

The tale of the two consorts is more than just a way to explain natural phenomena or to codify polygamy among the rich and royal. The heart of the story is one of sorrow: the inevitable sadness of change and knowing that all is temporary. It is also a parable of unmet desire, longing for the sun rays in the depths of a cold winter, or yearning for the quiet, cold silence of fallen snow while toiling under a July sun. Yet behind such longing is the constant turn of the cycle of the year, knowing there will be yet another chance to enjoy the return of a new set of seasons.

CHAPTER 5: CLEAR BRIGHT 清明

清明 / 청명 / せいめい / Thanh minh
Pinyin: qīngmíng
Literal Meaning: "clear bright"
Alternative names: Clear and Bright, Bright and Clear,
Qingming Festival, Tomb Sweeping Festival
Period: April 4 or 5 ~ April 19 or 20
Sun's Ecliptic Longitude: 15°

Qingming
Huang Tingjian
Song Dynasty

At Clear Bright peach and plum blossoms smile wide,
  yet mounds covered with weeds inspire distress.
Thunder has awoken dragons, snakes, and insects,
  and ample rains soften grasses and woods in the outskirts.
A tomb-beggar boasts to his wife of getting treated to dinner,
  an official refuses a promotion and gets burned alive.
Who knows if these men were poor and foolish, or virtuous and incorrupt,
  all they have left behind are mounds covered in weeds.

清明 | 宋 | 黄庭堅
佳節清明桃李笑，野田荒塚只生愁。
雷驚天地龍蛇蟄，雨足郊原草木柔。
人乞祭餘驕妾婦，士甘焚死不公侯。
賢愚千載知誰是，滿眼蓬蒿共一丘。

Clear Bright is a solar term characterized by contradiction. The name itself conjures up images of clear skies and sunlight, yet typically the weather of the time is anything but. It was traditionally a time of sacrifice during the Cold Food Festival (寒食節), as was the Qingming Festival following it. There are aspects of life-affirming joy in many of the traditional activities associated with the Qingming Festival, yet it is also a time of sorrow and remembrance of the departed, and has become chiefly connected to sadness and familial obligation over the course of time.

In terms of the natural world the name Qingming itself refers more to the quality of the air than to the weather[1], with gentle winds carrying clean air full of the fragrance of plants and flowers bursting forth thanks to the spring rains. Like an infant just opening its eyes, the word awakes. And yet it is at this time that people are reminded to think of those that came before us and are now gone -- a message that life is to be enjoyed, and is a process of birth, death, and rebirth. In this way, it is the most poetic of all the solar terms, and the only solar term that shares a name with a major festival. The most famous poem describing the quality of the solar term was written by Du Mu in the Tang dynasty:

Qingming
Du Mu
Tang Dynasty

Amid the constant drizzle of Qingming,
People walk the roads in a daze.
I ask, where where an inn can be found?
A shepherd boy points far away to Aprocot Blossom Village

清明 | 宋 | 黄庭堅
清明時節雨紛紛，
路上行人欲斷魂。
借問酒家何處有？
牧童遥指杏花村。

Pentads

> Vernicia begins to flower (桐始華)
> Voles transform into quails (田鼠化為駕)
> Rainbows begin to appear (虹始見)。

Vernicia is also known as the *tung* (tóng) tree. In Taiwan it is said to be the representative flower of the Hakka people (客家人), a Han Chinese subgroup who have established communities throughout Asia and beyond. The flower is named partly due to where it grows: the areas in between the high-mountains and plains, the geography which Taiwanese Hakka settled. The Hakka groups settled in Taiwan during the mid-1600s. When they came the plains were already occupied by Hoklo Han settlers (閩南人) , while the high-mountains were held by the island's indigenous peoples. This left the in-between areas, some plains and low mountainsides, typically with red soil that is very hard to farm. Vernicia, however, thrives in these areas, much as the Hakka did over the years. It is a fast-growing, vital plant and considered to have a strong life-force. It has many industrial uses such as oil and varnish. In this context, when the *tung* trees flowered, it was time for the Hakka to begin planting[2].

Voles, being creatures residing in burrows in the earth, are considered yin[3]. Quails, known for their fighting spirit, are yang. This pentad indicates the seasonal move toward the more active yang season of summer.[4] [5] Voles are also associated with the hidden, or trickery through seduction[6], while quails are associated with marital loyalty, echoing the reproductive qualities of the season. They also symbolize the hard study of scholarship[7], mirroring the hard toil required of farmers as summer nears.

Rainbows appear at this time of year for a couple reasons. One is the interplay of yin and yang as yang continues to advance during this solar term[8]. The other owes to weather, as during this time cloud-cover can be thin and patchy, allowing rays of light to hit the short showers common during the season.

Agriculture

This is the time when fruit trees start flowering, and farmers hurry around their orchards, helping with pollination. Melon, beans, corn, sorghum, and cotton are planted, while tea farmers guard against pests threatening their newly sprouting tea leaves. Grain farmers need to guard against late frost, or the worst possible combination of weather: a final freeze followed by a rapid warming up, which can damage grain crops and induce rot. In some areas grazing pasture is still limited. The immune systems of livestock are compromised, and the weaker animals need special care to survive until summer[9] [10].

Health

This is a time where health can be compromised by the emotional strain of visiting family graves. Exercise in loose clothing out in the clean air is advised. Otherwise, according to Chinese medicine, an overabundance of liver chi can affect the spleen and stomach, setting off a chain reaction of poor digestion absorption, imbalances in mood, and irregular blood flow, which then can result in illness. The key here is moderate exercise; over-straining or generating too much yang chi puts excessive pressure on the heart and is especially problematic for those with heard conditions, high blood pressure, inflammations, kidney stones, or any sort of communicable disease[11] [12].

In light of the above health considerations, arriving just after the Cold Food Festival, Qingming was an opportunity to go outside. In part to enjoy the fresh air, as well as to enjoy the advancing greenery of the season, which can counteract the deleterious effects of eating cold food during the previous days. Heading outdoors is also a time to pay respects to ancestors by tending their graves during the Tomb Sweeping Festival.

The Cold Food and Tomb Sweeping Festivals were celebrated together until the Tang dynasty,[13] [14] and the observance of the Cold Food Festival disappeared by the Qing dynasty[15], whereas observance of Tomb Sweeping continues into modern times.

Ancient Traditions

The third month of the lunar year was considered the last month of spring in the *Book of Rites* [16]. The emperor ritualistically presented robes dyed yellow -- the color of young mulberry leaves -- to the ancestral ruler and his queen.

Mulberry leaves are the main food of silkworms; this ritual was ensure productive growth of mulberry trees well into the summer to ensure enough food for the silkworms to produce plenty of silk. The empress fasted for a few days, carried out a vigil, and then went in person to fields in the east to care for the mulberry trees. She was accompanied by other women of the palace, who were not to wear ornamental dresses so as to be prepared for work in caring for the silkworms. No one was allowed to be idle, and their frenetic activity was both practical and symbolic of the season. The silk would then be distributed to the ladies of the palace to make robes worn during major rituals.

The Emperor also left the palace and stepped into a boat carefully examined for leaks by the official in charge – the text mentions flipping the boat over five times just be thorough. He caught a sturgeon and took it back to the ancestral temple to pray for a good wheat harvest.

In the natural realm the influences of new life and growth were considered fully developed. Warm, genial airs diffused across the land. The crooked shoots -- the harbinger of early growth -- were all grown out and the buds unfolded themselves. Life did not brook any form of restraint during this time. Nor did water: the superintendents of works needed to remove any obstructions from the ditches and larger channels carrying water away from dykes and dams, which also need to be repaired. Since this was the time of the rainy season, water came both from the skies and the ground, so any areas lying on low or level grounds needed to be inspected to prevent excessive flooding.

There was also a prohibition against nets for hunting animals and birds, hunting camouflage, and any sort of bait that would injure animals. Foresters were prohibited from cutting down mulberry tress, lest their destruction unduly influence the silkworm harvest.

Yet this was not just about economic production. The mulberry trees are also intended as places of rest for cooing doves and crested birds, intimating their value reaches beyond immediate human need and into the local ecology. Once again, certain restraints on humanity were cascaded through the empire to allow for the free movement and continued growth of nature.

In the human realm, the emperor set an example of kindness and warmth, distributing grain to the poor and fine silks or other presents to high-ranking officials, scholars, and men of talent and virtue.

Winter rituals performed during the last month of spring would invite unduly cold airs and the decay of plants and trees. A sense of terror would grip the populace. Summer rites brought disease, unseasonable rain patterns, and barren mountain farms and woods. Autumn rituals would cause the sky to fill with moisture and gloom, excessive rain, and warlike movements from rivals.

Customs

The major customs of the term all involved heading outdoors: grave-tending, tree planting, and kite flying. All are in some ways connected to the Tomb Sweeping Festival.

Festivals

TOMB SWEEPING FESTIVAL

Tending the resting places of ancestors has been a vital activity in Chinese culture for centuries, and annually maintaining graves likely preceded the establishment of the 24 solar terms[17]. Tomb Sweeping was first celebrated in the Zhou dynasty and was declared a national holiday in the Tang[18]. Tending of graves traditionally took place ten days before or after Clear Bright, or in some places up to a month prior or later[19]. In the Tang dynasty, although grave-tending was involved, the focus was much more on outdoor activities with family and friends. By the more impoverished Song dynasty, however, the focus returned to grave tending[20], along with the sorrow that accompanies such tasks: either sadness at the loss of the departed, or sadness that one could not return to family homes and tend the graves due to obligations in far-away towns.

The ritual of tomb sweeping, in addition to the clearing of weeds and dirt that have accumulated on the grave, involves kneeling down and praying before the tombstones, burning incense and paper money, and offering food, tea, and wine[21]. In some places there were different customs based on gender. In the north, women were not allowed on graves. Once paper money was burned, men were to take what was left, cut a door out of it, and place a mock door on the door of their home to protect against misfortune. In some areas, wives had to go back to their original homes, or risk inviting death to take the life of their father-in-law. In some places it was the exact opposite, where a return to one's original parents would bring death on one's mother-in-law. In some places, women weren't allowed to leave the house at all, in order to shield them from "Fierce Gods" roaming the land during this time[22].

Once respects were given at the tomb, families would then go out and enjoy the day together before they had to get back and work in the fields. The intensity of play likely differed from location to location, leading writer Xie Zhaozhe (謝肇淛) of the Ming Dynasty to say that Northerners took the observances very seriously, while Southerners used the holiday as an excuse to play, party, and stumble drunk around the graves[23]. For anybody who has witnessed Southern Chinese practices during the Tomb Sweeping festival, Xie's opinion has more to say about the universal mutual disdain between northerners and southerners of any nation than an accurate depiction of real southern practice.

When it comes to the traditional lore, the outdoor activities that took place after the serious business of tomb tending were numerous and frenzied: setting up swings from trees, flying kites, and *cuju* (蹴鞠) -- an early form of football or soccer -- rowing, placing willow branches on doors, and planting trees[24] [25]. In past times, women were not often allowed to leave the home most of the time, so this gave them a much-valued chance to go out into the world and enjoy the green of spring[26].

Kite flying was popular because Clear Bright is the last time of the year that the wind is considered predictable, and generally blows at an angle from low to high[27]. People would write their concerns and misfortunes on the kite, and once flying high in the air -- sometimes with a whistle attached -- they would cut the string, symbolically letting lose their problems. The practice was also believed to scare birds away from fields[28].

The frenetic activity of holiday inspired numerous poems and paintings, the most famous is *Along the River During the Qingming Festival* (清明上河圖). Over five meters in length, and long revered by emperors since its completion in the Song dynasty, the painting depicts the countryside and a dense city, all traversed by a winding river. People of every occupation and social station are depicted, from goatherds to jugglers to official scholars. The main focus of the painting is the crowded *Rainbow Bridge* (虹橋), where laborers scurry back and forth. Perfectly encapsulating the buzz and energy of the spring season, the painting is considered one of China's greatest artistic masterpieces.

Activities around the festival were not just about honoring the past at the graves of the ancestors, or enjoying the present by flying kites and swinging in trees. It was also a time to lay the groundwork for future well-being by planting trees. The Clear Bright period is ideal for planting trees due to the weather, which brings enough rain to ensure saplings are more likely to survive.

Tree planting had always been a culturally important activity in China, and planting trees in spring was referred to as a moral activity in the *Book of Rites*[29]. There was even a public official in charge of reforestation in ancient times.

The *Classic of Mountains and Seas* refers to Kuafu (夸父), the giant grandson of the Queen of the Earth (后土) , who tried catching the sun. In his pursuit, he became so parched that he drank all the rivers. Unsatiated, he died of thirst, and his stick fell to the ground, giving birth to a large peach tree forest which sustained humanity[30].

More folklore concerns Dong Feng (董奉), a famous doctor during the Three Kingdoms period. He would not accept any monetary payment for his services, instead asking only for apricot seeds if he successfully cured an illness: one for minor illnesses, five for critical ones. Each seed he received he planted near his house, until they grew into a forest of tens of thousands of trees, a testament to his healing skill. He then traded all the apricots that grew from the trees for grain, and distributed the grain among the poor. He was thereafter nicknamed the "Apricot Immortal of Dong Forest" (董林杏仙), and the "Apricot Forest" (杏林) has since been associated with the medical profession[31].

COLD FOOD FESTIVAL

The Cold Food Festival (寒食節) takes place one or two days before Qingming, and 105 days after the Winter Solstice[32]. One of the festival's names is therefore "105 Festival" (百五節), and also goes by "No-Smoke Festival" (禁煙節) " or simply the "Cold Festival (冷節). The event was observed by extinguishing all fires in the home for three days[33], and eating cold food prepared in advance. Foods might include porridge, noodles, barley rice, and cookies. A diet limited to cold food is generally anathema in Chinese medicine, and in climates where weather was still chilly, not eating warm foods or not stoking any fire with which to warm oneself was a dangerous prospect.

The festival likely originated from fire-worshiping practices in ancient times, when daily life was bound by aspects of fire: either its life-affirming gifts of warmth, cooking, and sterilization, or its destructive power and potential for disaster. Ritual avoidance of fire to prevent conflagrations is mentioned in the *Rites of Zhou* (周禮)[34]. During the Cold Food Festival, in honor of the Fire God, time was set aside where fire was given time to rest, as short as a day or as long as a month, and originally in mid-winter, when observing the custom could be fatal. In fact the festival was originally held in the depths of winter, and was a required observance even in cases of illness. [35] Many rulers tried to ban the practice -- unsuccessfully -- but it was eventually moved to three days before the Qingming Festival, and incorporated ancestor veneration by the Tang dynasty[36]. Observance as a separate festival virtually disappeared by the Yuan dynasty.[37]

In addition to eating cold food and venerating the ancestors, other activities included more uplifting pastimes like reciting poetry and painting eggs [38] -- an interesting synchronicity with Easter egg traditions in the West, which occurs around the same time. When the period of observance concluded, families would relight a "new fire," symbolizing resurrection of the fire spirit to heat their homes, cook their food, and prevent destructive wildfires[39].

One of the more important practices was carrying willow twigs or affixing them to doorways [40]. The willow tree is pregnant with symbolism throughout the world and is a symbol of spring and awakenings in Chinese culture[41]. The tree also symbolizes departure, hermitage, and reclusion [42], which connects it to its mythological significance as revealed in the tale below. It also is said to ward against evil and misfortune[43]. Both Taoists and Buddhists attest to the willow's power. *The Essential Techniques for the Welfare of the People* (齊民要術), states that placing young willow to the wall of a home keeps ghosts away[44], and in Buddhism the willow is called the "ghost-scaring wood" (鬼怖木), while in the *Consecration Sutra* (灌頂經) willow is used to subdue a dragon[45].

One reason willow is used is that the newly grown fronds are easily pulled away during this period of the year. Another is that protection is deemed necessary during the approach of Qingming, one of the three major underworld festivals, which include the Ghost Festival (中元普渡) in the seventh lunar month, and Winter Clothes Day (寒衣節) on the first day of the tenth lunar month[46]. In fact, willow is sometimes used any time someone is going to a funeral or any other activity involving death. In certain areas the willow is substituted with the Chinese banyan in places like Taiwan. Even in the absence of these particular trees, simply having green leaves or something natural on one's person are said to have protective qualities, and are to be thrown away once one has left the area where death lingers.

Folklore

THE CLEAR BRIGHT WILLOW

Jie Zhitui (介之推) was a musician and composer for the zither who served Jin Price Chong'er (重耳) during the Spring and Autumn Period. A conflict over royal succession drove the prince and his attendants away from court, and they spent the next 19 years on the run. At one point, having been robbed of their food by bandits, most of the Prince's attendants had run off, leaving only a small coterie of his most loyal advisors, which included Jie Zhitui.

The Prince eventually became ill due to lack of food. To nurse him back to health, Jie Zhitui cooked him a soup of herbs, cutting off flesh from his own thigh and adding it to the broth. Prince Chong'er's health was soon restored after drinking the soup

Realizing the impossibility of Jie obtaining meat, the Prince questioned him until he admitted to using his own flesh. The Prince was moved beyond words, but without royal title and no possessions but his own life, there was little he could do to reward Jie.

Years later, Prince Chong'er returned to the capital and was installed to his rightful place as Duke of Jin. He awarded many of his advisors with lavish titles, yet for some reason had neglected to reward his ever-loyal musician. Jie thereupon collected his mother, and carrying her on his back, went deep into the mountain forests and retired from official life.

An earlier song written by Jie was posted to the city gates by his friends, who were upset at the injustice suffered by the Duke's loyal official. "The Song of the Dragon and the Snake" told the tale of a dragon who invited the envy of heaven with its beauty and was stripped of its abilities and cast down to earth. In the earthly realm, it befriends five snakes. Four of the snakes help return him to Heaven, while one remains behind, forlorn at the dragon's departure. The song concludes that one cannot dwell on the past if one is to be cheerful.

When the Duke realized he had neglected his most loyal official who had sustained him with his own flesh, he sent numerous messengers into the woods to locate Jie and offer him a high position in line with his many sacrifices and long-standing loyalty. The messengers returned, saying there was no sign of him, other than some villagers who saw him going deep into the woods high on the mountain with his mother on his back.

One of the Duke's advisors suggested they set the mountain on fire on three sides, and wait for him to come out on the unlit side. Given Jie's duty to his mother, he would surely bring her out to save her from being engulfed in flames.

The Duke agreed, and the mountain was set alight. It burned for three days and three nights, yet neither Jie nor his mother ever emerged. The Duke himself went into the smoldering forest to search for him, and eventually found the man and his mother's burnt bodies next to a scorched willow tree.

The Duke threw himself to the ground and wailed, lamenting at the loss of a great official and for causing the death of a man and his mother. One of the Duke's retinue found a note stuffed into a hole under the willow tree, written in Jie's blood. It read:

"Cutting off my flesh and feeding it to your grace revealed my red-blooded loyalty to you. I trust my grace will forever remember to remain clear and bright.

"Although death has arrived and I will never again set eyes on my grace, let it be as if your humble servant still accompanies you. If you have me in your heart, I hope you can look inside yourself and act with virtuous conduct.

"I have no shame as I leave this world, and hope that my grace will forever remain clear and bright."

The Duke arranged to have a temple built and dedicated to Jie, and ordered everybody in Jin to refrain from lighting fire for a set period in memoriam for his loyal musician, and mandated his subjects to suffer the eating of cold food to remember the great loss of a loyal official of Jin. Owing to his sacrifice and loyalty, and with the adoration of the people of Jin, it was said that Jie became a Taoist immortal.

A year later, the Duke went back to the spot where Jie had died. The willow tree which had been badly burned remained, except a few new branches had grown out from the charred bark, long enough to catch the wind and sway back and forth with each gust, as if dancing. The Duke paid his respects to the reborn tree, and thereafter willow was known as Clear Bright Willow (清明柳).[47] [48] [49] [50]

***

Much occurs in this myth which may be perplexing to modern sensibilities, especially the virtue made of extreme loyalty and sacrifice for one's ruler. (Although perhaps those who have dedicated the bulk of their lives to cubicle habitation and digital serfdom might consider a chunk of thighmeat a smaller price to pay.) In a Confucian context his behavior would be considered highly meritorious, and Jie's installation as an immortal demonstrates respect for a certain toughness in sticking to one's principles, and enduring the trials of loyalty.

The poem Jie composes for the Duke is odd in its structure, mentioning "Clear and Bright" twice. Here the term could be translated as upright and incorruptible. By mentioning it twice, and in combination with the rest of the text, he appears to be admonishing the Duke, choosing to punctuate his criticism with his own death and a note written in blood. Some commentators have taken the Duke to task, saying his failure to give just acknowledgment or awards was the reason why he never became a powerful king[51]. Some give him the benefit of the doubt, explaining that he was likely busy fighting the continued resistance to his rule[52].

Jie himself also comes into some criticism. In one version of the myth, he departs the Duke because he is disgusted by all the other officials. Despite his mother's encouragement, he chooses not to return to court, realizing that going back would involve endless political infighting, especially given all the insults lobbed at him by the Duke's other advisors[53]. In another version he leaves in despondence at not being appropriately recognized by the Duke with a title. It is this sort of behavior which led the Legalist philosopher Han Fei (韓非) to describe Jie as ridiculous and "hard as a gourd,[54]" while Richard

Holzman calls him "rather petulant."[55] In other words, he is viewed by some like an angry child storming off into the woods to pout.

Regardless, it is a tragic tale that ends with Jie's immortal ascension and rebirth, along with the assumption that these rewards are deserved. The story's main lesson appears to be pointing at the final actions of the duke, and the importance of showing gratitude for those who are important to us in the here and now, before it is too late.

* * *

The time of Clear Bright is in many ways a microcosm of the seasonal cycle and the cycle of life itself. One side is an aspect of death, the other of birth. One set of activities call forth remembrance of those passed -- a sense of nostalgia, loss, and sorrow. Another set calls forth the present -- a seeking out of what is new, going out into nature and enjoying the gifts of the season. And by honoring those of the past, spiritual protection is brought down to those in the present. Meanwhile, fires are extinguished and then rekindled anew after the Cold Food Festival, and the cycle resumes for another year while young trees planted for future generations take hold in warming soil.

CHAPTER 6: GRAIN RAIN 穀雨

谷雨 / 곡우 / こくう / Cốc vũ
Pinyin: gǔyǔ
Literal Meaning: "grain rain"
Alternative names: Wheat Rain, Corn Rain
Period: April 19 or 20 - May 5
Sun's Ecliptic Longitude: 30°

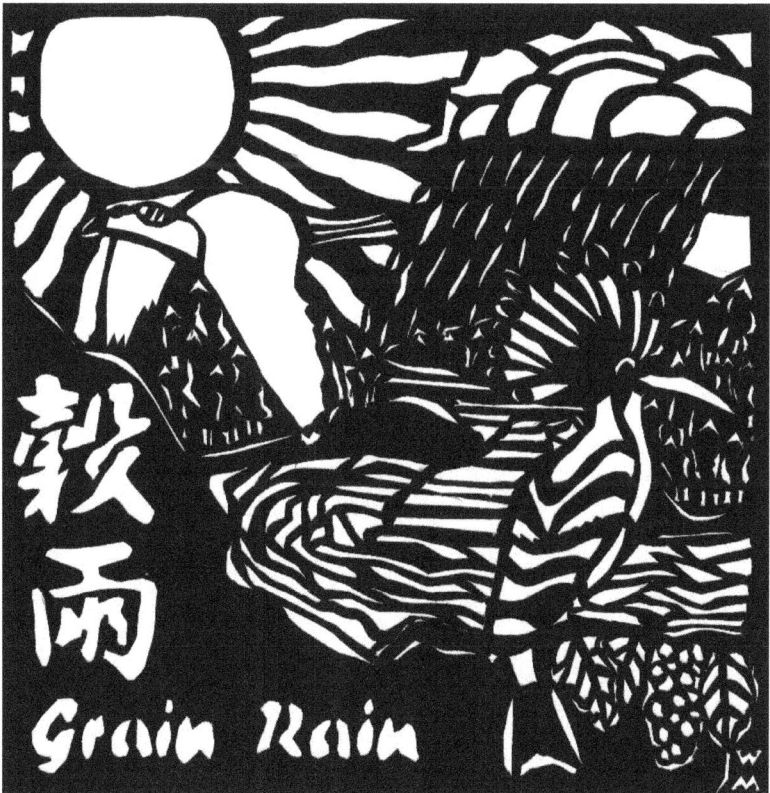

Western River in Chuzhou

Wei Yingwu
Tang Dynasty

Grass growing beside rivers is the most delightful,
*   along with the song of orioles from lush trees.*
Spring tides turn to rapids by twilight rains,
*   empty boats at deserted wharfs drift in the waves.*

滁州西澗 | 唐 | 章應物
獨憐幽草澗邊生，上有黃鸝深樹鳴。
春潮帶雨晚來急，野渡無人舟自橫。

The time of the Grain Rain is the last solar term of spring. All hint of cold is usually gone by this time, and temperatures have risen to summer levels in certain locations. As this is the season when grain is most in need of water, it is said the rain of this time "births a hundred grains" (雨生百穀), and is "more valuable than oil" (春雨貴如油)[1].

The much-desired rain can be heavy, leading to plenty of new growth. Cherry and peach blossoms turn their brightest red. Peony pistils extend far out of their buds. The fragrance of tea leaves sits heavy on the wind, and the cries of cuckoo birds ring out into the humid nights. It is considered the second most elegant solar term next to Clear Bright[2] owing to the sense of verdant growth along with a certain "Spring sentimentality" (傷春) described in many Tang and Song dynasty poems, where wind and rain destroy newly grown flowers -- a reminder that with growth comes inevitable decline.

Pentads

Duckweed begins to grow (萍始生)
Turtledoves clap their wings (鳴鳩拂其羽)
Hoopoe birds alight on mulberry trees (戴勝降於桑)

110

Duckweed is an aquatic plant that floats on the surface of still ponds. The presence of duckweed indicates lakes are completely thawed, and there is enough sunlight for the plant to grow as the season nears closer to summer. Since duckweed grows in still waters, it should be a time of light rains, and the torrent of water from spring melt should have eased to a slower pace.

More birds collect, usually perched together in rows on trees, a sign that late spring is arrived and the project of spring planting gains even greater urgency. Turtledoves also stand as a sign of benevolent rule and heavenly protection[3][4], which connects the time of Grain Rain with myths of the Jade Emperor. The term is also interpreted as cuckoo birds instead of turtledoves. The lore states that the cuckoo is a messenger of the Spring God[5][6].

Hoopoe birds are powerful symbols in many cultures. In Chinese culture they are associated with the Queen Mother of the West[7]. As covered in the chapter on the Spring Equinox, the mulberry tree represents the east, spring, the rising sun, and connection with the spirit realm. In the natural world, mulberry leaves are a primary food of silkworms; the reference to the mulberry tree is also referencing silk harvesting, which is a major activity during this time. In some areas, there is even a day where all works stops to ensure the silkworms are not disturbed as they grow[8].

Agriculture

This is the time to plant cotton, flowers, soy beans, potatoes, peanuts, sweet potatoes, and eggplant. Wheat is a major crop in the north, and farmers work to prevent the onset of rust, powdery mildew, and aphids. Corn needs protection from white grubs. Livestock also need to be fed liberally. It is the peak fishing season, so fishermen set out early and come home late.

Tea planters are usually harvesting and roasting spring teas at this time. Tea picked on the day of Grain Rain is considered second only to that picked during Clear Bright, and is often preferred by tea aficionados for its lower price and the look of the leaves when steeped. It is considered best to pick leaves in the morning, and according to traditional medicine the tea has cooling properties. Folklore makes even grander claims, saying it can improve eyesight, ward off evil, and even resurrect the dead. Tea farmers will usually steep and drink a few leaves the day of Grain Rain, and then keep some on hand for special occasions or special visitors.[9] [10] [11]

Health

This is a time when a lot of pollen is airborne, so a mask is usually necessary for those who are sensitive. Heavy rain and humidity can aggravate nerve pain, sciatica, and trigeminal neuralgia. Those with arthritis should avoid wet areas and wrap up joints. Temperature differences between night and day can extreme, so choice of clothing is a consideration when leaving early or returning home late.[12] [13] [14]

Customs

FIVE POISONS TALISMAN

On the day of Grain Rain, some households practice the placing of a "five poisons talisman" (五毒符) on their doors.[15] The "five poisons," also referred to as the "five noxious creatures," are the scorpion, the snake, the toad, the centipede, and the gecko. Usually there is a painting of a nail driven through their heads, or a rooster pecking at them. The talisman is placed at this time because the Grain Rain is a time of rising temperatures, when insects and reptiles become more active --usually reaching a fever pitch by the Dragon Boat Festival on the fifth day of the fifth lunar month. The talisman is intended to keep these poisonous creatures from entering the home.[16] [17]

One origin of the talisman is related to the famous novel, *Journey to the West* (西遊記). The two nearly-undefeatable heroes of the novel, the Monkey King Sun Wukong (孫悟空), and the Pig creature Zhu Bajie (豬八戒), are subdued by a scorpion demoness in the guise of a beautiful woman. Unable to defeat her, Guanyin (觀音), the Goddess of Mercy, called on the God of Pleiades (昴日星官) for help. He descended from heaven, changing into his rooster form. He crowed at the scorpion demoness, who immediately reverted to her original shape: a scorpion the size of Chinese lute. He crowed again, and she disintegrated [18]. This is one reason why a rooster is depicted on some talismans. But as any person who raises free-range chickens can tell you, real-world chickens are an excellent, practical measure for pest control as well.

The inclusion of the gecko on the talisman might seem like an odd choice to include among the others, but it was believed that the urine of geckos was highly poisonous and would cause skin to decay[19] [20], although scientists have proven this to be untrue. [21] Sometimes the image of the gecko is replaced by a spider.

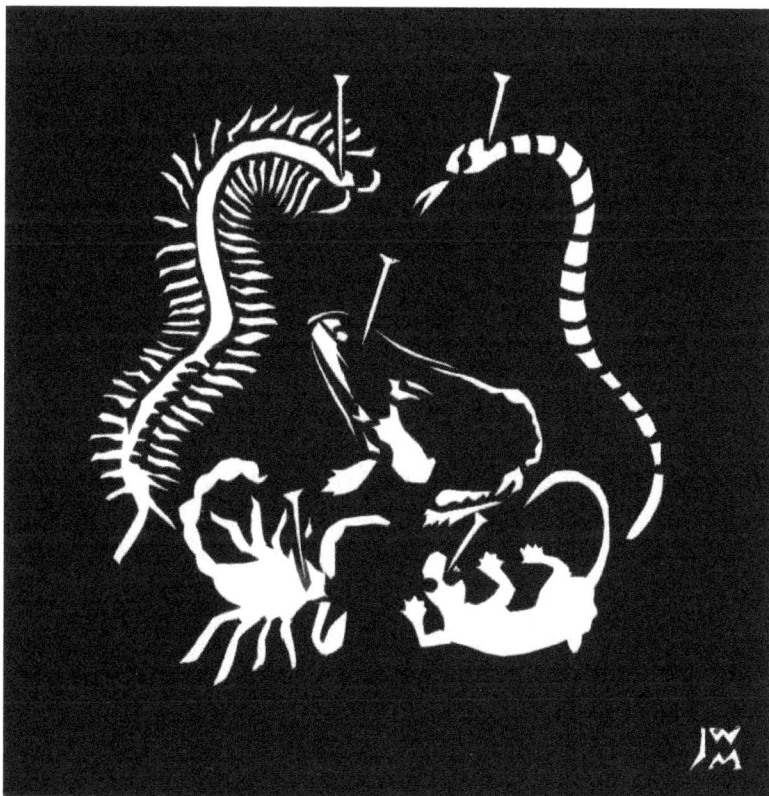

WALKING THE GRAIN RAIN

Traditionally this solar term was a time to go out and enjoy nature, particularly the peonies hitting full bloom. In fact another term for the peony is the "grain rain flower."[22] In the past the day of the Grain Rain was a time for women to set aside their work, take a basket, and head outdoors to collect flowers and herbs. Doing so was said to ensure good luck. People of the villages would often use the time to go out and enjoy the blooming peonies, creating a sharp contrast to farmers, who were working to furiously harvest silk. [23] [24]

Festivals

GAO MEI

Gao Mei (高禖) is an ancient goddess of marriage matchmaking and fertility. She is also called *Jiaomei* (郊禖) – jiāo being the word for suburbs, the usual location of her worship. In early depictions she is a mature, pregnant woman with thick thighs, large breasts, and a large belly. As society became more patriarchal she was conflated with the male Fuxi, and is conflated with Goumang as well. She was often celebrated in fertility and protection rites during the Double Third (三月三)/Shangsi Festival (上巳節)[25] [26].

DOUBLE THIRD FESTIVAL

On the third day of the third lunar month people in villages and those who worked the land would go down to the riverbank and give offerings and thanks for the precious waters that flowed during this time of year. Falling after or before Qingming and Grain Rain, in some areas tombs were swept, and so another name for the festival is Minor Qing Ming (小清明). Observances were typically led by priestesses, and were said to ward against calamity and boost good fortune. The rituals are now almost totally forgotten, save for a few minority groups scattered across China. The practice started during the Zhou dynasty as a simple observance mainly among the common folk, and then later became a more elaborate festival which included the emperor. [27] [28]

The water flowing in the rivers during this time of year was termed "peach blossom water," and washing in it before noon was believed to ward against misfortune, cure illness, and purify the soul. [29] Both common folk and royalty would rush down to the river in the morning, and after bathing, would enjoy banqueting, drinking, and poetry by the riverside. Drinking was not an affair of causal sipping, but rather a raucous drinking game where a cup was floated on water, and to whomever it floated was obligated to drink.

OCEAN WORSHIP

In the warming climate of Grain Rain fish migrate into shallower waters, making them easier to catch and kicking off the main fishing season. Meanwhile, it is a time of torrential rains and strong winds, making trips out on the ocean exceedingly dangerous. In an old practice fishermen pray to the Goddess of the Sea, Matsu (媽祖) -- an event just as important as the Spring Festival to fishermen. Worship takes place either at a temple dedicated to the deity, or more often near the ocean a day before going out to sea, with offerings of pork, cakes, and joss paper (金紙, lit. "gold paper") and plenty of fireworks. A toast of wine is offered three times: the first for safety of the boat and peace among the crew, the second for calm seas and good weather, and the third for a good catch and full holds. This is followed by a final bow to the ocean to give thanks for its generous nurturing.[30] [31]

Folklore

MATSU

Matsu goes by numerous titles: Granny Matsu (媽祖婆), Queen of Heaven (天后), or Holy Heavenly Mother (天上聖母). She is one of the most worshiped gods in the Chinese pantheon, with temples dedicated to her wherever large numbers have Chinese diaspora have settled, from Ho Chi Minh City to Melbourne to San Francisco. Many pilgrimages held every year in Taiwan involve tens of thousands of followers. She is so popular that she is one of the few Chinese gods that has been adopted by followers of Western religions, such as the Catholic Chinese communities in the Philippines where she is syncretized with the Virgin Mary[32], who also happens to carry the same title the "Star of the Sea."

Matsu is the deification of the young woman Lin Mo (林默) or Lin Moniang (林默娘), who according to tradition was a shamaness who lived from 960 to 987 CE on Meizhou Island near Fujian -- accounts differ as to the dates and location. Her name could be translated as Miss Silent Lin, and she was so named as she was a quiet, pensive child. Her birth, life, and death were marked by numerous miracles.

Her parents had originally wanted a boy, and after much praying her mother was visited by the Guanyin, the Goddess of Mercy who gave her a pill to induce pregnancy. Upon waking, she found the pill in her hand. She consumed it, and became pregnant with Matsu, who when born shot out of her mother in a flash of fragrant red light. As the mother's dream shows, legends of Lin Moniang attach her closely to Guanyin. Lin Moniang became a Buddhist adherent after being mesmerized by the goddess's statue in a temple as a child, and is said to be the reincarnation of the goddess.

Lin Mo displayed numerous talents as a child, and throughout her life quickly advanced in metaphysical skill thanks to gifts she received along the way. Visited by an aged monk who recognized her Buddha nature, he conferred on her abilities to foretell the future and astrally project to other locations. As a teenager, while her friends played she set about fixing her hair by looking at a reflection in a pool. A divine being emerged and gave her two bronze tablets inscribed with encrypted incantations. After prodigious study, she cracked the code and gained powers of exorcising ghosts, averting disasters, and curing disease.

Many legends tell how she helped villagers in need with her gifts, sometimes bringing rain, sometimes saving fisherman or guiding them in by wearing red clothes on the coast, rain or shine. Very often she fights off demons harrying the populace. Two particularly troublesome ones fell in love with her, and she made a deal with them that whichever one defeated her could take her as a wife. They agreed, and she thereupon handily defeated them with her martial and magical prowess, and in awe of Matsu they pledged themselves as her guardian generals. These two demons are the green-hued "Thousand-Mile Eyes" (千 里 眼) and red-colored "Wind-Following Ear" (順 風 耳), representing Matsu's sensitive clairvoyance in seeing future events and clairaudience in answering the prayers of her followers.

On Double Ninth day, also called Double Yang Day (重陽節), Lin Mo said goodbye to her parents and quietly went to the top of a mountain to meditate. As the sun reached its zenith the peak became shrouded in strange, heavy clouds. People below looked up to see a bedazzling light shoot out across the sky and then suddenly disperse. At the age of 27, Lin Mo departed the mortal world and ascended into Heaven as a goddess.[33] [34] [35]

Thereafter, the cult of Matsu grew, and people in coastal communities prayed to her to bring relief from drought, floods, epidemics, and piracy, or any serious personal difficulty. She is said to protect women during childbirth and to aid with conception. As the patron of the seas, she was often the first temple erected by overseas Chinese when they migrated. Today there are more 1,500 temples dedicated to her across the world, not to mention hundreds of dedicated events and activities -- some would say entire industries.

* * *

Grain Rain is one of the few solar terms to have so many activities concerned with water: water of the sky, the water of rivers, and the water of the sea. Taking place during the third month as described in the *Book of Rites*, it is also connected to all the water control work of ancient times. All practices are concerned with staying water's potential for destruction, while expressing gratitude and hoping for continued abundance and good luck. In some areas there was an old observance which prohibited any fires outdoors, for fear of offending the Thunder God, who would withhold rain as punishment[36] [37].

BIRTH OF A WRITING SYSTEM

When the Yellow Emperor ascended the throne there was no written language in existence with which to communicate ideas. A man named Cangjie (倉頡) hoped to remedy this situation. He traveled widely throughout the nine provinces, seeking to better understand the world and how it might take form in written language. During his trip he analyzed the characteristics of all things: the sun, moon, stars, clouds, lakes, oceans, and animals. Returning to his home town, he closed himself off in isolation near the bank of the river to devise a system of writing, working at it continuously for three years.

The Jade Emperor was deeply impressed with Cangjie's efforts, and while the man was sleeping he gifted him a gold statue. In the morning, the man awoke to a bright light as the morning sun glinted off the gift. He was shocked to find the statue at the foot of his bed, and realizing that it was a gift from the heavens could not accept it. He felt he did not deserve such a precious object, and that creating a writing system was not worth such a dear prize.

He sent the statue to the Yellow Emperor. Once it was set down in the throne room, the Jade Emperor came down from the heavens and took it back. All the Yellow Emperor saw was a bright flash of light, and was simply perplexed about what had taken place.

That night, while Cangjie was fast asleep, the Jade Emperor came to him in a dream, and asked that if he did not want the statue, what it was that he could gift him. Cangjie thought for a moment, and then asked that the people of the world be gifted an abundance various grains, so that everybody would have enough to eat. When daylight came, Cangjie awoke, washed up, and went outside. As he stepped out the door he saw that the ground was covered with golden grains a foot high. People were out with baskets, gathering as much as they could with plenty left over for planting future harvests.

Cangjie went to the Yellow Emperor and informed him that the grain came from the Jade Emperor. The Yellow Emperor ordered the establishment of the Grain Rain Festival, and required everybody in the kingdom dance and celebrate in a show of gratitude to the gods. Meanwhile, Cangjie's work on the written language was distributed to all the heads of the provinces for further teaching. [38] [39]

* * *

The development of the writing system was an occasion of rejoice by the Jade Emperor. Demons and ghosts, however, were terrified. The Fundamental Norms chapter of the *Huainanzi* (淮南子) explains that the demons wept in the night (鬼夜哭) upon Changjie's codification of the writing system[40]. It is said that the writing gave humanity the power to control the spiritual realm, and to this day textual elements in talismans are core to Chinese esoteric practices[41].

THE YELLOW EMPEROR

The Yellow Emperor (黄帝), also referred to as Xuan Yuan (軒轅) was a legendary Chinese ruler said to have lived around 3000 B.C.E. He was of miraculous birth: his mother, Fubao (附寶) conceived the emperor one night when a great bolt of lightning flashed in a circle around the stars of the Big Dipper (北斗七星). After 25 months of pregnancy, he emerged from the womb with the ability to talk. As a toddler, he was quick to learn and when he grew up, honest and clever; as an older man, he was especially wise. Legend states he was 300 years old when he died.

The Yellow Emperor is considered a main ancestor of the Chinese race, initiating a long list of skills and tools: seasonal planting, selective breeding, internal alchemy, medicine, housing, clothing, cauldrons, coins, measurement, time-keeping, the compass, football, rituals, and markets, among many others.

Although not a lover of violence, he is considered a war deity, focused on restoring order whenever it was challenged. And he was challenged frequently throughout his reign. The first was from his half-brother, the Flame Emperor (炎帝). Then the God of War, Chiyou (蚩尤). Next, a one-legged mountain demon called Kui (夔), and thereafter a vast assortment of would-be usurpers.

Typically in the old mythologies, challenges come from the south, with his opponent's army consisting of monsters and demons. The Yellow Emperor's army, meanwhile, was comprised of gods and animals: a vanguard of wolves, tigers, foxes, jackals, bears, and panthers with a division of eagles, pheasants, falcons, and phoenixes. The Yellow Emperor is closely tied to aspects of nature, and during the Warring States era, he was installed into the Taoist pantheon as a great saint -- and later a god -- advocating silence, inaction, and worship of nature.

The Yellow Emperor is also associated strongly with directionality and balance. During his campaign to defend against Chiyou, one of his officials invented the compass, so that within a thick fog they were able to find their way south to engage Chiyou's army. Within the pantheon of the five directional emperors, he is always in the center. The identity of the emperors of east, south, west, and north change from source to source, yet he is universally occupies the center role in every text. It is said that he has four faces, one facing each direction to meet any challenge from the other emperors, who he easily defeats whenever they try.[42] [43] [44]

This symbolism reflects the historical and political reality of China's dynastic cycle where the "Mandate of Heaven" enjoyed by an emperor is only good for as long as he or she can hold it, and the existing state of affairs is never without the potential for change.

The arrangement of five emperors also symbolizes the natural and cosmic realms. In the natural world, they represent the cardinal directions, east, south, west, north, and center, as well as the different seasons: spring, summer, fall, winter. They also stand for the five phases: wood, fire, metal, water, and earth -- the Yellow Emperor -- at the center. Within these systems, the center always holds a certain primacy to mirror the ideal of balance.

THE PEONY FAIRY

During the time of the Tang dynasty, the heavens opened up and rained without ceasing for days and days. The Yellow River swelled until it flooded and overtook the land.

A young man by the name of Guyu stood in front of his home, and watched as the approaching waters lapped nearer to his doorstep. He rushed into his house, had his feeble mother jump onto his back, and ran out of the house to seek higher ground. Once he found a safe place for her, he turned back and swam into town to help his neighbors. He was a gifted swimmer, and managed to rescue a large number of villagers.

As he made a final circuit around the village he saw an uprooted peony bush floating by. There was something distinctive about the bush which caught his eye, and as he watched it floating away it seemed to wave its little branches, as if begging to be saved. Disregarding his own incredulity at the sense of pity he felt for a floating bush, and ignoring his deep exhaustion and raging hunger, he swam over and pulled it out of the water and left it on the doorstep of a local flower farmer, who happened to be located on higher ground. He went back to his mother, and soon after the flood waters retreated and they were able to return to their home.

Two years later, his mother came down with a major illness. He went to every doctor in the village, but none was able to help. He resigned himself to fact that his mother would not be long for the world, and focused his efforts on collecting herbs that would bring her some comfort and escape from the pain that racked her body.

As he was picking herbs in a field, he was approached by a maiden dressed all in red. She introduced herself as "Red Phoenix" and asked what he was doing. He told her about his mother, and the types of herbs he was looking for. The maiden let him know that she was descended from a long line of healers, and she had some medicine that could treat his mother. She accompanied him back to his home, administered the medicine to his mother, and her situation improved. Every day the girl returned to check on Guyu's mother to administer more medicine and ensure her health was improving.

Once his mother was well, the maiden suddenly stopped coming. As each day passed Guyu thought about her more and more: how warmly she had treated his mother, and how easily and eagerly she had saved her life. He had been too distracted by his mother's health to notice at the time, but in her absence the maiden's beautiful face filled his vision when he went to sleep and when he woke up. He determined that he would marry her, and every day he set out to try to find her.

After days of looking, he found himself on the outskirts of town at nightfall. Dejected, he made his way back to town, passing the flower farm where he had dropped off the peony bush years before. As he went by, he noticed movement out of the corner of his eye. He turned to see Red Phoenix dancing with a number of other beautiful women in the moonlight, each women wearing different colors, their robes flowing back and forth as they danced in unison.

Guyu called out, and all the women vanished. Stunned, Guyu ran into the middle of the garden where they had just been. A red piece of paper floated down. He caught it. It read:

"Wait until the eighth day of the fourth lunar month next year. I will then go to your house to marry you."

Guyu looked around the field, silent and empty of people but redolent in the fragrance of flowers, and realized that Red Phoenix was a peony fairy. Her favors to him were most likely repayment for his saving that peony bush a few years before. And being a fairy, she must have divined his intent to marry her when he visited the garden.

Guyu was delighted, and there was not a day that went by when he did not think of her over the course of that year. One night he awoke to a frantic knocking on the door. When he opened it he was shocked to find an ethereal, semi-transparent likeness of Red Phoenix standing at his doorstep, panting, crying, and covered in wounds. She told him she had been captured by her enemy, the Vulture. The Vulture extracted her blood to make an elixir. Knowing she would soon expire, she used her last bit of energy to astrally project herself to Guyu's home and say goodbye. With that, her image dissipated.

Once Guyu shook himself out his state of shock, he felt his blood start to boil. He grabbed an axe and headed up to the Vulture's lair in the mountains.

After locating the Vulture's cave, Guyu roared for the Vulture to come out to meet him in battle. Amused, the bird flew out, expecting an *easy fight. But overtaken with a frenzy, Guyu defeated it, and the Vulture fell to the ground in a mass of blood and feathers. Scanning the area Guyu laid eyes on the limp body of Red Phoenix. As he ran over, she got up, smiled at him, and took his hand so that he could help her up.*

As Guyu leaned over an arrow shot through his chest, and he collapsed to the ground. Red Phoenix looked over to see the Vulture with a bow in its hands, eyes filled with hate. She launched herself at it, a red cloud of rage and sorrow, and pummeled the bird to death.

Returning to Guyu she held him as the light left his eyes as he died. Thereafter, the Peony Fairy caused all the peonies to reach full bloom during the solar term of Grain Rain in memoriam for her would-be husband. [45] [46] [47]

* * *

There is no overabundance of romantic love in Chinese legends, so the above story stands apart from many of the tales surrounding the solar terms. Of course, one might note that this love is born of filial piety to Guyu's mother, rather than the love born of romance and passion more common in Western folklore.

The most striking aspect of the story is Guyu's saving of the peony bush early in the tale. It describes a world where the boundaries between nature and the spirit realm are thin, and where the simple deed of saving the life of a small plant has far reaching consequences.

CHAPTER 7: SUMMER BEGINS 立夏

立夏 / 입하/립하 / りっか / Lập hạ
Pinyin: lìxià
Literal Meaning: "establishes summer"
Alternative names: Summer Commences
Period: May 5 ~ May 21
Sun's Ecliptic Longitude: 45°

Summer Begins
Lu You
Song Dynasty

Crimson banners raised on window sills across the city,
   as the God of Spring rides back to the east.
Noisy swallows build new nests from mud,
   flowers fall and honeybees scatter.
Scholar trees and willows thicken with new foliage,
   curtains keep the summer heat at bay.
Time to bathe in a sun-warmed bath,
   and once again try on some light clothing.

立夏 | 宋 | 陸游
赤幟插城扉， 東君整駕歸。
泥新巢燕鬧， 花盡蜜蜂稀。
槐柳陰初密， 簾櫳暑尚微。
日斜湯沐罷， 熟練試單衣。

The 24 solar terms system places the start of summer around May 5th with the term Summer Begins (立夏). There are many different ways to demarcate summer. From an astronomical view, it starts at the Summer Solstice (夏至) around June 20 or 21. Meteorologically, it is defined as the three months of June, July, and August in the northern hemisphere. In terms of seasonal temperatures, when the mercury consistently stays above 22°C or about 70°F. Some countries use modern national festivals, like Memorial Day weekend in the US (the last weekend in May).

It is during summer when the sun plays a lead role. Across all cultures and religions of the world, solar deities dominate, embodying the earliest sense of divinity among humankind[1] [2].

At Summer Begins, the myriad things surrender to the sun. Another meaning of the Chinese word for summer, *xià* (夏), is "big," referring to the size of crops that grow during this time[3]. Compared to the windy and often wet spring, the world of summer is drier and clearer as the skies open up and let the sun's rays soak the earth. Fruits such as cherries, watermelon, and tomatoes, swelling in the summer sun, deliver a range of tannic and sweet tastes.

Pentads

Frogs croak (螻蟈鳴)
Earth-worms surface (蚯蚓出)
King snakegourds grow (王瓜生)

The meaning of the term *lóu guō* (螻蟈) in ancient Chinese refers to a frog[4], referencing the concert of sounds that fill the summer air throughout the day and night.

Earthworms are considered yang[5], and are drawn out from their dark, wet home to the yang energy soaking the topsoil, thereby helping farmers loosen the earth. It is also a nod to the occasional heavy summer rain.

Earthworms are also called "earth dragons" (地龍)[6][7] given their resemblance to a dragon's body. According to Li Shizhen (李時珍), a Ming dynasty doctor and writer, the name is inspired from the myth that earthworms create cloudy skies and can predict the weather (陰晴), in the same manner as dragons[8].

Snake gourds[9] are a long, greenish melon which turns red when ripe. At this time of year its vines start creeping upward toward the sun[10].

Agriculture

The *Eight Treatises on Following the Principles of Life* (遵生八牋) states "In the first month of summer, heaven and earth begin to intermingle, and the myriad things bloom." (孟夏之月，天地始交，萬物並秀)[11] Winter wheat and rapeseed plant mature and it is time for the early summer harvest. It is the peak busy time for rice farmers, heeding a common saying: "the more seedlings planted at Summer Begins, the more grain fills our silos" (多插立夏秧，穀子收滿倉)[12]. Tea harvesters continue the pickings of the previous two solar terms.

With the heat and occasional rains, farmers need to watch out for anthrax and blight on cotton. Weeds proliferate, and a saying goes "weeding neglected for one day means weeding for three days" (一天不鋤草, 三天鋤不了).[13] Farmers hope it doesn't rain on the first two days of Summer Begins (初一落雨有花結無仔, 初二落雨有穀做無米).[14] Rain means that the whole season will be overly wet, decimating crops and preventing the flowers of fruits from getting properly pollinated. Wind kicking up from the southeast on the day is lucky; blowing from another direction portends misfortune.[15][16]

Health

As the year starts moving toward warmer temperatures, Chinese medicine warns that heat can harm one's vital essence (暑易傷氣) and that heat can invade the heart (暑易入心), which regulates yang energy. A time of growth, the season brings a peak of human metabolism, but also fiery tempers. It is a time to pay attention to one's mental health and stability, and if possible to adapt an easy manner. It is believed that vigorous exercise in the early summer prepares the body to better endure the high crest of temperatures coming later in the year.[17][18]

Ancient Traditions

In imperial times the Grand Recorder would declare the inauguration of summer and the ascendance of the energies of fire. On the first day of Summer Begins, the emperor, purified by some days of fasting, proceeded with his retinue to the south of the city to welcome the arrival of summer. All participants were adorned from head to toe in red. In addition to its role as an auspicious color, which drives its heavy use during the lunar new year, the color is also associated with the phase of fire, the southern direction, and summer. The use of red in these rituals carried an invoking quality to ensure a warm, productive harvest. After completion of the rituals and return to the palace, the emperor would award his princes with expanded territories.

This was the time for the Chief Music Master to commence ceremonial music, and the emperor would enjoy strong drink while watching performances.

In the natural world, what grew was encouraged to grow longer and higher, in keeping with the rising quality of the phase of fire. Animals could not be hunted or injured and the starting of earth works was forbidden. Trees were to be allowed to continue growing, so the felling of large trees was also restricted. This was a time to encourage the populace to stay close to home and the sending forth of great multitudes for war or any other large campaign was discouraged, lest their absence result in fewer crops. And to protect such crops, animals were to be chased away and not destroyed so that they did not eat all the grain. This was also an ideal time to collect medicinal herbs.

In the world of human affairs, foresters were to roam and inspect the woods, and officials were to stimulate the farmers in their work so that the season did not slip by unproductively. Officials would travel through the districts, making sure farmers were out vigorously working in the fields and not spending their time idly in the towns. The farmers were then required to send the first wheat crop to the emperor to offer the ancestors.

As a season of growth and abundance it was important to show leniency with criminals. Cases were reviewed to determine which merited lighter punishment, and those who had been convicted of minor offenses were sent free.

It was also a time of abundance for government coffers, and this is when silk taxes were collected. Taxes were based on the number of mulberry trees, and the *Book of Rites* emphasizes taxes were to be collected based on a standard rate regardless of social position or wealth. The bureaucracy also needed to be maintained, so the Grand Commandant (太尉) recommend eminent men to join the emperor's service.

Again, doing the wrong rituals during the summer would ensure havoc. Autumn rituals performed during the first month of summer bring pitiless rains, undernourished grains, and trouble for those living in the outerlands, so much so that they would need the emperor's aid. Winter rituals would cause plants and trees to wither early followed by great floods to an extent that would destroy the city walls. Spring rituals brought locust plagues, violent winds, and any plants in flower would not bear fruit. [19]

Customs

Historically, Summer Begins was also the day that ice sellers pulled their inventories out of storage and roamed the streets, touting some relief from the rapidly rising temperatures[20]. Ice was harvested from lakes in rivers in large cubes in the winter. They were stored in cellars prior to the eighth day of the twelfth lunar month, and covered in straw both to insulate the large cubes and to keep the ice blocks from fusing together. [21]

In the past, the harvests of the period such as cherries, green plums, and broad beans were offered to the ancestors and the gods worshiped to ensure fecundity and the success of future generations. [22] Five-colored rice was also common in ancient times: red beans, black beans, soy beans (yellow), and mung beans (green) mixed with peas (light green) and white rice. Over time the recipe evolved to include stewed pork, glutinous rice, amaranth, and yellowfish, taking on the name Summer Begins Rice (立夏飯).[23]

The foodways of Summer Begins are myriad and curious, and there are so many practices that even those born and raised in China are likely unaware of the various practices across geography and time.

In Jiangsu province, it was common to eat pea cakes while sitting on the threshold of the home, because pea cakes were said to improve stamina when laboring in the field, and given the similarity in the shape of peas with eyes, were believed to improve eyesight[24]. Sitting on thresholds stands apart from most customs. In most Chinese traditions, the threshold is held sacred and typically isn't touched at all when entering or exiting the house because it would be disrespectful to the door gods[25].

In keeping with this, in Taiwan, Summer Begins is considered the birthday of the door gods, so sitting on the threshold is expressly prohibited. [26] In Anhui province, it was forbidden to sit on the threshold as it would result in a bad mood for the rest of the year.

Children in Jiangsu were also had to avoid sitting on the threshold, as it was said to cause the bones of the legs and feet to wither.[27] They could, however, follow the practice in their native province of eating bamboo shoots, "the foot of the bamboo" and a near-homonym with the word "foot" (竹, 足) to fortify legs and feet. Bamboo shoots were eaten in pairs and uncut, each of equal width and about three to four inches long[28].

In Zhejiang it was popular to eat chicken or duck eggs, which symbolized healthy rotundity. More widely, eggs are said to be good for the heart given their resemblance to the shape of the heart. Zhejiang women would drink plum juice mixed with wine in order to maintain youthful skin. In Hunan, *Pseudognaphalium affine* (鼠麴草 lit. "mouse yeast grass") was mixed with glutinous rice balls to make Summer Begins Soup (立夏湯), which was said to give energy, prevent poverty, and make one "as light as a flying sparrow." Hoklo cultures eat shrimp noodles, since the word for shrimp (蝦, xiā) has a similar pronunciation to summer (夏, xià), while its reddish color is auspicious. In Suzhou, people go door-to-door among their neighbors, collecting one tea leaf from each house to make "Seven Family Tea (七家茶)." Boiled with the previous year's coal stored at the doorway, the infusion was said to keep the body strong and free from illness. In some places this was replaced with rice to make "Seven Family Porridge (七家粥) ." [29] [30]

Throughout communities in the south, it was common to weigh oneself on Summer Begins for comparison to the end weight on the first day of the Autumn Begins solar term. A higher weight indicated successful cultivation of the liver during the summer period. The practice is also a nod to a tale in *Romance of the Three Kingdoms* (三國演義) . As the story goes, Liu Bei's (劉備) deficient son and successor, Liu Shan (劉禪), retreated to Luoyang after losing to Sima Yan (司馬炎), the Emperor Wu of Jin. Meng Huo (孟獲), who had made a solemn promise to visit Liu Shan every year on Summer Begins, would make war against the state of Jin if Liu Shan was doing poorly. One way to ensure Liu Shan was being well taken care of was to weigh him, so Emperor Wu made sure he was fed copious bowls of rice and pea porridge to ensure his weight grew every year. [31] [32]

Festivals

BUDDHA BATHING FESTIVAL

Celebration of founder of Buddhism, Shakyamuni Buddha, takes place at different times in different countries. Traditionally in China it has been held on the eighth day of the fourth lunar month, which often falls during the Summer Begins solar term. Performing the ritual involves the pouring of fragrant water three times over a statue of the infant Prince Siddhartha, the founder of Buddhism. [33] The more common custom holds that the practice brings a fresh start for the year, and from a Buddhist point of view the observance is an outward ritual to remind followers of the importance of purifying the heart, or one's inner Buddha[34].

Temples hold elaborate ceremonies, usually beginning with welcoming the Buddha, placing his statue on palanquin, praying by monks circumambulating the statue, reading Buddhist texts, bowing three times, and then followed by a procession. When the statue is returned, monks circle the statue again and chant sutras.

The origin of bathing the Buddha comes from a legend telling of the Queen Maya's birth of Prince Siddhartha, who would later become Shakyamuni Buddha while meditating under a Bodhi Tree. According to legend, as the infant Siddhartha came into the world, he was bathed in fragrant water by nine dragons. He then walked seven steps to the north, and with one hand pointed to the sky and the other to earth, and said, "I am chief of the world, eldest in the world. This is the last birth. I will no longer be reborn." Within this story the nine dragons represent the nine virtues of Buddhism, and the seven steps symbolize the seven steps to enlightenment. [35]

While in common practice bathing the Buddha brings a fresh start to the year, the ritual is rich with symbolism to Buddhist adherents. Bathing is said to bring about a number of benefits, including diligence, wisdom, earthly and heavenly prosperity, numerous descendants, health and longevity, protection, and eventual enlightenment. [36]

Although originally an Indian holiday, the customs associated with the event took on their own practices in China, such as extensive banqueting and asking the gods for children. Releasing captive animals was also a popular pastime, usually by purchasing animals intended for use as food and releasing them into air, land, or water. This practice is now discouraged for a number of reasons: the negative ecological impact, the increased market demand the activities cause, and the unintended suffering that often happens when releasing captive animals into environments to which they are poorly adapted.

Folklore

THE OX GOD

The eighth day of the fourth lunar month is also the day of the Ox King (牛王), when he descended to the mortal realm to serve humans. This day is observed by giving the family ox a day off, thoroughly cleaning out its pen, and feeding it with top quality feed in gratitude for its service. Farmers also pray to the Ox God (牛神) to preserve the health of the ox, and for the arrival of more oxen. Another legend states that humanity primarily lived a hunter-gatherer lifestyle until one day a wild cow was captured. It was tamed, and eventually birthed a calf on the eight day of the fourth lunar month, which was then tamed to aid humanity in the drawing of carts and plows.[37] [38]

The Ox Demon King (牛魔王) appears as a fictional character in the classic novel *Journey to the West*, one-time friend of the protagonist, Sun Wu-Kong, and a match for the Monkey King in terms of guile and strength. At one point he even turns into a white bull, an impressive coincidence given the frequency with which white bulls appear in disparate cultures: as an object of sacrifice among the Druids[39], as a participant in Greek mythology as the Cretan Bull, and as a symbol of fertility and divine consciousness in Minoan culture[40]. The significance of the bull to Chinese culture far predates its presence in *Journey to the West*, and had been worshiped for thousands of years as a protection god.[41]

THE AZURE BULLS

In 739 B.C.E., Duke Wen of Qin (秦文公) commanded his officials to fortify the structures of the land to protect them from wind and rain. The builders required more materials, and so he sent over forty soldiers to chop down a grove of ancient trees. The soldiers set on their task, but soon found that the thick trunks would heal before they could finish cutting through. Realizing the attempt was pointless, they left and went in search of easier trees to harvest.

One soldier who had hurt his foot stayed behind. As he rested at the base of the tree, he heard a number of voices around him.

"If we keep getting chopped like this we'll all get tired and fall over," one complained.

"Duke Wen won't give up, will he?" asked another.

"It doesn't matter," said a third. "However strongly he insists, he is but a mortal. He won't have any idea how to do it."

A fourth voice spoke up. "Right. He doesn't know that in order to cut us down he has to tie our branches with red string. And that he would have to send three hundred men with their hair down, wearing brownish-red clothes and burning incense."

The voices then went silent as if returning to deep contemplation. The man quickly hobbled back to Duke's court and told him everything he heard.

The next day the Duke sent three hundred men attired as the voices described. They tied red string around the branches, and had no trouble chopping into the wood.

With the final cut, a number of azure-colored bulls burst out of the trunks and ran into river, never to be seen again. When told of what happened, the Duke took the omen to heart, and built a temple to the Ox God, recognizing the bull's potential for bravery, strength, and vibrant ch'i. [42] [43]

* * *

The myth above is obscure and there are no interpretations to reference. However, legend states the Azure Bull carried Laozi to Hangu Pass (函谷關)[44][45], where he wrote the *Tao Te Ching* (道德經) . Laozi is also symbolized by the Azure Bull, and it has appeared in many novels of the Ming and Qing Dynasties, such as *Journey to the West*[46], *Investiture of the Gods* (封神演義)[47], and *The Origin of the Eight Immortals and Their Journey to the East* (八仙出處東遊記) [48].

The tale might hint at the origin and transmission of the *Tao Te Ching*, with humanity guided by the forces of nature to enact a ritualistic sacrifice that passes on universal wisdom. The use of red clothes and red string on the branches ties the story back to the Summer Begins solar term. The use of brown mixed with red is a curious addition. Brown is not typically used in ritualistic settings and is underrepresented in Chinese color symbolism. Although yellow stands as earth in Chinese cosmology, brown is the literal color of soil, so the myth could tie back notions of land fertility.

CHAPTER 8: LITTLE FULLNESS 小満

小満 / 소만 / しょうまん / Tiểu mãn
Pinyin: Xiǎomǎn
Literal Meaning: little full/complete/filled/satisfied
Alternative names: creatures plenish,
corn forms, green buds form
Period: May 20 or 21 ~ June 5 or 6
Sun's Ecliptic Longitude: 60°

Returning to the Field in Spring and Summer

Ouyang Xiu
Song Dynasty

From the wilderness a southern wind blows all the grass,
    a small thatched cottage sits deep in the forest.
Young ears of wheat are as lovable as a child,
    and juicy mulberry leaves satisfy the silkworms.
Old farmers look forward to the annual harvest,
    but do the women who bring their meals see the beauty of the season?
Wild pear leaves grow in tight clusters amid the calls of night warblers,
    red camellia buds open and mingle with mountain bird song.
Who knows the joy living on a farm?
    But I know I returned too late.
Back then my body was strong and vigorous,
    I've squandered my time and now I'm already old.

歸田園四時樂春夏二首(其二)| 宋 | 歐陽修
南風原頭吹百草，草木叢深茅舍小。
麥穗初齊稚子嬌，桑葉正肥蠶食飽。
老翁但喜歲年熟，餉婦安知時節好。
野棠梨密啼晚鶯，海石榴紅囀山鳥。
田家此樂知者誰? 我獨知之歸不早。
乞身當及強健時，顧我蹉跎已衰老。

    The term "Little Fullness" takes its name from the grains of wheat and rice, which are ripening at this time but have yet to reach full maturation. [1] Many of the solar terms have "little" and "great" counterparts: Great Heat-Little Heat, Great Cold-Little Cold. At first glance the absence of "Great Fullness" may seem perplexing as the word mǎn (滿) has many positive associations related to fullness in Chinese: contented (滿足), satisfied (滿意), ample (豐滿), perfect (圓滿), as well as full and plump (飽滿). It is this latter term that is meant in the solar term context: the plumping heads of grain. So it might seem counter-intuitive that there is no auspicious-sounding Great Fullness to compliment Little Fullness.

138

The reason relates back to the pull of yin and yang in Chinese cosmology. "Great Fullness" would indicate a destructive extreme of polarity -- a state of maximum yang which demands movement toward the direction of withering decline, like an over-extended rubber-band. The use of the term "little" allows extra room for further growth. It shows how the importance of balance is built into the design of the solar terms, serving as a reminder that more is not necessarily better. And the gifts of nature, however modest, should be accepted with grace rather than greed.

Pentads

Sowthistle is in seed (苦菜秀)

Delicate herbs die (靡草死)

Winter wheat is harvested (麥秋至)

The Piya (埤雅) dictionary of the Song dynasty refers to using the sowthistle to make bitter tea[2]. In Chinese traditional medicine, bitter connects with the rising quality of the fire phase.

"Delicate herbs die" is a nod to the growing heat which wilts the plants that prefer cooler temperatures. The specific herb referred to is Draba nemorosa (葶藶[3]), a kind of whitlow grass, which thrives in the energies of yin and withers as the energies of yang ascend.[4]

Wheat planted in the fall has survived the winter and is ready to be harvested .

Agriculture

During this time of year, the climate patterns of north and south draw together as temperatures increase. This is a key time for wheat growers: if temperatures go above 30°C (86°F) and humidity below 30%, wheat can dry out and die, especially if there is a strong wind. The forces of rain and drought, heat and cool, seem at odds during this term. An old saying describes the fickleness of the sky as it tries to balance the heat enjoyed by silkworms and the relative cool preferred by wheat. (小滿天難做,蠶要溫和麥要寒)[5].

Accomplished 11th Century polymath Su Shi (蘇軾) wrote in the *Record of the Mutual Responses of the Things* (物類相感志) that silkworms cease producing silk after the Little Fullness term (蠶過小滿則無絲)[6], so while men traditionally worked the fields the *Qingjialu* (清嘉錄) notes that women were frantically making the final push to harvest the last of the silk. They would then take it to the markets, located in places like the front of the City God temple in Suzhou which would be packed with people trading silk until late in the evening. Meanwhile, farmers were either siphoning off excess water from the fields, or taking water from the river if the fields were too dry.[7]

Some of this practical activity made its way into a more ritualized context as described later in this chapter. In certain areas, people would speak of the three carts of the solar term: a cart for silk, a cart for water from the river, and a cart for the oil made from field mustard, some of which was used for cooking and the remainder sold to support the household[8]. All this shows the degree of intense activity at this time of year, both to secure income for the early harvest while ensuring longer term crops survive until the main harvest.

Health

The weather during this period presents its own challenges to the human body. A kind of pathogenic dampness (濕邪) is one of the Six Excesses of Chinese medicine, the others being wind, cold, summer heat, dryness, and fire (中醫六淫: 風邪, 寒邪, 暑邪, 濕邪, 燥邪, 火邪). Laboring in the summer climate consumes vast amounts of energy or essential essence. Bodily fluids need to be replenished to maintain blood chi, and the foods need to be eaten to fortify the spleen, including fermented foods like sauerkraut and kimchi, fats and oils, and lightly cooked vegetables and fruit.

In humid southern climates, measures need to be taken to prevent the build-up of moisture during heavy rains to avoid flare-ups of arthritis and joint inflammation. Food-borne illnesses proliferate owing to higher temperatures, and made worse by disease-carrying insects like flies. Spread of hepatitis A and E accelerate during the summer. Sanitation is key, as is plenty of sleep to keep the immune system humming. The spleen and stomach need to be fortified to protect against heatstroke.[9] [10]

Customs

In the traditional lore, if rain does not fall on the day of Little Fullness, the precipitation during the next few months will be light (小滿不下，黃梅雨少).[11] If so, crops might be overcome by locusts, and extra steps for prevention may be necessary. Another omen is whether the day of Little Fullness falls on a Yang Wood Rat (甲子) day or a Yang Metal Dragon (庚辰) day of the sexagenary cycle.[12]

The sexagenary cycle (干支), or the ten heavenly stems and twelve earthly branches （十天干與十二地支）, is a full cycle of sixty time periods of nested hours, days, months, and years. The system is an ancient method of time-keeping, starting from the 3rd century BCE, and evidence of its use can be found on Shang dynasty oracle bones from 1250 BCE. While no longer used officially to record time, it is referenced extensively for Chinese astrology and divination.

Explaining the intricacies of the cycle is beyond the scope of this book, but suffice it to say certain sexagenary times are associated with ups and downs, and some are associated with major change or cataclysms, like the locusts mentioned above. Some sexagenary years are significant, such as Yang Metal Rat (庚子), which has coincided with major defining events in China's history: the start of the opium war in 1840, the invasion of the Eight-Nation Alliance in 1900 which resulted in the Boxer Indemnities (庚子賠款), the middle of the disastrous Great Leap Forward in 1960, when 20 to 43 million people died of famine (estimates vary). The will of the cosmos, as if loathe to see the pattern broken, ensured 2020 was similarly eventful with the explosion of the COVID-19 pandemic.

Festivals

SILKWORM FESTIVAL

In ancient times, around the fourth lunar month, people in Zhejiang would hold a Silkworm Festival (祈蠶節). [13] [14] Timing depended on each household. Fruit, wine, and vegetables would be offered, "flour cocoons" (麵繭) in the form of dumplings would be placed on a hill of straw, and worshipers would pray for a good silk harvest.

Managing water levels in the fields was a critical activity during this time of year, and ritualistic activity developed around this agricultural practice as well, called "grabbing water" (搶水). In Zhejiang, people would take water carts, going to the river and back to irrigate the fields. [15]

One of the more involved celebrations occurred among the Bai minority of Dali in Yunnan province. In order to pray for more offspring and good health, various tribes would circumambulate three representatives of spirit in three different villages on three consecutive days (繞三靈): the Buddha in the first, then a local god, and lastly, an immortal. During the procession men and women went in pairs, one holding a willow branch in their right hand, and a fly whisk in their left, while the other held a willow branch in their left hand, and flicked a cloth in their right. Throughout there was a considerable amount of singing and dancing. [16] [17]

LEIZU'S GIFT OF SILKWORMS

Leizu (嫘祖), also known as Xi Ling-shi (西陵氏), was the wife to the Yellow Emperor. She is said to have taught humanity how to make silk[18] so that they had something better with which to clothe themselves than leaves and twigs. The introduction of silk to China by no less than a goddess shows how important silk was as an industry even in mythological or prehistoric times. Silk remains one of the greatest contributions of the Chinese to humanity. [19]

The *Records of the Grand Historian* (史記) notes that the Yellow Emperor took Leizu as his first wife.[20] After his defeat of Chiyou, they married, and she was responsible for domestic affairs while the emperor oversaw external matters. She bore him two sons, Xuan Xiao (玄囂) and Changyi (昌意), which in some versions of the five-emperor pantheon are two of the five emperors. [21]

Prior to her marriage, Leizu's tribe had been making silk, a process she discovered with her mother. When she and her mother went into the hills to pick wild fruit, she saw what looked like small white berries. She asked her mother what they were called, and her mother responded that they were in fact not fruit, but the cocoon of a worm.

Curious, the child took some home, fried them up, and noticed the thin threads become longer and longer. She thought that if sewn together with leaves and bark, they would make much better clothes than the rough vines they had been using. She worked on putting clothes together with her mother, and created the first attire which used silk.

After marrying the Yellow Emperor, one day she was inspired by the spider webs she saw in the forest. Using tree branches as a loom she was able to create whole pieces of cloth. Upon learning this new skill she traveled the land, teaching humanity how to make and sew silk. She was therefore widely revered, and temples were established in her honor in many villages.[22] [23]

Folklore

THE HORSEHEAD GODDESS

Traditionally men farmed and women sowed. But regardless of gender and even social class, all revered the Silkworm Goddess (蠶女). Most dynasties throughout the ages had a altar dedicated to the inventor of silk. The identity of the inventor changed with the times. It began as Leizu before the Han dynasty, but by the Northern Qi, it was said to be the Yellow Emperor himself. Then by the Northern Zhou it changed back again to Leizu.

However, there are those that say the silkworm goddess typically worshiped is not this "official" version recorded in the annals of history, but rather a horse deity which had evolved into a "silkworm maiden" with a horse head and human body.[24] The deity is also called the Bright Horse King (馬明王), the Silkworm Flower Goddess, or the Silk Maiden (蠶姑).

The book *In Search of the Supernatural* (搜神記) [25] and the *Extensive Records of the Taiping Era* (太平廣記) [26] tell of how a woman becomes a silkworm.

***

Long go in ancient Sichuan was a filial girl who lived in a small village. One day her father left the house and never came back. Concerned for her father's safety, the woman bought a stallion, and rode around the countryside and neighboring villages, desperate to find her father. After a couple days of looking she gave up and returned home. At a loss for what to do, just before going into the house she turned to the horse and said she would marry it if it could find her father.

Unknown to her, this particular stallion was divine, and upon hearing the woman's promise the horse galloped away. Within a few hours it located her father and brought him home. The daughter shed tears of joy to see her father again, and he was deeply grateful to horse.

The next day the father went out to feed the horse a rich and generous mix of grains. But the horse refused, simply turning away from the food and walking off a few steps. Every day the father went out to feed the horse, and every day the horse refused to feed. As time passed, the horse's ribs began to show, and the father grew increasingly confused and nervous. [27]

He asked the daughter what could be wrong. She hesitantly told him of the promise she had made the horse, that she would marry it if it found her father and brought him home. Her father was aghast. He took a knife rushed out of the house to kill the horse.

It was done quickly. As the dead horse lay there the father looked at its beautiful coat, and was loathe to let it go to waste. He skinned the

144

horse, and torn between the guilt which made it difficult to wear and the beauty of the leather too fine to give away or sell, he hung the leather on the wall of the house. But this was no normal animal skin. Sometimes he would notice the leather change places overnight, or sometimes flap out of the corner of his eye. But he convinced himself it was just the guilt he felt for murdering the animal which saved him.

One day while he watched his daughter sweeping the house, the leather leapt off the wall, wrapped itself around the woman, and vanished, leaving nothing but her broom toppling to the floor. The father ran out of his house and around the village, telling people what had happened and asking if they had seen his daughter. After a few days, a villager came forward saying they saw a girl wrapped in leather in a mulberry tree, entangled with white strings like a cocoon.

The father searched all over for her, but wasn't able to find his daughter. He returned home and spent several sleepless nights wondering where she went. One day he was sitting in front of his house, staring off into the distance and wishing he had handled the situation differently, when his daughter came to him, riding a cloud. She comforted him, saying that the Emperor of Heaven made her a silkworm fairy and a member of the heavenly immortal guard due to her filial behavior. She wanted to let him know she was very happy in heaven.

With that, she ascended back toward the sky, and in time the tale spread so that many small temples were built to the young woman, with statues showing a young maiden wrapped in a horse's skin.[28]. She was named the Horse-Head Goddess, and it was said that her temples were particularly powerful when answering prayers.[29] [30]

* * *

This tale contains many homonyms in the original Chinese. "Entangle" (chán 纏) is a near homonym for silkworm (cán 蠶), and the word for mulberry (sāng 桑) is a homonym with "grief" (sāng 喪), the feeling of the father when he heard his daughter was trapped in a tree, along with the general tone of sadness and loss that accompanies radical change and departure of those who are close.

Naming her the "Horsehead Goddess" would seem discordant with an origin tale describing her wrapped in horse leather, but the name is inspired by silkworms themselves. When a silkworm feeds on mulberry leaves, the way it angles its head looks something like a horse. It is an instance where the name of the goddess is inspired by the natural world. Curiously, she is rarely depicted with a horse's head. [31]

THE AZURE-ROBED GOD

The basins and mountains of Sichuan are filled with natural wonders -- a place of floating clouds and misty mountainscapes. It is the birthplace of many deities and religious practices in Chinese culture. And the contributions of the Azure-Robed God (青衣神) to the silk trade is one of the many origin deities that populate the Chinese pantheon.

The man who became the Azure-Clothed God is said to be the father of the silk trade. He was strong, brave, knowledgeable and a good hunter. As King of Shu -- shǔ (蜀) being the ancient name of Sichuan -- he turned the swamps to fertile grazing land. He is also said to have contributed many of the arts and skills commonly attributed to Chinese folk heroes: teaching animal husbandry and propagating the five grains.

In Sichuan it is believed he taught how to plant mulberry trees for silkworms, eventually leading farmers to diversify their livelihoods. He was said to wear azure robes, and rather than sit detached and away from the people in his throne room, often patrolled the kingdom. His ubiquity allowed the populace to witness his virtue, and thereafter they were thankful for the many improvements he made to their lives. After he died, he was worshiped as the Azure-Robed God. [32]

It was the silk trade that originally motivated Laozi to travel to Sichuan. The kingdom's roaring silk trade allowed it to secede from the Kingdom of Zhou, and connected it to central and southern China with bustling trade routes. Laozi intended to see the kingdom for himself, and traveled thousands of miles to visit the bustling trade center called Azure Goat Market (青羊肆) in the Hungu Pass (函谷關). He stayed for three years to write the *Tao Te Ching*. Later during the Tang dynasty the site would become the Azure Goat Daoist Temple (青羊宫).[33] [34]

Note that the mythology also states Laozi rode an Azure Ox into the pass, cementing the color's close associations with the divine. Given its frequent use and ambiguity in Chinese history, azure is the most Daoist of colors.

Sichuan was called the Kingdom of Silk, and silk production continues to be a major activity to this day. Some places carry on the old ways, with small groups of women gathered in dense mulberry groves, picking leaves while they chat, the sound of laughter echoing through the valleys. Indoors, lines of silkworms prodigiously weave their silk.

The Azure-Robed God is far less well known than Leizu, but what is clear is the profound impact silk has had on Chinese mythology. Whether concerning grand tales of the world's origin or more humble tales explaining the creation of silk, the mulberry tree adopts a weighty significance and stands as a tree attached to both the practical realm of wealth and to the greatest heights of divine connection.

CHAPTER 9: GRAIN RIPENS 芒種

芒種 / 망종 / ぼうしゅ / Mang chủng
Pinyin: mángzhòng
Literal Meaning: awn (of cereals) / arista (of grain) / tip (of a
blade) / Miscanthus sinensis (a type of grass)
Alternative names: Seeding Millet, Corn On Ear
Period: June 5 or 6 ~ June 20 or 21
Sun's Ecliptic Longitude: 75°

149

Grain Ripens in the Fifth Month

Yuan Zhen
Tang Dynasty

The arrival of Grain Ripens is visible today,
*   as praying mantises grow with the season.*
Colored clouds on high cast shadows below,
*   the songs of sparrows arrive.*
Lotus flowers bloom in clear ponds,
*   a mood of hot winds and summer rains.*
Passersby ask each other about silkworms and wheat,
*   fortune is found in human bonds.*

詠廿四氣詩 · 芒種五月節 | 唐 | 元稹

芒種看今日，螳螂應節生。
彤雲高下影，鵙鳥往來聲。
漉沼蓮花放，炎風暑雨情。
相逢問蠶麥，幸得稱人情。

The word *máng* (芒) can have multiple meanings which happen to match this period of the year. First is the awn, a botanical term referring to a bristle-like appendage you will see on grains and grasses. The bristly top of wheat would be the most common example. [1] The second is a kind of silver grass which flowers during this time, *miscanthus sinensis*, also known as maiden grass, zebra grass, or porcupine grass. The third meaning is related to its status as a homonym with the word "busy" (忙), as this is one of the busiest times for farmers.

Pentads

Mantises are born (螳螂生)
Shrikes begin to sing (鵙始鳴)
Mockingbirds cease their calls (反舌無聲)

Mantises reproduce in the deep autumn, so the arrival of mantises signal the forthcoming growth of the forces of yin, which will trigger the cycle of rebirth as the land begins its march toward the quiet of winter.[2] More generally, it refers to the proliferation of insects at this time of year.

In Chinese folklore the mantis is seen as formidable and courageous.[3] The "praying" aspect of its limbs are not that of divine contemplation; rather, they are a position of poise, getting ready to ambush its prey. It is well known to feast on cicadas, as covered in *The Zhuangzi* tale, where it is eaten by a bird while it focuses on a cicada (螳螂捕蟬, 黃雀在後)[4]. There is also a famous tale where the small animal raised its limbs to oppose a chariot about to run it over (螳螂擋車)[5]. Duke Zhuang of Qi (齊莊公), who was in the chariot, asked the charioteer what it was as they approached. The driver answered, "That is a mantis; it is an insect that knows how to advance, but never retreats. Without measuring its own level of strength, it looks down on its enemy." The Duke commented, "If it were a man, it would be the champion-hero of the empire." The Duke then ordered the chariot steered in order to avoid it. The act inspired numerous men from rival armies to come over to his side, since he clearly respected bravery and demonstrated mercy.

This time of year also brings the sound of shrikes, once again due to rising yin [6]. Shrikes are also called "butcherbirds" due to their macabre habit of impaling live prey on twigs and thorns, and methodically ripping them apart. Their victims are sometimes simply left to squirm and die a slow death. A research article published in 1894[7] describes a shrike killing a mouse and wedging the carcass into a forked branch. Once done with its meal, the shrike's "forehead and throat were matted and soaked with blood, the breast was reddened perceptibly and the bill was almost wholly of a carmine tint."

These habits are not a case of dark, sadistic play, but simply due to the bird's lack of effective talons,[8] and a desire to let its food cure and improve in taste.[9] In some cases it is to build a larder to attract mates for breeding.[10] So in typically cyclic fashion, this macabre-seeming behavior is also symbolic of life and rebirth.

Shrikes have appeared in poetry as far back as the *Book of Songs* (詩經) [11] and are viewed as "descended from heaven," bringing wealth if captured[12]. This dubious honor lead to large-scale hunting and growth of entire tourism industries based on barbecued shrike kababs -- a pastime the shrike would probably think far more macabre than its own elaborate foodways. One can imagine the shrike watching humans eat its kin, faces "matted and soaked" with barbecue sauce, their greasy tourist-lips "wholly of a carmine tint." Or perhaps it reveals another cycle, a sort of mimicry of predators impaling their prey on sticks.

Shrike-hunting in places like Taiwan has been curtailed as conservation laws take effect.[13] In the heart of the former barbecued shrike mecca of Fenggang Village (楓港村) of Fangshan Township (枋山鄉) in Pingtung County (屏東縣) the focus is now on the numerous totems to the bird erected all over the town, and the importance of the shrike to the local ecology[14].

The mention of mockingbirds connects to their calls, which change based on the season. At the beginning of spring their song is said to sound like "spring starts" (春起也) in Chinese, and by the start of the summer, "spring departs" (春去也)[15]. As the force of yin ascends in mid-summer, mockingbirds cease their songs.[16]

Agriculture

As mentioned earlier the word for this solar term (芒) is a homonym with the word for "busy" (忙), as it is a frenetic time of year for farmers, who are said to experience three summers (三夏): a time of harvesting crops like barley and wheat planted in spring (夏收), a time of planting for the fall with crops such as millet and broomcorn (夏種), and a time of managing what is still in the ground (夏管).[17] So in addition to the air of anxiety pervading agricultural communities as they race against time in the muggy heat, one must also endure and chuckle politely at an endless list of pithy sayings combining the puns for *mang* (芒) and *mang* (忙), deployed with ruthless frequency at this time of year.

Along with this intense period of work comes increasing heat made more oppressive by rising humidity, often exacerbated by occasional rains. And while the year up to this point has been about rise and growth and the manifestation of yang, we see inklings of the forces of yin across the customs and festivals this time of year. As farmers work feverishly in their fields, the approach of autumn lends not just an immediacy to their daily chores which will decide most of their annual wealth, but serves as a reminder that ultimately, from rise comes eventual decline. Farmers also watch the weather on the first day of Grain Ripens very closely: a wind from the northwest portends drought or will cut the life out of newly sprouting crops[18] (芒種刮北風,早斷青 苗根)[19], and a lack of thunder is an omen of a poor harvest. [20]

There are also agricultural folk customs related to tree girdling and plant propagation, which are described later in the section on customs.

Health

From the perspective of Chinese medicine, this is a time of delicate balance in managing the body's response to temperatures. Profuse sweating requires thorough showering, preferably not immediately after working or exercise, but following a period of cool-down. It is a good time to boost yang qi levels to get the blood circulating and to improve mood with sunlight, although preferably indirect sunlight, such as sitting out on a covered porch or in the shade of a tree. Heat and humidity tend to provoke lethargy, so occasional naps are encouraged to reduce fatigue and to keep the body healthy. Avoid sunstroke, and watch out for mumps and boils. Moreover, take care of one's emotional health which is easily compromised at temperatures rise.[21] [22]

Ancient Traditions

During the second month of summer high-level officers offered sacrifices to the spirits of the hills, streams, and springs, followed by grand summer sacrifices to the rain god, where musical instruments were played. There was considerable attention given to musical instruments, and the Chief Music Master oversaw the repair and tuning of hand drums, lutes, flutes, panpipes, organs, and bells. The farmers present their first millet harvest to the emperor, who would offer it up in the ancestral temple along with young chicken and peaches, representations of youth and longevity.

Near the end of the second month of the summer is the Summer Solstice, which is described in the next chapter. With the arrival of the longest day of the year the seasonal cosmology states that the influences in nature of darkness and decay and those of brightness and growth struggle together; the tendencies of life and death are divided. Owing to the abundance of yang at this point of the year, and the arrival of the forces of decline, many activities are curtailed to spur the smooth transition between these forces. Wood could not be burned for charcoal, and any fires in the southern section of any space – the quarter of highest yang – were prohibited to keep energies from growing out of balance. For similar reasons control needed to be exercised on horses.[23], which are of the phase of fire: impregnated mares were collected together, fiery stallions tied up, and the rules for propagating and raising them were promulgated. Cloth could not be bleached in the sun, and indigo plants used for dying could not be harvested, although this was for the more practical reason: the plant needed more time to grow.

With the exception of farming and teaching conscripts the handling of shields, pole-axes, and lances, too much activity was discouraged. Men of the higher social classes were to hold vigils and engage in fasts, while staying close to home, avoiding exercise, music, beautiful sights, rich foods and condiments, and even their spouses. To maintain balance and not encourage an over-expenditure of yang, they were to generally control desire and remain free from excitement. More "higher level" activities were advocated, both figuratively and literally, such as spending time in high, bright buildings, towers, pavilions, and hills to take in wide vistas.

To maintain the free flow of energies during this critical turning point of the year the city gates were all thrown open and could not be shut. Steps were also taken to prevent any injuries at the city gates or in the markets, which could invite misfortune. The spirit of generosity was also important as it was during other times of growth. Food allowances were raised, and prisoners – even those charged with major crimes – were shown a greater degree of leniency. Meanwhile, magistrates worked to stall any punishments and generally keep things quiet so as to bring about conditions in which the influence of darkness and decay could obtain full development. [24]

Customs

PLUM RAINS

While the sun grows hotter, the air also dampens with the plum rains (黃梅雨) of the East Asian rainy season. Meanwhile, the forces of yin advance, helping organisms that thrive in such conditions -- like mold -- flourish in the dark, stagnant places of the home. The most completely preserved of the ancient Chinese agricultural texts, *Essential Techniques for the Welfare of the People* (齊民要術) offers numerous tips to help ensure possessions survive the season. Bows are to be loosened so that they do not get mildewed and rotten. Leather and cloth can be buried in dry ash to draw out moisture. Rain gear can be placed on bamboo struts so that it is aired out, avoiding the accumulation of black mold in the creases and folds. [25]

Although modern folk might not have a bow to air out or a surplus of ash in which to bury their brand-name leather purses, inhabitants of the more humid climates place hordes of desiccant boxes in closets and cupboards, or run dehumidifiers day and night. Many still take out bedding to be purified by the winds and rays of the sun -- a common practice sadly lost only very recently in much of the US thanks to the proliferation of dryers and home-owners associations.

The Chinese calendar is said to have certain predictive qualities when forecasting the degree of mold that will occur. If the first day of Grain Ripens is the ninth stem of the Heavenly Stems (天干), which is Ren (壬), about a foot of mold will grow. If it occurs on the second day, one can expect two feet of mold, and so on, increasing by a foot a day until the tenth day, which means 10 feet of mold, or equivalent to mold growing overnight. Once the seventh Heavenly Stem Geng appears after the summer solstice, people can expect relief from the yellow plum rains and the resulting build-up of mildew.[26]

The plum rains are named as such for a good reason: it is the time when plums ripen and are harvested. Since the Xia dynasty plums have been processed this time of year, either cured whole or turned into juice with salt, sugar, and perilla. Another well-known drink is the thirst-quenching "Sour Plum Juice" (酸梅湯), containing licorice, hawthorn, and sugar.

FAREWELL TO THE FLOWER DEITY

With the peak of the flower season long left behind, the land is dotted with the last, withering remnants of the year's flowers. In earlier times, the custom on the first day of Grain Ripens was to offer sacrifices on the altar of the Flower Goddess, and engage in feasting and entertainments in observance of the flower deity's abdication. The scene is best described by a passage in the classic novel, *Dream of the Red Chamber* (紅樓夢) by Cao Xueqin (曹雪芹), where the morose protagonist of the novel, Lin Daiyu (林黛玉), holds a small funeral for the dying flowers, sobbing while reciting poetry[27].

Lin Dai-yu's poem captures the melancholy of early summer, when the ephemeral bursting forth of life in spring begins to draw to an end, bringing thoughts of one's own mortality.

As if to counter the sadness of inevitable decline, a common practice was to propagate daphne during this time.[28] Cuttings taken from the plant while in flower can be propagated by splitting the stem, inserting a grain of wheat -- a matter of symbolism as much as a practical matter of nutrients -- and planting it in well-draining soil. The cuttings need to be watered every few days during the course of the summer. Morning sun with afternoon shade is ideal. Daphne takes time to grow, but the act of propagation during this time serves as a reminder of rebirth and the continual march of the cycle of the year.

BREAKING TREE ARMOR

The agricultural practice of girdling -- cutting a ring into the bark so that more sugar accumulates in the fruit -- is practiced widely during this time of the year[29]. Called "cincturing" by orchardists, this technique was explored in the Lychee Grove legend of the Spring Equinox. Cincturing or girdling (環狀剝皮) is called "Opening the Armor" in Chinese (開甲), referring to the removal of its protective bark.

Another legend describes the origin of this agricultural procedure.

* * *

There once was a husband and wife who never produced any children. One day, they decided to obtain a date tree sapling, and bringing it home, they planted it tenderly into the ground. They treated it like a member of the family, doting on it nearly every day. When the weather was warm, they watered it. When the leaves lacked vibrancy, they fed it with their own nightsoil. They carefully pruned its branches, encouraging growth of more leaves, and helping it to attain a pleasing shape. They loosened the soil to make sure the roots had enough air and room to grow. Any weed that dared take up residence next to the tree was quickly removed.

The tree grew until its canopy covered the whole yard. Gorgeous blossoms appeared every spring, yet despite its beauty and prodigious flowering it never bore any dates. As each season passed, the couple grew sadder and sadder. They would spend their summer evenings sitting under the tree, the sigh of one feeding the other. One evening the wife suddenly stood up. "Enough!" she said. "There must be something we can do to get this tree to bear fruit."

The husband looked up at her with exhausted eyes, but said nothing.

"There's a new village magistrate who just took up the position," she said, taking her husband's arm and helping him up. "Everybody talks about how well he serves the people. Let's go see him and see if he can do anything."

The old couple puttered slowly toward the magistrate's office. When they arrived the magistrate received them with utmost politeness, and asked how he could help. The couple described the situation of the date tree, how well they had taken care of it, the beauty of its leaves and flowers, and how it seemed unwilling to bear any dates. They asked if there was anything he could do to help.

The magistrate struggled to keep a straight face, caught between amusement and anger that they would come to him with this complaint. But aged as they were, and knowing they had no children, he agreed to do what he could to help. Taking each one by the arm, he escorted the couple back to their home, trying to think of what to do when he got there.

When they arrived, the couple presented the tree to him. He looked around the yard, and saw an old branch lying on the ground. He picked it up, and feigning anger, began to hit the tree with a white-hot fury. After hitting it about forty times, he turned the stick over to the old couple, and told them to do the same. They did so, walking around and hitting it with the branch until the bark was hit away. The magistrate took his leave, went back to his office, and continued to work well into the night on the many tasks he had waiting for him.

That fall, the tree that had failed to bear fruit for dozens of years produced a bumper crop of dates. The husband and wife were delighted, and went around the village, praising the magistrate and telling others of the technique he used. Other people in the village copied the practice with their trees, and over time this evolved into cutting a circle of bark out of the tree, especially those failing to bear fruit.[30] [31] [32]

* * *

Festivals

DRAGON BOAT FESTIVAL

Commonly called the "Dragon Boat Festival" (龍舟節) in English, the Chinese name is "Duanwu Festival" (端午節). "Duan" (端) here refers to the word "initial" (初)[33], or the "initial fifth" day of the month (初五) within the earthly branches (地支) system. The "wu" (午) comes from the name of the fifth lunar month (五月) which was called wǔyuè (午月) in ancient times.[34] The Dragon Boat Festival is but one aspect of this holiday; it goes by a host of other less used names in Chinese: Double-Fifth Festival (重五節), Fifth Month Festival (五月節), Fifth Day Festival (五日節), Rice Dumpling Festival (肉粽節), Qu Yuan Day (屈原日), Poets' Festival (詩人節), and the Summer Festival (夏節). The number of names attests to the holiday's importance.

The word "dragon boat" (龍舟) first appeared in the Warring States Period in *The Tale of King Mu, Son of Heaven* (穆天子傳))[35]. Dragon boat racing was originally held as part of the Duanwu rituals and were a mixture of religious observance and entertainment.

Over time the festival expanded to adopt darker overtones after being ascribed different origin stories all characterized by tragedy. Chief among the folktales concerns Qu Yuan (屈原), where the rowing of the dragon boats and the throwing of rice dumplings into the river were to keep fish from eating his corpse. It is for memorializing Qu Yuan that this day goes by other names like Qu Yuan Day (屈原日), the Poets' Festival (詩人節) and the Rice Dumpling Festival (肉粽節). Other tragic folktales surrounding this day will be detailed later in this chapter, but they add to the general tenor of sadness attached to the holiday.

Nowadays the dragon boat aspect of the holiday is celebrated in different ways in different areas. In Sichuan and Guizhou, participants pray to a dragon head on the bank of the river, sacrifice a chicken, and drip its blood on the head of the boat. In Guangdong, the head and tail of the boat are paraded through Temple of the God of the South China Seas (南海神), while a pair of paper roosters are pasted to the boats to ensure a safe journey.[36] In Taiwan, participants pay their respects to the sea goddess Matsu.[37]

The fifth day of the fifth lunar month is considered a "wicked day" in Chinese (惡日). This is in part due to its sad origin stories. But also possibly due to the over-abundance of yang represented by the two number fives in the date (similar to Double Ninth later in the year), combined with the rising forces of yin described earlier in this chapter. There have also been numerous historical personages born on this day who have supplanted their parents in grisly fashion, so that it is considered an ill omen for a child to be born on the day of the Dragon Boat Festival[38]. Boys are said to bring ill upon the father, girls misfortune upon the mother.[39]

But there have been exceptions to this superstition. Lord Mengcheng (孟嘗君), one of the Four Lords of the Warring States (戰國四公子), was born on the fifth day in the fifth month of the lunar calendar. One of over forty children, his father wanted to let him starve to death because he was born on such an inauspicious day. But his mother raised him in secret, and he peacefully inherited his father's rulership owing to his intelligence and talent. [40] [41]

Concerns about the evil forces roaming about on this particular day and throughout this period of the year have lead to a number of customs. The most important of these is placing Chinese mugwort (艾草) and sweet flag (菖蒲) on the door. Chinese mugwort emits a fragrance which repels pests and purifies the air. Medicinally, Chinese mugwort regulates blood ch'i, warms the uterus, and removes excessive cold and moisture from the body.[42] Sweet flag is also fragrant in a way that heightens alertness and has antibacterial and insecticide properties[43]. Its herbal effects include the treatment of bronchitis, chest pain, cramps, digestive disorders, coughs, and inflammation.[44] Some locations add Chinese banyan (榕樹枝) branches, joining the other two plants in a trinity of herbs said to ward off evil. Chinese banyan is strongly yin, and as like attracts like, absorbs excessive yin from the household and promotes balance.

Given the way that energies interact during the holiday, in Taiwan the tradition has developed to balance an egg (立蛋) precisely at noon on the day of the Dragon Boat Festival. Doing so is said to bring luck for the rest of the year. The tradition actually descends from doing the same observance on Spring Begins, which eventually moved to the Summer Solstice, when the gravitational pull from the center of the earth was believed to be strongest. Given the proximity of the Dragon Boat Festival to Summer Solstice solar term, the tradition was eventually observed on the day of the festival.[45]

In earlier times herbs were placed on one's person. For example in Shaanxi women would sew together fragrant sachets containing such herbs. They would create all sorts of shapes: tigers, butterflies, sparrows, peacocks, peaches, plum blossoms, squash, deer. More widely, herbs were sewn with flowers as a way to prevent miasma, termed "Plucking the Hundred Herbs" (採百草). Another tradition are "Herb Battles" (鬥百草).[46] The more physical version involved two children fencing with plant stalks: the winner being the last one with their stalk remaining intact. [47]

There was also a more literary version, where a player would say a line of poetry involving a plant name, and the opponent would need to respond with a line containing another plant with a similarly themed name. This game is depicted in *Dream of the Red Chamber*. An example of the game is excerpted below, although translation does not do justice the meter or rhyme scheme — an impossible task — nor the inventiveness and challenge in regards to the players' encyclopedic knowledge of botany and poetry:

I have Guanyin willow (我有觀音柳)
I have Luohan pine (我有羅漢松)
I have gentleman's bamboo (我有君子竹)
I have lady's canna (我有美人蕉)

I have green starwort (我有星星翠)
I have red moonflower (我有月月紅)
I have a peony from the Peony Pavilion (我有牡丹亭上的牡丹花)
I have a loquat from the Tale of the Pipa (我有琵琶記裡的枇杷果)

Dream of the Red Chamber, Chapter 62
Cao Xueqin 曹雪芹

These games present the lighter side of the holiday, yet they are but a short pause sandwiched between the darker aspects of this time of the year. Three origin stories, all typified by sorrow, have made the rounds at different times and places.

Folklore

THE WRONGED POET

Qu Yuan is considered one of China's greatest poets. He was the first to have poems attributed to his authorship -- prior to that poems were collectively authored or otherwise anonymous -- and he broke free from the confined, four-word verse (四言詩) of earlier traditions and created Chu Ci (楚辭) a new form of verse of different length and meter. He was one of the literary tradition's most prominent romanticists, and his works went on to inspire some of China's best poets such as Li Bai. His work was collected in the *Songs of Chu* (楚辭), a poetic compilation covering autobiography, political allegory, mythology, religion, and some shamanistic elements of the local Chu culture where he had been exiled.

He is described as a deeply loyal official who was unjustly slandered and sent into exile, at least twice. He eventually committed suicide by walking into the Miluo River (汨羅江) with a rock. Different motivations have been used to explain his suicide: martyrdom for his weakening homeland, failed political dreams, or a way to demonstrate his sincerity, innocence, and sense of principle. Modern interpretations suspect love-sickness after his relationship with the king.[48]

Although unable to save the poet-official, the people on the banks used the oars from boats to scare off evil spirits that might inhabit his body and packets of rice to feed the fish and shrimp that might otherwise consume him. Using oars to scare off the spirits is said to be the origin of the dragon boat festival. Throwing rice packets into the river is believed to be the origin of preparing and eating glutinous rice dumplings (粽子).

The practice of throwing rice dumplings into rivers and the dragon boat activities are suspected to relate to earlier dragon totem practices among the Baiyue (百越) people. [49] [50] The Baiyue were excellent boat builders and sailors, and used rice dumplings to feed the water dragon to ward off maritime calamity. It is likely that these earlier traditions were assimilated by the Han majority of China and other groups over time. The observance of the holiday from places as far from each other as Vietnam and North and South Korea hint at a practice that far predates or has a separate origin from the suicide of a poet-official.

THE CAO'E STELE

A poor fisherman lived with his daughter, Cao'e (曹娥), in a small unknown fishing village below Phoenix Mountain. During the time of the plum rains it rained non-stop for days. The Shun River (舜江) began to flood, its water swelling over the banks. Having stayed at home for so many days to avoid the weather, the fisherman considered going out. One advantage was the swelling waters brought with it a potentially bigger catch of fish and shrimp. But going out in such weather was especially dangerous.

After deliberating for a few hours, and concerned by their thinning larder, he decided to make his way out into the river. As he punted his small boat out into the rushing waters, his daughter stood at the banks, watching him float at a dangerous pace down the river until the roiling river obscured his progress. For seven days and nights she waited by the bank, her tears and the sound of her sobs increasing with each passing day until she had no more tears to spare.

On the eighth day she erupted in cheers as she saw a dark form in the waves. Knowing that it was her father, she jumped into the rushing river to grab him and disappeared into the water. Nearby villagers, who had witnessed the girl's long vigil and her disappearance into the river, all knew the father and daughter were good people and worried about their fate. Once the waters had finally receded three days later, the villagers went looking for their bodies.

They found the bodies ten miles downriver. Father and daughter were together, back to back. The searchers were amazed that even in death, the daughter managed to find her father and remain with him. Impressed with her filial piety, they built a temple to the "Filial Goddess" (曹娥廟) and erected a stele (曹娥碑) memorializing the event. From the woman's death in 143 A.D., every year on the fifth day of the fifth lunar month the village would host large celebrations at the temple, and thereafter the nearby landmarks and the Shun River took on Cao'e's name (曹娥江). [51] [52]

THE WAVE GOD

Wu Zixu (伍子胥) was born in the Kingdom of Chu. At an early age his father and brothers were killed by the King Ping of Chu (楚平王). As a young man without power he could only accept his fate despite his desire for revenge.

Once he came of age he defected to the Kingdom of Wu and helped them defeat Chu. After seven intense battles he managed to lead an army into the Chu capital. The former King of Chu had long since died, denying Wu Zixu the opportunity to exact his revenge. Undeterred, he led his men to the king's tomb, pulled his corpse out of the earth, and whipped the body at least 300 times while his 6,000 soldiers stood in witness. Wu did not cease until his anger was assuaged.

This macabre scene was only the start, however. After defeating Chu, the Kingdom of Wu gave vent to their longtime hatred of another rival kingdom: the Kingdom of Yue. During one of the battles, the King of Wu (吳王闔閭) was killed, and his son Fuchai (夫差) installed. After three more battles, they finally took the capital of the Yue Kingdom. The King of Yue (越王勾踐) pleaded for the occupying army to take him prisoner and to leave the people of Yue unharmed.

Wu Zixu, long familiar with the threat posed by those who craved revenge, advised Fuchai to kill every person that could pose a threat, murdering the whole capital if necessary. Somebody in the Yue camp, however, bribed another of Fuchai's ministers to slander Wu Zixu so that such action would not be taken. The slander worked -- Fuchai ordered Wu Zixu to kill himself.

Wu Zixu had no choice but to take his own life. But before he died, he cursed the king and court, asking that his eyes be dug out of his freshly dead face, and hung from the east gate to watch and enjoy Yue's defeat of Wu. Hearing this, the angry King ordered Wu Zixu's body wrapped in leather and thrown in the river to feed the fish on the fifth day of the fifth month. Soon after, nearby villagers, taking pity on the man who tried to protect the kingdom, built a temple to him near the river. Thereafter he was worshiped as the God of Waves (迎涛神), his anger and thirst for revenge satiated by the taking of the occasional hapless swimmer. To appease his angry soul and prevent more drownings the people of Wu held an annual ritual on the anniversary of his death, the fifth day of the fifth lunar month, which later became the Dragon Boat Festival. [53] [54]

* * *

These three stories all contain characters giving up their lives, and at first glance would seem odd or even disturbing in a modern Western context. Qu Yuan's suicide might seem ineffectual, melodramatic, and even petulant. But the point of the observance is less about the act than the expression of loyalty and idealism the act represents. Cao'e, throwing herself after her father's body might seem wasteful for someone so young. But not so within the tightly wrapped bonds of Chinese filial piety, the annals of which are a pageant of one-upmanship of bodily harm to demonstrate respect for parents. The action is one of more universal application: the grief that comes from love, and one of the many tragic ways that grief might be expressed when facing the immutable fact of losing a parent.

The story of Wu Zixu is the most curious tale of the three, ending with the deification a man consumed with hate and revenge. As opposed to Qu Yuan, it is hard to apply loyalty as the lesson of the tale, since Wu Zixu is keen on destroying every sovereign and kingdom he serves. Rather, he comes to personify the fatal aspects of nature, in this case the dangerous tides that pull swimmers down in undertows, or engulf those innocently walking on river banks or beach shores -- a warning that the ways anger and vengeance can engulf our own lives if gone unchecked.

CHAPTER 10: SUMMER SOLSTICE 夏至

夏至 / 하지 / げし / Hạ chí
Pinyin: xiàzhì
Literal Meaning: "Summer Solstice"
Alternative names: Summer Maximum
Period: June 20 or 21 ~ July 6 or 7
Sun's Ecliptic Longitude: 90°

Escaping Summer Solstice Heat at the Northern Pool

Wei Yingwu
Tang Dynasty

The shadow on the sundial has reached its farthest point,
  from here the nighttime water-clock drips ever longer.
I have barely had time to effect my plans,
  yet am already worried about the change from hot to cold.

Occupants of government offices are idle,
  while it is the time for farmers to be busy.
One privileged as me feels respect for those in the fields,
  how can they ward off the bitter heat?

They all gather together at noon for a rest,
  while I enjoy the pond all to myself.
Closed city gates bring stillness and silence,
  city walls stand high and trees grow verdant.

Green bamboo is still covered in powder,
  plump lotuses start dispersing their fragrance.
Here I can dispel all my worries,
  and regard a beautiful glass of wine.

夏至避暑北池 | 唐 | 韋應物

畫晷已雲極，宵漏自此長。未及施政教，所憂變炎涼。
公門日多暇，是月農稍忙。高居念田裡，苦熱安可當。
亭午息群物，獨游愛方塘。門閉陰寂寂，城高樹蒼蒼。
綠筠尚含粉，圓荷始散芳。於焉灑煩抱，可以對華觴。

The Summer Solstice is the longest day and shortest night of the year. From here the daylight diminishes with each passing day and the nights grow longer. This continues up until the Winter Solstice, the time of shortest day and longest night, after which daylight begins to grow again. The Earth reaches the aphelion in relation to the sun within a couple weeks of the solstice -- in other words it is the farthest distance from the sun over the course of its elliptical orbit, which translates to longer summers in the northern hemisphere by about four days. The opposite is true in the winter, when the sun is closer and therefore moving faster, hence the Chinese phrase "summers are long and winters are short" (夏長冬短). The situation is reversed in southern hemisphere, with longer winters and shorter summers.

This solar term is associated with the farthest extreme of yang. Although we saw the first inklings of yin in the previous solar term of Little Fullness, it is at this point that yang starts its decline in earnest and yin begins its rapid ascent as the earth moves toward autumn and winter. After the Summer Solstice, yin flowers start to bloom. Flowers like Chinese clematis, leopard lily, resurrection lily, and gardenia. These flowers are considered yin due to their even number of six petals -- even numbers being a manifestation of yin just as even numbers represent the passive in Western esoteric systems. Five-petaled plum, peach, and apricot flowers, which are odd-numbered and thus yang, bloom after the Winter Solstice.

The Summer Solstice is China's oldest solar term and festival, more ancient than the Shangyuan, Dragon Boat, Mid-Autumn, and Double-Nine festivals.[1] [2] Its original name was simply the "Summer Festival" (夏節) or "Summer Solstice Festival" (夏至節).[3] In the Zhou dynasty it was a time rest in order to prepare for the forthcoming rise in heat as well as deity worship to ward away illness, famine, starvation, and death. By the Han dynasty it was a national holiday.[4] Officials would take time off, stay at home, wash up, spend time with their families, and banquet with neighbors.[5] This was also a time for making and consuming rice dumplings, as the food was not originally exclusive to the Dragon Boat Festival; rather, it was first a Summer Solstice activity in the Jin dynasty,[6] adding further evidence that the attribution of the food to Qu Yuan's death was a later addition.

Pentads

Deer shed their antlers (鹿角解)
Cicadas begin to chirp (蜩始鳴)
Crow-dipper herb grows (半夏生)

Deer are considered a very yang animal,[7] so the shedding of their antlers indicates of the rise of the forces of yin.[8] The deer is sometimes depicted as mount for the Old Man of the South Pole (南極仙翁), also known as the Star of Longevity (壽星).[9] This association with longevity as well as yang has led to heavy use of deer antler in traditional Chinese medicine. [10]

Like the deer, cicadas are considered yang, but their singing grows louder as if to compete with the rising forces of yin.[11] Cicadas feature prominently in Chinese culture for multiple reasons. Hibernating in the fall to feed on roots for months or even years, cicadas emerge again from a state of near-death in the spring, reborn to ascend the heights of trees, and so serve as a potent symbol of rebirth as well as transcendence. They also represent purity, since they are believed to subsist on dew (actually, tree sap), and are therefore associated with the ideal official: [12] sitting on high, consuming a pure diet, and keenly observing the world from above. Finally, they are a poignant reminder of the circle of existence. The Taoist philosopher Zhuangzi, while hunting a jaybird, is distracted by a cicada. While looking at the cicada it is captured and eaten by a praying mantis, which is then in turn eaten by the jaybird he was hunting (螳螂捕蟬, 黃雀在後). Disturbed by the event and his role in the cycle of predation, Zhuangzi declines to kill the jaybird. [13]

Crow-dipper (半夏- *Pinellia ternata*) is a poisonous herb often used as a "hair of the dog" (以毒攻毒) curative for other poisons, like scorpion stings. The Chinese name can be literally translated as "mid-summer herb," since it sprouts at the approaching center of the solar year. Ground up and applied to wounds, it helps alleviate pain, giving it the nickname "scorpion grass" (蝎子草).[14] It is considered an yin plant, preferring bogs and paddies, and its growth is another signal that yin is on the rise.[15]

Agriculture

For the farming community this period means plenty of sun and lots of rain, so crops grow especially fast and weeds even faster. A

170

common saying goes that any weed not pulled is like raising a poisonous snake to bite you (夏至不鋤根邊草，如同養下毒蛇咬)[16]. Insects are numerous, and according to the *Record of Jingchu* (荊楚歲時記) -- before the arrival of chemical pesticides -- farmers in the south would burn chrysanthemum leaves and stems, using the ash to kill pests.[17] [18]

Health

As temperatures rise, it is important to maintain a positive disposition, and enjoy what the world of summer has to offer outdoors. In the face of growing heat the Chinese have a saying: a placid mind naturally cools (心靜自然涼). It is a time when the extra light and heat results in late bedtimes and early rising, so naps are a must. Exercise is best done early in the morning or later in the evening when temperatures recede. Getting fresh air in parks, forests, and beaches is advised. In terms of food, it is a time of advancing mold and more bugs, so it is best not to eat cold, raw foods. The Summer Solstice is not the hottest solar term of the year. Those come later. However, a number of customs described later in this chapter have evolved to prepare for the inexorable rise in temperatures that are around the corner.[19] [20]

A common custom practiced in Chinese medicine is *sanfutie* (三伏貼), where patches containing medicinal herbs are applied to acupuncture points, usually on the back, and left there for a number of hours. The practice is a preventative one, helping people avoid illnesses that crop up in the winter, according to the principle of treating winter illnesses in the summer (冬病夏治)[21] by removing excess cold from the body during the hottest days of the year. The initial patch is applied at the first *fu* period (初伏 or 頭伏), also called "Entering Fu" (入伏), between the third and fourth *Geng* (庚) day after the summer solstice. The next occurs during the second *fu* period (中伏 or 二伏) between the fourth *Geng* (庚) day and the Autumn Begins solar term. The final *fu* period （末伏 or 终伏), also called "Departing Fu" (出伏) between Autumn Begins and the first *Geng* (庚) day of the same solar term.

Meta-analyses of randomized controlled trials show the practice to be helpful in treating allergic rhinitis.[22] [23]

Customs

In ancient times the Summer Solstice was a time to worship agricultural deities. The book *Dong Yang Yin Zhi* (東陽縣志) describe offerings made to a Field Goddess (田婆) in the middle of the family field[24]. The *Records of the Grand Historian* (史記) speaks of worship of the Land God with singing and dancing. [25]

Modern observances, however, are centered on foodways, and there are many different practices throughout China. In northern China, some regions serve noodles on the Summer Solstice and dumplings on the Winter Solstice, while others prefer wontons over dumplings. The main difference between dumplings and wontons are the thickness of the skin and the method of wrapping. In Taiwan, tangyuan are preferred, as described in the later chapter on the Winter Solstice. In Shandong, cold noodles (涼麵) are eaten as a reminder to protect against the hotter weather to come[26], and children use wheat stalks to fish out cooked wheat from soup.[27] In Jiangsu, pea cakes made with peach, apricot, and red flowers are said to help with fatigue.[28] In Zhejiang, it's crepes, cucumber, and boiled eggs to ward off the "bitter summer" (苦夏).[29]

In the south Lingnan areas of Guangdong, Guangxi, and Hainan Island, the traditional food of the period is dog meat. Dog meat has been eaten in the area since the Warring States period. In the second year of Duke De of Qin's reign (秦德公), the sixth month of the year was abnormally hot and disease was rampant. He ordered that dogs be killed, because they are considered yang and killing them can prevent misfortune. This turned into the practice of "Summer Solstice Dog-Killing" (夏至殺狗). Dog meat is also said to have medicinal properties, fortifying the body and preventing illnesses by blocking cold from entering the body. Being yang, it wards against evil. It is generally advised to not consume too much because it can cause indigestion. [30] Although still eaten in China, the practice is dwindling as urbanization has resulted in closer relationships with canines, and as animal protection organizations work to curtail the eating of dogs and cats. [31]

There are a number of other observances associated with the Summer Solstice. The *Qingjialu* (清嘉錄) notes that people are prohibited from cursing or cutting their hair -- doing otherwise invites misfortune. [32] In Hunan, thunder on the Summer Solstice means drought will come in the sixth lunar month, and if it rains the Sanfu (三伏) period will be extremely hot (夏至有雷, 六月旱; 夏至逢雨, 三伏熱).[33] The Sanfu period comes twenty to thirty days after the summer solstice and lasts through Little Heat, Great Heat and early Autumn Begins. In Henan, if the solstice is at the beginning of the fifth lunar month, grain will grow well; if at the end of the fifth month, it will grow poorly (夏至五月頭,不種芝麻也吃油; 夏至五月終,十個油房就個空). [34] In Shandong, farmers feed their oxen extra helpings of wheatberry, which is supposed to make them strong, and lowers its perspiration as it toils in the steamy summer fields.[35] One of the more curious beliefs comes from the *Miscellaneous Morsels from Youyang* (酉陽雜俎), which states that cats' noses are always cold, except for the Summer Solstice, the only day when their noses are warm.[36]

Festivals

LOTUS VIEWING FESTIVAL

The Lotus Viewing Festival (觀蓮節) takes place on the 24th day of the sixth lunar month, and is considered the lotus's birthday. The festival has been in existence since as early as the Song dynasty, and typically involved a number of activities: boating in lakes to appreciate the flowers, the making of lanterns with long lotus stems and leaves for children to carry, and the hollowing out of lotus seed heads to hold candles for floating on the river at night.[37] [38] The plant is also eaten, and according to traditional medicine, its leaves dissipate heat. The flowers invigorate the blood and reduce phlegm. The seeds are said to fortify the kidneys and calm the nerves.[39] In the Song dynasty the lotus petals were crushed and put in rice noodles and cakes, and lotus wine was brewed in the Ming dynasty. [40]

Why is the lotus in particular singled out for its own holiday? Aside from the time of year, when the flowers are in full bloom, the lotus is a major flower in Chinese culture. The flower embodies a long list of attributes. One is its status as a general symbol of purity. It also crops up in poetry as a symbol of feminine purity and love.

In the eyes of Cao Xueqin, the author of the famous novel *Dream of the Red Chamber*, women embodied the purity and virtue of the lotus, while men represented the muddy base, full of greed and sullied by the affairs of the world.[41] Women, like the lotus, were proud and fearless, born of mud yet elegant (出淤泥而不染), embodying perfection, containing the seed of love, and symbolizing sacred purity. Associating women with purity was a common view at the time, and extended beyond ideas of virginity. Among families of means, women were kept at home to protect them from the taint of the outside world. They pursued household and artistic affairs, only leaving the household grounds on special occasions.

THE LOTUS LOVERS

Chao Cai (晁采) was a talented young girl who was especially adept at composing poetry. She lived next door to a boy named Wen Mao (文茂), and the two played together in their childhood. But as they grew older, propriety mandated that they rarely saw each other.

Missing her childhood friend and wanting him to know she still thought of him, Chao Cai gathered ten lotus seeds from the pool in their yard and placed them into a brocade bag, along with a poem, and had them secreted over to Wen Mao.

When Wen Mao received the bag, he was overjoyed and rushed outside to a quiet area to see what she sent. He placed the bag of seeds on his lap and read the poem. Lost in the beauty of the verse, unbeknownst to him one of the seeds rolled out of the bag and into their family pond.

A few weeks later a lotus flower surfaced from the dark pond water. But this flower looked different: two conjoined buds grew from a single stalk. He was delighted and he wrote back to Chao Cai, sending her a poem describing the lotus.

Chao Cai's mother, seeing the packages going back and forth, eventually realized their feelings for each other. She was filled with joy but at the same time unsure of how to bring them together. Marriage was a complicated matter and usually required delicate arrangements between two families. She engaged the services of a well-known matchmaker, who managed to arrange the necessary meetings, and eventually obtained agreement between both families.

The children were ecstatic, and they were married on the Summer Solstice, when the pool in Wen Mao's yard was brimming with lotus flowers. Given the common challenge of arranged marriages, the coupling of the young man and woman were held up as an example of an excellent match, and the day was celebrated by viewing and picking lotuses. Thereafter the Summer Solstice also became the time of the Lotus Viewing Festival.[42] [43] [44]

THE ORIGIN OF THE LOTUS

Jade Belle (玉姬) was an attendant to the Queen Mother of the West, and was nearly always by her side. Over time, Jade became bored with the myriad wonders of the heavens and began to envy the coupling that mortal men and women enjoyed.

One day, the Queen was occupied with other matters, so Jade went down to West Lake in the mortal realm. She was so captivated by the sights and sounds she forgot the time. When the Queen returned, she was furious to find out Jade had secretly left.

Once Jade finally returned, the Queen seized her and thrust her deep into the mud of West Lake as punishment for her transgressions. Jade grew back out of the fetid mud and transformed into the proud, pure lotus immortalized by countless poets, and bringing yet further beauty to West Lake.

* * *

175

Although the pentads of this solar term hint at the rise of yin and the ascent of darkness that is to come, the lotus and its associated stories show that celebration of life is still in full swing at midsummer. Stories about the lotus are characterized by tales of brave rebirth and young romance. Throughout many cultures in the world, the Summer Solstice is also a way to mark the peak of light for the year. Bonfires are common. In Christianity, it is celebrated as St. John's Day[45], with fires as an emblem of St. John the Baptist. These celebrations carry on pre-Christian traditions that are even more ancient, but are similarly centered around marking time, celebrating light, and warding off misfortune. Chinese minority cultures have similar traditions, such as Torch Festival (火把節).

TORCH FESTIVAL

There are many origin stories for the Torch Festival, but the celebration most likely derived from a primal veneration of fire. It is most reverently observed by the Yi (彝族) and Bai (白族) minority groups, and is their most important holiday. These groups have traditionally divided the year into 10 months of 36 days each. On June 24th or 25th, they celebrate the Summer Solstice, which is also called the Star-Returning Festival (星回節)[46] and effectively acts as their new year.

Whether derived from ancient veneration of fire or to observe the changing of the year, the rituals center around recognizing the passage of time and dispelling darkness. These practices are seen as critically important: vulnerability to agricultural disaster increases after the Torch Festival, posing a major influence on their fortunes linked to the upcoming harvest.

The ritual lasts for three days, and all the villagers emerge from their homes with pine branches and other assorted kindling, placing them in a large pile. Flowers, fruit, and written words wishing a good harvest are placed on the top. After a gong is rung, the pile is lit and all villagers gather around it, children often dancing and singing. Later, the festival incorporated other activities like bullfights, wrestling, horse riding, and archery. [47] [48]

As is common with origin myths -- particularly among China's minority cultures -- the tales describing the origin of the Torch Festival are a colorful mix of love and tragedy.

THE MAGPIE MAIDEN

Long ago a beautiful maiden lived among the Yi people (彝族). She was pursued by many men from many different tribes, but she refused them all because she was promised to another young man, whom she loved.

A bloodthirsty chieftain known for his murderous ways came to their tribe, demanding the woman's hand. He threatened to annihilate the whole tribe if he was refused. Her parents, despondent but with little recourse, agreed to his demands, and set the wedding date for June 24th.

Early on the day of the wedding the woman wore a white top, black coat, and a dress of woven flowers. She went to where the wedding was to take place and made a giant bonfire. As the flames licked the sky and smoke spread throughout the mountains and valleys, people were drawn from all the surrounding tribal lands.

Soon a large crowd gathered, watching as the flames burned hotter. The woman stood nearby, her eyes on the crowd. Scanning their confused faces, her eyes landed on the man for whom she was originally intended -- the man she loved. Just as their eyes locked, and before he had a chance to even nod in acknowledgment, the woman jumped into the bonfire.

The crowd gasped in horror. Her lover jumped into the fire to save her, but her body was buried too deep into the pile. All he was able to get was a small piece of the clothing she was wearing.

Thereafter, the women of Yi wove the woman's cloth into their own belts, to commemorate the maiden's unyielding loyalty to the man she truly loved. It is said by the Yi that the smoke from the woman's burned body can be seen as the early morning fog coiling through the mountains, and her memory is preserved in the call of morning magpies.[49] [50]

* * *

This myth shows the very different shade of proper conduct than what might be expected in the Han majority culture where patrilineal Confucianism dominates. The behavior is somewhat transgressive, in that the maiden goes against the arrangement agreed to by her parents, placing them and possibly her whole community in danger. One can sense a different set of rules, where keeping ones word and the power of romantic love play a larger role.

The Yi (彝), also called the Nuosuo (諾蘇) or Lolo (倮倮), are a minority ethnic group living in China, Vietnam, and Thailand. Like the Han, they pay respects to their ancestors but also worship nature gods taking the form of fire, hills, trees, rocks, water, earth, sky, wind and forests. [51] The specific symbolism of the magpie to the Yi is now obscure, but in the Han culture it represents joy, happiness, and good fortune -- a somewhat discordant set of symbolism considering the tragic aspects of above story. In traditional Yi observance we could speculate that the magpie symbolizes fidelity, which would match both the story above and the bird's monogamous mating behavior.

Folklore

THE FIERCE GOD

There once was a deity named the Fierce God (凶神), who would come down from heaven and harass the Yi people. The people eventually had enough, and selected a hero to fight the god.

The next time the Fierce God descended from heaven, the Yi people readied for battle. To aid their champion, thousands of villagers brought torches to the heavenly stairs, and burned them down to the ground so that the Fierce God had no retreat. They then hunted him down and engaged in a pitched battle, the hero fighting him while the tribes people assaulted the god with fire. After nine days, the god was finally killed.

The King of Heaven was livid when he learned the Fierce God was killed. He sent a plague of heavenly insects in the form of locusts to consume all of their crops right at the time when the potatoes, taro, corn were ready for harvesting.

After three days of eating through their crops, the tribes people used the same strategy they had deployed on the Fierce God, using fire to burn the locusts. Most of insects were set alight, and the few that remained burrowed underground to resurface the following year to battle with the torches of the Yi tribes people. This eventually evolved into the Torch Festival.[52][53]

BURNING PINE-BRIGHT TOWER

The *Unofficial History of Nanzhao* (南詔野史)[54] tells of a tribal queen of the Bai people (白族) named Lady Baijie (白潔夫人) in their origin story of the Torch Festival.

***

A loyal, brave, and wise woman, Lady Baijie was alarmed to hear her husband, King of Tengtan (邆賧), had received an invitation from the rival king Piluoge (皮邏閣), to a banquet to celebrate a new tower Piluoge had built. Lady Baijie sensed it was a trap. She made every effort to persuade her husband not to attend, but he felt it would be more dangerous to refuse. Seeing that she could not persuade him, she gave the king a bracelet to wear for good luck.

The King of Tengtan went to the banquet, and the rival king Piluoge showed off his newly built structure, which he named Pine-Bright Tower (松明樓), and they all ascended for a grand banquet. Halfway through, Piluoge snuck away and his warriors set fire to the building. Made of pine, it burnt quickly and everybody inside was burned alive in short order.

Lady Baijie, upon hearing the news, refused to believe that her husband was trapped like all the others. She rode her horse to the location of the banquet, searching for her husband until she came across a smoldering pile of ash. She dug through the ash and dirt until her fingers *bled and her fingernails shredded away. As she overturned a charred piece of pine, she saw the bracelet she gave her husband. She grabbed it in her hand and wailed with so much force that the whole tribe felt incredible sorrow.*

Unphased by Lady Baijie's sorrow but impressed by her beauty, Piluoge asked her to marry him. Aware of her limited options to refuse Piluoge, she threw herself into the Erhai Lake (洱海). The Bai people built a temple to her near the lake, revering her as the Holy Consort of White Purity (白潔聖妃) for her display of loyalty to her assassinated husband. Every year on June 25th, the people of Dali (大理) raise torches and ride horses, circumambulating the town just as Lady Baijie searched for her husband. Women also paint their fingernails bright red, to commemorate the shredding of her fingernails as she clawed through the ash and dirt in search of any object with which to remember her husband. [55] [56] [57]

* * *

The Bai people (白族), also referred to as the Pai or Baipho, are an ethnic minority centered around Erhai Lake (洱海) in Yunnan province mentioned in the above legend. They currently number about two million. [58] They have traditionally been Buddhist since the establishment of the Nanzhao Kingdom in 8th century CE. They also have a native religion comprised of local gods, ancestors, folk heroes. [59]

THE FIRE-WIELDING SKY GOD

The Jade Emperor felt a growing unease that the mortal world would pollute the grandeur of his heavenly realm. Thinking the best solution would be to isolate the heavens from the filth of the mortal realm, he ordered his guard to shut the gates of heaven. Secure in knowledge that the heavens were safe from the mundane world's influence, he whiled away his time exploring the glories of the heavens and the oddities of the eighteen hells. Over time he grew bored, and wished to see how the mortal realm was doing.

The Jade Emperor had the doors unlocked, and he descended down to Earth, flying from place to place to inspect what had changed. He soon became consumed with jealousy, observing that the beauty of the world now surpassed that of his heavenly kingdom. He sought out the Fire-Wielding Sky God (掌火天神) and ordered him to burn the world.

The God went down to the mortal realm as ordered, taking a look around to see what had so upset the Jade Emperor. He was struck by the world's beauty and the kindness of its people, and couldn't bear to set it ablaze. Hoping to spare the world from destruction, he returned to heaven and lied to the Jade Emperor, saying that the job was done.

The Jade Emperor in time found out that the Fire-Wielding God did not burn the world, and in fact the world had become even more beautiful since he had last seen it. Furious, he killed the god who would dare contravene his orders. But as the god died, a single drop of blood fell from heaven and landed into a temple. The drop of blood transformed into a toddler, who walked out of the temple and told the people of the Jade Emperor's plans to destroy the world. He advised them to make fires for three days and three nights, the bigger the better. Astonished at the eloquence of the small child, the people understood it was in fact the advice of a god, and did as advised.

The Jade Emperor soon cast his eyes again on the mortal realm. Seeing it ablaze, he assumed one of his subjects carried out his order. He watched intently for three days and nights to be sure the world was burned away. After the three days, he returned to his throne room, satisfied that the beauty of heaven was now again unrivaled.[60][61]

* * *

This legend shares aspects with the origin myth of the Lantern Festival, but rather than a story of divine retribution, it is a commentary on the meddling of heaven. Once the gate of heaven is closed and the mortal realm is left to its own devices, it thrives. The lesson is that the earth and nature are themselves a reflection of a greater force even above that of reigning deities. In Chinese culture, this could be named the Tao, a primal force that sits above even the highest gods. It could also fit many other religious cosmologies, providing comment on too frequently looking to the heavens for aid while overlooking the existing gifts of the secular realm.

CHAPTER 11: LITTLE HEAT 小暑

小暑 / 소서 / しょうしょ / Tiểu thử
Pinyin: xiǎoshǔ
Literal Meaning: "little summer"
Alternative names: Moderate Heat, A Bit Sweltering
Period: July 6 or 7 ~ July 22 or 23
Sun's Ecliptic Longitude: 105°

Dispelling Heat
Baiju Yi
Tang Dynasty

How does one extinguish the tormenting heat?
    Simply sit in the middle of the courtyard.
Nothing but blank space before my eyes,
    fresh wind blowing from under the window.
Heat is dispelled with a calm mind,
    while the cool is born in an empty room.
At this moment I am content,
    and it is difficult to be the same as others.

消暑 | 唐 | 白居易
何以消煩暑，端坐一院中。
眼前無長物，窗下有清風。
熱散由心靜，涼生為室空。
此時身自得，難更與人同。

The name "Little Heat" refers to sweltering temperatures while hinting much more is to come. At this time of year the flowers that bloom -- sunflowers, hibiscus, moonflower, Chinese trumpet vine, lotus -- get more colorful as the sun burns hotter. There are also fruit flowers: watermelon, eggplant, pumpkin, tomatoes, peppers. Yet despite their color and beauty, their time is short, and after a few days of budding they quickly start to wither, much like the prime of human youth that burns by in a flash.

The weather at this time of the year can be uncomfortable, but is not yet suffocatingly hot. Thunder and rain are unpredictable, and if the sound of thunder does indeed occur during the time of Little Heat, it is said the yellow plum rains will return, and regular precipitation can be expected. (小暑一聲雷，倒轉做黃梅).[1]

Pentads

Warm winds arrive 溫風至
Crickets live in the walls 蟋蟀居壁
Young hawks learn to hunt 鷹始摯

"Warm winds arrive" refers to gusts of wind getting warmer, canceling any hope of cool winds to offset the blazing sun. [2]

The cricket is a rich symbol in Chinese culture. The *Classic of Poetry* (詩經) details the lifecycle of the cricket,[3] which explains this pentad. Using a different calendar system, the classic states that crickets stir in the fifth month, beat their wings in the sixth, fly out into the wilds in the seventh, sit under the eaves in the eighth, then into houses in the ninth (to escape the cold), and then under beds in the tenth (when it is even colder). At this time of year their wings are still not yet fully formed, and so they stay near walls until it is time to go out into the wider world. This movement into the world is said to result in crickets fighting one another, driven by the "murderous energy" (殺氣) rising at this time. In other words the darker energies of yin.[4]

The cricket in Chinese culture shares much of the symbolism of insects introduced in previous chapters: bravery for their willingness to fight, rebirth and longevity for their cycle of life, death, and resurrection from the soil, fecundity and success for their numerous eggs, and the cycle of the seasons given their appearance when it is time to plant and disappearance in the autumn when it is time to harvest. Their summertime song was used by poets as an indication of happiness, and their last autumn chirping as a symbol of melancholy and loneliness. [5] [6]

The first mention of crickets appear in records from 1000 B.C.E, and they have long been carried around in small bamboo cages or gourds as pets, both for their song and to participate in cricket fights. The latter runs from casual get-togethers between friends to professional-level tournaments. Rules are strict, and are based on a 13th century manual *The Book of Crickets* (促織經) While the practice sounds brutal to the uninitiated, the bouts are rarely lethal. There are rules in place to protect the safety of combatants, and their owners display a level of sentimentality for their cricket pets rare among some of the crueler animal fighting sports. [7]

The final pentad refers to hawks or eagles, which are also an animal affected by the rise of "murderous energy." As the forces of yin accumulate, young eagles turn their attention toward the hunting and capturing of small animals.[8] They will then be skilled at the hunt to survive the difficult winter that arrives later in the year. Within the pentads of the 24 solar terms they are associated with the severity of winter, and to some extent, death. More generally in Chinese culture, however, eagles are a symbol of strength and advancement.[9]

Agriculture

Some local traditions ascribe significance to the relative temperatures between Little Heat and Great Heat. If it is very warm during the Little Heat term, Great Heat will be hotter, which is better for crops as they will get plenty of sun during the peak growth period. If it gets too hot during Little Heat, some crops will not mature correctly. If it is not hot enough during Great Heat, the winter will bring damaging rains and snow.[10]

Southwest winds are bad omen in Jiangsu, as they collide with the southeast winds and indicate the crops will not grow well and the "three machines" (三車) – the oil cart, the rice windmill, and the ginning machine – will not be needed to transport oil, mill grain, nor process cotton (小暑西南風, 三車勿動).[11] This likely refers to the type of rain at this time of year, which can be more concentrated, raining at damaging volume in shorter bursts.

There are also typhoons which supply the necessary water for rice but can damage cotton, beans, and leafy vegetables.[12] The weather also encourages the growth of aphids and red mites, necessitating careful preventative measures. [13]

Health

According to *The Esoteric Scripture of the Yellow Emperor* (黃帝內經), the internal organs suffer from a lack of balance between joy and sorrow.[14] A calm mind is critical in the growing swelter in order to maintain organ function. Profuse sweating causes blood viscosity to increase, leading to blood clots and cardiovascular problems. Drinking ample water prevents such problems while helping to lower body temperature. In the realm of folk remedies, drinking a cup of fresh warm water is said to enhance longevity and prevent major illnesses. A bit of salt added to cold water can also lower body temperature. [15]

Ancient Traditions

In the third month of summer, four inspectors were sent by the court to collect rich fodder from all the districts, which were used to fatten sacrificial animals. The animals were then used to worship heaven and the spirits of famous mountains and great streams, as well as the four quarters. Sacrifices were also made to ancestral spirits of temples and the spirits of the land, while prayers were offered to bless the populace.

In the natural world the ground was said to be steaming and wet due to the combination of heat and heavy rain. Floods covered the roads. The trees at this time grew luxuriant with leaves, and foresters were ordered into the hills to examine them, to ensure they were not cut down nor the branches stolen. For a prosperous autumn, as well as to appease the God of Agriculture, farming was to be attended to with all diligence. Certain agricultural techniques were encouraged, like the burning of cut grass on fields with water poured over the flaming mounds. The descending hot water was said to kill the roots of weeds, while at the same time fertilizing the soil.

In the human realm, officials in charge of women's work oversaw the dying of silk to make robes for ceremonies, done meticulously and exactly according to the ancient practices.

Like previous months the undertaking of great affairs was prohibited to avoid disturbing the natural growth proceeding at this time. There were to be no major assemblies of officials, or convening of state matters, military movements, or any such projects would cause general excitement. Any major orders were to be delayed. Failure to keep the empire calm and quiet would invite the curse of heaven.

Performing the rites of spring at this time would bring about scanty grain yields, colds and coughs among the populace, and the migration of the populace elsewhere. Autumn rites would cause floods, unripe grain, and miscarriages. Winter rites brought unseasonable wind and cold. Hawks and falcons would prematurely begin to hunt prey, and subjects living on the empire's borderlands would require sheltering. [16]

Customs

There are many customs associated with Double Sixth Festival (六月六, 天貺節) as described below, but some locations have customs related directly to this solar term. In Shandong and Jiangsu it is eating summer goat (吃暑羊).[17] The meat is especially fragrant and tender after the goat has spent months drinking fresh mountain spring water and eating the tender grasses of the spring months. These places have a saying: "One soup-bowl of summer lamb, no need to see the medicine man" (彭城伏羊一碗湯，不用神醫開藥方). [18]

Some places celebrate a similar form of "Eating New"(食新) from the last term, making offerings of newly harvested rice and wheat and freshly brewed wine to the God of Five Grains (五穀大神) to offer thanks and ensure a good future harvest.[19] The Tang dynasty doctor Su Gong (蘇恭) claimed that fried noodles made from newly harvested grain in this period could relieve heat, treat diarrhea, and improve function of the large intestine.[20]

The Miao people (苗族) hold certain food prohibitions during this time. Pork, beef, and lamb are fine, but eating chicken, duck, fish, softshell turtle, and crab will result in misfortune.[21] [22] Among the Yao people (瑤族) and the Tujia people (土家族), however, chickens and ducks that are eaten as part of the Double Sixth Festival. [23]

Festivals

DOUBLE SIXTH FESTIVAL

The Double Sixth Festival (六月六), which takes place on the sixth day of the sixth lunar month, goes by a number of names in Chinese. It is called the Insect King Festival (蟲王節) by the Manchu people (滿族), hoping to placate the Insect King so that he does not send pestilence to destroy their crops before harvesting.[24] The Bai people (白族) call it the Azure Sprout Festival (青苗會), and pray to the Azure Seedling Prince (青苗太子) at the Five Grains Temple (五穀廟) for his blessing on the processes of seeding.[25]

The Muslim Hui people (回族), along with the Monguor people (土族), and a number of other minority ethnicities in China celebrate it as the "Flower Fair" (花兒會), based on a sad legend about a couple that would sing to each other about flowers. The man was forced to sing by officials until his voice broke, and his lover cried tears that created a magic spring that helped the people of the land.[26] Among the Buyi people (布依族) the Flower Fair serves as a mini-New Year.[27]

More broadly, the Double Sixth Festival is a time to pray to the flower deity, pick and appreciate lotus flowers, and set lotus lamps afloat on the water. Among the Han people (漢族) and some other ethnicities it is recognized as the Heavenly Gifts Festival (天貺節), Homecoming Festival (回娘家節), or the Auntie Festival (姑姑節).[28] The Heavenly Gifts Festival has a number of origins, and revolve around the sacred texts of Taoism and Buddhism.

One origin is that Emperor Zhenzong of the Song dynasty (宋真宗), a major promoter of Taoism, claimed to have received heaven's blessings and scriptures on this day. Among Buddhists, it is associated with Xuan Zang (玄奘) of the Tang Dynasty, when he had to dry the waterlogged holy scriptures he brought back from India.[29] In Taiwan it is said to be the day when the Gates of Heaven open (開天門), so people go to the temple and supplement their luck. The day is said to be a particularly powerful one for having requests granted.[30]

This brings us to the main activity for this holiday, which is the sunning of clothes and books. It is the day the "dragon suns its scales" (龍晒鱗),[31] when the sun's rays are strongest -- or in Chinese terms when the sun is its most "bitter" (苦)[32] -- and most effective at killing mold and mites. It is an ideal day to sun household items: the weather is usually clear, summer is in high gear, and the weather takes a break from the frequent rains that cause mildew. In the past, as soon as the sun came out, people would rush outside to get a good spot and lay out clothes and bedding, ideally for two hours or more.

The practice of sunning used to be a raucous community event, leading to the inevitable "keeping up with the Jones's" complex satirized in a couple of folktales.

SAGE OF THE BAMBOO GROVE

Ruan Xian (阮咸) was a famous scholar and musician who lived in the 3rd century C.E. He was a highly talented lute player, and altered an older version of the pipa (琵琶), or Chinese lute, into a different instrument which was named after him called the ruan (阮), ruanxian (阮咸), or ruanqin (阮琴).

Despite his fame and the high regard he received in his own time, he spent most of his life in poverty. He lived on the south side of the main street in his village, along with all the other impoverished inhabitants.

On Double-Sixth day, all the wealthy people brought out their finery, and set them out on slats to capture the rays of the day's hot sun. The majority of the inhabitants of the south side of the street did not dare do the same, ashamed as they were considering the shabbiness of their attire.

Unperturbed, Ruan Xian brought out the few clothes he owned, mostly tattered and in poor shape. The wealthier people on the north side of the street, examined the finery of their immediate neighbors -- each comparison provoking a sense of glee or shame. They then ambled over to Ruan Xian's items. They laughed at the thinning material, and poked their fingers through the holes in his clothes, telling him that they weren't even worth the effort of sunning, and should just be thrown out.

Each time a neighbor made fun of him, he came back with a single reply:

"Just can't help but follow the old custom, and that's all there is to it." (未能免俗,聊復爾耳)[33] [34]

* * *

Ruan Xian's quotation has two implications. The first is that his wealthier neighbors, by focusing on the quality of his clothes, demonstrated that they missed the point of the annual custom, which was to clean and air out their clothes, not show them off. It is a comment on how customs become twisted from their original purpose by greed and the passage of time -- a concept familiar to many in the West who dislike the modern versions of seasonal holidays. Second, it is a hint at the folly of looking at the surface level, and that material riches are not something to boast about compared to one's level of learning and virtuous conduct, qualities that Ruan Xian had in spades.

READING BREEDS ELEGANCE

Hao Long (郝隆) was a highly learned man who lived during the Jin dynasty. He had memorized the classics of poetry, but lived in grinding poverty. The custom was similar to story described above: the villagers vying for space to place their household items to air in the sun.

Hao Long carried out a bamboo settee, and then lay down on it and opened his shirt to expose his belly to the sun. The villagers, confused, all stared at him until one of the neighbors went over to ask him what he was doing. "You're all sunning your clothes, I'm sunning the books in my gut."[35] The exchange one of the stories connected to the idiom sometimes translated as "knowledge in the belly breeds an elegant air" or "wisdom in the hold, elegance in the mold" (腹有詩書氣自華).[36] [37]

Again, like the story of Ruan Xian, the historical figure is an impoverished scholar of great talent. This is a theme repeated frequently throughout Chinese intellectual history, the most famous being Confucius. The respect for learning over material wealth reflects class hierarchies in ancient China, where scholars occupied the top and merchants the very bottom no matter the size of their coffers, below struggling farmers and craftsman. It also connects well with Buddhism and some aspects of religious Taoism, which valued the richness of spirit and mind over the material -- particularly the branches leaning heavily on sacred texts.

ELEPHANT WASHING

Double Sixth was not originally about sunning books and clothes; rather, in its initial form the custom was to take household dogs and cats to nearby rivers to wash them off, ridding them of mites and fleas (六月六, 狗馈浴).[38] This eventually evolved into sunning household items, a custom not just practiced by the populace at large, but by the emperor as well.[39] [40]

In Beijing during the Yuan, Ming, and Qing dynasties, washing the elephants of the emperor's stable was a major event. Elephants were considered auspicious by both the common folk and royalty alike, and the emperor kept a large stable of elephants given as gifts from Vietnam, Thailand, and Myanmar, along with teams of imported handlers charged with their care and training.

A reader encountering the dog meat section above or any visitor to a modern zoo could be forgiven for imagining the animal stables as a chamber of horrors, but the elephants had much better lives than they did back home as laborers. They were generally well-treated, and engaged in lighter duties, like pulling the emperor's chariot during grand ceremonies, or standing a guard at the Forbidden City, their trunks interlocked to block unauthorized entry and exit. One exception was a major flood in 1890, when rains brought the city to a standstill: elephants were enlisted to open the gates and clear the roads.

On Double Sixth day, elephants were led out of the stables in a grand procession, winding their way through the streets of Beijing to the city moat where they were bathed. It was a major event for the city, with banners, gongs, and tents by the moat where the wealthy reserved spots to watch and have tea. Hawker carts wended their way through the assembled crowds selling their goods.

Allowing elephants out on the streets ended in 1884, when one of the elephants, annoyed with his training, escaped and rampaged through the streets. They ultimately did not survive the ravages of war in the early twentieth century, but traces remain in the names of local streets, like Elephant Way (象來街) and Elephant Stable Alley (象房胡同).[41] [42]

HIDING IN THE MOUNTAINS

Among the Buyi people (布依族) in Guizhou (貴州) some of the respected elders lead young men to pay their respects to the creator god, Pangu (盤古), and chase ghosts out of the village.[43] The others don traditional garb, and take glutinous rice, chicken, duck, fish, meat, and wine up into the mountain, a custom named "Hiding in the mountains" (躲山). [44]

Up in the mountains they engage in singing and dancing. At sunset, celebrants sit on the ground with their families, entertaining each other with food and wine. Later in the evening, four groups of young men are sent to retrieve four ox legs that were used as part of the ritual to venerate the mountain god. Each family takes a piece of the meat to gain the mountain god's blessings. [45]

Folklore

PANGU: SUNDERING HEAVEN AND EARTH FROM CHAOS

At the beginning of time the universe was formless chaos. Over eons it coalesced into a moist darkness contained within a giant egg, where Pan Gu the Creator took form. He slept amid the chaos, continually growing, until he woke up after 18,000 years. A short, stout man, he held a chisel in one hand and an ax in the another. Thrashing around in the darkness, he spit the egg, releasing the elements of creation into space. The lighter parts, or yang, rose upwards to become Heaven, and the heavier aspects, or yin, sank to form Earth.

Pan Gu stood on the Earth and rested his head on the sky, and with his hammer and chisel he cut asunder the link between Heaven and Earth, which continued to part due to the force of his blows. Heaven moved higher by ten feet every day, the Earth grew thicker by ten feet a day, and Pangu grew taller and wider at the same rate. With each day he became more divine than heaven and more sacred than the Earth. He refused to move from where he stood lest Heaven and Earth once again pair together and descend into chaos.

After 18,000 years, satisfied that Heaven and Earth were separated, he lay down on the Earth and died of exhaustion. His body then became the natural phenomena that gives the world life. His breath became the wind, his voice, thunder, his left eye the sun and his right eye the moon, his hair and beard the stars, his sweat, the rains. His hands and feet became the four corners of the square earth. His blood became the rivers and streams, his flesh, soil, and his body-hair the grass and trees. His teeth and bones became minerals and stones. His semen and bone marrow formed into pearls and jade. The fleas on his body became animals, including the human race [46].

* * *

There are many variations of the above myth. In another, the egg is similar to a chicken egg, the white of the egg representing the lighter yang and the yolk the heavier yin. Unable to bear the stuffiness of the confining egg, Pangu breaks out. The shell mixed into the white to become stars, and the yolk to become stones, while larger pieces of the shell became the sun and the moon. [47]

There are other tales describing the origin of the sun and moon. One states that the humans Pangu created lived in darkness. He made his way east, attracted by beams of light coming from that direction, and came across two sisters, one fair, and one that glowed. The fair one was the elder, and called Moon. The younger sister who glowed was called Sun. They agreed to Pangu's request to stand on a mountain, taking turns by day and night. Sun was afraid of the dark, leaving the night to the Moon. Yet the Sun was also shy, and ashamed to show herself during the daylight. Her older sister, Moon, gifted Sun a fistful of fiery needles which she could cast at the eyes of anybody who dared stare at her. [48]

An interesting aspect of this story is the overlap with the Sun and Moon Goddesses as described in the chapter on the Spring Equinox. Despite conceptions of the sun and moon as male yang and feminine yin -- in Chinese thought as well as many systems in the West -- many legends depict both as feminine. This is likely a representation of yin as the material aspect of sun and moon, and the male yang as the more abstract creative or initiating principle. Such is the case with Pangu here and Di Jun, the Sun-Moon God, in the spring equinox legend, who act as broader forces driving the moon and sun.

Another sun-moon tale begins similarly, with the world shrouded in darkness, but with sun and moon deities much less willing to cooperate. At the direction of the Buddha, Pangu goes to the sea where the deities are hiding. He writes the word for "Sun" in his left hand, and "Moon" in his right, and alternately displays his hands, chanting divine words seven times, until the deities ascend and take their place in the sky, separating day and night. [49]

There are many other tales of Pangu's efforts to create the world, including the assistance of supernatural creatures of the four directions: the Azure Dragon in the East, the Vermilion Bird in the South, the White Tiger in the West, and the Black Tortoise in the North. [50]

Another tale tells of the aid he received from an ox, formed of mud and saliva and animated by his breath, who helps hold up the weight of the world. With the ox prone to naps, Pangu sets a rooster to peck the ox when it nods off. Every once in a while, when pecked by the rooster, the ox shakes his body three times, sending earthquakes through the world. [51]

Pangu is also sometimes conflated with the Nüwa and Fuxi legend, marrying his sister to help populate the world.[52] In some traditions he is a living god, responsible for the weather, bringing sunshine when happy and storms with angry or sad. In some areas he is worshiped as a rain god, such as the Tongbai Mountains (桐柏山), where droughts rarely occur. [53]

Pangu is also ascribed many different forms. The most common representation, paradoxically, is as a giant dwarf. He is clad in a bearskin and wears an apron of leaves and sports horns on his head. In some regions it was believed humans also had horns in Pangu's time, mirroring their creator, and they used such horns for hunting and as a signal of death, the horns growing soft and loose toward the end of life. Those that felt their horns failing would often quit working, since death was approaching. This upset the God of Heaven, who took their horns so that humans would remain industrious. One early source, the *Wuyun Linianji* (五運曆年紀), describes Pangu as having a dragon's head and a serpent's trunk, in many ways matching his name: *pan* means "to coil" and *gu* means "ancient." In other variations, he is depicted as a giant with a cat's head, a serpent's trunk, and a tiger's paw. One can see how early representation of deities readily combined aspects of humanity with those of the wild.[54]

Despite describing the creation of the world, the Pangu myth was not actually recorded until the third century C.E., during the Three Kingdoms Era. The source of the myth is one of controversy. Some say it comes from the ancestral myths of the Miao (苗族), Yao (瑤族), She (畬族), and Li (黎族) ethnic groups in southern China, and was later transmitted to the Han (漢族) majority, or vice versa. Others point to India, where Rig Veda and Aitareya Upanishad contain similar stories. Some insist that the tale is Han, and derived from a figure described in the *Classic of Mountains and Seas*. The figure was called Torch Dragon (燭龍) or Torch Shade (燭陰) -- either name rich with symbolic connotations. The book described his appearance and role in the world: a human face with red serpent's trunk, eyes that created daylight when opened, and night when closed, as well as breathing that formed the winds of the seasons. [55]

Further supporting a Han Chinese origin is that the key themes -- an egg-shaped chaos and a world created from the corpse of a deity -- are key concepts in ancient Chinese mythology, and ideas around formation out of chaos and correspondence between humans and the universe can be found in Zhou dynasty texts. Regardless, one cannot help but see the overlap with other cultural myths, such as that of Ymir, the giant whose body forms the universe in Norse mythology.[56] Or the

Babylonian Tiamat, the embodiment of the archaic sea, which produced all life on Earth out of desire to create order out of chaos. There are also themes matching modern scientific conceptions of the universe's origins such as the Big Bang Theory.

DAUGHTER'S HOMECOMING

Similar to the second day of the first month of the lunar new year, Double Sixth is a time for married women to return to their ancestral home, along with their children. In some places a child will get a red stamp on their forehead for good luck. In Henan province, women make dumplings, dig four holes in the graves of their ancestors, and put a dumpling in each one. In Gansu province, new brides hoping for a child go to the Taibai Spring (太白泉), pull out a stone from the water, wrap it in red cloth, and take it home.[57][58]

The tradition of wives returning to their ancestral home has its practical aspect. Given that traditionally a woman lived with her husband's family, this gave the woman a much-valued opportunity to visit her parents halfway into the year after the last visit six months prior during the Lunar New Year, particularly if the wife's home was far away. There are also origin myths explaining the genesis of this holiday.

THE REDEEMED OFFICIAL

Hu Yan (狐偃) was an accomplished official attached to Chong'er, the Duke of Jin -- the same Duke who failed to recognize Jie Zhitui in the chapter on Clear Bright, resulting in Jie Zhitui's death by forest fire and transformation into a willow tree. Hu Yan, however, was one of the officials who was recognized by the Duke. Some would say Hu Yan's advancement was at the expense of Jie Zhitui, or that Hu Yan was even one of the reasons Jie refused to return.[59]

* * *

Due to his impressive achievements and service to the Duke, Hu Yan was eventually promoted to the high position of Prime Minister. Initially, he was an excellent administrator and respected by both his superiors and subordinates. Hu's birthday was on the sixth day of the sixth lunar month, and he would often receive numerous gifts, at first due to genuine admiration of his leadership skill, but over time by people looking to get into his good graces. He succumbed to these charms and was soon surrounded by smiling sycophants and groveling toadies, stoking his pride and making him more arrogant with every passing day.

Concerned, Zhao Shuai (趙衰), an accomplished official and father to Hu's son-in-law, tried to counsel Hu, with limited success. Infuriated, Hu Yan humiliated Zhao in front of his respected peers. The embarrassment and shock overwhelmed Zhao, and he soon fell ill and died. Zhao's son, who was also Hu's son-in-law, harbored deep resentment toward Hu, and waited for the optimal time to seek his revenge.

The next year famine swept through the kingdom. The Duke wished to distribute emergency grain rations to the starving. Hu announced he would go and personally oversee the distribution of the grain, and would return just before his birthday. The son-in-law realized it was a perfect opportunity to assassinate Hu.

As he made his preparations, his wife, Hu's daughter, found out about her husband's plans and hurried over to her parent's home to inform them of the plot. Hu was shocked when he heard what his son-in-law had planned, and was overcome with sadness rather than anger. He had already regretted causing the death of a family member, and his mood had worsened when he witnessed the misery of the starving populace.

He quickly called all the officials, including his son-in-law, and in front of all he recounted his errors and emphasized that the family should live together in peace. From that day forward he worked to gain the trust of his son-in-law and daughter, and over time their mutual love and respect grew.

Every birthday, on the sixth day of the sixth lunar month, Hu invited his daughter and son-in-law to his home to mend their relationship and to grow closer. News spread to the citizenry, and moved by the tale, the common folk copied the practice. Ever since the festival has been observed to dissolve family enmity, ward off difficulty, and facilitate luck.[60] [61]

GOD OF THE RICE FIELD

June is a critical time for harvesting rice, and to ensure protection of their crops, the Zhuang people (壯族) pray to Yawang (婭王). The Zhuang originally eked out a challenging life as nomads. After they discovered rice farming, over time they began to see rice paddies as a form of divinity, which if not worshiped appropriately would invite the destruction of their crop. The legend tells of a goddess, Yawang, who witnessed how the Zhuang struggled in their nomadic wanderings. She settled among them, introduced agricultural technologies, and taught them the necessary skills.

After a few years among the people, rice paddies planted by Yawang crisscrossed the landscape. She taught the people how to cook rice, make porridge and rice noodles, steam rice cakes, and ferment spirits. Yawang gave the Zhuang the means of obtaining food, warmth, and stability. They built temples in her honor to show their gratitude, and they celebrated her contribution on Double Sixth day.

In September of 2012 the oldest recorded statue of the goddess was found on Daoshan Mountain (稻神山) in Nanning city. It was highly degraded, but appears to be in the form of an elderly women with some avian characteristics, which matches the legend describing Yawang as coming from a bird tribe.[62] [63]

* * *

As Little Heat reaches its end, the hot sun grows yet hotter. Whatever discomforts affect humankind -- as they seek escape the swelter, or sun their possessions, or pay their respects to a creator god

-- the crops are happy. And fortunately for the crops, they have more sun to look forward to as the year moves into the time of Great Heat.

CHAPTER 12: GREAT HEAT 大暑

大暑 / 대서 / たいしょ / Đại thử
Pinyin: dàshǔ
Literal Meaning: "big summer"
Alternative names: Most sweltering
Period: July 22 or 23 ~ August 7
Sun's Ecliptic Longitude: 120°

Great Heat
Zeng Ji
Song Dynasty

The day of crimson has passed,
a fresh breeze is impossible to find.
Leaning against a pillow made of piled books,
staring at melons and plums floating in water.
The temples are silent,
my straw hut is secluded.
As hot and steamy as it is,
one is grateful for slivers of time.

大暑 | 宋 | 曾幾
赤日幾時過，清風無處尋。
經書聊枕籍，瓜李漫浮沉。
蘭若靜復靜，茅茨深又深。
炎蒸乃如許，那更惜分陰。

The time of Great Heat, as the name implies, is the extreme of high temperatures for the year, and the zenith of those most universal of human pastimes: complaining about the weather. Those in North American or North European climates are increasingly familiar with the discomfort of hot summers, but the misery experienced by those in the southern US and southern Europe comes closer to the Chinese climates birthing the title of Great Heat. Humidity soars, particularly following afternoon rains. The air is stifling, the heat inescapable.

As Xie Zaihang (謝在杭) writes in the Wenhai Pisha (文海披沙) "the winter is bearable, the summer is not" (寒可過，暑不可過).[1] During the winter one can cozy-up at home, bundle up in some heavy clothes, and light a fire. For those who lived in pre-industrial times before air conditioners, summer heat was inescapable. Even throwing off all one's clothes and fanning oneself is useless if the flowing air is hot and humid. And as temperatures near and exceed that of the human body, perspiration is more of a burden than an aid, blanketing the body in a damp, sauna-like swelter. As Zhao Yuan (趙元) describes in his poem, Great Heat (大暑).

Great Heat
Zhao Yuan
Jin Dynasty

Parched flying clouds ignite heaven's expanse,
  the white-hot sun makes the world a rice steamer.
Unless you retreat to some icy cold cave,
  a fan can only kick up so much cool breeze.

大暑|金| 趙元
旱雲飛火燎長空，白日渾如墮甑中。
不到廣寒冰雪窟，扇頭能有幾多風。

The list of poets and historians complaining the challenges of summer weather is a long one. It is best captured by Liu Zongyuan (柳宗元) when he visited Yongzhou in Hunan province, and had not experienced its characteristically moist swelter in decades.

Ascending the West Tower in the Bitter Heat of a Summer Night
Liu Zongyuan
Tang Dynasty

The bitter heat wakes me in the night,
  I ascend the tower with my robes cinched up.
Mountains and marshes torpid in the summer air,
  the Milky Way clear and radiant.
The sun's fire has dried out all the dew,
  stillness out in the wilds has calmed the blow of wind.
Draw water from cool wells,
  in this furnace open the doors for air.
Leaning on a railing unsure what to do,
  sweat is flowing everywhere.

Speak not of creative forces and growth,
*   I look up at the Pole Star to beg relief.*
Understand that I am not some mountain fairy,
*   there is no hope for calm to prevail over heat.*

夏夜苦熱登西樓 |唐| 柳宗元

苦熱中夜起，登樓獨褰衣。
山澤凝暑氣，星漢湛光輝。
火晶燥露滋，野靜停風威。
探湯汲陰井，煬灶開重扉。
憑闌久傍徨，流汗不可揮。
莫辯亭毒意，仰訴璿與璣。
諒非姑射子，靜勝安能希。

    The frustrated voice of the poet stands in stark contrast to the genteel man of observant repose that can be found in so much Chinese poetry. It is a man driven almost mad by heat, running around near-naked, seeking out some relief on higher ground, and practically screaming in annoyance at suggestions that he remain calm in order to keep cool. "Staying calm" refers to the *Tao Te Ching*, which states "stillness overcomes heat" (靜勝熱)[2]. This Taoist ideal becomes ridiculous and almost maddening to contemplate when dripping in suffocating heat.

    Dai Fugu (戴復古) is another poet to capture the season, although rather than focusing on misery he looks outside the self, and reminds the reader not only how the weather benefits our survival, but there are always those in professions that sustain us who must bear the full brunt of it.

The Great Swelter
Dai Fugu
Southern Song

Heaven and earth are one giant furnace,
*   the sun rakes the sixth month over the coals.*

Myriad things comprise a crucible,
  but why would anybody resent the heat?
The many grains you see in the fall,
  are born in the midst of swelter.
Paddy fields boil like soup,
  perspiration splashes down one's back.
Knowing the toil of farmers in the summer,
  how can I just sit here and eat?

大熱 | 南宋 | 戴復古

天地一大窯，陽炭烹六月。
萬物此陶鎔，人何怨炎熱。
君看百穀秋，亦自暑中結。
田水沸如湯，背汗濕如潑。
農夫方夏耘，安坐吾敢食！

Regardless of the discomforts humanity must endure, Great Heat is also a time of great beauty in the realm of flowers. The air is heavy with the smell of blooming jasmine, and lotus flowers come to peak bloom, looking particularly striking at night under the rays of the moon.

Great Heat is a time of extremes, the very peak of temperature and vegetation growth. There is also a tension as the land reaches the peak of heat that has intensified after the Summer Solstice, and will soon turn and descend its way once again to the decline of autumn.

Pentads

Decaying grass transforms into fireflies (腐草為螢)
Ground is wet and air is humid (土潤溽暑)
Heavy rains are frequent (大雨時行)

Ancient Chinese thought that fireflies were born of rotting grass, rising at night to carry their little glowing lanterns. This belief stems from the fact that fireflies lay their eggs on dead vegetation.[3]

It is believed that during this time of year the ethers from the earth are moist, creating a simmer of melancholy and wet heat -- a sort of "filthy heat" (齷齪熱) as described by Lang Ying (郎瑛) in the Qixiu Leigao (七修類稿).[45]

This period is typically a time of colliding weather fronts, resulting in torrential afternoon rains. The sense of sudden downpour is captured in the painting *Homeward Oxherds in Wind and Rain* (風雨 歸牧), depicting two anxious young oxherds trying to ride their oxes home before the rainstorm intensifies. Grass and willow trees in the background are buffeted by strong winds. One of the boy's hats is blown away, and he is desperately crawling on the back of the ox to retrieve it. Anybody who has been caught unprepared in an afternoon rainstorm will be able to empathize.

Agriculture

Whatever discomforts humanity is experiencing, plants are happy, growing at their fastest rate under the blazing sun and the torrential rains. The precarious weather encourages early harvesting to prevent loss from storm damage. A common saying is "during Great Heat, any grain not cut on any given day is one less basket harvested." (大暑不割禾，一天少一籮).[6]

Yet farmers cannot count on constant afternoon rains, and another saying notes that "during the days of Great Heat, three days without rain turns the ground into brick" (大暑天，三天不下乾一磚),[7] so watering crops during this time is critical. Another notes that if the rain of Little Heat is as valuable as silver, the rain of Great Heat is as precious as gold (小暑雨如銀，大暑雨如金).[8] Many crops have particularly sensitive water needs. Cotton, for example, needs soil with water saturation of 70% to 80%. Less than 60% and the crop will wither. Timing of watering is important as well. Watering at noon should be avoided, as the rapid temperature change can damage plants. [9]

The traditional practice was to adjust activities around the day's weather, harvesting when it was clear and sowing seeds on cloudy or rainy days. But in some locales the pace required is relentlessness, and the saying goes "no sweating during Great Heat means harvests are reduced by half" (大暑無汗，收成減半). [10]

Health

The need to avoid heatstroke is key for this solar term. At 35°C / 95°F the chance of heatstroke greatly increases, and spikes after 37°C/98.6°F.[11] As mentioned in previous chapters, winter illnesses are treated in summer, when yang is at its highest point, especially chronic illnesses exacerbated by the yin of winter. Escaping into air conditioned environments is a common solution, but ensuring the temperature changes are not too drastic will help keep the immune system from becoming compromised.[12] [13]

Ancient Traditions

While the *Book of Rites* does not advise any particular rituals or imperial commands during this period, the text does note that this period is the middle of the year, representing the phase of earth and standing in the middle of heaven above, earth below, and at the center of the five phases. [14]

Customs

Lychees are often eaten during this period, and in Fujian their consumption is referred to as "Passing Great Heat" (過 大 暑). According to Chinese medicine, lychees in Great Heat are as beneficial as ginseng, greatly fortifying the body. In imperial China, lychees were not to be just gobbled up, but enjoyed for their aesthetic qualities as well. Song Biyu (宋比玉) in the *Treatise on Lychees* (荔枝譜) says, "the lychees must be covered with dew when picked. Once picked, place them in a cold spring to soak. When it is time to serve them, place the lychees on a white ceramic plate. The white of the plate contrasting with the red of the lychees is the best way to highlight the fruit's vibrant color and elegance." Written in the early 1600s, it is clear that the importance of the presentation of food is not just a modern obsession.

While the southerners toil under oppressive heat and rain, northerners like those in Shandong get a chance to rest, and celebrate by partaking in lamb soup, called "Drinking Summer Lamb" (喝暑羊), as well as enjoying the newly harvested wheat.

Festivals

HALF-YEAR FESTIVAL

An important festival in the ancient past, second only to the Spring Festival, the Half-Year Festival (半年節) is now nearly forgotten. It was typically celebrated between the first to fifteenth day of the sixth lunar month, with offerings to thank the gods for the summer harvest. [15] Merchants would hold banquets for employees, who would also get the day off. A few ethnic minorities like the Yao people (瑤族) of Guangxi Province hold a large family dinner, along with banquets for guests featuring lamb and chicken, heavy drinking, sprinkling of lime powder, pasting of couplets, and lighting fireworks -- much like the Spring Festival.[16]

Vestiges of the holiday survive in pockets of Taiwan, with Half-Year Yuan (半年圓). The sweet balls in soup are first offered to the ancestors, and then eaten to invoke family unity and sweetness. [17]

GREAT HEAT BOAT

This time of the year is also the time of epidemics. According to Yu Quyuan (俞曲園), writing in the *Youtai Xianguan Biji* (右臺仙館筆記), people of the coasts would hold a boat ceremony to drive out illness and misfortune, and appeal to the gods for blessings. Boats were loaded with pillows, blankets, and other associated bedding items, pigs, chicken, fish, shrimp, rice, grains, beans, spears, swords, guns and cannons. They would then send them out to float into the ocean in offering to the Five Saints (五聖).[18]

The most well-known of these saints is Zhao Gongming (趙公明), who in the *Investiture of the Gods* (封神演義) was listed as responsible for gold, silver, and various riches, as well as for attracting wealth. He is now commonly considered to hold the center of the five directional wealth gods, and named the Martial Wealth God (武財神).[19] He is often simply referred to as the God of Wealth (財神爺), and more exotically as the Black Tiger of the Mysterious Altar (黑虎玄壇).[20] Although he considered the primary wealth god, there are many other wealth gods in the pantheon, each tied to different aspects of wealth or various methods of its accumulation.

Folklore

WEALTH GODS

The pantheon of wealth gods can be subdivided into Literary Wealth Gods (文財神), Martial Wealth Gods, Windfall Wealth Gods (偏財神), and Buddhist gods from other Tibetan and Thai traditions.

Literary Wealth Gods are associated with wealth accumulation through scholarship, writing, or civil service. These would include deified advisors like Bi Gan (比干), who dared to speak truth to power. Another is Lord Wenchang (文昌帝君), also known as Lord Zitong (梓潼帝君), who was a model of filial piety, deified as a the God of Literature, and is said to answer the prayers of test-takers, as is Great Master Kui (魁星). The Land God, although not literary, is usually placed among this gentle group since he personifies the gifts of nature, and is associated with the fruition of goals, health, wealth, and safety of the home.

Martial Wealth Gods are connected to military service, policing, and most business activities. The aforementioned Zhao Gongming is the prototypical Wealth God and is placed in the Martial category for exploits as a Taoist magician. One of the most popular is Lord Guan (關聖帝君), the deified general Guan Yu (關羽) from *Romance of the Three Kingdoms*, and the patron deity of a businesspeople, accountants, law enforcement, and gangsters.

Windfall Wealth Gods are those deities appealed to when a one-off injection of funds are needed, usually obtained not with merit or skill but with luck, like lotteries, gambling wins, and unexpected gifts. These include Master Sea-Toad (海蟾祖師), Lord Han Xin (韓信爺), and the "Little Ghosts" (小鬼) that inhabit the smaller temples. Chinese religious culture, being highly syncretic, also look to Buddhist traditions in other countries for wealth gods with a track record for granting wealth, such as the Four-Faced Buddha from Thailand.

* * *

The above sampling of wealth gods is in many ways representative of the solar term of Great Heat. While traditional Chinese cultures worshiped gods throughout the year, it was in the sweltering temperatures and driving rain of Great Heat, when crops grow their fastest, that many fortunes were made and lost over the millennia. A lone farmer, toiling in the heat with a few tools -- and an ox if lucky -- would look to the sky and to the earth, hoping the gods would favor the family with abundant crops. And as he prayed, sweat dripping into the soil, he looked forward to the end of heat and the coming of cooler temperatures and a bumper harvest to come in autumn.

CHAPTER 13: AUTUMN BEGINS 立秋

立秋 / 입추/립추 / りっしゅう / Lập thu
Pinyin: lìqiū
Literal Meaning: "establishes autumn"
Alternative names: Autumn commences
Period: August 7 ~ August 22 or 23
Sun's Ecliptic Longitude: 135°

Autumn Begins
Fang Hui
Yuan Dynasty

The departure of heat is like the arrival of fine music,
the first cool beloved by all.
Although the parasol trees have not dropped their leaves,
in the end we have the chirp of crickets.
Tonight the cowherd and weaver girl meet in the Milky Way,
tomorrow morning the sun's rays shine as constellations fade.
The imperial court hopes to find the Master of Obscured Reality*,
in a waterside village a fisherman wearing a straw cape,
is shrouded by mist and rain.

立秋 | 元 | 方回
暑赦如聞降德音，一涼歡喜萬人心。
雖然未便梧桐落，終是相將蟋蟀吟。
初夜銀河正牛女，詰朝紅日尾觜參。
朝廷欲覓玄真子，蟹舍漁蓑煙雨深。

There is a Chinese saying which goes "spring is best painted in ink, autumn is most suited to the strum of a zither" (春宜繪墨,秋宜操琴). The phrase speaks to the fleeting nature of both seasons. Spring comes and goes so fast that the only way to capture it is to paint the season's thriving life in ink. The warmth of autumn departs so quickly that the associated sadness can only be kept at bay with the strum of music.

The autumn is when the myriad things start quietly storing their energy, building a hard encasement to carry life into to the other side of winter, much like the nuts harvested late in the season. As for the solar term of Autumn Begins, the sense of change has yet to begin in many places. In Chinese this time of year is known as the "Autumn Tiger" (秋老虎),[1] and corresponds to what is called "Indian Summer" in North America. Particularly in southern China, buffeted by

---

*Refers to recluse poet Zhang Zhihe 張志和 (ca. 730 - ca. 810), famous for fishing without any bait and his preference for living among nature

typhoons during this time along with the blazing sun that comes from the cloudless skies before the storms, or the oppressive humidity that arrives during and after typhoons blow through, it does not feel cool at all. During some years the "Autumn Tiger" prowls the land, preventing the arrival of cool winds until late September.

To give a sense of the variation in temperatures, in Northern China in places like Heilongjiang and Xinjiang, fall comes around mid-August. In Beijing, early September. In Nanjing, mid-September. October in Hunan. Early January in Guangdong, and not until almost Lunar New Year in China's deep south in places like Hainan Island. Regardless of the temperature, with this solar term the forces of change are set in motion, and Autumn Begins is a reminder that cooler days are on the horizon. [2]

Pentads

Cool winds arrive （涼風至）

White dew descends（白露降）

Cold cicadas chirp（寒蟬鳴）

The winds at this time are said to come from the west -- the western wind being one of cold and desolation. Warmth recedes, and the cold ethers of the western direction bring a sense of grief. [3] *The Discourses of Zhou* (周語) mentions that it is the time that fires appear, and cool breezes show it is time to prepare for cold (火見而清風戒寒是也). [4]

Mention of cold winds and the building of fires might seem preposterous at this point in August, when much of the world is caked in sweat and stifling heat. One reason is the differing weather systems of China, but it also refers to the metaphysical dimension of the solar terms, when unseen forces are set in motion and the natural world will eventually absorb and express those same forces. Much like the withered leaves of a parched plant: the leaves do not immediately perk up after watering, but take time before they show a sense of relief and vibrancy.

"White dew" in this pentad refers to the mists that gather once cooler breezes arrive. White in this case refers to the metal phase of the five phases, the phase corresponding to autumn and the west.

"Cold cicadas" are a type of cicada which are smaller than the cicadas that come earlier in the year and are of greenish-purple hue (寒蟬，蟬小而青紫者). Another tract states these creatures are born in the summer, and emit a different sound than their earlier counterparts (物生于暑者，其聲變之矣.) [5]

So no matter how much heat greets the land on the first day of Autumn Begins, beneath it all flows the first tinges cooler winds, the accumulation of white dew, and a rising crescendo of late-year cicadas. All signify the rise of yin and the themes of death and rebirth of the autumn period.

Agriculture

Practices remain unchanged from earlier terms: water is key to bringing crops to maturity. A number of phrases are applied in a farming context. "With three rains in Autumn Begins, autumn paddies produce rice" (立秋三場雨，秋稻變成米) and "the pitter-patter of Autumn Begin's rain ensures plenty of gold to gain"(立秋雨淋淋，遍地是黃金). [6] Other than the usual maintenance of crops as the major harvest nears, farmers need to watch out for pests, like the yellow stem borer, moths such as *syllepte taiwanalis*, and planthoppers. [7]

Health

This is a time of yang withdrawing and yin advancing, and as with any time of transition, exercise, diet, and emotional health are key points of maintenance. The sorrowful tone of the season can be a challenge, as in Chinese medicine sadness hits the lungs hardest. Seek out activities that improve one's mood, and get to bed early in order to match the rhythms of withdrawing yang. Rising early also opens up and expands the lungs, counteracting the common chest ailments that can occur during this time of year. [8] [9]

Ancient Traditions

In ancient times the changing of the solar term was celebrated with a great deal of fervor. The Grand Recorder would announce the arrival of autumn three days prior, noting that the character of the season was of metal. The emperor would devote some time to self-cultivation and as early as the Zhou dynasty he would lead all his major officials to the west side of the capital to welcome the fall. All the chariots, horses, banners, and clothing would be white, the color representing metal and the season of autumn.

After the ceremony, they sacrificed animals to the gods, and watched soldiers perform martial feats like horse archery and generally ensure that the soldiery were ready for national defense.

This period also marks a change from the spring and summer: where generosity had its place in the earlier part of the year, this is a time for reserve. There could be no appointment of high ministers nor issuing of great titles or gifts. Only the chief general and military officers -- those who served in the martial domains and matched the "murderous energy" of the season -- could enjoy gifts from the emperor on his return from the western outskirts of the city. It was recognized that Heaven and Earth at this point in the year turned more severe, and while there was to be no excess in emulating that same severity, there was also to be no excess in engaging in the opposite quality of indulgence.

The Book of Rites is mute on changes in nature, other than to discuss human activity related to it. Farmers were to present the first grain to the emperor, and officers went into the countryside to collect and store the farmer's contributions. In preparation for floods, embankments, dykes, and dams were fortified.

The classics have much to say directly about human activities, however. With the exception of encouragement to refit houses and strengthen walls, in light of the character of the season most of the commentary concerns war and punishment. Military leaders and commanders were to sharpen their weapons and select men for service -- particularly those of distinguished merit who had proven themselves trustworthy. Being careful with appointments was said to better inspire righteousness. The emperor was to punish the oppressive and insolent, making it clear the model for good and bad behavior. Officers revised laws and ordinances, repaired prisons, forged handcuffs and fetters, and were to be active in preventing crime and capturing criminals. Judgments for criminal and civil cases were to be correct and just, with close examination of forensic evidence such as wounds, sores, broken bones, and dislocations.

If winter rituals were incorrectly done at this time of year, the autumn would be overtaken by a dark and gloomy influence. Shelled insects would destroy the grain and warfare would erupt. Spring rites would bring drought and an overabundance of yang, keeping the five grains from maturing. Summer rites would bring calamities of fire, unruly heat and cold, and fevers among the people. [10]

Customs

Autumn Begins was celebrated in ancient times by the emperor as described earlier. But the populace also had their own set of activities. Out among the common folk, the *Dreams of Splendor of the Eastern Capital* (東京夢華錄) describes the cutting of *Manchurian catalpa* (楸 qiū) leaves into the shapes of flowers and placing them in their hair, since the plant has the same pronunciation as autumn in Chinese (秋 qiū). The streets would be bustling with sellers and celebrants, enjoying red beans, melon, jujubes, chicken heads, and prickly waterlily (芡), and asking one another how the harvest was going. [11]

During the Southern Song dynasty, on the first day of Autumn Begins a high official would stand in front of a Chinese parasol tree and announce "Autumn has arrived!" If one or two leaves happened to drop after the announcement, fall had truly arrived. [12] Certain customs changed over time. During the Song it was advised to drink fresh well water, which was said to keep illness away. [13] By the Ming, drinking unboiled water in this way was discouraged, as it was thought to cause rashes. The Ming also saw the arrival of other customs, like eating lotus root and dried ginger, and admiring jasmine, cape jasmine, and hibiscus flowers. [14] [15]

By the Qing dynasty, the tradition was to weigh oneself to see if any weight was lost since the Summer Solstice, since the stifling heat of summer meant a general loss of appetite. This was followed by the consumption of heavy meat dishes, a tradition translated roughly as "Adding Autumn Fat" (貼秋膘).[16]

Other customs include eating peaches on Autumn Begins (秋日食秋桃). Each person receives one peach and keeps the pit until the Lunar New Year. On New Year's Eve, they burn the pit, which is said to dispel sickness for the coming year.[17] Similarly, another custom is "Biting Fall" (咬秋), observed by eating melon, which are in season at this time of year.[18]

In certain areas, such as Yunnan, Hu Pu'an (胡樸安), in *Customs of China* (中華全國風俗志) tells of prohibitions such as going out into the fields on the day of Autumn Begins. To do so would cause a poor harvest. To counteract the inauspicious energies in the air, people would put up red paper, with the words, "Today Autumn Begins, may one hundred illnesses end" (今日立秋，百病俱休).[19]

In other parts of China, showering on this day is discouraged, because it is believed to cause heat rash and diarrhea. Farmers throughout the country keep a keen eye on the skies on this day. In Hebei, rain means the crops will be flooded. In Hubei, Henan, and Zhejiang, thunder means heaven will cut the harvest in half with surging flood waters. In Shandong, Jiangxi, and Jiangsu, rainbows are a bad omen, foretelling lower crop yields.[20]

Festivals

DOUBLE SEVENTH FESTIVAL

The Double Seventh Festival or the *Qixi* Festival (七夕節) is typically translated into English as Chinese Valentine's Day. In Chinese it goes by many names: Qiqiao (乞巧節), which could be translated as "Seeking Skill," Daughter's Festival (女兒節), Fragrant Day (香日), Star Cycle Festival (星期節), Eve of Skill (巧夕), Woman's Festival (女節), Orchid Night (蘭夜), and Meeting on the Fragrant Bridge (香

橋會).[21] This last, rather poetic name refers to the tale associated with this holiday, referenced in the *Classic of Poetry*.[22]

The Cowherd and the Weaver Girl

In ancient times, when the worlds of the gods and humanity were much closer than they are now, there was a river filled with sparkling stones of myriad colors. Humanity lived on one side, the gods on the other.

On the human side lived a young, handsome cowherd. The youngest of three brothers, he inherited a poor parcel of land next to the river after his father died. He spent his days farming it, and tending his cattle, his favorite of which was a large ox.

Unknown to him, the ox was actually the star Venus, sent to earth to live as an ox as punishment for disobeying orders. The ox observed the young man working the soil every day, sometimes pausing to look across the river as if looking for someone. Over time the cowherd grew more and more despondent, clearly suffering from loneliness.

One day the ox approached the cowherd and broke his silence to tell him a star maiden would come to the river to bathe that night, along with her six star-sisters. This particular maiden was the Weaver Girl of the Heavens, granddaughter of the Queen Mother of the West, responsible for weaving the clouds that filled the sky. He advised the cowherd to hide behind some trees and watch as they arrived.

The cowherd did as the ox suggested, and was shocked to see seven beautiful maidens approach the river bank. They removed their clothes and jumped into the water as quick as a flash, the opaque waters hiding their nakedness. As they giggled and splashed in the water, the ox quietly ambled up to the cowherd, and told him to take the weaver maiden's clothes, and to return them only if she agreed to marry him.

The cowherd followed the ox's advice. Occupied as they were with swimming and bathing, the ladies did not see him taking their robes before he darted back behind a large stone to hide. Once the women finished, the Weaver Girl was shocked to find her clothes missing. The cowherd jumped out, holding her clothes, and said he would give them back if she agreed to marry him.

Once she came over her shock, the Weaver Girl looked the cowherd up and down. Pleased by his handsome appearance, she happily agreed to his demands instead of smiting him where he stood. The two were soon married, and lived happily together, producing two children.

The Queen Mother of the West eventually noticed she had not seen her granddaughter in a while. The attendant she ordered to search for her quickly reported back what had happened. The Queen Mother was livid when she found out that her granddaughter, a goddess of considerable breeding and rank, had not only married a mere mortal, but had also produced children with him. She sent her guards to the cowherd's home to bring the Weaver Girl back.

The guards grabbed the Weaver Girl out of the house while she kicked and sobbed. As they carried her back to the Queen Mother across the river, the cowherd collected their children and pursued her captors, the boy and girl wailing at the loss of their beloved mother.

As he approached the river he noticed it was gone: what was once a rushing stream had become nothing but a bed of soggy mud. The Queen Mother of the West had caused the river to ascend into the heavens, making the large expanse of the Milky Way that is today visible in the night sky.

The cowherd returned home and put the children to bed, and as he walked to his room the ox stood there, blocking his way.

"I will die tonight," said the ox. "After I die, take my skin and wear it. My hide has magical properties which will allow you to ascend to the heavens."

The cowherd, despondent and distracted by the night's events, said nothing in response. He went to his room and spent a few sleepless hours staring in shock at the ceiling.

Late in the night he heard a loud thud. He got up, and as foretold the ox lay dead on the ground. With great sorrow, he skinned the dead ox. Cleaning it up as much as he could, he gathered the children, and wrapped the three of them together in ox hide. After a few moments he *found himself in front of the Milky Way, his wife the Weaver Girl visible on the other side.*

As he attempted to cross, the Queen Mother of the West caused the river in the heavens to turn into a bubbling torrent. Undeterred, the cowherd fashioned a ladle and ladled out the water as fast as he could. He worked and worked, unceasing in his effort to get the river to a low-enough level so that it would be safe for him and his children to cross.

The Queen Mother watched the cowherd, over time growing touched by the man's effort, however futile. She ordered a flock of magpies to ascend into the heavens and create a bridge between the Weaver Girl, seen today as Vega in the night sky, and the Cowherd, visible as Altair. The magpie bridge allowed the cowherd to safely cross the Milky Way. The family were once again reunited, embracing each other in tears of joy. Although still against their union, thereafter the Queen Mother of the West allowed the family to reunite once a year on the seventh day of the seventh lunar month.[23] [24]

* * *

This very old myth is packed with meaning. A modern reader would no doubt be disturbed by the cowherd's blackmailing of the maiden into marrying him, and many scholarly theses about the "male gaze" could be written on his creepy skulking and voyeuristic ogling. But it is important to observe of this tale both in its historical context and the greater themes on which it touches.

In the cultural context in which this myth emerged, the mores at the time required that the woman play a passive role in the lead-up to marriage. Normally marriages were arranged, so romantic courting was less of a factor, and determining one's own marriage outside consultation with the family was highly frowned upon, unless there could be some circumstance that forced the woman to make a decision. The act of blackmail provides that circumstance.

What is interesting is that, as a goddess, she would presumably have the power to destroy the thieving cowherd, yet she doesn't, and plays along, desiring to marry the handsome young man. This choice manages to subvert the typical roles. It is also less of a problem within the context of ancient Chinese morality because she is a goddess rather than mortal woman.

The relationship between goddess and mortal man reflects the major theme of this tale: the connection between earth and heaven, the mundane and the spiritual.

The physical closeness of humanity to the gods in the tale -- just across the river from one another and able to interact on the material plane -- and then the loss of that closeness when the river is turned into the Milky Way, points to a loss of divine connection. It describes a world where ancient humanity was once able to interact directly with the gods, and through some fault or transgression on the part of humanity, that connection was taken away or made more difficult by an angry god -- a theme prevalent in so many of the world's religions.

The story is also about the challenge humanity encounters when trying to believe, comprehend, or access the spiritual realm, and the need for extreme measures to bridge the gap: anything from rigorous asceticism, deep meditative states, prolonged silence, psychedelics, hairshirts -- the list goes on. Any means that allows a person to move beyond the physical realm and inhabit the spiritual. In this story it is an animal hide that provides the vehicle, a common accouterment among shamans the world-over.

So while this old myth is an origin myth of the Milky Way, and tale of love, loss, and reunion, it is also an allegory of humanity's unceasing effort to understand and connect with the cosmos. An effort that is always challenging, and even if successful, joyous but mercilessly brief.

Among the population it was the romantic tones of the tale and the power of the Weaver Girl to confer skill that resonated most deeply, especially among young women. Most women in ancient China were confined to the home, and lived lives of domestic toil that could be incredibly boring. For those who were unmarried, their attractiveness and the happiness of their marriage would depend on their skill in the domestic arts, particularly needlework. Double Seventh was an opportunity to pray to the Weaver Girl for skill in needlework, as well as one of the few nights they had to escape the home and engage in various games and activities with friends late into the night. [25]

Young women would gather at a friend's home and worship the Weaver Girl, the moon, and the stars in the night sky. The women would set up a table with tea, wine, melon, and other sacrifices, a bottle filled with flowers and covered in red paper, and a small incense burner. After praying, they would gather around the table and chat about the latest happenings around the village in hushed tones, late into the night, and munch on the goodies laid out for the goddess. In southwest China, women would crush *Impatiens balsamina* flowers, and paint their nails red, chatting while they waited for the dye to dry. [26]

A common pastime for unmarried women on this evening was to go out into the fields, either alone or with friends. They would sit quietly under the night sky and listen for the whispers of the Cowherd and the Weaver Girl. If a woman heard the lovers whispering on the wind or among the rustling of the leaves, it meant she would fall in love a few days later.[27] [28]

Both married and unwed women would gather river water or spring water for bathing on this day. The water collected was believed to be water from the Milky Way, imbued with sacred and purifying powers of the seven star maidens who had bathed in the river in ancient times. Washing in it would earn the Weaver Girl's protection, and held all sorts of magical benefits, such as the prevention of illness, treatment of burns, healing of sores, exorcising of evil, and general good luck, happiness, and beauty. Many women made an effort to store as much of this water as they could hold. In some areas, the dew that collected over the night was said to be the tears of the lovers. Rubbing the dew on one's eyes and hands was said to improve eyesight and make the hands quick and nimble.[29]

Back at the home, one custom was to place a certain species of long-legged red spider named Joy Spider (喜蛛) or Joy Mother (喜母) into a box overnight after praying to the Weaver Girl to gain skill in needlework. If there was a spider web in the box the next morning, it meant the woman's prayers were answered. [30] The spider was generally seen as very auspicious, and having this species fall onto one's clothes from above -- or any other long-legged spider -- was an auspicious omen, regardless of the paroxysms of terrified screaming the spider's landing likely inspired.

A number of games to gain luck were a highlight of the year for many women. One game included threading needles toward the moon, successfully threading the needle an indication of favor from the

Weaver Girl. Another divination game used needles floating on water, the arrangement of the needles casting shadows on the bottom of the bowl. The shapes of the shadows indicated good luck if they landed in a particular area or formed certain shapes. Shapes like scissors or shoes were auspicious for needlework. There were also many other contests – with the low-light conditions usually a key element -- to see who was the best at needlework. Losing involved the giving of presents. [31]

Yet another game involved seven women and seven dumplings, matching the number of star fairies in the story above. One dumpling would contain a coin, one a jujube, and one a needle. Receiving the coin indicated a future of wealth, a jujube early marriage and children, and a needle, skill in handicrafts. [32]

Double Seventh is considered a day to memorialize the sacrifice of the ox who aided the Cowherd's union with Weaver Girl. Children would decorate the horns of the family ox with flowers. In most places the ox would also be excused from working in the fields on this day. [33]

In modern times, in Fujian and Taiwan, girls at the age of sixteen engage in a coming of age ceremony, and visit temples dedicated to the Seven Mother (七娘媽).[34] Another important tradition in Taiwan is worship of the Bed Deity (床神), composed of male and female deities: a Bed Mother (床母) and a Bed Lord (床公)[35]. In addition to the protection of children, they also look after all aspects of the bedroom: sleep, rest, sex, fertility, and recovery from illness. It is for this reason that the bed is one of the most carefully placed pieces of furniture in the house. In addition to ideal alignment according to the principles of Feng Shui, even moving the bed can only take place on certain dates deemed acceptable by the Chinese astrological calendar.[36]

Folklore

LAND GOD AUTUMN CELEBRATION

The Land God Autumn Celebration (秋社) is the second Land God celebration of the year, following the first one in spring. Whereas the spring version is about asking for a good harvest, the fall event is about thanking the Land God for his generosity. And as the horizon is enveloped in vistas of golden fall light, and as the harsher, cold winds pick up, it is easy for the departure of summer to depress ones mood, making it a perfect time to hold a celebration. This was a holiday typified by lots of drinking, feasting, games, dancing, and general merriment. However it is no longer observed by the larger populace owing to the ruling Mongols banning the festival in the Yuan dynasty, since they were not keen on their Han subjects gathering in large, excitable groups.[37][38]

DEITIES OF AUTUMN

Withering plants, shriveled leaves, and the general decline of vegetation as it moves toward slumber give autumn an air of sorrow. Even the romantic legend that marks this time, that of the Cowherd and Weaver Girl, is characterized by loss, the two lovers separated in the sky, reunited for a short time with tears of joy and sadness. The two major deities associated with this time of year described below are similarly contradictory, cast in tones that are bleak and mysterious yet also connected to the harvest and its abundance.

Rushou and Shaohao

During the Shang dynasty, divination was a widespread practice to ascertain the will of heaven, which is the main reason for oracle bones bearing early Chinese writing. The Duke of Guo (虢國公) was particularly taken with their use, and in addition to frequent divination would often beg the gods to turn his declining kingdom into a powerful one.

One night he dreamed of a fearsome-looking man with white fur, tiger claws, and a human face. In one hand he had a large battle ax resting on his shoulder. The Duke was terrified, but as he was about to run the fearsome man ordered him to stay. He let him know that the Kingdom of Jin would eventually attack, and the Heavenly Emperor favored this enemy kingdom to win in the battle. The Duke fell to the ground and begged for mercy, and with that, he woke up from his dream.

The Duke called all his ministers to help him interpret the dream. After hearing the king's tale, one of his most loyal ministers determined that it was Rushou (蓐收), the punishing deity of heaven in charge of killing, and that his appearance in the Duke's dream indicated heaven was making arrangements to change the order of power. The Duke was furious that the minister would speak such an inauspicious omen, saying it would bring misfortune. He had the minister taken away and locked up.

He then turned to his other ministers and proclaimed the dream was an auspicious omen. The Duke's kingdom fell six years later. [39] [40]

* * *

This tale is one of many examples of the Mandate of Heaven at work: the idea prevalent since early Chinese dynasties that the right to rule was determined by divine mandate and maintained by the moral behavior or governance of the ruler. The perceived gain and loss of this mandate has played a large role in China's turbulent history of dynastic change throughout the centuries, and continues to be a source of political anxiety in the modern era. The concept says much about Chinese culture. Compare this with the more sedate and orderly succession of emperors in Japan. Conversely, China's history is steeped in chaos, change, large-scale war, cataclysmic disasters, and the fickle preferences of the divine world as reflected in the natural and political realms.

Apart from this larger idea, the tale itself says something about the process of appealing to the divine for aid. The Duke, despite his avid praying and divination, refuses to listen to straight-forward advice direct from the heavens. It demonstrates the folly of wishful thinking, and the pitfalls of ignoring real dangers while wrapped in a cloak of procrastination and denial. It also is an example of the pithy but apt phrase: "God answers all prayers. And sometimes the answer is "no."

The identity of Rushou varies. Some sources describe him as the Guardian God of the White Emperor of Shaohao (少昊), or the son of Shaohao himself. [41] *The Huainanzi* (淮南子) describes him as responsible for the fall season, the western direction, and the phase of metal. He guards the White Emperor and brings order to autumn. [42]

In *The Classic of Mountains and Seas*, he is depicted with a snake on his left ear, a giant battle ax propped on his right shoulder, and riding two dragons. [43] The snake represents propagation of descendants.[44] The ax represents the aspect of punishment -- referring to the executions carried out during the autumn (秋決). [45]

***

Shaohao's mother was a beautiful fairy name Huang'e (皇娥), who was responsible for working the heavenly looms. When at rest, she would while away her time on a raft, floating across the Milky Way to visit the Qiong Mulberry Tree (窮桑)† near the Western Sea.

Under the tree stood a good-looking young man, who was actually the embodiment of Venus, the morning star which rises in the east. The young man joined her on the raft. Together they fashioned a mast for the raft out of cassia, upon which they placed sweet-smelling grasses, enjoying the fragrance when the wind blew across the leaves. They also carved a dove out of a piece of jade, and placed it on top of the mast so that they could determine which way the wind blew. It is said this was the first invention of the weather vane.

They would then position the boat to get the best of the wind. Enveloped in the fragrance of grasses, they leaned against one another, floating along the Milky Way and singing to the tones of a delicately plucked zither, lit only by the bright full moon above. Not long after, Shaohao was born.

When Shaohao came of age, he traveled to the five mountains of the eastern paradise, and established a kingdom of birds. He took the form of a vulture, and stood as ruler. The phoenix acted as Lord Chancellor, the hawk was in charge of law, and the pigeon, education. The pheasant, quail, shrike, and swallow managed the four seasons.

Shaohao ruled the bird kingdom with wisdom, but over the course of time left to the West, leaving his son Chong (重) in charge of the birds.

---

† While qiong [窮] means "poor" in modern Chinese it also meant "extreme" or "thoroughly" in older forms of the language.

His son, Rushou, went with him, and they settled on Everstay Mountain (長留山). Thereafter father and son ruled over the western heavens and took responsibility for the sunset, leaving rule of the kingdom to his other son. [46]

* * *

In this myth the union of father and son in the western quarter of the sunset is intended to embody the cyclical nature of day and night, and death as a prelude to rebirth. However, usually the west is associated with feminine deities, and in the Taoist canon one of the most powerful female deities: the Queen Mother of the West.

Queen Mother of the West

The Queen Mother of the West, or Xiwangmu (西王母), is one of China's most ancient deities, mentioned in Shang dynasty oracle bone inscriptions.[47] Evidence of her worship was geographically widespread from the Qilian Mountains (祁連山) in Gansu, Northwest China to the Central Plains, where legends about her were widespread even as early as the Spring and Autumn and Warring States periods. She was a major deity by the end of the Western Han, and had inspired numerous searches for the elixir of immortality by Qin and Han dynasty sovereigns. During the Eastern Han, she was adopted by religious Taoism given her general popularity. [48]

After the Han dynasty she appeared in a wide variety of Taoist literature, and came to take on a large list of titles: Lady Queen Mother (王母娘娘), Golden Mother of the Jade Pond (瑤池金母), Queen Mother of the Western Spirit (西靈王母), and many other variants. Among the populace she went by less ornate names, like "Queen Mother" or "Divine Mother."

By the Wei and Jin dynasties, she became the leader of all female immortals in the Taoist pantheon.[49] She was at that point designated as the daughter of Primeval Lord of Heaven (元始天尊).[50]

Early depictions of the goddess presented her as the savage embodiment of nature. *The Classic of Mountains and Seas* describes a woman with tiger teeth, a leopard tail, and disheveled hair braided in jewels. She lived in a cave in the wilderness and roared, befitting her status as a fierce deity originally responsible for pestilence and punishment. [51]

On her head she wore an ornament called a *sheng* (勝).[52] There are different interpretations of this ornament. Some say it is a victory crown,[53] others that it is an animal hide, and yet others say it is a part of a loom,[54] linking her to sericulture, as well as to the weaving deities so frequently connected to autumn.

Other legends describe the head ornament as a hairpin that forms the Milky Way, again linking her to the formation of the celestial bodies as in the Weaver Girl legend.[55] She is said to be in possession of three azure messenger birds and one three-legged crow, which fetches food for her, among other animals.[56] [57]

Her depiction would change markedly over time. In the *Tale of King Mu, Son of Heaven* (穆天子傳), King Mu of Zhou was obsessed with finding her. After extensive traveling and adventures to lands in the west, he discovers she is not a fierce goddess but a real queen, although a vestige of her ancient depiction remains: she lives with wild animals and birds. He has a pleasant banquet with her and their dialog consists of singing and poems. He finds her elegant, gentle, and kind-hearted.[58] [59]

This kicks off a long tradition of describing the goddess as beautiful and refined. *Stories of Emperor Han Wudi* (漢武故事) and *Anecdotes of Emperor Han Wudi* (漢武帝內傳) both depict her as an exceedingly beautiful, graceful young goddess followed by a large group of fairy maidens.

King Mu also began another tradition of depicting kings as enjoying positive interactions with her to demonstrate the divine legitimacy of their reign. However much she was respected by kings and historians, she was revered by the populace at large, attributing many miraculous tales to her and creating a legend shrouded in mystery.

One her most mysterious aspects is her location itself: Kunlun Mountain. Although there is a present day Kunlun Mountain range, the location of Kunlun Mountain varies in mythology. Tradition held that waters from Kunlun mountain fed the four corners of the world with the Yellow, Red, Yang, and Black rivers,[60] and that drinking these waters would confer immortality.

Kunlun Mountain stretched from earth to sky, its base set as deeply into the earth as it was high, covering nine levels. Winds blew from doors on the side of the mountain, and the eastern door, the door of light, was guarded by a creature with nine human heads and the body of a tiger. This was where the Lord of the Sky lives, reigning over a kingdom of birds who would do his bidding.[61] One can easily see the connection to bird kingdom of the Shaohao and Rushou myth.

The Queen Mother of the West lives in a majestic palace of pure gold at the peak of Kunlun. She commands the Lord of Rain or the Rain Master (雨師), an armor-clad warrior using his sword to flick water onto the thirsty earth,[62] embodying the generative five-phase principle of metal creating water.

The most famous feature of her palace is the peach garden and the Queen Mother's peaches of immortality. A peach that had ripened over 3,000 years would bring one health. A peach that was over 6,000 years old would bring long life, and a 9,000 year-old peach would allow one to live as long as heaven and earth. [63]

Over time, depictions of the Queen Mother continued to be embellished. She is shown as a compassionate and merciful Bodhisattva or a white-haired Taoist immortal. Sometimes she is depicted on a cloud, or mounted on a dragon or a tiger, or flying a white crane. She is often surrounded by any number of fantastical creatures: a jade rabbit, toads, birds, a three-legged crow, deer, dragons, a nine-tailed fox, wigged servants, a rabbit taking mortar and pistil to grind out an immortal elixir, and a number of fairy maids. [64]

Her general personality is depicted as an elegant, poised, and loving mother, and for this reason she was prayed to for wealth, health, safety, longevity, honor, fertility, personal salvation, and avoidance of calamity. Mothers would affix a yellow or red strip of paper reading "The Spirit Tablet of the Queen Mother of the West" to bless their babies. [65]

The Queen Mother of the West has been assigned as consort to different personages at different times. The Tang and Song dynasties saw her married to the Jade Emperor. One myth collected in Sichuan in the 1980s described her as the mother of the sun and the moon. The two siblings worked together: one moving from east to west, the other from north to south. However, the sun would frequently harass and proposition his sister, the moon. Annoyed, she confronted her brother in front of their father, the Jade Emperor. The Emperor was furious, and nearly destroyed the sun, but the Queen Mother begged him not to. A minor god suggested that the sun could work during the day, and the moon at night, so that they would not have the chance to interact. The Jade Emperor accepted the advice, and ever since, the sun and moon cross the sky at different times. [66]

Earlier, in the Han dynasty, she was depicted as a consort to the King Father of the East (東王公). In one tale they live under a huge bird called "Rare" (xiyou, 希有), the King living under the left wing and the Queen under the right. They would climb up on the wings of the bird and onto its back whenever they wanted to meet. Another tale describes the King as living in a large stone house on the East Barren Mountain (東荒山). He was a man ten-feet tall, his hair was snow-white, and he had the general form of a man, but with a bird's face and tiger's tail, and rode a black bear. He sometimes would appear with the Queen Mother on early bronze inscriptions, providing evidence that he was viewed as the original consort. [67]

From the standpoint of Chinese cosmology, the King Father of the East makes a far more fitting counterpart. Associated with the east and with the phase of wood, he is depicted as the male principle of yang; the Queen Mother is associated with the west and the female principle of yin. Together, they engender the myriad things and all being. [68]

Much like the season over which she reigns, the Queen Mother of the West is a bundle of contradictions: animalistic yet refined, fierce yet beautiful, dangerous yet protective, and a bringer of both death and immorality. She is the perfect encapsulation of the themes of autumn, symbolizing the death of the harvest, and the sustenance and life-giving energy for those who consume what falls.

CHAPTER 14: HEAT DEPARTS 處暑

处暑 / 처서 / しょしょ / Xử thử

Pinyin: chùshǔ

Literal Meaning: "depart heat"

Alternative names: Heat Withdraws, End of Heat

Period: August 22 or 23 - September 7 or 8

Sun's Ecliptic Longitude: 150°

Yangze River in Two Poems (1 of 2)
Su Jiong
Song Dynasty

Not even three days into Heat Departs,
*   a fresh cool breeze is more priceless than gold.*
The white-haired have experienced the world,
*   green grass is imprinted with a meditative heart.*
Let cranes perform their dance,
*   hear crickets sound staccato chirps.*
Those of deep benevolence enjoy long lives,
*   even the depths of the ocean cannot compare.*

長江二首 (其一) | 宋 | 蘇洞

處暑無三日，新涼直萬金。
白頭更世事，青草印禪心。
放鶴婆娑舞，聽蛩斷續吟。
極知仁者壽，未必海之深。

The sun by this time of year is eye-piercingly bright, and the leaves take on an even deeper shade of emerald as the sun moves lower in the sky. In some places something in the air has changed. According to the *Qixiu Leigao* (七修類稿),[1] the *chu* (處) of *chushu* (處暑) means "ending" or "retreat."[2] The word not only assures that the heat will eventually fade, but that the year is heading toward quiet, peace, and stillness.

Yet in most places, the weather can remain frustratingly hot. The time is a last gasp for insects, who engage in a furious orgy of noise and activity particularly vexing to humans. One might say that this sense of calm and peace is aspirational rather than a reflection of reality during this awkward, transitional time. As a saying goes "Heat Departs, Heat Departs, so hot rats melt apart" (處暑處暑，熱死老鼠).[3] As the heat continues and summer refuses to let go, approaching this time with a calm, peaceful mind is the best -- perhaps the only way -- to sense the cooling flavors of fall.

There are two signs in the natural world that Heat Departs has come: the Queen of the Night flowers (*Epiphyllum oxypetalum* 曇花)[4] and the clouds. Queen of the Night flowers are especially sensitive to both frost and sun, and usually choose one of the quiet evenings of Heat Departs to display their otherworldly buds.[5] Clouds take on a wispy look, compared to the blocky, bloated, heavy-looking clouds of summer.[6] While clouds transform to different shapes during the day, the night sky during the course of the seventh lunar month reveals the move toward autumn with the position of Antares (七月流火).[7] The star appears directly south at twilight on the Summer Solstice; its slow move west indicates summer is ending.[8] During the fall, once it lowers to the horizon in the west, and is covered in mountain mists, it signals the change of weather from hot to cold. [9] [10]

Pentads

Hawks sacrifice birds (鷹乃祭鳥)

Heaven and Earth become severe (天地始肅)

Grains become ripe (禾乃登)

From ancient times the hawk was a "righteous bird" (義禽).[11] While their hunting of prey embodies the murderous air of the metal phase of autumn, they are called "righteous" because of the belief that they avoid killing pregnant birds or those still caring for their young. And prey that is captured is presented to the gods in sacrifice before eating.[12] The details of how this is done are obscure,[13] but one would assume ancient observers noticed a period of pause once the prey is captured before the hawk has its meal.

In the human realm, as the fall brings the accumulation of desolation and murderous energy between heaven and earth, it was traditionally a time to set out and kill. In other words, go to war. Autumn and its association with death was not only thematically optimal for war, but also practical, as some portion of the crop had been harvested in certain locales, meaning soldiers were well supplied, and avoiding disruption of agricultural activities lowered the chance of a fallow winter. And as if mirroring the activities of winter preparations on the farms and in nature, it was the time for "fall executions" (秋決), when prisoners sentenced to death were killed.[14]

Along with themes of death are themes of gratitude to the gods for the harvest, and grain was often placed on altars and thanks given to the Field God, the Land God, and the ancestors for their protection and generosity over the course of the growing season.

Agriculture

Farmers still need to worry about water levels. Continuous rain can ruin the harvest but lack of water is just as much a problem, and the changing weather makes it a delicate balance, as noted by a common saying, "the grain fields during Heat Departs can change overnight" (處暑禾田連夜變).[15] Rain patterns change in southern China, from the previous state of heavy rain in the west and lighter rain in the east, to heavy rain in the east and lighter rain in the west. While protecting their crop, it is also a time to store water. Rain on the day of Heat Departs carries different omens in different locales. In Jiangsu, rain is preferred as without it the crops won't mature (處暑若還天不雨，縱然結實也無收).[16] In Henan it is the opposite, where rain will cause major losses (處暑若連天下雨，縱然結實也難留).[17]

Out in the fields, farmers prune back dead leaves to improve air flow in crops, especially those that easily rot, like cotton. The extra moisture in the air causes fungus growth and requires the use of fungicides. [18]

Health

It is best to continue the habits of summer and dress lightly, except at night, when temperatures might suddenly drop. During the day the humidity of summer and the dryness of autumn conspire to harm the lungs and upper respiratory tract. Some traditional Chinese medicine doctors suggest a drink with *ophiopogon japonicus* (麥冬) and chrysanthemum (菊花) to moisten the lungs, improve the stomach, and clean and calm the mind.[19] Keeping windows open to let in fresh air, and washing out the nose with cool water can prevent colds.

In some places, like Beijing, duck is consumed for its cooling properties to counteract the final flare-ups of heat during this solar term,[20] although Beijingers aren't known for requiring excuses to eat duck. Exercises that produce mild sweating are preferred: Tai Chi, light jogging, and calisthenics. Moderate alcohol and medicine can be taken to quicken the blood and cast out cold. The belly should be kept protected and warm, as the many nerve-endings in that area can cause reproductive problems in both men and women if they get too cold.[21]

Customs

GIFT OF LAMB

On the fifteenth of the seventh lunar month, the old tradition in northern China was for a maternal grandfather or uncle to give a live goat or lamb to one's grandson or nephew. The practice has changed to two bowls of lamb noodles in modern times, but the sentiment is the same: to bring the families together and observe the tradition initiated from the fairy tale of the Magic Lotus Lantern (寶蓮燈).[22] [23]

THE MAGIC LOTUS LANTERN

Third Sacred Mother (Sanshengmu, 三聖母) was so-named because she was the third and youngest child of the Emperor Xiyue (西嶽大帝). When traveling the land disguised as a common maiden, she fell in love with a mortal man -- a scholar. Hoping to spend her life with him, she took a Magic Lotus Lantern (寶蓮燈) from the heavenly palace and descended back down to earth, where she lived with her husband, enjoying the humble simplicity and beauty of the earthly realm. She soon gave birth to a son, and the couple named him Eaglewood (沉香).

Her brother, Yang Jian (楊戩), also known as Yang Erlang (楊二郎), or more popularly known as the Erlang Diety (二郎神), disapproved of the union as well as his sister's pilfering of the Magical Lotus Lantern.

After seven years he was able to find the family by following the light of the lantern. As punishment, he imprisoned his sister under Mt. Hua (华 山).

The Third Sacred Mother's son, Eaglewood, too young and powerless to stop Erlang, could only watch in sorrow. As he grew his every effort was dedicated to saving his mother, and he worked to find the Magical Lotus Lantern which could be used to find and free his mother. The Monkey King was impressed with Eaglewood's effort to save his mother, so he granted him a magical ax with which he could challenge Erlang.

Eaglewood eventually found Erlang and they battled with a ferocity that shook the heavens. But Eaglewood's strength began to flag, and just as Erlang was about to deliver a killing blow, the light of the Magical Lotus Lantern penetrated Eaglewood's body and merged with him, providing the power needed to defeat Erlang and rescue his mother.[24] [25]

* * *

This tale of family discord is the genesis of the practice of maternal relatives giving lamb to their sister or daughter's son. Lamb (羊) is a homonym with Yang (楊), the surname of Erlang, so by gifting a lamb the discord caused by Uncle Erlang is dissolved. The practice also ameliorated the distance between maternal in-laws and her new family, given that the women were considered as belonging to her husband's family after marriage. The gifting of lamb reaffirmed the biological connection, while expressing familial love through symbolic action rather than professed words, as was often the custom in China. The word *yang* (羊) also is part of the word *xiang* (祥), so it has an added benefit of wishing luck to one's sister or daughter.

The tale itself, in addition describing challenging family dynamics, is also a tale of spiritual growth. Her son, interestingly, is named Eaglewood -- a wood commonly used for incense in Buddhism and religious Taoism for meditation, chanting, and prayer, The wood is generally considered the most powerful incense for connecting to the spirit realm. It is also used to make Buddhist rosary beads. Given this connection, the tale is also an allegory of gaining spiritual balance with the forces of yin -- forces that are growing particularly active at this point of the year.

Festivals

GHOST FESTIVAL

The Ghost Festival or the Hungry Ghost Festival are the names given to the observance that goes by a slew of names in Chinese: Zhongyuan Festival (中元節), Sacrifices to the Lonely Ghosts (祭孤) Mid-Seventh Month Festival (七月半), Yulanpen Festival (盂蘭盆節). Aside from the commonality of referring to ghosts in the English name of the festival, the word "ghost" is assiduously avoided in the Chinese language, especially during this time. Sometimes friendlier euphemisms are used, like the "Good Brothers" (好兄弟).[26]

The ghost festival is one of three festivals concerned with the dead in Chinese culture, the other two being Tomb Sweeping (清明節) and Double Ninth (重陽節). While Tomb Sweeping usually involves going out to pay respects to the dead, during the Ghost Month the dead come and visit the living. Similar to Samhain in Celtic culture, which evolved into Halloween, the veil between the underworld and the living world grows thinner. Yet instead of one night the Ghost Festival occurs over the entirety of seventh lunar month, and is therefore sometimes referred to as "Ghost Month" (鬼月).

Beliefs about the afterlife in China have varied by region and over the course of time, and have been complicated in some respects by Buddhist notions of reincarnation. Generally speaking, souls of people who have behaved righteously in life and whose memory is cherished with proper ritual have an easier time in the spirit world. Those whose lives were cut short unnaturally or who have no relatives to tend their graves turn into restless, hungry ghosts, condemned to wander the realms until their next reincarnation [27] -- usually into a more challenging life or lifeform. This is the main reason why continuation of the family line is viewed as so important in Chinese culture, to insure people are prayed to by future generations.

On the first day of the seventh lunar month the doors of the Underworld are thrown open, and ghosts of all kinds -- from angry, hungry ghosts to recently departed saints awaiting their next reincarnation -- come barreling out looking for food and other goodies. Many are not exactly in a good mood, and latch on to the living out of loneliness, their powerful yin energy causing all sorts of misfortune to their newfound "friend." The more aggressive actually kill the living, so that their victim can take their place in the Underworld and allow their souls to move on.

Because of this, there are a host of prohibitions during the course of the month. Below are a sample of the main ones.[28] [29] [30] They are intended as examples of the rich folklore of this period of the year, and are not intended to impose any behavior on other belief systems, or to introduce a litany of obsessive-compulsive behaviors or fears about supernatural phenomena. In modern Chinese cultures attitudes toward these old ways range from seeing them as complete nonsense to something to keep in mind and avoided if possible.

GHOST MONTH PROHIBITIONS

Swimming

Going out into bodies of water is strongly discouraged. Swimming in rivers and oceans invites those that have previously died a watery death to drown the living so that they may take their place in the Underworld. Naturally, Ghost Month occurs during one of the hottest periods of the year, the time of summer vacation -- August -- when swimming is a popular activity. There are many who throw caution to the wind and go anyway. In Taiwan, drownings show a consistent peak in July every year, with about half the number during August, when Ghost Month occurs. So either the data does not support the notion of ghouls gurgling out from the gates of hell to grab the naked ankles of hapless swimmers, or enough people heed the superstition to keep the numbers down.

Going Out Alone at Night

Leaving the house at night is to be avoided since the dead are more active. This is especially the case for the young or pregnant, as they are vulnerable to the attentions of wandering dead. If one must go out, it is advised to take a friend. If you hear any strange sounds, like soft whispering, sobbing, or notice any strangely sweet smells, ignore them.

Whistling

In Western culture whistling in the dark is associated with bravery -- a signal of nonchalance and a carefree manner, most evocatively used in the phrase "whistling past the graveyard." In Chinese culture whistling at night is generally frowned upon; even more so during Ghost Month. Whistling near a graveyard at night would be considered the absolute peak of stupidity. Hungry ghosts love high-pitched sounds, and whistling acts like a homing beacon. A sharp whistle ringing out in dark causes the dead to snap their disheveled heads in the direction of the whistler, stop whatever they are doing, and then follow the individual home, causing all sorts of illness and havoc. For this reason it is usually best to refrain from playing musical instruments at night as well.

Patting Shoulders

In some traditions of Chinese lore there is a life-flame burning on each shoulder. What can be intended as a friendly pat on the shoulder can turn into a curse, especially during Ghost Month. Extinguishing of a shoulder flame can open one up to all sorts of illness and misfortune. If one is the victim of this type of friendly pat during Ghost Month, it is advised to continue looking forward, as looking back can also snuff out the flame, and the friendly shoulder-pat might not be coming from an entity you want to see.

Finding Money or Red Envelopes on the Ground

If there is money on the ground, especially ghost money used in ritual burning, leave it alone. Picking it up will anger the ghosts for whom it is intended and they will spend whatever energy they have on making the thief's life miserable. If one comes across a red envelope on the street, they are usually intended as an invitation to marry a deceased person.

Hanging Clothes Outside at Night

This is less of an issue in this day of ubiquitous dryers, but there are always delicate items that retain their size and shape better when hung out to dry. Such items should be taken in before nightfall, as clothes twisting in the night breeze invite ghosts to inhabit them, resulting in a nasty surprise the next morning when the ghosts stick to their victim and cause an accident on their morning commute. This bit of folklore has become more controversial recently, and some Taoist priests claim that ghost aren't any more interested in used underwear than the living. Whatever advanced knowledge such priests have of the denizens of the Underworld, they clearly have much to learn about the curious preferences of the living.

Walking Near Walls

When walking around at night, stay away from walls. The dead are said to "stick" to walls, drawn in by their cold, yin nature.

Urinating Outside

With the land populated by wandering unseen ghosts, it is best not to relieve oneself outside, lest you offend any of them. Trees are especially dangerous, and if a pet or a child needs to relieve themselves before it can be stopped, it is best to ask the tree's forgiveness.

Major Events

Avoid doing anything major during Ghost Month: starting a new business venture, traveling, getting married, moving house, parties, going to the hospital -- and dying if it can be avoided. Doing any of these activities during Ghost Month increases the chances to encounter misfortune because the elevated emotions associated with these events draws the unwanted attention of the dead.

Killing Insects

If an insect enters the house do not kill it. It is likely to be a reincarnated relative coming to visit. The rarer the insect, the more likely it is the embodiment of somebody known to occupant. More common bugs, like cockroaches and ants, are said to be just that, and can be dealt with in the usual way.

Clothing and Accessories

High heels are discouraged. The heels of the feet are exposed and ghosts can get at the vulnerable entry points in the heel.

Do not open umbrellas in the house because ghosts will fly close to take shelter under it. Red and black umbrellas are particularly bad.

Similarly there is a prohibition against red or black clothing, but also white. Red, black, and white accents are fine, but avoid wearing all of one color, which will not only attract undead wraiths but also the condemnation of anybody with any fashion sense.

Grooming

Haircuts should be done before or after the Ghost Month, not during. Similarly it is best to avoid nail cutting, especially at night. Hair and nails are said to retain enough of residual life force to attract spirits, driving them to attach themselves to the original owner. Shaving, however, is not an issue because the hairs are too fine or too short to attract ghouls, and supposedly are neutralized when they are washed through the drains and sewer system.

Do not paint fingernails or toenails dark colors. Spirits will think the wearer is one of them and will follow the person around. Bangs are discouraged: the forehead projects powerful yang energy and covering it creates an opening for ghouls.

Doors and Windows

It is fine to keep windows opened for fresh air, especially if they are screened, but avoid keeping doors open, or the dead will take that as an invitation into the home.

Photographs

Like the living, the dead have a complex set of reactions to cameras. Some are offended and will cause the photographers harm, some are attracted, and will enter the camera as some sort of spectral photobomb, tying the fate of the subjects of the picture to their own. So avoid taking photos at night, especially outside. Taking pictures during the day is fine.

Talking to Yourself

As enjoyable as it can be to mumble to yourself, this should be avoided during Ghost Month. The lonely dead see it as an invitation to interact with you. Otherwise, why *else* would you be talking out loud when you are alone?

Ghost Stories

Avoid telling ghost stories or watching horror movies. The terror or mirth that accompanies such activity offends the dead. In that vein it is best to avoid talking about the dead at all, or even saying the word "ghost".

* * *

The above is a long list of prohibitions. One might ask, what *can* you do during Ghost Month? The list is much shorter, but some options are as follows:

- Visiting temples. Preferably large, well-visited ones. Temples dedicated to Guanyin, Matsu, and Guangong tend to be the best for exorcising any harmful spirits.
- Burn ghost money. Since money can be spent in the underworld it can placate hungry ghosts. They will be grateful and tend to leave the person offering the money alone.
- Adopting a vegetarian diet. Vegetarianism, with its notions of purification that derive from Buddhist practice, is said to keep ghosts at bay.

- Give to charity. Similar to the virtue that vegetarianism confers in Buddhist belief, charitable giving offsets negative karma and will keep the giver safe.
- Wear a protective amulet. Those dedicated to Zhongkui (鍾馗) and Guangong are considered powerful when warding off ghosts.

PUDU

The main observance of Ghost Month is Pudu (普渡), where sacrifices are made to the ancestors, hungry ghosts, and the Pudu Lord.

The Pudu Lord (普渡公) has a couple of origin stories. One is that he is reincarnation of Guanyin, the Goddess of Mercy. Another is that he was originally the King of Ghosts. He is in charge of all the affairs around Ghost Month, and is appealed to ensure the safety of the living and order among dead during this period. [31]

Sacrifices to the ghosts – the "Good Brothers" – are made in the afternoon and into the early evening before dusk. A table is usually set up in front of the home holding cookies, fruit, and meat, with incense attached to each group of offerings, and a pennant of blue, green and red to indicate the victuals are for the visiting spirits. Three sticks of incense are burned in an incense burner, and prayers are voiced to the gods to protect the home.[32][33]

Sometimes new toiletries are placed under the table.[34] In addition to ghost money, the more enthusiastic celebrants offer burnable paper-model versions of all sorts of goodies that the dead can use in the underworld: tuxedos, sports cars, mansions.

The protocol for burning various types of paper money is fairly strict. Larger sheets are reserved for gods, in this case the Pudu Lord, to ensure he keeps the ghost-visitors from the world of yin in order. Next are mid-sized sheets containing pictures of clothes and other items the dead might need in the underworld. Finally, the smallest sheets are the actual money the departed can use in the afterlife. [35]

During the process observers are to avoid looking under the table, because the Good Brothers don't like to be watched when they eat. And everything on the table is fair game for the visiting ghosts, so never place a child on the table.

In Hoklo-speaking communities, certain fruits are avoided because they are homonyms with attributes undesirable for spectral visits. One is pineapple, because it sounds like "increasing" (旺來); this sentiment is fine when praying for wealth, but less ideal when dealing with the dead. Bananas, plums, and pears sound like "come on over" (招你來), and guava and tomatoes contain a word that could be construed as "willful" (番). Apples (蘋果) are preferred as the word contains a syllable that sounds like "peace" (平). Oranges are fine too since they are associated with good fortune (吉).

Different places have different observances. A peach made of flour and rice play a bigger role in some locations. Once respects are paid in front of the home, the peach and rice are cast in the four directions. At nightfall sticks of incense are stuck in the ground; the more the better as they stand for accumulation of the five grains. In the older traditions observance was an all-day event, with prayers at dawn, noon and dusk, rather than the one or two hours typical in modern times. Some places put floating lights on the river, called lotus lights, so that ghosts can find their way back to the underworld. There are similar decorations on land, with lights in front of the home to guide the ghosts but also to keep them moving along and not entering residences. [36]

YULANPEN

While the above activities have a very Taoist folk religious flavor, Buddhism is believed to have a powerful set of practices for dealing with the departed. Yulanpen (盂蘭盆) is a major one with close connections to Pudu given its focus on those in the underworld and the observance on the same day of the fifteenth day of the seventh lunar month.

The festival derives from a monk by the name of Mulian (目蓮).

Folklore

MULIAN

Mulian was a devoutly religious boy, and when he came of age he donated all his worldly possessions, leaving a good portion to his mother, and went on to become a monk. He eventually became a disciple of the Buddha.

After his mother died he used supernormal capabilities (神通) to visit the Underworld to ensure she was doing well. He went on a long journey, asking various deities as to her location, and eventually found her.

What he saw shocked him. His mother looked extremely emaciated. Her cheeks were sunken in, and her ribs showed through her torso. Her eyes bulged from their sockets, darting back and forth wildly, looking for something to eat.

Horrified, Mulian used his powers to produce food for her. She took it with a ravenous greed and stuffed into her mouth whatever he caused to appear. She would then spit it out, the food having turned to coal in her mouth. Unfazed, she continued to wolf down food, but the result was the same, and she would cough out the coal along with blood from her shredded mouth.

Mulian went to the Buddha to find out what he could do. The Buddha said that his mother was being punished for living a greedy life. While he went off to live the life of a monk, his mother coveted more wealth. When monks came begging for alms, despite the fate of her own son, she refused to offer them anything. If she did, she would trick them into eating meat and rejoice at the joke she played on them.

The Buddha went down to the underworld to see if he could help. He released many souls from their torment. But Mulian's mother was still consumed with greed and was unable to ascend.

Returning to Mulian, the Buddha said that it would take more than just the individual efforts of Mulian or the Buddha to absolve his mother and release her from torment. It would take numerous monks, nuns, and other devout worshippers -- assembled on the fifteenth day of the seventh lunar month -- chanting scripture among the fragrance of living flowers. This act of compassion could generate limitless virtue by which his mother could be saved.

Mulian did as Buddha described, setting out vases of orchids, fruit, and vegetarian dishes for the masses of chanting people. His mother was then able to consume food again, and in time went on to her next incarnation as a dog. Discovering this, Mulian recited scripture for seven days and nights, and she was finally reincarnated as a human. [37] [38] [39]

* * *

There are multiple ways to read this tale. Filial piety is the most obvious theme shining through this story. A devout monk, who as required in the Buddhist monastic tradition has stepped away from family, still does his utmost to save his mother. This was the context under which the Yulanpen Festival was appreciated by so many emperors, and implemented as early as the Northern and Southern Dynasties.

In line with the above, the tale advocates certain behaviors; namely, filial piety, avoidance of greed, vegetarianism, and the importance of chanting, especially in groups.

Note the festival's timing during the same day of Pudu. This is in part a grafting together of two traditions: Taoism and Buddhism. Both Pudu and Yulanpen highlight an overarching theme, which is one of compassion. The compassion of setting out a table laden with food and other offerings to beings unseen and unknown to those offering prayers. Moreover, one might consider the sacrifices involved: time and the discomfort of standing under the hot sun at the tail-end of summer, sweat dripping down one's neck and back waiting for an hour or two. It is a time not just of compassion and respect for those that came before us, but also a reminder to join with others in expressing that same respect and compassion in the world of the living.

CHAPTER 15: WHITE DEW 白露

白露 / 백로 / はくろ / Bạch lộ°
Pinyin: báilù
Literal Meaning: "white dew"
Alternative names: Dews
Period: February 7 or 8 ~ September 22 or 23
Sun's Ecliptic Longitude: 165°

White Dew
Du Fu
Tang Dynasty

White dew beads together on oranges,
    as I saunter out on horseback at dawn.
Flowerbeds bloom against stones and trees,
    ferry boats enter the river.
Leaning on a table watching fish play,
    then rushing home with the crack of the whip and scattering birds.
I gradually understand the true beauty of autumn,
    and fear losing my way on the many secluded footpaths.

白露 | 唐 | 杜甫
白露團甘子，清晨散馬蹄。
圃開連石樹，船渡入江溪。
憑几看魚樂，回鞭急鳥棲。
漸知秋實美，幽徑恐多蹊。

    At this time of year the light and buzz of summer remain and the soil is soaked with the heat of the season. As the forces of yin become heavier, cooler air sinks to the ground and against flat surfaces, condensing moisture out of the air and accumulating as droplets. This is where the "dew" of "White Dew" gets its name. "White" corresponds to the fall, the phase of metal, death and decay, and all the aspects of western direction.[1]

    The weather usually begins to change more markedly at this time, with bigger differences between night and day. One saying describes the steady drop in nocturnal temperatures around White Dew and the next solar term, the Autumnal Equinox, every night colder than the last as colder air migrates from north to south and the daytime heat readily dissipates during cloudless nights (白露秋分夜，一夜冷一夜)[2].

    Another saying highlights the rapid change in weather from the previous solar term. While you need eighteen basins of water in Heat Departs to clean yourself from the constant sweat, by White Dew you need to take care to fully cover yourself to avoid the intrusion of cold yin airs into the body. (處暑十八盆，白露勿露身) [3]

Pentads

Wild geese go south (鴻雁來)
Swallows return north (玄鳥歸)
Flocking birds store up provisions (群鳥養羞)

As northern waters freeze over wild geese flock together and head south for food. As the birds pass overhead, their calls tell of the arrival of cooler weather. At night they land on riverbanks or sand bars to rest. Their calls to the moon in the darkness is another sound of that mirrors the desolation of autumn. Wild geese can be a symbol of separation, and hence death, although they are also a symbol of fidelity,[4] reflecting the dual yin-yang nature of loss that can accompany the generative character of love.

The migratory patterns of the swallow are the opposite of the wild goose: they head for the south in spring and return home in winter. [5] Swallows are associated with the spring, and embody good luck and success.[6]

Observation of birds frantically storing away provisions reminds humanity to prepare and store what is necessary to get through the lean winter.

In addition to this particularly avian-heavy trio of pentads, two other birds are connected to the White Dew solar term: the White Crane (白鶴) and the White Heron (白鷺鷥). Often confused with one another, these two birds are from different families. Cranes are the larger of the two.

The crane is a symbolically rich animal in many cultures, and in Chinese culture it shares the symbolism of being a messenger of the gods with other world traditions.[7] It also embodies ascension of the soul during funerals. [8] In China it also represents longevity and wisdom, and the word for heron (鶴, hè) is a homonym with the word harmony (和, hé).

The word heron in Chinese (鷺, lù) is a homonym with the word "road" (路, lù), and therefore means "path," usually an upward path of promotion or achievement.[9] It is also a homonym with good fortune (祿, lù).[10]

In the past people would adopt cranes when they landed in their courtyards, much as somebody would adopt a stray outdoor cat, feeding them and letting them go where they pleased. They would usually stay near of their own accord because they like to have a home base.[11] Tradition holds that they emit a high-pitched sound on the day of White Dew.[12]

Herons were raised at the home for amusement, and are considered a mild-tempered bird which prefers to return to its own nest every evening. But many ancient texts advise that herons need to be caged on the day of White Dew, since it is a time they turn wilder and will depart their caretaker's home for good.[13]

Agriculture

Farmers will keep watch for the formation of dew in the days before and after the start of White Dew, as according to a saying the appearance of dew in White Dew portends a good harvest during the Autumnal Equinox (白露白迷迷，秋分稻秀齊).[14] The weather typically dries out after White Dew, which can help prevent crops from rotting in the fields. If not, there are a number of idioms which tell of disaster should too much rain occur during this period:

- The fall of rain on the day of White Dew, horrible through and through. (白露日落雨，到一處壞一處)[15]
- Rain before White Dew means ghosts after. (白露前是雨，白露後是鬼)[16]
- The rain of Heat Departs is sweet, the rain of White Dew is bitter. (處暑雨甜，白露雨苦)[17]

Health

A saying of this time of year is "cover in spring, chill in fall" (春捂秋凍、不生雜病).[18] This expresses the idea of how to handle attire during the change of seasons. As winter turns to spring, the temptation is to dress lightly and enjoy rising temperatures of early spring. Similarly, as fall turns to winter people are over-eager to wrap themselves in their chic-looking winter wardrobe. During these transitional times, according to Chinese medicine the body is compromised and it is important to ease into the new temperature. So in early spring it is best to stay covered to keep the remaining chill of winter from entering the body, and in early fall it is advised to risk a bit of chill to avoid wearing too much and overheating. The exception of course are the frail, such as children and the elderly, or people with asthma or arthritis.

Those with allergies, asthma, or arthritis should avoid shellfish or scaleless fish like cutlassfish. As White Dew is a time of dryness, drink plenty of water. Certain fruits offset the drying effects of the weather, such as pears, apples, grapes, oranges, pomelos, persimmons, and longans. [19]

Longans are particularly prized for their fortifying effects during the time of White Dew. In Fujian, longans are mixed with rice porridge. This dish is said to nourish the blood and calm the nerves, fortify qi and invigorate the spleen, and beautify the skin, along with addressing anemia, insomnia, and neurasthenia.[20] Sweet potatoes are eaten in Wenzhou to prevent heartburn and promote fecundity.[21] [22]

Ancient Traditions

During this second month of autumn the emperor held ceremonies against pestilence to secure the development of the healthy airs of autumn. Offerings would consist of grain seeds and dog meat. While all times of the year had their various rules for ritual and management of the empire, rules were particularly strict during the autumn to emulate its severe air. All offerings and sacrifices had to meet exacting requirements of measurement. Garments and accessories used in rituals had to be carefully verified by the Superintendent of Robes to ensure they were made to fixed embroidery patterns passed down from previous times.

This second month of autumn includes the next solar term -- the Autumnal Equinox -- so it was a time nearing equal day and night. As such, death and decay were on the ascent and yang in decline. Following the Autumnal Equinox, water would begin to dry up, so it was a good time to dig underground passages and grain pits, repair granaries, and send the court officers out to receive crops for storage. They were to accumulate as much as possible, and any delinquent farmers were punished. It was also a time to encourage the sowing of wheat before the planting season slipped away.

In the human realm it was a time of busy commerce. The imperial bureaucracy was to do its utmost to facilitate trade from even the farthest reaches of the empire, and all gate, bridge, and road tolls were paused to encourage movement of goods. In terms of humanitarian action it was a time to look after those consumed with "decay"; in other words, the elderly, who were issued items to ease the burden of their decline, like stools, staves, and congee.

In keeping with the seasonal qualities of rules it was a time to repair walls and unify systems of measurement. The establishment of cities and towns were encouraged, along with any major undertaking, so long as the timing was in accord to "the movements of the sun." In other words auspicious according to the astrological calendar. It was also a time to draft and revise laws concerning criminal punishment, and this was the ideal time for beheading, executed "without excess or deficiency" to avoid bringing down the harsh judgment of Heaven.

The second month of autumn came with the typical injunctions against rituals for other seasons. Spring rites performed during this time would stop all rain. Plants and trees would not blossom and there would be a general panic among people of the nation. If summer rites were performed there would be droughts and insects would not retire to their burrows. Grain would grow prematurely. Winter rites would bring unseasonable winds, thunder before its time, and the death of immature plants and trees. [23]

Customs

For tea aficionados the tea of White Dew is the best of the year. Having soaked up the rays of the summer sun and harvested just as the weather turns dry, the tea of White Dew has a characteristic mellow and fragrant taste enjoyed by tea lovers.[24] A saying goes, "spring tea is bitter, summer tea is astringent; if you want to drink tea, make autumn tea of White Dew" (春茶苦，夏茶澀，要喝茶，秋白露).[25]

The fall is also a great time for brewing and distilling, and rice wine brewed during White Dew is said to be particularly sweet.[26]

Festivals

Among the wider Chinese populace there are no major rituals or festivals during the time of White Dew, with one exception: the people of Lake Tai in Jiangsu Province, who hold a White Dew Festival (白露節). The populace prays to Yu the Great (大禹), the legendary figure who introduced flood control to China during the Xia dynasty,[27] and according to the *Book of Gods and Strange Things* (尚書), relieved the area of years of constant flooding.[28] He is also called the Waterway Bodhisattva (水路菩薩).[29] Next to the Spring Festival and Qingming, it is one of the largest celebrations for the area: a week of temple offerings, gong ringing, and dancing. In Shanxi, people gather along the Yellow river and pay their respects to a number of other Deities: the Land God, the Flower Goddess, the Silkworm Maiden, the Door Gods, the Household deities, and Jiang Ziya (姜子牙).[30][31]

Folklore

YU THE GREAT

Yu the Great is the last of the three mythological sage rulers of China, succeeding the virtuous Shun (舜), who previously succeeded the moral Yao (堯). What is notable is that all three of these early rulers were not related to one another and chosen on merit, although Yu would be the king who initiated China's hereditary line of succession when he established China's first known historical dynasty, the Xia.

One of Yu the Great's most well-known accomplishments was taming the Great Flood of China. This is a project he took up from his father, who failed in the task despite his best intentions.

Yu's father was named Gun (鯀), and was an immortal grandson of the Yellow Emperor.[32] In some sources he is described as taking the form of a white horse.[33] As an immortal less unaffected by the travails of the material world, he watched in sorrow as humanity suffered from the Great Flood that had begun under the reign of Yao. [34]

* * *

Flood waters covered the land, rising so high people retreated into the mountains. With no land to grow crops and few remaining animals upon which to feed, humans suffered terribly. Gun could not think of any way of helping until he was a approached by two spirits taking the forms of a black turtle and a horned owl. They told him there was a substance owned by the Yellow Emperor called Swelling Soil (息壤) which could magically expand to soak up all water until commanded to stop.

Gun knew that it was the Yellow Emperor himself who had ordained the Great Flood, and there was no hope in the heavenly sovereign granting his request to use Swelling Soil. He mentioned his dilemma to the turtle and the owl, and they advised that he just steal a little of Swelling Soil, since it would be just as effective and the Yellow Emperor would not notice its absence.

Gun did as they advised and set to work staving off the flood with the Swelling Soil. The substance worked as well as had been described. Over time he had made great progress in clearing the flood.

The Yellow Emperor, realizing Gun had stolen the Swelling Soil, sent the God of Fire and of the South, Zhurong (祝融), to execute his grandson. Catching wind of the Yellow Emperor's fury, Gun fled, and managed to elude his assassin for nine years. Zhurong eventually tracked Gun down at Feather Mountain (羽山), and promptly murdered him, depriving Gun of his immortality.

But some aspect of his godly nature remained, and the body lay on the ground, exposed to the elements but not decomposing. After three years, his son, Yu, emerged from his belly. (In some tales Yu is born on the back of a dragon and in others he is a dragon himself.

By the time Yu was of age he had already made a reputation for himself. Shun, who was ruler at the time, was advised by his ministers to recruit Yu. Once recruited, he carried on his father's legacy of aiding the world by dispersing the Great Flood, and he set his every effort to that project.

His first stop was a visit to the Yellow Emperor. Laying prostrate he politely asked the ruler of the heavenly realms if he could use some of the Swelling Soil to help the people of the earth. The Yellow Emperor was impressed by Yu's manner and attention to protocol. He granted Yu his request, and Yu left with a small satchel of the substance.

Yu immediately set to work. He dove deep into the rivers and found the source of the problem: the water surging into the world came not from the skies, but from the ground. He stuffed the exits and found the outlets to be limitless and unpluggable with normal mud. This was not ordinary ground water, but the Yellow Springs (黄泉), the underground stream on which the sun traveled back eastwards to the Sacred Mulberry Tree where it rose every day. Only the Swelling Soil was up to the task, and he used it to staunch the holes.

The waters receded. People came down from the mountains and found newly dry, rich soil. They set about cultivating the land; a rich bounty of crops burst from the ground.

Yu labored daily until all the spring vents were plugged and was close to finishing. But a peasant came to him and reported that the lands he had already cleared were now filling up with water again. It turned out that Gong Gong (共工), the same Water God that inundated the earth with water in Nüwa's time, had set about unplugging the outlets and letting the water flood the earth once again.

Yu used his powers to summon an army of spirits. They descended on Gong Gong and chased him into Mt. Kuaiji (會稽山). Knowing he was no match for Yu and his army, Gong Gong ran back to the heavenly realm to hide.

Shun was deeply grateful to Yu for plugging the vents of water and subduing Gong Gong. To show his appreciation as well as to ensure smooth running of the kingdom, he made Yu joint regent.

But Yu's career was only just beginning. Although the bulk of the spring vents were plugged, rains still brought flooding. The next stage of his grand project was to plow the earth to make channels to the ocean, allowing the water to drain out. For this he enlisted the help of the Responding Dragon (應龍), who furrowed the earth with his tail, as well as a giant black turtle, who carried the green mud dug out the channels to the sea. He was further aided by a map provided by the River Master (河伯), the god of the Yellow River, a human who drowned and was turned into a god with a fish body and a human face.

As he was tunneling through a mountain he came across a bright light and followed further into the earth. He eventually emerged into a cavern filled with light and occupied by a creature with a snake's body and a man's face. It was no other but the god Fuxi.

Fuxi informed Yu that he was greatly pleased with the work he had completed, but there was much more work to do. He gifted Yu two jade tablets to measure and map the kingdom, and eventually impose political order. But the use of those tablets would have to wait until after a number of other adventures.

As Yu approached thirty years of age, he felt it was time to find a wife. This thought was in the back of his mind while he ambled through a forest. As he rounded a tree he noticed a nine-tailed fox dart through the brush. The sighting was a positive omen, as a local song containing reference to a nine-tailed fox spoke of a woman in Tushan (塗山). He ventured to the area and was happy to discover there was an eligible maiden named Nüjiao (女嬌) whose family was seeking a husband.

A meeting was arranged and Yu was pleased with her beauty and her bearing. She perfectly embodied her name: tender and lovable. Their marriage was off to a good start, and soon Nüjiao was pregnant.

But Yu was nowhere near done with his grand project. Every morning he woke up early and came back late. His wife tired of spending so much time alone and was also curious about what he was doing all *day. His constant admonitions to not follow him only served to heighten her curiosity.*

One day she secretly followed him. Yu, completely unaware his dear wife was approaching, used his ability to transform into a bear so that he could continue digging a tunnel he was working on. His wife screamed when she saw the bear, and Yu reflexively jumped up and roared. She turned around and fled, Yu in hot pursuit. He caught up to her and changed into his regular form, but she was so terrified she turned into stone.

Yu was horrified. Not only was his beloved wife turned to stone, his child was still inside. He commanded her to release the baby, and some vestige of her awareness caused the north side of the stone to crack, revealing Yu's child inside. He named his child after the event, giving him the name Qi (啓), meaning "cracked open."

Around this time Shun's health was failing, and so he chose Yu as his successor before he died. Using the jade tablets bequeathed by Fuxi, Yu went about measuring the world. Different sources give different measurements, but the key finding was his discovery that the world was square while the heavens were comprised of a circle (天圓地方).

The rest of Yu's reign was focused on bringing order to the world and recovering from the natural catastrophes that had wracked humanity for so many years. He divided the kingdom into nine separate provinces and had tripod cauldrons cast in each province. Each finished cauldron was then sent back to Yu in the center. The cauldrons were said to be extraordinarily heavy when the kingdom was well-governed and light when administrated poorly.

But the challenges were not over. Officials found smaller spring vents -- more than anyone could hope to close no matter how many people or mythical beasts or magical soils were used. The people of the country would have to live with it, and this is said to be the cause of many future floodings.

Gong Gong was still keen on seeking revenge for the humiliation he suffered at Yu's hands. He sent Xiangliu (相柳), a serpent with nine human heads. The beast ravaged the land, trying to destroy what Yu and his subjects built. Yu called forth the Responding Dragon and rode high in the sky. Normally the serpent could not be caught off guard because of all its heads looking in all the directions, but it never looked up, assuming nothing could attack from that direction.

Mounted on the dragon, Yu attacked from above. Flying in circles around the nine heads, he severed each one, his sword flashing in the sunlight. As each disembodied head spun to the ground and the long headless necks flapped around wildly in their death throes, Xiangliu's venomous blood spurted out into the soil. The blood killed everything it touched, rendering the land infertile.

To keep the venom from spreading over the land, Yu buried Xiangliu's body. But over time, the blood trickled down into the groundwater, and spread the deathly effects of the blood yet further. Eventually, the poisoned soil was formed into mountains, and the body placed in a lake with enough water to insulate the land from the effects of the creature's blood. It is said this battle and the placement of the beast's body resulted in many of China's geographic landforms.[35] [36] [37] [38]

* * *

Yu would have many other battles with fearsome creatures. He defeated the spirit of the Huai River, the Wuzhiqi (巫支祁), which appeared as a monkey with a green body, white head, yellow eyes, and white paws. The Wuzhiqi said to have the strength of nine elements. Then there was the Yellow Dragon (黃龍). While Yu was traveling by boat on the Yangzi River, other passengers cowered upon seeing the Yellow Dragon. But Yu confidently stared it down, not fearing the dragon because he knew it was not of the material world and could only materialize temporarily. He announced to the dragon his mission to save the people on behalf of the heavens, and he beheld the dragon as he would an earthworm. Terrified, the dragon fled. [39]

Despite his divine heritage, miraculous birth, and incredible powers, Yu the Great was not an immortal. He eventually died, ceding his kingdom to one of his capable ministers. The people, however, insisted that his mantle be passed to his son, Qi. His son was placed on the throne as the second king of the Xia dynasty, starting the patriarchal line of royal succession that continued for thousands of years.[40]

At the time of Qi's installment, the nine cauldrons required ninety oxen just to move one, reflecting his competence in ruling the kingdom. By the fall of the Xia, it was said each tripod could be easily carried by a single person, indicating the kingdom had lost the Mandate of Heaven. So despite initiating a tradition of hereditary succession, hereditary rule was not a permanent fixture and subject to change. And change it would over the following centuries.

* * *

There are many motifs that appear in this mythological tale that are shared with folklore the world over. There is the son (Yu) birthed from the corpse of his father (Gun): lineage as a form of rebirth. The son redeeming the mistakes of the father, extending the theme of rebirth to notions of karmic debt. Then there is seeking the power of the gods with the magic soil, and doing so respectfully and humbly.

Above all, this is a tale of imposing order on chaos, a key dynamic in Chinese philosophy. In this case chaos is represented by the raw, dangerous aspects of nature embodied by the flood and the various monsters which Yu must fight. The flood is managed, the monsters are dispatched, and then the world is organized in a political grid, preparing the land for humanity to flourish and dynasties to unfold.

It would be easy to misread this tale as the need for humanity to impose its will on nature: to control it and bend it fully to humanity's advantage. Rather, Yu the Great is in constant struggle with the natural elements, indicating both the inevitability of continual struggle and also the futility of thinking nature can be mastered. In addition to his constant tribulations, the vents between the bubbling Yellow Springs and the world above remain open, too numerous to plug fully. Humanity will just have to live with them and the occasional tragedy they bring.

Then there are the aspects of Yu working with nature. Realizing that plugging every vent underground is a futile project, he creates channels that let the water move as a natural process, adapting to its qualities rather than fighting it.

The tale is rich in esoteric aspects and those themes reverberate through centuries of Chinese culture. Yu divides the kingdom into nine provinces with the king at the center, mirroring the construction of the Lo Shu Square (洛書), the magic square which gave rise to China's major system of divination in the I Ching, rules of building placement with Feng Shui, and many aspects of placement and movement in Taoist ritual.

Nine is the number of wholeness, and so the nine tripod cauldrons, in addition to representing a united empire, are associated with ancient rituals practiced since the earliest of times. Yu is an exemplar of using magic to bring order to the chaos of natural and spirit realms, and a key step sequence in Taoist ritual is named after him: The Yu Step (禹步) or Seven-Star Stepping (七星步). The pattern mirrors the stars of the Big Dipper, and in some cases are performed with a limp. Yu is said to have walked with a limp due to the rheumatism he suffered as the result of all his labors. Another explanation is that he was imitating the gait of the divine birds he encountered. [41]

Lastly is the curious theme of Yu's transformation into a bear. One reading is that this form reflects Ursa Major, the Great Bear, connecting Yu to the seven stars of the Big Dipper, the step sequence named in his honor described above.

Another reading is that this form is a comment on humanity's connection to nature. Other than Taoist texts, many early Chinese mythological tales are at pains to describe the importance of humanity's transition from hunter-gather lifestyles to agriculture and civilization, and display a somewhat anxious preoccupation with moving away from the time when "men lived no differently than beasts."[42] Some texts describe Shun as a man of the deep mountains, a forester who lived in nature among beasts, while Yu is the initiator of civilization. [43]But the bestial transformation of Yu reminds future generations that the boundaries between man and the natural world are arbitrary, and the delineation between the material and spiritual are just as porous as bottom of the river bed, where the yellow springs bubble up into our world.

Yu the Great, while a prominent mythological figure, is not worshiped as widely as some of the other deities described in this book. But those that do pay their respects on the 15th day of the seventh lunar month, which commonly falls in the solar term of White Dew. It is also the time when the earth starts to dry, as if Yu's spirit has once again arrived on the land to bring the waters under control.

THE POWERS OF WHITE DEW

As explained in earlier chapters, autumn and its associated color white correspond to both the death aspect as well as longevity and purity. The "white" of "White Dew" invokes the latter quality. The dew collected on the first day of White Dew was believed by Taoist alchemists and Chinese medicine practitioners to boast properties of longevity and immortality. *The Compendium of Materia Medica* (本草綱目) says the substance cures hundreds of illnesses, treats diabetes, unburdens the body, staves off hunger, and enhances flexibility. [44]

Emperor Wu of Han (漢武帝), who ceaselessly searched the world for immortal elixirs, was advised by his sorcerers to build statues of immortals carrying bronze plates to collect the morning dew. Presumably he had the statues built, and drank the dew collected from the plates. He was undoubtedly disappointed to discover he wouldn't live forever, but he did live a relatively long life of 70 years. The original statues have never been found, but an easily overlooked replica stands in Beihai Park in Beijing, called the Immortal Dew-Collecting Plate (仙人承露盤).[45]

This legend matches closely the five-phase system of Chinese cosmology, where metal produces water through condensation, and the resulting water nourishes wood, emblematic of the rebirth and outgrowth of spring.

As White Dew nears its end, people turn their attention from the morning earth to the evening skies. The Autumnal Equinox nears, as does the Moon Festival, and the moon will soon illuminate an ever longer night.

CHAPTER 16:
AUTUMNAL EQUINOX 秋分

秋分 / 추분 / しゅうぶん / Thu phân
Pinyin: qiūfēn
Literal Meaning: "autumn center"
Alternative names: N/A
Period: September 22 or 23 ~ October 7 or 8
Sun's Ecliptic Longitude: 180°

Poems of the 24 Solar Terms
Autumnal Equinox, Middle of the Eighth Month
Yuan Zhen

Tang Dynasty

A zither strummed in major sixth,
the sound of the wind high and clear.
Clouds disperse and cast bobbing shadows,
thunder withdraws its angry roar.
Heaven and Earth go still and solemn,
chill and heat attain balance.
Were geese to suddenly arrive,
who would not be startled?

詠廿四氣詩 · 秋分八月中 | 唐 | 元稹
琴彈南呂調，風色已高清。
雲散飄颻影，雷收振怒聲。
乾坤能靜肅，寒暑喜均平。
忽見新來雁，人心敢不驚?

The *fen* (分) of *qiufen* (秋分) means half,[1] and in this case the midpoint or center-point of fall. The time is more commonly referred to as the Autumnal Equinox in the West, where it kicks off the start of fall, whereas in the solar term calendar the autumn started weeks prior, a reflection of the subtle, overlapping seasonal gradations of the solar term tradition. Day once again equals night, as it did at the Spring Equinox. In Chinese metaphysics the forces of yin and yang and summer and winter are once again in balance. (秋分者，陰陽相伴也，故晝均而寒暑平).[2] Plants and trees start to wither. Skies tend to be clearer and the winds are chillier. In more northern climates or in high elevations, rivers start to ice up.[3]

One of the most emblematic flowers of this solar term is the equinox flower (彼岸花),[4] which goes by a number of other names: red spider lily, hell flower, red magic lily, hurricane lily. The Chinese name literally means "flower of the opposite shore," evoking its otherworldly quality.

The flower is said to bloom next to the Yellow Springs, the river of the Underworld.[5] As departed souls walk by the river in the afterlife, memories fall away into the soil and equinox flowers bloom in their wake. The bright blood-red petals of the flowers are the only color in the drab landscape of the underworld.

Buddhists texts refer to the flower, saying it blooms for a thousand years and withers for another thousand, while the flower petals and leaves never meet.[6] This refers to the plant's growth pattern. The flower petals appear during the fall after a rain shower, much earlier than the leaves. This pattern mirrors the rebirth cycle inherent in the symbolism of fall and winter, the flower petals representing death and rebirth, and the leaves embodying the growth of new life.

Pentads

Thunder restrains its voice (雷始收聲)

Hibernating insects close burrow entrances (蟄蟲坏戶)

Waters begin to dry (水始涸)

As seen during the solar term of Insects Awaken, thunder is born out of the interaction of yin and yang,[7] and active when yang is rising, as thunder is analogous to creative principle. Thunder typically ceases after the Autumnal Equinox, driven by the retreat of yang and the advance of the energy of yin.

Insects burrow into the mud, drilling a hole small enough for them to enter and exit. As the temperatures drop, the insects head down into their burrow sand block the entrance with a small piece of earth so that they can slumber undisturbed until thunder sounds the following spring. [8]

Rains become either less frequent or change to a lighter drizzle. The start of freezing rivers also diminishes the amount of water coursing through waterways. [9]

Another sign of the solar term is the large hawk-cuckoo (鷐鳩). According to the ancients the call of the bird tells the plant world it is time to withdraw for the winter. [10]

Agriculture

According to farmers there are "three autumns": one of harvesting, one of plowing, and one of sowing.[11] Some crops need to be harvested early enough to not suffer frost and rain damage. Meanwhile, there is often enough remaining heat to get more seeds into the ground for one final harvest, or to plant crops hearty enough to get through the winter or the early cold snaps that can arrive during the Autumnal Equinox (秋分寒).[12]

In Anhui and Jiangsu, farmers hope for rain on the day of the Autumnal Equinox, because clear skies portend drought (秋分天晴必久旱). In northern China, the saying is that wind from the east on the day of the Autumnal Equinox will bring drought as well (秋分東風來年旱). [13]

According to tradition, timing of the Autumnal Equinox before the Mid-Autumn Festival is preferable, as this would signal a good harvest. If the Mid-Autumn Festival occurs prior to the Autumnal Equinox, the harvest would likely be poor. [14] No explanation of this reasoning is evident, but perhaps the Autumnal Equinox's association with the sun and the Mid-Autumn with the moon might reflect the energies of yin and yang on the crops. In which case it is preferable that -- yang being a force of advance – precedes those of yin and the forces of decline.

Health

Just as the Autumnal Equinox is a time of balanced yin and yang, it is important to maintain the same in the body. This time of year can bring an excess of dryness which can be offset by exercising and drinking plenty of water. A general sense of twilight settles on the land, which can affect mood. One must remain calm and optimistic to keep the murderous energies of fall from overcoming the body.[15] [16]

Potential health concerns include intestinal diseases, malaria, and Japanese encephalitis. Watch out for the recurrence of old ailments, particularly stomach problems, chronic bronchitis, asthma, high blood pressure, coronary disease, diabetes, and other ailments that affect the elderly. [17]

Customs

With the arrival of equal day and night, there is a tradition that repeats the egg-balancing observance (立蛋/豎蛋) on the Dragon Boat Festival, although the eggs are said to achieve balance for different reasons. On the Dragon Boat Festival, egg balancing is aided by the increased gravity at the center of the Earth. However, on the Autumnal Equinox, eggs can be balanced due to the balance caused by the equal time of day and night. [18]

Festivals

CELEBRATION OF THE MOON

In ancient times the moon was the only light in the sky at night, and consequently is referred to by many names: "Night Bright" (夜明), "Extreme Yin" (太陰), and "Big Bright" (大明). The last character in this latter term, *ming* (明), combines the characters for sun (日) and moon (月), because "sun and moon create brightness" (日月為明),[19] indicating the two celestial bodies are both a unity in generating light and a dualism of the poles of yin and yang.

The moon has been worshiped since the very earliest of dynasties. According to the *Rites of Zhou* (周禮), the ruler would worship the sun at the Spring Equinox, and the moon at the Autumnal Equinox (天子常春分朝日，秋分夕月).[20] Rituals were held at dusk on the 15th of the eighth lunar month (中秋), before the breathtaking moonrise in the night sky, usually referred to as the Harvest Moon in the West. This was a time to worship the moon goddess, who rules the forces of yin between the autumnal and spring equinoxes.[21] [22]

Later in the night was a time when rulers and officials would send their prayers to the star Canopus in the south of the city, called the Star of the Old Man of the South-Pole (南極老人星) or Old Man Star (老

人星). In the northern hemisphere Canopus is not visible after the Spring Equinox, and then emerges at the Autumnal Equinox. Seeing the star was said to bring peace and longevity, and greeting the southern energies more associated with yang possibly provided a balance to the preponderance of death energies associated with fall and the numerous ritual activities carried out on the western quarter. In keeping with this theme, if the star was not visible, it portended war. [23]

Emperors in ancient times practiced the custom of praying to the sun on the Spring Equinox (春分祭日), to the earth on the Summer Solstice (夏至祭地), to the moon on the Autumnal Equinox (秋分祭月), and to the heavens on the Winter Solstice (冬至祭天).[24] By the Ming and Qing dynasties, emperors prayed to the earth on the Summer Solstice, in the north to welcome the yin of fall and winter, and to heaven in the south to greet the yang of spring and summer[25]. Evidence of these practices, where rulers worshiped the sun, moon, heaven and earth, can still be found in the layout of Beijing, with the Temple of the Sun (日壇) in the east, the Temple of Earth (地壇) in the north, the Temple of the Moon (月壇) in the west, and the Temple of Heaven (天壇) in the south. Although now all tourist destinations in varying states of neglect or refurbishment and rapid commercialization, at one time these areas were considered sacred nexus of great power.

This tradition was carried forth through subsequent dynasties, and was fixed in the festival calendar by the Tang and continued well into the Song dynasty, when the streets were choked with night markets, children emerging into the night with lanterns, and numerous moon-gazers. Rituals at one point switched to celebrating the arrival of the moon at mid-heaven, and a whole host of celebrations emerged out of the time spent waiting for the moon to pass overhead. Over time, as with many of China's traditions, what started off as an activity reserved for royalty and high officials eventually trickled down to the literati, and eventually into common folk-practice, evolving into the Mid-Autumn Festival celebrated today. [26]

MID-AUTUMN FESTIVAL

In addition to worship of the moon and metaphysical aspects of yin and yang, the Mid-Autumn Festival (中秋節) is at heart an agricultural festival to celebrate and give thanks for the harvest. This can be seen in many local practices. In Nanning, Guangxi province, children carry hollowed out painted pumpkins or pomelos with candles inside[27] -- as if expressing humanity's universal urge to stick candles in gourds in the fall. In Guangzhou lamps of bamboo and paper are hung in a tradition called the Tree of the Mid-Autumn Festival (樹中秋).[28] They are decorated in many ways, but are often painted with rabbits, an echo of the practice of worshiping the Toad Master (蟾蜍) and the Jade Rabbit (白玉兔) in Beijing and Tianjin during this time of year.[29] Both of these animals, in addition to their association with the moon, are connected to the Queen Mother of the West, all aspects of the autumn, death, longevity, and immortality.

Mooncakes are a ubiquitous delicacy at this time of year. Round like the moon, they represent good fortune and family unity.[30] The tradition came from the various cakes offered to the moon goddess. The origin is attributed to the early Tang dynasty, when Emperor Gaozu (唐高祖李淵) and his ministers met a Tibetan merchant who handed them the cakes, pointed to the moon, and said they should use the cakes to invite the Toad of the Moon.[31] [32]

Nowadays moon cakes come in a variety of styles: sweet, savory, meat-based, vegetarian, and so forth. They are often imprinted with the characters for fortune (福), achievement (祿), and longevity (壽). Sometimes they are imprinted with the characters Chang'e (嫦娥), the Chinese moon goddess who is the lead character in the holiday's central origin myth.

Folklore

CHANG'E THE MOON GODDESS

After Houyi (后羿) shot down nine of the ten suns, the Queen Mother of the West wanted to show her gratitude. She gifted Houyi two elixirs of immortality. Taking one elixir would grant unparalleled longevity in the human realm; two would grant immortality.

Houyi rushed home to his wife, Chang'e, and showed her the elixirs, and suggested they each take one so that they could live together to an advanced age. Chang'e, deeply in love with Houyi, was delighted. They decided to each take one, and selected an auspicious day in the calendar to properly bathe, put on a set of new clothes, and embark on a new stage of life together. He told her to hide them well until the proper date.

Houyi's apprentice, Feng Meng (逢蒙), found out about the elixirs and wanted them for himself. He waited for a day when Houyi left the house, and once he was sure Houyi was gone, burst through the door and demanded Chang'e give him the elixirs. Chang'e went to the hiding spot and knew that once she had given them up, Feng Meng would kill her. There was no way he would let her live to tell Houyi.

She grabbed the two elixirs and swallowed them before Feng Meng could get his hands on them. Feng Meng watched in a mixture of envy and terror as Chang'e's body was filled with a white-golden light. She began to float, her form flickering and fading while she went up through the ceiling. Neighbors who happened to be outside watched her continue ascending in the night sky, eventually reaching the moon and charging it with a new radiance.

When Houyi returned his neighbors told him what they saw. He looked up and was overcome with sadness as he saw Chang'e's outline in the moon, confirming what his neighbors had told him was true. Added to the sadness of losing his wife was a deep sense of her betrayal. He had no idea Chang'e had taken the elixirs to escape the murderous clutches of Feng Meng.

Still, he remained devoted to her. When the moon reached its peak of brightness in the eighth lunar month and Chang'e was at her most visible he would set out incense and her favorite treats on a table in the courtyard. The townspeople witnessed Houyi's devotion and did the same, asking her to grant them luck and security.

It said that Chang'e, while deeply appreciative of the devotion, is often filled with longing for Houyi at the Mid-Autumn Festival. This is *why the moon is sometimes obscured at this time of year, her mood creating clouds hiding her face and her tears raining down on the world.*[33] [34]

* * *

The above origin myth derives from more modern versions which capture Chang'e's popular symbolism of feminine beauty, gentleness, and elegance. Earlier legends describe Chang'e in a much less favorable light. She was first depicted in Warring States era texts as stealing the elixir. [35]

By the early Han dynasty, the *Huainanzi*[36] tells of her marriage to Houyi. Both were gods cast down to live as mortals as punishment. Chang'e, unhappy with their situation, becomes a source of never-ending whining, forcing Houyi to appeal to the Queen Mother of the West for help. She pities them, gives him two elixirs, both of which Chang'e steals and drinks herself. Hou Yi (后羿) is depicted thereafter as bitter and angry at Chang'e's betrayal.

She ascends to the heavens, but halfway there realizes questions will be asked about why she abandoned her husband, so she stops on the moon. She ends up stuck there, and the moon for all its brightness is a desolate prison-scape: a large, cold palace (Guanghan Palace - 廣寒宮) where she is accompanied only by a toad and a rabbit. Another prisoner, a man named Wu Gang (吳剛), was banished there as well, doomed to work for eternity by chopping down an immortal osmanthus tree which heals after every ax strike.

In some tales, Chang'e was the toad, transformed into that shape for betraying her husband, and forced to pound the elixir of immortality with a mortar and pestle for eternity. [37] In earlier sources it is the rabbit doing the pounding, and is shown with the Queen Mother of the West. By the Jin dynasty the rabbit was moved to inhabit the moon with Chang'e, and is often shown in Chang'e's arms, laboring to produce the elixir while Chang'e is an image of leisure and elegance. [38]

Chang'e's original name was Heng'e (姮娥), but was changed because her original name was too similar to that of an emperor, which was seen as disrespectful.[39] There are sources that say Chang'e is a later retelling of the precursor moon goddess, Changxi (常羲), also referred to as Changyi (常儀) and Shangyi (尚儀) . This goddess bears a relationship to a more primal version worshiped by many matrilineal tribes who took the moon as their totem. As society became more patriarchal this version was left aside in favor of Chang'e, a more domesticated version connected to Houyi.[40]

As described in the chapter on Spring Equinox, Changxi was the second consort of Di Jun (帝俊), she gave birth to twelve moons, one for each month of the year. In *the Classic of Mountains and Seas* she is referred to as the Harmonizing Moon Mother (女 和 月 母), [41] responsible for harmonizing yin and yang within the lunisolar calendar. To keep both methods of time-keeping in balance, she births a leap month every three years. Within the old pantheon she is considered equal to Nüwa. [42] While Nüwa is creator of humanity, Changxi manages the cycle of the moon by which humanity marks the passage of time.

CHAPTER 17: COLD DEW 寒露

寒露 / 한로 / かんろ / Hàn lộ
Pinyin: hánlù
Literal Meaning: "cold dew"
Alternative names: N/A
Period: October 7 or 8 ~ October 22 or 23
Sun's Ecliptic Longitude: 195°

Watching Cold Dew on Moonlit Leaves of a Parasol Tree
Dai Cha
Tang Dynasty

On the dreary leaves of the parasol tree,
  shines the light of a newly risen moon.
The dripping dew glows brightly,
  bringing brilliance to the drab colors of winter.
Trembling from the wind it resembles crumbling jade,
  with pearls of dew hanging from the rustling branches.
The cold air falsely hints the end of autumn,
  even the smallest sound can be heard in the night.
Dew gathers and disperses through the air,
  coating the world making it clearly visible.
Don't rue the scene for it casts away fatigue,
  when dawn comes the dew will all disperse.

月夜梧桐葉上見寒露 | 唐 | 戴察
蕭疏桐葉上，　月白露初團。
滴瀝清光滿，　熒煌素彩寒。
風搖愁玉墜，　枝動惜珠幹。
氣冷疑秋晚，　聲微覺夜闌。
凝空流欲遍，　潤物淨宜看。
莫厭窺臨倦，　將晞聚更難。

Dew was often used by the ancients as a marker for the change of seasons.[1] A few weeks prior was White Dew, a foreshadowing the death of autumn and winter with the color white. By this time of year, chill skies and slumbering earth conspire to make cold dew get colder, nearing a temperature of frosting but falling short of a morning freeze. As with many of the solar terms, this term speaks of gradual change, bridging what has come before and hinting at what the weather has in store.

Cicadas have long since ceased their chirping. And as mentioned in the poem by Li Shang-yin (李商隱), "withered lotus flowers listen to the rain" (枯荷聽雨聲),[2] painting a picture of drooping buds and the lost vibrancy of the land now cloaked in decayed vegetation and grayer tones, signs of life departing just as quickly as they arrived in spring. Despite the welcome relief of cooler weather, one will soon long for the heat and color of the past few months.

In China, the northeast and northwest are already feeling the temperatures of winter. Mountainous areas are snowing. People in Beijing are waking up to the first morning frosts. In southern China, high pressure cold fronts push out much of the rain, making the air dry and crisp.[3]

Pentads

The last wild geese fly south (鴻雁來賓)

Sparrows enter the sea and become clams (雀入大水為蛤)

Chrysanthemums display yellow flowers (菊有黃華)

The original Chinese of the first pentad is something more to effect of "wild geese come as guests." In this usage guest (賓) means something that comes after something else. In this case, the stragglers who eventually follow the earlier flocks south for the winter.[4] Another interpretation is that the word is equivalent to the word "shore" (濱), and that the pentad refers to their flocking on southern shores.[5]

The enigmatic second pentad of birds becoming clams reflects the various animal transformations that were said to occur in the dance between yin and yang. In this case, as yang yields to yin, sparrows -- emblems of spring, the sky, and yang -- cast themselves into the water and transform into clams, representing the dark, moist, cold depths of yin. Many texts such as *Discourses of the States* (國語)[6] and the *Wuzazu* (五雜俎) by Xie Zhaozhe (謝肇淛) mention this phenomenon,[7] and the pentads and Chinese legends have many examples of such transformations, such as hawks to doves, rotting grass to fireflies, pheasants to sea serpents, sharks to tigers, fish to yellow sparrows, and carps to dragons.[8] Some say the tales are born out of superstition and poor observation of nature. [9] Under this understanding the transformation was nothing but a simplistic explanation of why sparrows disappeared during the season and why clams -- which had the same coloring as sparrows, were so plentiful. [10] Rather, the transformations are instead metaphorical representations of the change of the changes of yin and yang and the seasons than a literal description of the world.

The final pentad mentions chrysanthemums: a fall flower blooming near the close of Cold Dew, just as most of the other flowers are withering away. The flower is also closely linked to the death and renewal aspects of fall. Chrysanthemum wine is drunk to promote longevity, and conversely, the flower is worn during funerals. It is for this reason that chrysanthemums are never given to the living in Chinese culture, and are reserved for grave sites. Like many of the common motifs of fall, the flower combines symbolism of death as well as the longevity of both body and spirit. The flower is also associated with unsullied noble character, or the seclusion of a scholar-official uninterested in seeking power. [11]

Agriculture

Some areas benefit from the dryness of this period. Others, particularly in parts of southern China, are still hit with the occasional late-season typhoon. Otherwise, farmers must contend with long periods of heavy cloud cover and little sunlight and drizzly rain, which can be disastrous for the harvest. In these areas farmers might have to harvest earlier to be safe.[12]

A saying goes "if cotton isn't picked at Cold Dew, don't rage at heaven when it dies of frost" (寒露不摘棉，霜打莫怨天).[13] Potatoes often need to be pulled in advance. Rice farmers in the south need to be sure rice paddies stay wet, and do what they can to prevent damage from the dreaded Cold Dew wind (寒露風). Another proverb states that "grain fears Cold Dew winds like people fear poverty in old age" (禾怕寒露風，人怕老來窮).[14]

Health

The colder and drier weather creates a higher probability of colds. A saying advises that it is best not to expose the body during White

278

Dew, while in Cold Dew one must keep one's feet covered (白露身不露，寒露脚不露).[15] According to Chinese medicine feet are entry points for cold due to their distance from the heart, their thin skin, and lack of protective fat.[16]

Ancient Traditions

In the third month of autumn the Emperor would once again present offerings of dog meat, this time with rice, and ritually consume them after the ritual. Mirroring the martial character of autumn, he was to model – through act of hunting – adept handling of horses and the wielding of the five weapons (五戎): bow and arrow (弓矢), pike (殳), spear (矛), dagger-axe (戈), and halberd (戟). Any game collected was to be offered to the spirits of the four directions. This was also the time for the Director of Music to prepare students to play wind instruments for ritual use.

Leaves continue to yellow and fall so that the past injunction on tree cutting was lifted since it was a good time to cut branches for the use of charcoal. With winter closing in, it was the final push to gather the harvest. Officers were sent to ensure both nobles and peasants exerted themselves to take in the crops, which was seen as being in proper harmony with the storing character of heaven and earth in fall. Nothing was to remain out in the fields. The Chief Minister took account of all collected produce and grain and had them stored in an act that was as much religious as it was practical. Goods were moved from "the acres of god to the granary of the spirits" with the utmost reverence and correctness.

In civil affairs, the increased harvest activity meant it was also the time to revise and enforce taxation laws, collection of which was supposed to be carried out without any special privileges. Decisions on criminal cases were to be hurried before the end of autumn. And remaining in harmony with the need for strict balance during the season, any salaries given incorrectly were to be rectified and anybody who was facing great need were to be attended to. The ministers would then announce the beginning of the hoar-frost, and that soon labor would cease for a season. As cold airs arrived, people were to draw up into their homes.

If summer rituals were mistakenly done at this time there would be great floods, winter stores would be damaged, and viral epidemics would erupt among the people. Winter rites would encourage thieves and robbers. The empire borders would be threatened and territory lost. If spring rites were performed, warm airs would come, making the people overly relaxed and languid, while stimulating harmful troop movements. [17]

Customs

In the north in places like Beijing, cricket fighting reaches its last crest of activity[18] before slowing down for the winter. In the south, female crabs are at their peak of flavor.[19] This time of year is also associated with the consumption of various cookies and cakes. Otherwise, most of the customs are associated with the Double Nine Festival.

Festivals

DOUBLE NINTH

The Double Ninth Festival (重陽節) typically coincides with Cold Dew. Taking place on the ninth day of the ninth lunar month, the Chinese name translates to "Double Yang". Nine is considered a yang number, so with the number nine for both the day of the lunar month and the day of the solar year, this particular date is considered to bring an over-abundance of yang (日月並陽).[20] A large number of customs have arisen to commemorate the date.

In ancient times it was actually deemed an auspicious date. Before the Qin dynasty, *Master Lü's Spring and Autumn Annals* (呂氏春秋) described Double Ninth as a time to celebrate the harvest, pray to the Emperor of Heaven, and revere the ancestors.[21] Many looked to the stars, and Antares (大火星) was the celestial body whose departure marked the arrival of autumn. Grand ceremonies were held to call for the return of the star in spring, when it would reappear after suffering through the barren cold of winter. Some say these ceremonies might have been the precursor of Double Ninth. [22] [23]

The ceremony transformed into a wider festival by the Han dynasty, and the *Miscellaneous Records of the Western Capital* (西京雜記) first describe the customs carried on to this day: wearing dogwood and drinking chrysanthemum wine.[24] The practices were carried out into the Han, and in the Three Kingdoms Period was the first to refer the festival as "chongyang" (重陽節).[25] During the Wei and Jin dynasties, Tao Yuanming (陶淵明) wrote his famous poems about the beloved chrysanthemums which filled his garden (秋菊盈園) and the spirits he fermented with the flowers.[26] It became an official national festival by the Tang, which appended reverence for the elderly to the day. Observance followed in the Song, Ming, and Qing and continues today, with people ascending mountains, drinking chrysanthemum wine, eating cakes, and less frequently, wearing dogwood. [27]

CHONGYANG CAKE

Eating Chongyang cake (重陽糕) started in the Tang dynasty, and by the Song its production had become a very exacting process according to the *Mengliang Lu* (夢粱錄).[28] Chongyang cake is made of rice flour and sugar and decorated with jujubes, chestnuts, and almonds. The cake is prepared and eaten because the word "cake," (gao 糕) is a homonym with the word "high" (gao 高), matching both the practice of hiking on high mountain tops on this day, and to grant people a higher position in career, wealth, or life. They are sometimes constructed with nine layers, or in the shape of a pair of twin lambs, another homonym meaning "twin yang" (重羊, 重陽).[29] It is also called flower cake (花糕), chrysanthemum cake (菊糕), and five color cake (五色糕).[30]

There are two origin stories surrounding the custom. The first is that Emperor Wu of Song (宋武帝), Liu Yu (劉裕), gave such cakes to his soldiers when he reviewed the troops on the ninth day of the ninth lunar month. The other is relates to Kang Hai (康海), a scholar during the Ming dynasty. He traveled to the imperial capital of Chang'an to take the imperial exam, which he passed. But before he could return home he fell ill, and was stuck in the capital until he recovered. As was standard practice, messengers were sent around the country to inform the test takers of their positive result. The messenger sent to Kang Hai's residence found nobody there. Desiring a reward for his effort, he refused to leave empty-handed and camped out on Kang Hai's doorstop. Kang Hai eventually returned on the ninth day of the ninth lunar month to find the messenger still there. He gave the man payment and fed him cakes for his effort, and from then on word of the tale spread, and people ate Double Yang cakes to effect their own progress and achievement.[31] [32]

WEARING DOGWOOD

The wearing of Dogwood (茱萸) was prevalent by the Tang dynasty and often worn on the Double Ninth Festival by women and children and sometimes men. It could be put in the hair, on the shoulders, or in a pouch. The plant is believed to ward off evil and prevent cold from entering the body.[33] In the Song, paper cuttings of chrysanthemums and dogwood were gifted to others or worn. [34]

Dogwood is a plant with many associations across a number of cultures. Its wood drips with black blood in the *Aeneid*.[35] Within Christianity a legend states it was the wood upon which the crucifix was built[36] -- although this is attributed to the wood of many different trees. It is also called "Hounds Tree" in reference to Hecate's Hounds.[37] In certain parts of North America, it is a harbinger of spring and their blossoms a sign to begin planting; otherwise, one's crops might be destroyed in the cold snap of a "dogwood winter." [38] Dogwood enjoys high status in North America as the official flower of many locales, and has a host of other medicinal and practical uses.

DRINKING CHRYSANTHEMUM WINE

There is an old custom of drinking chrysanthemum wine during the Double Nine Festival. When the chrysanthemum blooms, the stems and leaves are harvested, mixed with millet and fermented.

Traditionally chrysanthemum wine was brewed on the ninth day of the ninth lunar month and fermented over the course of a year and consumed on the following Double Ninth Festival.[39] It was considered a powerful elixir, with all sorts of benefits attributed to it, including sharpening eyesight, alleviating headaches, lowering hypertension, weight loss, treating stomach ailments, and preventing colds. When combined with dogwood it was said to alleviate pain and regulate the flow of vital energy. It was also believed to have more powerful esoteric qualities like promoting longevity and protecting from evil. [40] [41]

ADMIRING CHRYSANTHEMUMS

Tao Yuanming (陶淵明) is the Chinese poet most associated with the chrysanthemum,[42] and some would say that he helped popularize the flower. Tao was originally a government official during the darkest days of the Jin dynasty. Sick of the constant sniping and bitter politics among scholar officials in a fading kingdom, he retreated to live in the countryside, becoming one of the foremost "Poets of the Field,"[43] a tradition of poetry capturing a slower life close to nature.

His influence not only extends throughout the generations of Chinese poets, but also across the Pacific to American Beat poets.[44] He took on the name Tao Qian (陶潛) later in life to reflect his break with court life, the new name meaning something akin to "Recluse Tao."[45] However, his new life was not one of squalid poverty and ascetic denial, but about simplicity and enjoyment of nature and life. The following poem -- his most famous one mentioning chrysanthemums -- gives a sense of his style.

From the "Drinking Wine" series - Part 5

Tao Yuanming
Six Dynasties Period

Building one's house among humanity,
  yet absent the bustle of wagon or horse.
Ask me how can this be?
  The mind directed far finds its seclusion.
Picking chrysanthemums under the eastern fence,
  calmly looking at the southern mountains.
The mountain air of dusk is fine,
  flying birds weave about and return.
Within this is true meaning,
  I want to explain but lost the words.

飲酒•其五 | 六朝 | 陶淵明
結廬在人境，而無車馬喧。
問君何能爾？ 心遠地自偏。
採菊東籬下，悠然見南山。
山氣日夕佳，飛鳥相與還。
此中有真意，欲辯已忘言。

Tao was said to spend his days farming, drinking, writing poetry, and chatting with friends. He cultivated numerous varieties of chrysanthemums, nurturing a garden of such beauty that neighbors would continually seek him out to admire the flowers, drink wine, and talk. [46]

On one particular Double Ninth day, Tao was without wine. Despondent, he went to view his garden of chrysanthemums and was allayed by their beauty. He made a wish that from then on, chrysanthemums bloom on Double Ninth Day. Thereafter, the flowers did just that, and the day became a day to go out and appreciate chrysanthemums.[47]

ELDERS' DAY

Double Ninth has some aspects in common with Tomb Sweeping and the Ghost Festival: setting aside time to pay respects to the ancestors. But added to this notion is time to appreciate the living;

namely, the elderly on Elders Day (老人節). Originally practiced in the Tang dynasty, the observance has been revived in modern times. It is a day to spend time with the aged and get them out and about, especially up to higher elevations, combining the observance with the Double Ninth tradition of ascending the heights. In addition to the physical benefits of exercise and the emotional benefits of socializing, going to higher elevations is said to be an ideal place to absorb qi and a process which nurtures longevity and the ascension of personal character.

Folklore

ASCENDING THE HEIGHTS

The custom of hiking in mountains comes from a story told in the Liang dynasty in the Xuqixieji (續齊諧記) about Huan Jing (桓景) of Runan (汝南) in Eastern Han.[48] The initial version of the tale offered scant detail, but was embellished over time and evolved into many different versions. The tale below is the most common one.

* * *

Long ago the people of Runan were plagued by a demon. Whenever the demon would emerge from the depths, many would die of plague. The people lived in constant terror, worried they would be the ones to contract the illness. The demon ravaged and tortured the populace in this way for countless years.

A man named Huan Jing watched the latest wave of plague take his parents. As a filial son he was consumed with fury, and determined to put an end to the demon's reign of terror. He left his wife and the town, and headed out into the wilderness to try to locate an immortal who would teach him in the ways of suppressing demons.

He traveled through wet swamps and high mountains. He fought his way through thick brush and climbed dangerous sheer cliffs. He endured hunger and thirst. He asked every fellow traveler he encountered about the immortal's whereabouts, and eventually learned of an eastern mountain peak which was home to a Taoist immortal named Fei Zhangfang (費長房). The stories were that he was able to travel the clouds, dispel evil, treat illnesses, and even bring people back to life.

Huan Jing was delighted and went to find him. Soon an immortal crane came across his path, and carried him to where Fei lived. Once Fei heard all that Huan Jing had endured in his effort to find a teacher he was touched, and took him on as a student. Fei taught him swordsmanship and esoteric techniques to take down monsters.

The student was profoundly appreciative of the opportunity and did his utmost to learn the techniques, working tirelessly to the point of neglecting to eat. Slowly he began to master the esoteric techniques of the swordplay necessary to put down demons, aided as well by a bejeweled demon-suppressing sword gifted to him by Fei.

When the immortal Fei observed that Huan Jing had learned everything he could teach him, he knew it was time to part ways. Fei called his student before him and said, "Tomorrow is the ninth day of the ninth lunar month, when the plague demon will once again emerge from its den. You have learned what is required and must go back to alleviate the people's misery."

Fei gave him a satchel of dogwood and a pitcher of chrysanthemum wine, telling him they would provide protection against evil. Huan Jing accepted the gifts and took leave of his master. He rushed back to Runan on the back of the immortal crane.

On Double Ninth, he led the townsfolk up to the top of the nearest mountain and gave each of them dogwood and chrysanthemum wine, saying the demon would not dare come close.

The demon, who was sleeping soundly in the mountain, was awakened by the smell of dogwood and chrysanthemum, odors highly disagreeable to him. As he emerged out of his den Huan Jing set upon him, killing him with one slash of the gem-encrusted sword.

Thereafter, the people ascended mountains with dogwood and chrysanthemum wine on the ninth day of every ninth lunar month to escape danger and promote long life.[49] [50]

* * *

This tale contains many elements of the Double Ninth Festival: chrysanthemum wine, dogwood, and ascending to high places for self-cultivation and health. And the frequently-occurring motif of longevity -- in this case the longevity that occurs when one avoids falling victim to the plague -- once again emerges to counter the overriding theme the autumn season: that of murderous energy and death. These customs provide more than just a way to mark the calendar as one cycles through time; they also show that despite the inevitability of death and decline, there are methods to forestall its arrival in ways that are enjoyable as they are effective.

CHAPTER 18: FROST FALL 霜降

霜降 / 상강 / そうこう / Sương giáng
Pinyin: shuāngjiàng
Literal Meaning: "Frost descends"
Alternative names: Frost
Period: October 22 or 23 ~ November 6 or 7
Sun's Ecliptic Longitude: 210°

The Cold of the First Four Days of Frost Fall
Lu You
Song Dynasty

Grass and wood begin to yellow and fall,
  wind and clouds come and go.
Children finish hoeing the wheat,
  neighbors hold processions for the gods.
Hunting hawks hold dear the approach of frost,
  the call of cranes foretell the arrival of rain.
Do not sigh at aspects of rise and decline,
  for flames have resurged from sparks in the ashes.

霜降前四日頗寒 | 宋 | 陸游
草木初黃落，風雲屢闔開。
兒童鋤麥罷，鄰里賽神回。
鷹擊喜霜近，鶴鳴知雨來。
盛衰君勿嘆，已有復燃灰。

Like the American usage of "fall" to refer to autumn, "Frost Fall" refers to the descent of cold and desolate qi congealing on surfaces and turning dew into frost.[1] This is the coldest solar term of fall, when a winter chill fills the air which can penetrate the bones. Soil and plant life are covered in a thin gray-white crystalline frost.

The phrase "heavy frost, fierce sun" (濃霜猛太陽)[2] refers to the cloudless skies at this time of year. At night the bare heavens sap the earth of its warmth, laying the perfect conditions for frost. Leaves, formerly showing off their remaining vibrancy in an array of fiery colors, grow heavy with the weight of frost and drop off their branches. They fall momentarily to the ground and then swirl around like butterflies borne on the northwest wind.

The cloudless night sky reveals a moon that – while not as large as the harvest moon -- can glow even more brilliantly. The moon at this time of year has been the subject of many poems, and often carries an air of change with a tinge of desolation. One example is best encapsulated by Li Shang-yin (李商隱), comparing the beauty of the fall, represented by the Moon Goddess, to that of the Azure Lady, goddess of frost and snow:

Frost Moon
Li Shang-yin
Tang Dynasty

Cicadas are absent amid the first sounds of migrating geese;
  above the one-hundred-foot tower water meets the sky.
The Azure Lady and Moon Goddess endure the cold;
  a contest of beauty among the moonlight and frost.

霜月 ｜唐｜ 李商隱
初聞微雁已無蟬，百尺樓高水接天。
青女素娥俱耐冷，月中霜裏鬥嬋娟。

Another old saying goes "Frost Fall kills myriad plants" (霜降殺白草).[3] This phrase refers to the lowering temperatures of this time of year, which freeze and dehydrate plants, causing cell walls to degrade. The frost itself protects the plant up to a point by releasing warming heat energy during the course of its formation. Yet usually ambient temperatures are low enough for the heat energy to make little difference. Still, the idea of the encasing and protecting qualities of ice is a theme that will come up as the year moves into winter.

The weather expresses itself very differently throughout China. The term is less relevant in places like Tibet where it snows 200 days of the year. In the south, temperatures hover around 16° C, so there are a couple weeks to go before frosts arrive. In places like Hainan Island there won't be any frost at any point throughout the year.[4]

Pentads

Mountain wolves sacrifice prey (豺乃祭獸)
Grass and plants yellow and fall (草木黃落)
All insects bow in hibernation (蟄蟲咸俯)

As the buzzing of insect-life departs and vegetation withers, predators sit silently among the groves and awaiting their desperate prey. Mountain wolves, more commonly referred to as dholes, are an endangered reddish canid that look like a cross between a gray wolf and red fox. Other names include Asian wild dog, Indian wild dog,[5] whistling dog, red dog,[6] and red wolf.[7] They are highly social creatures -- more social than gray wolves -- and emit a whistling sound that sounds similar to fox calls.[8]

Early observers of the species in China claimed that after capturing and killing prey, they would lay their bounty in a square formation, as if to give thanks to the gods.[9] [10] Again, whether these animals actually behave his way is less the point of the pentad, and like many other themes of this type, indicate connection between the natural world and the divine. The square formation is a symbol of earth and the material world, which could either reflect appreciation to the heavens for the gifts of the land, or respect offered to the earth, presaging the themes of earth-worship in winter.

In ancient conceptions of the cosmos, the withering and falling of vegetation was as much the result of the advancing forces of yin as the result of weather and seasonal change. One might say that there was considerable ambiguity as to the cause-effect relationship between these physical and metaphysical forces.

Pentads earlier in the year told of the insects' preparation for dormancy. As the insects tuck into their tiny burrows, they drift off to sleep, protected by the hard, icy earth around them.

Agriculture

In the north, even cold-resistant crops like spring onions have no hope of growing. A phrase goes that the time of Frost Fall cannot give rise to spring onions; the more they grow, the more hollow their stalks (霜降不起蔥, 越長越要空).[11] In the south, however, it is the time of the third autumn (三秋), a time of cross-breeding and harvesting of late rice, planting wheat and harvesting rapeseed.[12]

It is also the time for picking cotton, although folk proverbs advise a certain fastidiousness with the remaining cotton straw, saying that if it is not cleaned up, insect eggs and bacteria will wreak havoc (滿地秸秆拔個盡，來年少生蟲和病).[13]

In the Yellow River Delta, Frost Fall is the optimal time to breed goats. Females are in heat during the fall and winter. When the doe's kid is born in spring, it is greeted by a green world with plenty of grass for the mother, providing her the nutrients needed to produce rich milk.[14]

In places where frost does occur, the appearance of frost on the first day of Frost Fall is a welcome event. In Yunnan, the saying goes that no frost on the day of Frost Fall means there will be no rice (霜降無霜，碓頭沒糠).[15] In Jiangsu, the saying is that frost on Frost Fall means there will be so much rice it will rot in the silos (霜降見霜，米爛陳倉).[16] Conversely, seeing frost before Frost Fall will ensure rice sellers become tyrants (未霜見霜，糶米人像霸王).[17] In other words, the timely appearance of frost means there will be more surplus than anybody can possibly consume, and an early frost ensures so little rice harvested that prices will skyrocket.

Health

Taking care to fortify the body during this solar term is said to pay dividends. A saying goes that fortifying the body throughout the year is not as effective as simply doing so in Frost Fall (一年補透透，不如補霜降).[18] It is likely this phrase is simply meant to highlight the importance of taking care of one's health during this transitional period of the year. Skipping opportunities to fortify one's qi during the other months would make for a very boring and bland year given the variety of foods and practices in Chinese culture centered on this ever-pressing concern.

The dramatic change in temperatures between night and day present risks for people with myocardial infarction, as the cold causes the blood vessels under the skin to constrict, hampering circulation, increasing blood pressure, and impacting the heart's ability to pump blood. The elderly are susceptible to changes in weather and need to be careful to avoid stroke.

Most people will need to keep an eye on blood pressure, cholesterol, stomach ailments, asthma, and arthritis. Keep warm, drink liquids and use plenty of lotion to prevent autumn dryness, and as always engage in an appropriate amount of exercise.[19] [20]

Customs

RED LEAVES
Because falling temperatures around the first frost trigger fall colors, Frost Fall was often a time to venture out and appreciate the red leaves. The most common red foliage in China is displayed by maple trees and Chinese tallow trees, the latter of which also goes by a number of other names: Florida aspen, chicken tree, gray popcorn tree, and the candleberry tree. Maples and tallow trees lined rivers and dotted hills in ancient China, and were a rich source of inspiration for poets and painters for many generations. [21] [22]

Night-Mooring at Maple Bridge
Zhang Ji
Tang Dynasty

The moon descends as crows caw, frost sparkling in the heavens;
  Fishermen's fires under riverside maples disturb my melancholy sleep;
Outside the walls of Suzhou sits Hanshan Temple;
  The tolls of midnight temple-bells ripple over my boat.

楓橋夜泊 | 唐 | 張繼
月落烏啼霜滿天
江楓漁火對愁眠
姑蘇城外寒山寺
夜半鐘聲到客船

One can imagine a shivering Zhang Ji, half-lidded eyes watching the red leaves of the maples river bank alight with the fires of his noisy neighbors. Du Mu, one of the most revered Tang poets, wrote specifically about the beauty of red maple leaves when visiting in the suburbs of Chang'an during Frost Fall:

Mountain Travels
Du Mu
Tang Dynasty

Far away in late-autumn mountains on a steep stone path;
  family homes emerge through white clouds;
My carriage stops for I enjoy admiring maple trees in the evening;
  the frosted leaves are redder than February flowers

山行 | 唐 | 杜牧
遠上寒山石徑斜,
白雲生處有人家,
停車坐愛楓林晚,
霜葉紅於二月花

   It is not clear if Du Mu has somewhere to go, or is simply traveling aimlessly for the sake of it. Either way he takes the time to stop and admire the fall scenery, finding its beauty comparable and even exceeding the colors of spring on the other side of winter.

   During the Ming dynasty, artist Qiu Ying (仇英) painted *Waiting for the Ferry on an Autumn River* (秋江待渡). This painting depicts a broad riverscape surrounded by high mountains. A scholar sits on the bank on the left side and fishermen work from a dinghy on the other, close to a small house near the shore, all dwarfed by the outlines of nature towering above. The green-gray toned vista is dotted with red trees, indicating the arrival of deep fall.

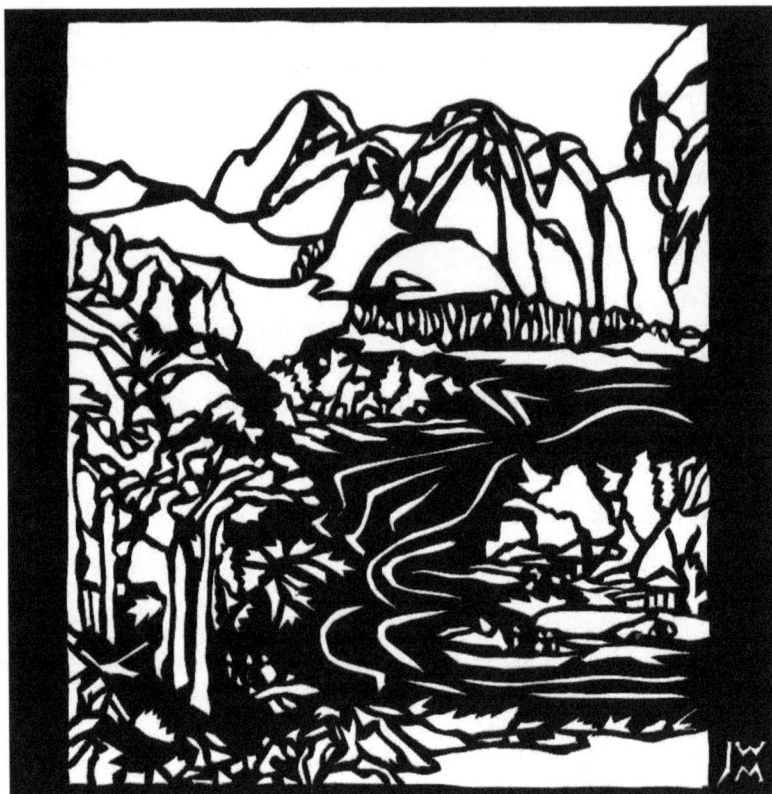

Sima Gong (司馬公) advocated the liberal planting of maple and Chinese tallow trees in youth so that when one is old, at the times frost covers the rivers, a vibrant red will adorn the mountains and sky.[23]

CHRYSANTHEMUMS

As during Cold Dew, chrysanthemums are a reemerging theme in Frost Fall. In addition to going out to appreciate the flowers, the devout place chrysanthemums on a table, in a courtyard, or in front of their home, along with offering of food and wine. They then bow to the Chrysanthemum Gods. Festive eating and drinking followed the formalities, along with admiring the flowers. In Beijing, flower festivals were held at Tianning Pavilion (天寧寺) and Taoran Tower (陶然亭),[24][25] the latter acquiring its name from the Tang dynasty poet Bai

Juyi (白居易): "Wait till the chrysanthemums are yellow and home-made wine is ripe; I'll drink with you and be carefree."(更待菊黄家釀熟，共君一醉一陶然).

PERSIMMONS

No fruit better captures the spirit of Frost Fall and the late fall like the persimmon. The fruit reaches a peak of red after the first frost and their peak of taste during Frost Fall.[26] In Chinese culture they have many positive associations, namely joy and longevity.[27] The word *shi* (柿) is a homonym with the word for "matters" (事), so they are connected with matters going according to one's wishes (事事如意).[28] The fruit also looks like the head of a type of ancient scepter -- also called the ruyi (如意) -- an item symbolizing power and good fortune and carrying a rich array of connotations in Buddhism.[29]

According to volume ten of *The Erya Yi* (爾雅翼)[30] the fruit and its tree are said to be gifted with seven virtues:

1. Longevity, as the tree lives around 80 years (一多壽)
2. Providing good shade (二多陰)
3. Avoided by birds for nesting (三無鳥巢)
4. Resistance to pests and parasites (四無蟲蠹)
5. Frosted leaves that can be enjoyed (五霜葉可玩)
6. The tastiness of the fruit itself (六嘉實)
7. Leaves broad enough to write on (七落葉肥滑可以臨書)

It is this last quality above which made it especially popular among painters and the literati. *The New Book of Tang* (新唐書)[31] tells of Zheng Qian (鄭虔), a master painter, poet, and calligrapher beloved by literary giant Du Fu, who was an eager but poor student in his youth. He was fortunate to live near a temple which had rooms and rooms filled with persimmon leaves, all of which he exhausted to perfect his calligraphy, poetry, and painting skills. This led to the idiom "using persimmon leaves to study" (柿葉學書), meaning committing to a grueling project of study until it is learned.[32]

One of the most famous zen paintings takes persimmons as its subject: *Six Persimmons* (六柿圖) by the 13th-century monk Muqi (牧谿). Best embodying the spontaneous style of this school of art, and described by Arthur Waley as "passion...congealed into a stupendous calm,"[33] the painting displays all the aesthetic and moral ideals of zen painting first described by Shin'ichi Hisamatsu (九 松 真 一): asymmetry, simplicity, lofty dryness, naturalness, subtle profundity, freedom from attachment, and tranquility.[34] The painting depicts six persimmons in black ink, seemingly floating in space against a white background, each fruit a different shade. The brushstrokes, such as the way the stems are shown angled in a style reminiscent of Chinese calligraphy, are said to be a peak of technique for the genre. [35]

Within paintings, the persimmon's appearance with other fruits connote different positive meanings, often appearing with other auspicious fruits like peaches and apples. Like other seasonal produce there are a large set of curative properties assigned to the persimmon. According to the *Manual for Gastronomy* from the Suixi Studio (隨息居飲食譜) when dried in the sun the fruit cleans the spleen, fortifies the stomach, moisturizes the lungs, treats diarrhea, stops bleeding, satisfies hunger, and cures various other diseases. [36]

That said, there are a vast array of terrifying prohibitions around the fruit, particularly its more freshly-picked version, which Chinese medicine attributes to be "cold" and can cause complications depending on other foods with which it is paired. Eating persimmons with sweet potatoes, spinach, acidic vegetables, foods high in calcium or protein-rich seafood like crab, fish, and shrimp are said to cause calcified growths in the body. Combining persimmons with white wine, potatoes, or seaweed causes heartburn and indigestion. Crabs, along with goose meat, are said to cause stomach pains, diarrhea, and vomiting when eaten with this fall fruit. [37] [38]

The above is a long, somewhat anxiety-producing list, but for those careful to note what they are eating alongside the fruit, there is nothing quite like the taste of in-season persimmons. And fittingly for this time of year, with its positive attributions and warning of mortal danger, folklore around the fruit combines the contradictory ideas of longevity and death, the core themes of the Chinese autumn season.

Festivals

Aside from the various ways Frost Fall is enjoyed among the Chinese Han majority through its manifestation in nature with red foliage, chrysanthemums, and persimmons, the solar term is not otherwise celebrated and brackets no major festivals. But as with many of the solar terms, the arrival of Frost Fall is an opportunity for minority cultures such as the Zhuang people to celebrate the Frost Fall Festival (霜降節).

The festival's most colorful celebration occurs in Xialeiwei (下雷圩) in Daxin County, Guangxi Province. Around October 23rd, people gather to celebrate the harvest, worship the gods, and enjoy time with friends and family. One of the major activities is making "Welcoming Frost" rice dumplings (迎霜粽), and the general atmosphere is similar to the Spring Festival for the Han, with lots of drinking, eating, singing, and shopping.

In the past the event was held over three days: the day before Frost Fall, called "First Fall" (頭降), the day of, called "Proper Fall" (正降), followed by "Ending Fall" (尾降). Here the Chinese word uses the "fall" as in descent rather than "autumn."

The ox is the center of activity for First Fall. Respect is shown to the ox by feeding it well, washing it, and adorning his horns with red ribbons. The feeding of the ox is said to "open fall" (開降). The ox must be allowed to rest and cannot be used for labor, let alone whipped. If the ox happens to die during this time, it is buried with full honors, and certainly not eaten. The Yi minority as well have a prohibition against allowing oxen into the fields on this day.

Proper Fall is a day of prayer and devotions. Meat, wine, rice dumplings, and cakes are offered to a golden statue of the Oxen Antie, or Yamo (婭莫), to which many come to pray for good fortune. Men dress up as warriors, carrying banners and beating drums, parading the portrait of the Oxen Antie around the town. When it stops in front of a home, firecrackers are lit.

"Ending Fall" is the climax of festivities, accompanied by a maelstrom of fireworks, sports, singing duets, puppetry, and dragon and lion dances. It is often a favorite time of the year for young men and women of these ethnic groups.[39] [40]

Folklore

OXEN AUNTIE

The word ya (婭) in the Zhuang language means a middle aged woman, and the word mo (莫) is the Mandarin phonetic used for the local language term for "ox." The heroine Cen Yuyin (岑玉音) was given her nickname after her exploits in defending the tribes against

Japanese pirates (倭寇) during the turmoil around the end of the Ming and beginning of the Qing dynasty.

During this time Japanese pirates were a scourge terrorizing and pillaging the southern coast of China and coastal communities throughout Southeast Asia. Concerned about the pirates' unchecked plundering, Cen Yuyin went off with her husband, Xu Wenying (許文英) to fight them off.

Cen Yuyin was a warrior woman from the Zhuang tribe, said to be as tall and muscular as a man, and excelled at horseback archery. She set out to the coastal provinces on the back of an ox, and rounding up soldiers from Guangdong and Fujian, she took the fight to the Japanese pirates. A superior military strategist, she lead the vanguard in many battles, finally defeating the pirates and freeing the people of the coast from their years of constant harassment.

She returned home triumphant. The Qing emperor was grateful, and wanted to festoon her with honors and titles. She refused, and returned to her tribe to continue working the fields as she had done before the war. Thereafter, the Qing dynasty mandated a three-day festival in honor of the Oxen Antie who had little need for honors and rewards, and simply desired to end the suffering of the people.

This tale reflects one other aspect bound to the death aspect of fall: war. Even in times of peace, the fall is a time for military parades and displays of martial prowess to assuage or curry favor with the murderous energies of the season. Even to this day, national military parades are held at end of autumn. For as much as war is an affirmation of death, the military is an affirmation of life and longevity of the nation, and preparation for the inevitable hardship embodied by winter.[41][42]

CHAPTER 19: WINTER BEGINS 立冬

立冬 / 입동/립동 / りっとう / Lập đông
Pinyin: lìdōng
Literal Meaning: "Establishes winter"
Alternative names: Winter Commences
Period: November 6 or 7 ~ November 21 or 22
Sun's Ecliptic Longitude: 225°

The Winter-Begins Routine

Lu You
Song Dynasty

A hovel so small it can barely fit my knees,
*   walls so low they can hardly clear a shoulder.*
The autumn break has passed,
*   and already it's time to wear furs.*
A pile of coal measured in inches,
*   a smidgeon of cotton for my clothes.*
Living all one's life in a humble alley,
*   one can be happy anywhere.*

立冬日作 | 宋 | 陸游

室小才容膝，牆低僅及肩。
方過授衣月，又遇始裘天。
寸積籌爐炭，銖稱布被綿。
平生師陋巷，隨處一欣然。

The word *li* (立) means beginning, and the word *dong* (冬) in its older meaning connotes conclusion and ending.[1] Thus this solar term is the beginning of the final segment of the cycle of the year before the arrival of spring.

In many places the feeling of winter has not quite arrived, and the day of Winter Begins can be bright and sunny, carrying the crispness of late fall. Perhaps the land and streams are choked with dead leaves, some still blown about in the wind and others wet, matted in piles on the ground. But the active quality of spring and summer is certainly long gone, and the romantic, moon-lit air of autumn has departed. The names of the solar terms, however weakly they describe what we see in the weather around us, are often a prelude, reminding us of the slow, inevitable arrival of a new season. Once the final leaves blow away, the air becomes as crisp as mint, and even chiller airs soon arrive. [2]

Winter Begins is a time of increasing quiet, concealment, rest, and storage. The fields return to an untended, wild state. Fish go deeper where the ice has not yet frozen, and animals rest in their dens and burrows. All beings collect and hoard the fruits sown in the spring, grown in summer, and harvested in the fall. The earth's energies are said to draw in and slumber as well, awaiting for another rebirth in spring.

Pentads

Water begins to freeze (水始冰)

Ground begins to harden (地始凍)

Pheasants enter the water and become mollusks (雉入大水為蜃)

In the phrase "water begins to freeze" the word "begins" is key here, and reflects both the quality of beginning in Winter Begins and the reality that the most intense cold is yet to come. At this time of year the surface level of lakes and ponds freeze over while the lower levels remain fluid.

Cold ethers start the process of freezing and hardening the ground. Up to this point, the freezing was mostly a temporary morning frost, but at this time of year the top layer is hard throughout the day.[3]

The final enigmatic pentad once again reflects the withdrawal of yang as represented by the pheasant, and the advance of yin symbolized by what has been translated here as "mollusk." The word *shan* (蜃) is an ancient word with numerous meanings. One meaning describes a giant clam,[4] with the coloring and pattern of a pheasant on its shell.[5] The *shan* can be anything from a real-life giant mollusk to a more mythical being. The mythical version of the clam is said to produce ethers that form sea mirages,[67] known in English as the "Fata Morgana," or "The Fairy Morgana," referring to Morgan Le Fey of Arthurian legend.

Fata Morgana are formed by distortions of rays of light when they pass through layers of air with different temperatures. Depending on whether the light is reflecting a coastal town, a rock, or even another small craft, from a distance the mirage looks eerily like a large phantom building inexplicably floating on the horizon.[8] Early sailors in the West believed these mysterious fairy castles -- which would appear and quickly disappear and could never be reached -- were the product of Morgan Le Fey's witchcraft to lure sailors to their deaths.[9] Morgan Le Fey, also called the Mistress of the Fairies of the Salt Sea, has a long association with the Sirens.[10]

In Chinese legend the mirage was given similarly otherworldly provenance, and believed to be the palace of the Sea God (海神). In *Sea Mirages at Dengzhou* (登州海市) by Su Shi (蘇軾), otherwise known as Su Dongpo (蘇東坡), the poet describes an answered prayer to the Sea God, asking the god to reveal a mirage for him, even though it was winter rather than spring or summer,[11] when such mirages usually occur. Throughout the poem, Su describes a cosmos where Heaven, rather than an arbiter of misfortune and destruction as is so often the case in Chinese mythology, is far removed from the affairs of humanity, granting wishes out of occasional pity rather than a desire to shape the events of the world. Meanwhile, it is not the gods but humanity who is the cause of all the world's troubles.[12]

One might wonder why an optical phenomenon appearing during warmer weather is mentioned in pentad at the start of winter. The traditional explanation of these mirages was a release of qi which later accompanies the opening and flourishing of the world in the spring and summer seasons. Winter, meanwhile, connected to closure and storage conserves the vestiges of qi. This is represented by the mythical pheasant, as it descends into the sea, where it starts its new life, safe and enclosed in the deep, sleeping soundly in a shell. It is also now of water, matching the particular phase with which winter corresponds in the five phases system.

Agriculture

Although the daylight is shorter, the temperatures which keep the ground frozen have not arrived, and the residual heat in the earth combined with clear skies and a soft wind can stir up a "Little Spring" (小陽春)[13]. These conditions can be good for crop growth.

A good time to water crops is when the ground is close to freezing at night. Water is scarcer this time of year, so watering nourishes the crops while protecting their roots from freezing damage.[14] Good drainage is required to avoid pools freezing over. Farms in the north are still riding out the winter, but in the south farmers are harvesting the wheat grown as part of the "third autumn." A saying goes "vegetables not picked in Winter Begins will succumb to frost" (立冬不拔菜，終究受霜害),[15] indicating how quickly the weather will be changing in forthcoming weeks.

If temperatures fall below 15°C (59°F), crops like red potatoes will stop growing, and will need to be harvested and stored. Foresters need to keep an eye on fires, as the dryness and winds of the season can kick off destructive blazes despite the cold.

On the day of Winter Begins, farmers in Hebei and Shandong do not want to feel a wind from the southeast blowing. If so, the next harvest will be bad. In Sichuan, if the skies are clear rather than cloudy and rainy, it means the family ox and horse won't be hurt by the cold. In Hunan, Zhejiang, and Jiangxi, a clear day on Winter Begins means it will be a clear-skied winter (立冬晴，一冬晴).[16] In Sichuan the situation is exactly the opposite (立冬有雨一冬晴), and rain will bring clearer skies during the winter months.[17] [18]

Health

The start of the change of seasons, particularly from fall to winter, are a critical time for fortifying the body to ensure strong immunity, metabolism, and the prevention of a "cold stomach" (胃寒).[19] It is a good time for increasing one's intake of carbohydrates, fats, protein, and foods high in calcium, iron, and vitamins. It's best to have foods considered hot or warm by Chinese medicine as they are especially good for the kidneys and build resistance to cold. Some traditions state raw, cold radish and fruit should be avoided on Winter Begins.

As with any fortifying, balance is the key. Overdoing it can cause more harm than good.[20] Those with inflammation, constipation, or serious medical conditions are better not eating fortifying foods at all, or if so only in very sparing, token amounts. Most of all, sleep is critical and necessary for any attempts at fortifying the body to be successful.

Different regions practice varying foodways to fortify the body. Southerners generally eat chicken, duck, lamb, and pork. In Taiwan people head out to restaurants to eat braised lamb or ginger duck, or stay at home and make stewed chicken soup with four Chinese medicinal herbs (四物雞).[21] The four herbs are *Paeonia lactiflora* (芍藥), *Rehmannia glutinosa* (地黃), *Angelica sinensis* (當歸), and *Ligusticum sinense* (川芎). More broadly in Minnan culture married women return to the family to give gifts of chicken, duck, pigs feet, and pork belly to fortify their parents' health and to express filial love.[22] In Chaozhou culture, it is the time to fortify with sugarcane, which is said to prevent toothaches when gnawed on this time of year (立冬食蔗，不會齒痛). Fragrant fried rice (炣香飯) -- made with lotus seeds, mushrooms, Chinese chestnuts, shrimp, and carrots -- is also a favorite seasonal dish among the Chaozhou people. [23][24]

Ancient Traditions

Winter Begins is not just solar term; it has been a traditional holiday among the Han people of China since the Zhou dynasty. The *Book of Rites* refers to the time as the first month of winter. Three days before first day of the term the Grand Recorder would announce the inauguration of winter, calling the character of the season as the arrival of the phase of water. Much like the first month of autumn, the emperor would devote time to fasting.

On the day of Winter Begins, he and his retinue would proceed to the north of the city, garbed in dark robes and black emerald, to greet the winter. The emperor would lead the assembled officials in praising the Land God as well as a deity known as the Black Emperor, Xuanwu (玄武大帝). The emperor would also wear furs at this point of the year to embody the spirit of the season, and signal to the empire that it was a time to greet and guard against the cold. Upon returning to the palace, the more benevolent rulers gifted their advisors leather jackets, or in some cases five-colored brocade coats.

The character of the time was a mix of the severe and the generous. Matching the drawn-up, hidden quality of winter, there is a preoccupation with deception. The Grand Recorder would smear tortoiseshells and divining stalks with blood, and use them to augur crimes and deceit. The use of the shells and stalks was to remove the effects of human bias so easily swayed by flattery and partisanship. The Chief Director of Works would also arrange the production of sacrificial vessels according to exacting measures and capacity. No "licentious ingenuity" was allowed, which might distract the mind. Every article was engraved with maker's name to certify its genuineness. In cases where works that were improperly made or counterfeited, the artificer would be held guilty and any deception would be met with a violent end.

At the same time it was a period of grand festivity. The Emperor would praise heaven to receive blessings for the coming year, with oxen, rams, and boars sacrificed to the spirits of the land at public altars and town gates. This was followed by banquets and drinking. On the third day of Winter Begins, the spoils of the chase were offered to ancestors and spirits of the home, hearth, soil, door, and pathways. Farmers were also encouraged to pause their toils and enjoy some rest.

Views of the natural realm were that the airs of heaven ascended on high while those of earth descended beneath, leaving no interplay between heaven and earth. Nature was shut closed, and winter completely formed. The Superintendent of Waters and the Master of Fishing went to collect the gifts of rivers, springs, ponds, and lakes. But were to do so without encroaching on the bounty belonging to the people. Doing otherwise would risk awakening feelings of discontent against the emperor. Any officer over-harvesting the waters to a degree that offends the people would be punished without forgiveness. The *Book of Rites* clearly acknowledges here the priority given to a certain ecological balance, not just to keep the waters teeming with life, but that to abuse the gifts of nature can have far-ranging consequences in the realm of human affairs, cascading from the populace right up to the stability of the emperor's rule.

In the human realm it was a time to continue paying attention to military matters, although softened with strains of generosity. The state was to demonstrate compassion to widows and orphans, especially those who lost husbands or fathers to war in service to the empire. Due to this custom the time of year became associated with the honor of martyrs, and like many of the autumn ceremonies was a time to prepare the public for the challenges of war and protection of the nation. Commanders were ordered to instruct the military, train soldiers in archery and chariot driving, and to hold trials of strength.

There was also frenetic activity to shore up anything symbolizing notions of storage, fixity, and containment. Food stores were examined, gates and walls repaired, nuts and bolts secured, locks and keys fixed, field boundaries strengthened, frontiers secured, mountain passes and bridges inspected, and byways and cross-paths closed. Similar care was taken in revising the rules and measures of funerary practices: mourning rituals were revised, dimensions of upper and lower garments defined, thickness of inner and outer coffins confirmed, as was the size and depth of graves. All these practices mirrored the limiting quality of the natural world, while also invoking limits against the deathly advance of winter which will arrive soon. One can see within these practices human attempts to exert control or gain balance against the seemingly chaotic and destructive advance of nature during its most destructive season.[25]

Customs

Among the common folk in ancient times it was time to welcome winter by praising the Land God and pickling freshly harvested vegetables to ensure enough food for the lean days ahead. Vestiges of these traditions live on in the food-ways of the people in Beijing who eat buckwheat noodles on this day with freshly pickled cabbage and radish or cucumbers mixed with sesame oil and vinegar. In Tianjin they eat dumplings. [26] As is the case with the traditional lunar new year, Winter Begins marks the change between autumn and winter, and since dumplings, jiaozi (餃子) are a homonym with "exchange" (交子之時), it is the time to celebrate the transition with food.[27] In Tianjin squash dumplings are popular. Usually this is made from squash picked in the summer and stored on the windowsill until Winter Begins. Squash cured in this way is said to be sweeter.[28]

Prior to the availability of indoor plumbing, "washing scabies" (掃疥) was a common tradition in Shanghai. In the past it was inconvenient to shower regularly in the winter. It wasn't just a simple matter of heating water and sponging down. Due to concerns in Chinese medicine around the body's vulnerability to cold, bathing needed to take place within a warm room. That meant collecting firewood and stoking the fire until large and hot enough to heat a bathroom as well as heating up large amounts of water soaked in chrysanthemums, honeysuckle, and vanilla. It was believed by washing in this way on Winter Begins, scabies and fleas would be less likely to infest one's body during the winter.[29]

Festivals

Winter Begins is one of the few solar terms that is a festival itself, although in modern times a small one mainly associated the consumption of fortifying foods for the change of seasons, as described above.

Folklore

THE BLACK EMPEROR

The Black Emperor (黑帝) appears in different Chinese traditions, and has different names and origin stories. In Taoism he is called the Emperor of the North (北帝), Xuandi (玄帝), True Martial Great Emperor (真武大帝). Mysterious (or Black) Martial Emperor or *Xuanwu Dadi* (玄武大帝), and Xuantian Shangdi (玄天上帝). The word *xuan* (玄) means both black and mysterious,[30] essentially something occluded, an appropriate moniker for a god that is so highly revered but about whom so little is known and characterized by conflicting origin stories.

He is a powerful god in the Taoist pantheon, and temples dedicated to him throughout China are only surpassed by the Land God, Goddess of Mercy Guanyin, and Guangong.[31] He is one of the five directional emperors of mythical history occupying the north and responsible for water and winter.[32]

Taoist traditions describe Xuantian Shangdi (玄天上帝) as a crown prince, sometimes mortal, sometimes superhuman, in either case achieving immortality after several decades of Taoist meditation in the mountains.

In one tale he is all too human, growing bored with his meditations and descending the mountain to see how the world has changed in his absence. He comes across an old woman sitting next to a well, grinding away on a thick iron bar. Curious, he asks what she is doing. She tells him she is making a needle. Perplexed, he asks her how long she expects to be at it before she's done. The old woman pauses, looks up at him, and says, "constant effort yields success." Realizing he was being chastised, the prince hikes back up into the mountains to continue his meditations until he becomes immortal.[33]

In even more ancient times the Black Emperor was said to be Zhuan Xu (顓頊), also known as Gaoyang (高陽), the grandson of the Yellow Emperor, the son of Changyi (昌意). [34]

Sources present conflicting stories about Zhuan Xu's parentage. The *Classic of Mountains and Seas* says he is the great-grandson of the Yellow Emperor, the grandson of Changyi (昌意) and the son produced from the coupling of the half-human, half-beast Hanliu (韓流) and Anü (阿女), also known as Daughter of the Mud People (淖子).[35] There are other versions as well. Whatever his lineage, his link back to the Yellow Emperor mark him as a powerful deity.

Songs of Chu (楚辭) by Qu Yuan state in early times he was something closer to a nature god or animal totem, associated with the tortoise or snake. The former is the animal guardian of the north, an animal often playing a role in disaster myths. The latter, the snake, is connected to water and river gods like its cousin, the dragon.[36]

The Black Emperor also has a lead role in early myths, ordering Zhong (重) and Li (黎) to separate heaven and earth. [37] Rather than the Pangu myth of separating dark and bright, heavy and light out of chaos to form the world, the emphasis on the Black Emperor's project was concerned with the ordering of the planes of existence, separating heaven and earth to prevent humans from ascending the sky and deities from frequently descending to earth.

He also said to have arranged the position of the sun and stars, and defeated and executed the Water God Gong Gong, the deity that commits so much havoc throughout China's mythology. [38] The Black Emperor is therefore prayed to for the control of floods, [39] and given his association with water, the control of fires.[40] In some traditions he is so exalted as to be credited as the progenitor of humanity.

With this sense of power comes darker aspects as well. The book *In Search of the Supernatural* (搜神記) says Zhuan Xu had three sons who transformed into ghosts of pestilence: the malaria ghost (瘧鬼), the goblin ghost (魍魎鬼), and the child ghost (小鬼).[41]

The Black Emperor embodies a rich mix of traits: protection from the destructive powers of nature, particularly floods, fire, and illnesses; participation in the ordering of the material and spiritual planes, and a representation of the difficult work required for spiritual attainment and reconnecting the material and spiritual in the self.

WINTER GOD

The Winter God (冬神), also called Xuan Ming (玄冥) -- literally "mysterious dark" -- is also connected to the Black Emperor. [42] In addition to representing the season of winter, he is considered the God of the North Wind (北風之神) as well as God of the Sea (海神). In the *Classic of Mountains and Seas* he is described as having a bird's body and a human face, along with azure snakes adoring his ears and two red snakes under his feet.[43] Some sources say he rides two dragons. [44]

Li Bai described winter and the role of the Winter God in bringing snow to the land:

Great Hunt Rhapsody
Li Bai
Tang Dynasty

Winter is severe, miserable and piercing,
*   chilling ethers of biting cold;*
Upon the Northwest Wind,
*   the Winter God wields the snow.*

Plants shed their leaves,
*   grasses loosen their joints;*
Caves encase shaded cold air,
*   the well of fire is frozen shut.*

大獵賦 | 唐 | 李白

若乃嚴冬慘切，寒氣凜冽，
不周來風，玄冥掌雪。
木脫葉，草解節，
土囊煙陰，火井冰閉。

Li Bai's poem describes that once winter arrives, the Winter God rules the affairs of the world. It is a time when the crisp cool autumn gives way to a severe northwest wind, the god of the frigid watery depths blowing snowflakes across the land. The wilds turn to ice, hail falls from the sky, earth hardens with frost; plants, roads, and buildings become shrouded in crystal, silver, and white.

CHAPTER 20: LIGHT SNOW 小雪

小雪 / 소설 / しょうせつ / Tiểu tuyết

Pinyin: xiǎoxuě

Literal Meaning: "Little Snow"

Alternative names: Snows a bit

Period: November 21 or 22 ~ December 6 or 7

Sun's Ecliptic Longitude: 240°

Surprise Snow
Lu Chang
Tang Dynasty

Why does the north wind blow with such urgency?
  The front yard is as bright as the moon.
Denizens of the heavens are so skilled,
  cutting snowflakes out of water to fill the sky.

驚雪 | 唐 | 陸暢
怪得北風急，前庭如月輝。
天人寧許巧，剪水作花飛。

A dark gray sky sits atop a land shrouded in a chilly haze as temperatures continue to drop. The spring is a time of green. Summer is the domain of flowers. The moon rules autumn, and the winter is of course the time of snow. According to the pentads, rainfall at this time of year thins due to cold ethers coalescing into the snow that will soon cover the land. Within the name of this solar term, the word "light" of "Light Snow" might be more accurately translated as "small," indicating the full bloom of winter is still a ways off.

Temperatures in Northern China have dropped well below freezing, while the first dusting of snow appears along the Yellow River. Unless a warm front moves in, carrying moist air, in which case a massive snowfall might occur. Southern China might be wintry, but will only see five days or so of snow; snow does not typically stick because the ground temperature is usually above freezing. Sleet and even snow pellets are common, however.[1]

Painters have also worked to capture the mood of the solar term. [2] *Mountain Pheasant in a Snowy Winter* (寒雪山雞圖) by Lü Ji (呂紀) shows a pheasant on a snow-covered stone, feathers ruffled against the cold. The sky is white, snow covers branches, leaves, and rocks -- all is white with freshly fallen snow.

Pentads

Rainbows hide and are unseen (虹藏不見)
Heaven's ether ascends, Earth's ether descends (天氣上騰，地氣下降)
All is closed up and winter formed (閉塞而成冬)

There is a clear meteorological explanation for the lack of rainbows this time of year: the absence of sun and the decrease in rain. In terms of Chinese metaphysics, rainbows form during the ascendance of yang over yin, which occurs during the spring and summer. Rainbows are therefore absent as the yang yields to the advance of yin during winter.[3]

The symbolism of rainbows in Chinese culture is complex, embodying a mixture of good and bad omens. It can either portend romantic love and pregnancy, or infidelity as one partner seeks out new pastures.[4] In both senses it involves the intermixing of yang and yin energies and the creative principle. While spring represents creation, summer symbolizes growth, and autumn symbolizes death and immortality, winter embodies the principles of inaction, or "non-creation" and a time of quiet rest. The winter is not a time of intermixing; therefore, no rainbows appear during this time.

The second pentad aligns with the creation myth presented in an earlier chapter: the separation of ethers by Pangu, where the inhabitable universe is formed by ascendance of lighter yang ethers, and the descent of heavier yin ethers, creating order out of chaos. On the surface this would seem to be a paradox: if winter is the time of non-creation and non-action, how can this theme be connected to the idea of creation of the universe? The paradox is solved by the balanced nature of yin-yang cosmology as well as the cyclical turning of the seasons of the year. The world cannot have infinite co-mingling, a perpetual spring and summer of non-stop birth and growth. Unchecked growth and creation would spin the universe back into a state of chaos. In winter the lighter heavenly ethers move up, and the heavier earth ethers move down, reestablishing order so that they regenerate and come back together at a future time to intermix for a new cycle of growth.

The final pentad reflects the dual meaning of "winter" (冬) in Chinese, which means both the season as well as "end," in this case nearing the end of the year. The final pentad, also evokes the idea of rest and inaction, the earth sealed off and asleep for the winter.

Agriculture

For farmers, snowfall on the day of Light Snow is critical. A saying goes that a Light Snow without snow means there will be no need to hire farm laborers next year (小雪不見雪，來年長工歇). Another states "snow filling the sky during Light Snow guarantees a great harvest" (小雪雪滿天，來歲必豐年).[5] Both of these sayings show that snow is not just tolerated, but dearly welcome, since the cold is said to kill locust eggs.

318

This is the time of harvesting cabbage. The crop will not be watered for up to ten days before harvesting to prevent freeze damage. It is picked on a clear day, set out in the sun, root side up, for three or four days. Finally, it is placed root-side down and covered with leaves or corn stalks to insulate the heads from the cold.

In the south, it is a key time for planting wheat, this activity usually completed three to five days later. Lower temperatures and less daylight are ideal conditions for sprouting wheat seeds. Moreover these liminal times of the year between seasons are a good time to take advantage of fast-growing crops like wheat and barley, which will mature in time and not interfere with the planting cycle of other crops later in spring. [6]

In the north, the saying goes that "the ground is sealed at Light Snow, and the rivers are sealed during Heavy Snow" (小雪封地，大雪封河).[7] Although the ground is off limits, orchardists are busy pruning fruit trees to protect them against cold.[8]

Health

Constant gray skies and lack of daylight can create dark moods. This is a time to find ways to manage one's emotional state and control one's temper. Participating in outdoor activities can help and for the frail or those who can't take the cold, music can help.[9] [10]

Customs

Pickling vegetables has already started in Beijing in Winter Begins. Light Snow is the time for same activity south of the Yangtze.[11] [12]

In Suzhou and Nanjing, due to the relative dryness this period, Light Snow is an ideal time to make sausage, ensuring it will cure in time for the Lunar New Year. In the more southern provinces, glutinous rice was offered to the Ox god in earlier times. Nowadays, it is simply eaten without any religious fanfare.[13] It is also used to ferment spirits, a particular spirit called 10th Month White (十月白), as spirits fermented during the tenth lunar month are said to taste particularly good. "Three-White Wine" (三白酒) is also produced at this time of year, the "three whites" referring to rice, flour, and water. These spirits are imbibed as much for enjoyment with friends are they are for health reasons. [14] Three-White Wine is said to be especially good for treating an upset stomach.[15]

But cozying up at home, away from the chill of winter, was as good a motivation as any for drinking booze, as described by poet Bai Juyi.

An Invitation to Mr. Liu Shijiu
Bai Juyi
Tang Dynasty

Green trub bubbles up from a fresh bottle of wine,
   warmed on a red earthen stove.
It's getting late and snow is coming;
   why don't you come here for a drink?

問劉十九 | 唐 | 白居易
綠螘新醅酒
紅泥小火爐
晚來天欲雪
能飲一杯無

Festivals

XIAYUAN FESTIVAL

Earlier festivals like the Lantern Festival, also called Shangyuan Festival (上元節) along with the Zhongyuan Festival (中元節), are the more widely known and celebrated of the three observances throughout the year which ends with the lesser known Xiayuan Festival (下元節). All three are Taoist holidays, and could be roughly translated as the Year-Beginning, Mid-Year, and Year-End festivals due to their observance on the fifteenth days of the first, seventh, and tenth lunar months. Folk customs around the Xiayuan Festival have fallen out of practice, and where it is celebrated at all, carries a more specifically religious Taoist flavor than the first two festivals, which are observed more broadly within the culture.

The three festivals celebrate what could be translated as the Three Officials. The Heavenly (or Sky) Official (天官) for Shangyuan, the Land Official (地官) for Zhongyuan, and the Water Official (水官) for Xiayuan. There are many different descriptions of the deities occupying these ranks. One is that it is the tri-part expression of the Primeval Lord of Heaven (元始天尊).[16] Some traditions say it is one of the Pure Ones (三清),[17] the Heavenly Lord of Dao and its Virtue (道德天尊),[18] also known as Taishang Laojun (太上老君).

Another assumes the ranks are respectively occupied by China's mythological sage-kings: Yao, Shun, and Yu.[19] This attribution matches aspects of their roles in mythology. Yao was the first benevolent, moral ruler and the initiator of China's understanding of celestial phenomena. In other words, that which is above in the heavens. Shun is credited with bringing order to the land with sacrifices to the hills and rivers, the setting of uniform measurements, and reinforcement of ceremonial laws. Yu the Great delivered humanity from the deluge of destructive floods. There are other gods occupying the roles as well, but common folklore usually casts Yu in the position of the Water Official.

Regardless of the personage occupying these roles, and aside from the tendency for Chinese Taoism to envision the pantheon of deities as operating within a heavenly bureaucracy, these "officials" are in the end conceived more as key realms which structure the universe in Taoist cosmology: heaven, earth, and water -- a three part structure shared with other spiritual traditions.

Those observing the three-festival cycle are seeking a different outcome from each realm. Shangyuan was a time to seek good fortune from the heavens; Zhongyuan was for appealing to the earth and the underworld for forgiveness; Xiayuan is an opportunity to ask for protection. [20]

Traditionally there were a set of careful practices. As is typical for any form of worship, and altar was set up to the Water Official and prayed to for deliverance from harm or calamity.[21] Matters concerning physical and mental hygiene were strict: no meat or alcohol could be consumed leading up to the ritual. One had to bathe beforehand, and wear a freshly laundered set of clothes. Just as important was one's frame of mind. Observance had to be approached with a sincere attitude, emotions needed to be controlled, and the mind ordered into a state of peace and calm.[22]

Over time, observances were simplified to the laying out of sacrifices and praying to the ancestors and departed. No matter how the ritual procedures changed, the aspect of maintaining a calm and peaceful mind and reigning in one's emotions is just as appropriate for facing calamity as it is for dealing with the lower mood that can occur at this darkening time of the year.

Folklore

THE AZURE LADY

The Azure Lady (青女) first appeared in the *Huainanzi* (淮南子), where she is described as a sky goddess controlling frost and snow,[23] and was immortalized in the earlier poem, "Frost Moon," by Tang poet Li Shang-yin.[24]

Li's poem points to the Azure Lady as the bringer of cold, symbolizing grace, beauty, and fortitude amidst hardship. The poem also hints at the distance of the goddess, sitting high in the frigid skies above the world, basked in moonlight.

The origin legend of the Azure Lady starts not with her, but with another goddess: Wu Luo (武羅).[25] [26] Wu Luo was made a goddess by the Jade Emperor and put in charge of a certain area of the earth. She was bright and warm deity who cared deeply for the people populating her corner of the world. However, years of war had only just ended, leaving farms in tatters and rivers polluted with blood. There were no seasons, and the world was consumed in perpetual heat. Diseases were rampant and the people of the world suffered miserably.

Witnessing the plight of the people, Wu Luo flew to the moon to ask the occupant of the Cold Palace (廣寒宮) -- the Azure Lady -- to bring down frost and snow to purify the world and put and end to the plague. The Azure Lady was the sister of Wu Gang (吳剛), the Sisyphean deity punished to an eternity of chopping down the self-healing osmanthus tree. She was originally called Wu Jie (吳潔), which translates as "Clean." Responsible for frost and snow, she was known among the court of the Heavenly Palace as the "Cold Beauty."

She was uninterested in helping, but after persuasion by Wu Gang and Wu Luo she descended to the world on the 14th day of the ninth month. She landed on Qingyao Mountain (青要山) and strummed her seven-string zither. The notes rang out in all four directions, and snow began to fall, covering the world in pure white. The unclean things withdrew and the pestilence ended.

Every year thereafter, the Azure Lady would descend to earth on the ninth month of the lunar year to create frost, doing the same on the twelfth month to produce snow, and again in the third month until she is driven totally away by Great Heat in the sixth month. Thereafter, there four seasons were set, and the world was delivered from the oppressive heat which baked the earth.

Wu Luo built the Pavilion of Cold Purity on Qingyao Mountain in her honor, giving the Azure Lady a place to stay when she descended to the earth as well as to commemorate her service to humankind. The building was located near a spring called the Spring of Jade Purity (玉潔泉), and according to local legend, she bathes there before she strums her zither, ensuring the falling snow is pure and clean.[27][28][29][30]

The legend of the Azure Lady points to necessity of winter in the cycle of the year: a time for rest and a time for the world to be purified by cold and ice.

CHAPTER 21: HEAVY SNOW 大雪

大雪 / 대설 / たいせつ / Đại tuyết

Pinyin: xiǎoxuě
Literal Meaning: "Little Snow"
Alternative names: Snows a bit
Period: December 6 or 7 ~ December 21 or 22
Sun's Ecliptic Longitude: 255°

325

Night Snow
Bai Juyi
Tang Dynasty

Surprised by the chill of my bedding,
   I once again squint at the bright window.
So deep into the night, I know the snow is heavy,
   when I hear the sound of snapping bamboo.

夜雪 | 唐 | 白居易
已訝衾枕冷，復見窗戶明。
夜深知雪重，時聞折竹聲

In northern areas temperatures are well below freezing and the world is covered in a thick blanket of white; hence, the name Heavy Snow for this solar term. All the creatures that crawl have long since burrowed deep into the earth, every trace of them gone. Those that fly or walk the earth have found places to evade the cold. In Shandong there is a saying to describe the deadly fate of those who are not equipped to handle the cold: "When the snow flies, when the snow flies, it's like Heaven murdering with falling knives" (白雪飄，白雪飄，老天下的殺人刀).[1]

Bai Juyi, the poet who so famously invited a friend in the warmth of a home to enjoy some wine, wrote the poem which begins this chapter. Even tucked safely away at home, he lies sleepless as the cold invades his covers and the window glows with the light reflected by the snow. The sound-absorbing quality of the snow amplifies the deafening silence, broken occasionally by the startling sound of snapping branches.

Evening Snow and Winter Birds (暮雪寒禽) by Ma Lin (馬麟) depicts a similar scene of early winter, with dried bamboo covered by a dusting of snow and two birds huddled on a crooked branch. [2]

Both Bai in his room and Ma in his painting capture the still beauty of the term. Song dynasty poet Bai Yuchan describes a drearier picture.

Snowy Window
Bai Yuchan
Song Dynasty

The weak lamp on the stark wall darkens,
*   the flame in the red stove glows deep in the night.*
White snow outside the window,
*   is as pure as my integrity.*

雪窗 | 宋 | 白玉蟾
素壁青燈暗，紅爐夜火深。
雪花窗外白，一片歲寒心。

The poem is rendered even more melancholy given that the phrase speaking of his pure integrity seems contains the words sounding akin to "chilled heart" (寒心) and relates to the ideas of disappointment.

Another nursery rhyme from Sichuan describes the inescapable cold.

Sichuan Nursery Rhyme

Snow spouts and spits from the sky above,
  falling on the crops like a white quilt.
It falls so much the sparrows fly into enter the house,
  black dogs run all over the hills,
Chicks sit in the corner of the room,
  naked children help their mothers tend the fire.

四川童謠
噴噴雪,滿天落
落得青菜穿白袍
落得麻雀飛進屋
黑狗滿山跑
小雞蹲屋角
娃兒沒衣服
跟着媽媽,守火格篼

Yet for all the season's discomforts, it has its pleasures. As hinted in the final line of the nursery rhyme, this solar term is a time to withdraw into the home and light a fire. It is a time when idleness is permitted, even encouraged; a time to spend with family and friends, drinking tea or wine, and enjoying leisure of watching the snow fall outside. Once everyone is nice and warm, and the snow has stopped falling, it's time to enjoy the white-filled landscape.

The *Ancient Matters of Wulin Garden*, also called the *Wulin Jiushi* (武林舊事), a description of the city of Lin'an (臨安) during the Song Dynasty, now modern day Hangzhou, describes how women of the palace enjoyed playing in the snow, decorating snow lions, and lighting lanterns.[3] But nowhere in the China's prose literature are the diversions of snow better captured than in the Ming dynasty novel *The Golden Lotus* (金瓶梅), considered one of China's great novels.

The Golden Lotus
Chapter 21
Lanling Xiaoxiao Sheng
Ming Dynasty
Translated by Clement Egerton, 1939

Yueniang had wine and food set before him and soon the whole family was enjoying a very merry time. Through the window Ximen Qing looked out upon the snow. It was as white as cotton wool and the falling flakes seemed like the whirling petals of the pear blossom. It was a very beautiful sight.

Snow like tender willow seeds
Snow like down from a goose's back
Falling softly with no more sound
Than a crab that creeps over the sand.
Piling up mountains of powdered jade
And dressing wayfarers with glittering spangles
Till they look like bees covered with pollen
And the palaces are covered deep.

The snowflakes whirl like a dragon of jade
Tossing his scales high in the air
The white powder scatters like the feathers
That fall from a stork
The lofty mansions are a mass of ice.
So cold is it that the body tingles

The earth shines like a silver ocean
And the flame of the candle seems like a flower upon it.

Yueniang noticed that the snow lay deep upon the mound in the garden. She sent a maid for a teapot and herself put snow in it, and, from the snow, made boiling water with which she made the most fragrant tea for all of them.

This poem from *The Golden Lotus* is a more glowing description of the wonders of snow and this time of year, and the making of tea from fallen snow shows just how earlier generations whiled away the time and made sure to enjoy the natural elements around them.

Pentads

Flying squirrels are silent　(鶡旦不鳴)
Tigers begin to pair (虎始交)
Milky iris sprouts　(荔挺出)

The pentad referring to flying squirrels uses the word "bird," something akin to a crossbill or a nightingale.[4] But the popular folklore states it refers to the flying squirrel. Their fur is said to fall off in winter, and the weather is so cold by Heavy Snow that they are unable to even emit their calls.[5] The Ming dynasty text *Leijingtuyi* (類經圖翼) states that flying squirrels are of yin, and seek yang energy. At the first inkling of yang, they are silent while it begins to manifest.[6]

Tigers are yang, and at the first stirrings of yang energies, they mate[7] to produce the cubs who will be born in the spring.

There are different possible translations of the milky iris named in the third pentad. James Legge translated the word as broom-sedge.[8] It is sometimes described as a kind of Eupatorium fortunei (蘭草的一種),[9] and older texts refer to what would be called milky iris in the U.S., or white flowered iris in the U.K. (馬藺).[10] Regardless, the plant is a variety first sprouting once the first yang energies start to advance, similar to snowdrops (galanthus) in Western countries, although appearing earlier in the season.

All three pentads describe the rise of yang energies, which might seem odd before the world has even entered the depth of winter at the solstice. But as in earlier parts of the year, the energies which will build to the next high peak on the other side of the year start early.

Agriculture

Ground covered thick with snow on the first day of Heavy Snow is a welcome sight, and the phenomenon is accompanied by the usual sayings: "a winter without snow means ungrown wheat" (冬無雪，麥不結)[11] and "heavy snowfall portends a rich harvest; no snow brings calamity" (大雪兆豐年，無雪要遭殃).[12] Snow keeps the ground warmer and insulates the crops from temperature fluctuations[13]. More snow also means a longer time until thaw so that farmers do not need to worry about the onset of an early spring. As in Light Snow, snow also means fewer pests in the growing season.

In China, the northwest is lower than -10°C (14°F). In the Yellow River valley, winter wheat no longer grows. In most cases a thick blanket of snow protects the fields, but if there is not enough snow, farmers will douse the wheat in water once or twice to improve its resistance to cold. Snow also contains more nitrogen than rain, so it fertilizes the field as it melts.[14]

In the east, wheat and rapeseed grow, albeit slowly. The crops are usually helped along with fertilizer and winterizing, such as clearing irrigation channels so that ice doesn't form and covering the crops. In the south and southwest, wheat enters the tillering phase, so ventilation is important to avoid rot. Temperatures as close to possible to freezing are ideal, but too far below freezing and the crops are destroyed. This is also the time to prep livestock to help them ride out the winter. [15]In the very deep south crops can still be planted, but just a bit farther north the harvest has already been taken in and the fields are at rest.[16]

331

Health

To accord with the rhythms of the season it is best to follow the example of the myriad things, which have withdrawn into hiding. Stay warm, keeping skin moisturized due to the dryness of the season combined with the drying effects of indoor heat. Layers are important to avoid overheating, which can open up the pores and result in the loss of yang energy. Getting to bed early and rising early is preferred, and during sleep heavier bedding is ideal to keep the blood flowing to all the limbs, helping to prevent blood clots and colds. Those with high blood pressure, high cholesterol, or diabetes need to watch out for stroke. In places where outdoor air quality is poor, it is best to avoid exercising in morning fog.[17] A hot foot-soak and foot massage is recommended.[18] In an earlier time, people prayed to the Pox Goddess (痘疹娘娘) so that their children would survive any breakouts of chicken pox or small pox during this time of year.[19][20]

Ancient Traditions

In the second month of winter, officers would take time to pray and sacrifice to the spirits of the four seas, great rivers, deep ponds, lakes, and all wells and springs. It was imperative to close up and secure the genial influences of the season by certain forms of inaction. Nobles were to commit themselves to fasting, stay at home, and not indulge in any music or beautiful sights. They were repress all desires, maintain a state of physical repose, and avoid excitements of the mind.

The main activity of the courts was brewing, and the Grand Superintendent of Liquor was to ensure the quality of the six important aspects of brewing: the ripeness of rice and grains, the seasonality of yeast cakes, careful soaking and heating of equipment, the sourcing of fragrant water, the soundness of vessels, and the ideal temperature of the fires. This might sound like a great deal of activity given the mandated repose of the season, but as anybody who has brewed beer, wine, or spirits knows, the bulk of the time is comprised of storage and quiet waiting.

The second month of winter also encompasses the next term, the Winter Solstice, and so is nearing the time of the shortest day of the year. This is when yin and yang are in a state of contention and reversal, and marks the period when the elements of life will once again begin to move. In preparation for this future reemergence, humanity is to cooperate with nature -- or in the words of the *Book of Rites*, cooperate with Heaven and Earth -- to ensure the genial influences are allowed to rest. Any uncollected produce in the fields, or stray oxen and horses, could be assumed to be for the taking, and stored or housed as one saw fit. Wardens and foresters were to guide people to take any remaining produce or surplus game from the hills, forests, and lakes. The key idea here was securing of surplus or that which was remaining uncollected; attempts to rob or steal would be severely punished.

In the realm of civil affairs, funerary practices were to be revised and regulated. There were to be no earthworks, or exposure of anything previously covered. Apartments and halls were to remain shut, and the masses were to be kept in a state of peace and not roused to action. Offices with no active trade were to be closed, and women's work was to be lessened, and any undertaking of an extravagant nature was not permitted. Repairing pillars, gateways, courtyards, doors, gates, and prisons was allowed but otherwise everything was to remain generally quiet and shut. Failure in this regard would result in the death of beneficial insects and imperial subjects would fall ill from pestilence, and various losses would ensue.

If summer rites were done at this time, the empire would suffer from droughts, grim fogs, and unseasonable thunder. Autumn rites would bring damaging rains and slush, preventing crops like melons and gourds from attaining full growth. They also bring great war. Spring rites would cause locusts, dry the springs, and create illnesses like leprosy and ulcers among the people. [21]

Customs

A saying goes that Little Snow is the time for curing vegetables, while Great Snow is the time for curing meat. (小雪醃菜，大雪醃肉).[22]

Festivals

CELEBRATIONS AMONG CHINA'S MINORITY CULTURES

The Nashi people (納西族) of southwest China have carried on a very old custom of venerating the God of Animal Husbandry (牧神) on the twelfth day of the eleventh lunar month (建丹節/牧神節), which usually falls around the solar term of Heavy Snow. All households prepare a large breakfast feast, the most important constituent of which is a pig's heart. The pig's heart is offered to the god of animal husbandry, and then consumed by the worshipers at breakfast. Those who raise livestock for a living must wear new clothes on this day, and in gratitude for their service to the community receive from the various households a sack containing the best food they can muster, usually sausage, pig's tongue, pig's feet, candied rice (米花糖) and fruit -- enough food to last six or seven days.[23] [24]

The following day, the thirteenth day of the eleventh lunar month is a major day for Tungusic people (通古斯民族) in the far north, such as the Evenks (鄂溫克族) and the Oroqen (鄂倫春族), the former from whom we get the term "shaman." Both are known for their husbandry and hunting of reindeer. At this time of year snow is already thick on the ground with more to come, along with lower temperatures. So this is an important day to prepare for the deathly winter by slaughtering enough animals and storing their meat in order to make it to the spring.[25] [26]

In the south, a "Little New Year" is celebrated among the Kam, also known as the Dong (侗族). In the local language it is called "the changing of the year" and is celebrated over the course of three days and up to a week.

The timing of the celebration differs based on family surname. For example, the Luo (羅) family might celebrate on the 27th day of the 10th lunar month while the Zhou (周) family 1st of the 11th lunar month. Generally the timing occurs around the Heavy Snow solar term.[27]

334

Activities are similar to the Lunar New Year, including prodigious cleaning the day before and the cooking of glutinous rice, fermenting of wine, and the steaming of dessert. Lambs or cows are slaughtered on this day as well. Respects are paid to the ancestors followed by heavy banqueting, drinking, and gaming. Sons-in-law give presents to their wives' parents or friends and family. The unmarried go out into the hills to engage in duets across the valleys. The villages are busy with bull-fighting, dancing, and celebrants decked out in traditional clothing.[28] Yet as with many traditional practices, observance has fallen out of favor as young people move to the cities to find work. [29]

SUN CELEBRATION

Most cultures across the world have a one time worshiped solar deities, and the Yi people are no different with their own Sun Celebration (太陽會), a festival maintained since antiquity.[30] Around the 29th day of the 11th lunar month, all people of the tribes converge on a village and worship the sun god, giving him offerings of meat and fruit while chanting their indigenous sun scripture.

The origin of the sun deity has some overlap with the Han version but also has key differences. Both tales have multiple suns: the Han nine, the Yi seven. But the similarities end there, for while the multiple suns of the Han are a source of endless heat and misery, the Yi's seven suns fostered a long-lost evergreen world of verdant vegetation, perennial flowers, and fertile fields. The seven suns produced seven harvests annually and livestock birthed offspring seven times a year. [31]

These are interesting differences. The following story concerning the ancient past among the Yi were a time of prosperity and blessings, a utopia or heaven on earth. Yet for the Han, the past is portrayed as riddled with natural disasters and misery. (With the exception of some Taoist texts, which describe humanity as fallen from earlier times). Oftentimes in Han mythology, as demonstrated by the sage kings who delivered the people to a cultured existence devoid of grass-made clothing or living in beast-like ways, the past was a time of benighted ignorance from which humanity was saved by the march of progress, which is a myth certainly not limited to the Han. The Yi, however, follow that other familiar pattern: the fall from paradise.

Folklore

THREE MAIDENS SEEK THE SUN

In ancient times seven suns burned brightly in the sky, bathing the world in life-giving light. A dark cat demon hated the suns, hanging as they did so high and arrogant in the heavens. He made plans to kill them, training himself to transform into an eagle-beaked warrior. After years of training, he set off to kill the suns, firing arrows made of feathers.

The suns went down one by one until the seventh realized his six brothers had been killed. He ran off to hide, casting the world in darkness. Realizing the harm this would cause, all the strong, able-bodied men of the tribe assembled and went out to find the hiding sun. They searched high and low, but were unable to find him.

Three maidens of the village came forward. They were known for their wisdom, and told the people the sun would not come out until the cat demon was gone. They suggested that all the tribespeople burn torches to flush him out. All did as they advised, and with torches burning in the four corners of the world the cat demon was terrified. It ran all over the hills, trying to find a place to escape from the light. Overtaken with fear, the cat found himself trapped by a group of tribespeople, who burned him alive.

The sun, however, still refused to come out, so the three maidens ventured into the hills and mountains to find him. After weeks of grueling travel, they eventually found the sun, still cowering and trembling with fear. Eventually the maidens were able to convince him to come out, and the seventh and last sun ascended the heavens to retake his usual place.

The maidens, exhausted from their labors, died. Their bodies turned into the three-peaked Sanjian Mountain (三尖山). Thereafter the Yi every year celebrated their sacrifice and the return of the sun to the sky.
32 33 34

* * *

As much as the legend is a tale of labor and ingenuity, and the power of fire to ward off the darkness and the dangerous creatures who would hide in it, it is also a tale of appreciation of the sun and the gifts it gives. And as the winter advances toward the longest night of the year, the Sun Festival acts as an invocation, calling for the sun to return in the spring.

CHAPTER 22:
WINTER SOLSTICE 冬至

冬至 / 동지 / とうじ /Đông chí
Pinyin: dōngzhì
Literal Meaning: "Winter Solstice"
Alternative names: winter maximum
Period: December 21 or 22 ~ January 5 or 6
Sun's Ecliptic Longitude: 270°

27th of the Eleventh Month, Winter Solstice
Zhu Derun
Yuan Dynasty

Wind wailing like angry thunder sweeps the earth,
  a single night's sky heralds the return of yang.
Daytime sun weaves an extra line of shadow on the dial,
  while notions of snow grip mountains eager to grow plums.
Twin watchtowers lean on the sky taking in the palace gate,
  the five phases a colorful book beheld from the observatory.
South of the river waters warm and ice no longer builds,
  and the old men of the creek trade speared fish for wine.

十一月二十七日冬至 | 元 | 朱德潤
捲地顛風響怒雷，一宵天上報陽回。
日光繡戶初添線，雪意屏山欲放梅。
雙闕倚天瞻象魏，五雲書彩望靈臺。
江南水暖不成凍，溪叟穿魚換酒來。

After months of contracting daylight hours, the Winter Solstice marks the shortest day and longest night of the year. In the eyes of the ancients the sun was the creator of the myriad things, not only providing warmth and growth but also destroying malevolent ethers. As the world is cast in its greatest darkness, a bone-chilling wind whistles out of the north, and the forces of yin hit their peak. Yet this is also the time when the sun, reaching the far extremity of its path away from the earth, starts to turn back. The rise of yang begins to accelerate, bringing assurance that the even colder days ahead will also reach their end. It is for this reason that the first day of the Winter Solstice solar term is an auspicious day.

The character of the solar term was captured by various poets. In the poem which opens this chapter, Zhu Derun describes the cold desolation combined with the change in yin-yang energies, noting in the final lines that warmth is already beginning to stir in the rivers and ends with themes of celebration and abundance.

The ground is said to still retain some of the heat of summer, so the weather has not reached its coldest for the year, but it is losing more heat than is absorbed by the weak and distant sun, so temperatures continue to fall. In astronomical terms, the Winter Solstice is only the very start of winter,[1] further indicating there is much cooler weather left to endure before the spring. In the northern hemisphere, January is when temperatures reach their lowest, and a Chinese saying is that it isn't really cold until after the Winter Solstice (不過冬至不冷).[2]

Pentads

> Earth-worms coil together (蚯蚓結)
> Milu deer shed their antlers (麋角解)
> Springs begin to flow (水泉動)

The way worms cluster together is attributed to two different phenomena. One is that as the soil has reached its point of deepest cold, worms can do nothing but coil together for warmth.[3] The other explanation is the nature of how worms express the forces of yin and yang, twisting in yin and straightening in yang (陰曲陽伸).[4] Although this solar term marks the beginning of an acceleration of yang, it is also the time when yin is still very much dominant, and so worms continue to display this behavior.

Milu deer, also called Père David's deer, are considered creatures of yin,[5] opposite to their common deer cousins, who are considered yang. The animal is also called the "the four unlikes" because its body looks like it is comprised of many different animals, and yet in total looks nothing like them. It is said to have the hooves of a cow, the neck of the camel or the head of a horse, the tail of a donkey, and the antlers of a deer.[6]

At the end of the solar term the energies of yang ascend just enough to melt the springs of the deep earth, allowing them to begin flowing again.[7]

Agriculture

In China, the northwest is encased in ice and the Yellow River basin is covered in snow, so there is no farming to worry about. Southern China is still over 5° and the earth is remains covered in green crops. The coastal regions remain above 10°C; not only green, but filled with flowers and birds. In Hubei farmers look to the skies, hoping for rain, as a saying goes "If there is no rain on Winter Begins, look to the Winter Solstice. If there is no rain on the Winter Solstice, it will be a clear winter" (立冬無雨看冬至，冬至無雨一冬晴).[8] In other words, the future will bring drought.

Farms that experience the colder temperatures are busy repairing and building infrastructure, fertilizing, and winterizing. Any earth that hasn't frozen can be plowed so that it can retain more water. Livestock enclosures are repaired to ensure they have a place to stay safe and warm. The farms of the southern coast have already started spring planting.[9]

Health

With the change in yin-yang energies it is a critical time for health. Yang energies arouse movement, warming, protection, and absorption, and are the basis for keeping the body alive. Since the forces of yin are at their extreme, it is advised to get to bed early and rise late if at all possible, and be sure to bundle up against the penetrating cold. This is also a time of year that can exacerbate respiratory and urological problems. [10] [11] [12]

Customs

The Winter Solstice is a sensitive time of year, and there are many prohibitions on behavior to ensure protection from the forces of yin. In Huzhou (湖州) the children and elderly need to get to bed early as the ethers of yin are at their heaviest and these groups do not have sufficient yang to compensate. [13] In Yunnan, animals cannot be butchered. In Zhejiang, it is taboo to sweep the floor on the Winter

Solstice, and any sweeping and cleaning must be done the day before.[14] In most regions, this is a time of year to change one's fortune, so it is strongly advised not to get upset, lose one's temper, argue, curse, or say anything inauspicious[15] lest the powers of yin take hold and cause decline in one's fortunes.

Festivals

WINTER FESTIVAL

The Winter Solstice is one of the oldest solar terms, noted by astronomers in the Spring and Autumn period about 2,500 years ago. It was recorded as an official holiday by the Han dynasty.[16] It has gone by many names over the course of time: the Winter Festival (冬節), *Yasui* (亞歲), and Change to Winter (交冬).[17]

During the Han it was primarily a festival of rest and merriment. Government and business activities were halted and drinking and feasting were encouraged.[18]

The day took on more religious overtones in the Tang and Song dynasties, with the emperors praising heaven and the common folk turning to the ancestors, careful to respect the divine chain of command mandated in earlier times.[19] For this ritual, the emperor would first bathe, and then don a flat-top crown, azure dragon robes, and jade ornaments. He would then go to the altar in the south of the city, leading a train of high officials to engage in ritual directed at the sky. It was a very grand and serious ritual, accompanied by music and gongs.[20]

For the common folk, many of whom depended on the sun for their livelihoods, it was a time of year when the sun seemed gone, almost in a state of death, and in the long darkness of winter it was believed malevolent forces roamed the land[21] as the cracks between the worlds of yin and yang widened. These fissures between worlds was an opportunity for the ancestors to better hear the prayers of their descendants and receive their offerings. And for the living, such respect not only ensured the protection of their forebears, but was a proper demonstration of filial piety.[22]

In the Northern Song, time was also made for merriment, much like the Lunar New Year, with feasting, visiting, drinking, and gambling. By the Southern Song, it was a three-day holiday, and families made winter wontons (冬餛飩) while wealthy families ate multi-colored wontons (百味餛飩).[23]

The *Qidan Guozhi* (契丹國志), written during the Song, describes the festivities of the Khitan (契丹人) -- a Mongolic, nomadic people -- who would butcher three beasts of white: a horse, a goat, and a goose. The animal's warm blood would be mixed with wine, and their tribal leader, cup in hand, would give reverence to the mountain spirit of the black mountains in the north. The Khitan believed that the black mountain god looked after the dead of the tribe in the afterlife.[24]

By the Ming, for imperial and court officials it was a time of great feasting, raging altar fires, and beautiful attire -- a thousand households banging gongs and welcoming the return of lengthening days. *Scenery and Monuments in the Imperial Capital* (帝京景物略) by Liu Dong (劉侗) describes ancient practices of the common people, held over from the Wei and Jin Dynasties. In their spare time women would knit shoes and hats over the course of the year, which would be given to their aunts and uncles on the day of the Winter Solstice. Over time the giver and recipient were reversed: aunts and uncles gave shoes to their nieces and nephews. Girls would receive shoes embroidered with flowers and birds and hats with phoenixes; boys' shoes would be embroidered with fierce animals and hats with tigers. However, it should be noted that gifting shoes is frowned upon in the modern day, as it is equivalent to telling the recipient to "take a hike."[25] [26]

By the Qing the tone became more formal, and temples were not allowed to ring bells and the populace were prohibited from banging gongs or setting off fireworks. [27] One record remarks that the people in old Beijing did "nothing but eat wontons," giving rise to the practice of eating wontons on the Winter Solstice and noodles on the Summer Solstice. [28] More jovial attitudes continued in the south, however, protected by their distance from the capital.[29] The atmosphere was similar to the Lunar New Year, and a number of traditions flowered in different ways across the regions, especially foodways.

In the Chaoshan (潮汕) area of Guangdong province, people would revere the ancestors with offerings of meat and fruit, then eat together as a family afterward. On the coasts, fishermen would pray to the gods and ancestors for protection just before the crack of dawn, and then head out to sea. In Hui'an (惠安), Guangdong province, ancestor worship was accompanied by tomb sweeping.[30] Among the Hakka in Taiwan, the ancestors are offered nine-layer cake (九層糕)[31] made out of a mixture of long and short grain rice powders, corn starch, and brown sugar.

Tangyuan are also a must-have on this day, and are eaten in even numbers, since during this occasion even numbers represent fulfillment and odd numbers, loneliness. Red tangyuan are auspicious for attracting happiness, and white for dispelling harm. [32] Other interpretations are that red brings love[33] and white attracts riches.[34] The two colors represent the balance of yin and yang (陰陽兩全), and accordingly, balanced with flavors both savory and sweet, indicate a transition from difficulty to luck (運勢苦盡甘來).

In the north, people eat dumplings to memorialize the Han dynasty physician Zhang Zhongjing (張仲景), the Sage of Chinese Medicine (醫聖). The legend goes that Zhang went back to his hometown around the Winter Solstice, when it was snowing heavily. The town was wrapped in bitter cold, and everybody was starving and their ears were horribly frost-bitten.

Zhang set up a clinic in a tent, and on the Winter Solstice gathered some lamb, chilies, and herbs which were capable of driving out cold. He put everything in a boiling pot and cooked it thoroughly, then pulled out the herbs and meat and chopped them into a fine mince. He wrapped the mince in a wide noodle dough, and folded them up so that they looked like little delicate ears (嬌耳). He gave each person in the town two of the dumplings in a small bowl of hot soup.

After consuming the soup and the "delicate ears" their own ears started to get hot, driving away the frostbite and healing the damage, not to mention driving the cold out of their bodies. These "delicate ears" are of course dumplings, and were thereafter connected to the Winter Solstice in certain areas.[35] [36]

But this connection to dumplings varies from region to region. Some say that eating them on the Winter Solstice will cause one's ears to fall off from frostbite,[37] while other regions say the exact opposite.[38]

Red bean rice (紅豆米飯) is a popular dish in the south. The Water God Gong Gong's son was said to have died on the Winter Solstice and became a pestilence ghost. Pestilence ghosts hate red beans, so they are cooked in rice on the first day of the solar term. [39] [40] Dog meat is also popular, although that has given way to mutton as more people view dogs as pets.[41]

After years of evolution, the holiday lost much of its religious character and foodways took central stage: wontons, glutinous rice balls, or dumplings, depending on the region. They are now an inseparable aspect of the holiday among modern Chinese and the variety of older practices are mostly unknown.

Folklore

THE RAT: FROM FRIENDS TO ENEMIES

In some areas of Fujian province people have been eating tangyuan for centuries, offering them to the gods and ancestors and even sticking them on door-frames. The origin of this latter practice stems from an old legend about the small animals who live alongside us, like the rat.

***

In ancient times, not long after the goddess Nüwa repaired the sky, humanity survived by hunting and gathering. Life was difficult, and there was never enough food to go around.

During this time in the evolution of our world, rats were benevolent creatures. Greatly moved by the plight of mankind, the rats grouped together and traveled far away to the lair of the black cat. While the ferocious cat slumbered, they stole the seeds of the five grains it was guarding, and brought them back to the humans.

With these grains people were able to develop farming, creating a surplus of food which sustained them. In gratitude for the rats' gift of grain, the humans promised to give a portion of their harvest to the rats every year.

For years humans kept their promise, not only setting aside grain but also forming it into delicious, soft spheres. Enjoying the surplus of food the rats soon multiplied and lived happily alongside humans.

One year the rats noticed no food had been set aside for them, even though the fields had yielded a bumper harvest. They scrounged for what they could until the following year, when again there was no food set aside.

It was becoming clear humanity had become greedy, keeping the entire harvest for themselves and not giving the rats so much as one grain. Angry, they traveled to see Guanyin, the Goddess of Mercy, telling her how humans had become greedy, untrustworthy, and ungrateful.

After patiently listening to the rats' story, she gifted them with sharp, perpetually-growing teeth and powerful jaws unparalleled in their ability to chew through any substance on earth: dirt, fabric, wood, and even metal and stone. They returned to the world of men on the Winter Solstice, and set about chewing into their bags of grain. People began to create structures to house the grain and keep the rats away, but nothing worked; the rats could chew through everything.

Once rats began to take humanity's food, they became a target of disdain and disgust. When humans weren't able to kill them, they tried to supplicate them with offerings of tangyuan on the Winter Solstice. Over time, the tangyuan became associated with observation of the Winter Solstice, and were eaten by humans to represent sweetness and family unity. Unfortunately, the rats never got over what the humans did to them, and continue to steal their food to this day. [42] [43]

* * *

The central theme of this legend is clearly one of keeping promises and avoiding the folly of human greed -- and the consequences of that greed in the form of divine punishment and blowback from the natural world when it is not given due respect. Another reading is man's perennial, adversarial relationship with some aspects of nature that can only be acknowledged and accepted -- or at best mitigated rather than solved. A third angle might be the easy interchangeability of the rats in the story with humankind: creatures capable of eating through everything in sight -- a disturbing notion for those that might place humanity a more vaunted position in the grand scheme of the world.

THE KILN GOD

The Kiln God (窯神), also called the Lord of the Kiln (窯王爺) is in charge not only of kilns for the firing of bricks and pottery, but also of coal in general. In ancient times people worshiped the Kiln God on the Winter Solstice to recognize his birthday (although other traditions place his birthday on the 18th of the 12th lunar month). Another reason was to thank the Kiln God for the warmth of coal before its increasingly heavy use over the course of the winter.

In the past, worship of the Kiln God required the resting of all furnaces for a day, along with cessation of work by all coal miners. People raised colorful lanterns and held large banquets with whole-roasted pig or lamb. The barbecued animal was placed in front of the kiln to ask for the Kiln God's blessings. This would include not only kiln owners, but coal miners as well, who would ask for abundant, high quality coal and good coal prices.

There are many legends of Kiln Gods around China, each attributing the role to a different personage along with colorful backstories. Temple statuary of the god varies: in some he looks like a cultured civil official, some like a fierce, armored, black-robed dark-faced god with a whip. Some hold a string of coins to signify his ability to bless the coal industry. Some traditions attribute Laozi as the creator of coal and consider him as God of the Kiln given the vast amount of the substance required for the alchemy of immortal elixirs.[44][45]

In Shanxi province there is a legend about worship of the Kiln God and the blessing of coal from the deity to humanity.

* * *

There was once a woman who lived in an old cave, alone save for a small lamb to keep her company. She was largely ignored by the townspeople, and she spent most of her time on the hillsides around her home with her lamb to find new patches of grass on which the lamb could graze.

One day, while watching her lamb feed on grass deep in the hills, she was overtaken by a local man who was as wealthy as he was wicked. He tried to capture the woman so that he could take her back to his mansion. There was nothing she could do but run, and taking her lamb, she fled deep into the hills.

The man would not give up, and recruited a number of henchmen to kidnap her. As they followed her into the mountain a howling, bone-chilling wind kicked up, followed by a blizzard. The wealthy man and his gang soon froze to death, but the woman was led into the safety of a nearby cave by her lamb.

The lamb pulled her deeper and deeper into the cave. As they walked the air grew warmer, until they entered a room filled with light, occupied by a kindly-looking old man. Without saying a word he placed into her hand a shiny, dark stone.

The woman was surprised to find that it was not just warm to the touch, but warmed her whole body the longer she held it. She examined it to see where the warmth was coming from but was unable to find what made the black stone so special. She looked up to ask the old man what he had given her, but he had vanished.

She made her way back to town, the warmth of the stone keeping her and the lamb warm through the cold mountains. She told the townspeople what had happened, and then broke the stone up into pieces, giving one to each household so that they could use it for warmth.

The people of the town named the old man who gifted the magical stone "the Kiln God," the deity bestowing the warmth of coal on the common-folk. Henceforth, nobody needed to fear the cold of deep winter enveloping the world after the Winter Solstice. [46] [47]

* * *

The two Winter Solstice tales above present two views of the world: one where humanity's greed and untrustworthiness create the dual torments of plague and famine, and one where the gifts of nature are passed through the hands of an outcast who eagerly shares such gifts. The latter is a theme aligning with similar Western traditions at this time of year -- the sharing encouraged at Christmas, and no doubt reflecting the importance of community ties in lean times.

Interestingly, the tale presents a positive take on a substance so deeply maligned in our modern world, blamed for pollution and even holding a starring role in the collective imagination as the worst possible Christmas gift for wicked children. One might suspect the projection of the shadow, a simmering hate and disgust for the substance that has powered a good share of our modern comforts. The lesson of both tales is that it is not the gifts of nature that should be maligned, but rather handled responsibly.

CHAPTER 23: LITTLE COLD 小寒

小寒 / 소한 / しょうかん / Tiểu hàn
Pinyin: xiǎohán
Literal Meaning: "Little Cold"
Alternative names: moderate cold
Period: January 5 or 6 ~ January 19 or 20
Sun's Ecliptic Longitude: 285°

Cold Night
Du Lei
Song Dynasty

Drinking tea in place of wine with a guest on a winter night,
*   the first red flames on the stove heating the water.*
The moonlight outside the window would look ordinary,
*   were it not for the contrast of plum blossoms.*

寒夜 | 宋 | 杜耒
寒夜客來茶當酒，竹爐湯沸火初紅。
尋常一樣窗前月，才有梅花便不同。

The world is getting close to the depths of winter, the temperatures lower than at any other point during the year with the lowest yet to come, as hinted at with the word "little." In China, the thermometer plummets lower than -30°C (-22°F) to -50°C (-58°F) below zero. The northern area around the south of the Yangtze is less than -5°C (23°F), while the rest of the south is just touches the freezing point.[1]

Despite the growing cold weather stealing every spark of warmth, the atmosphere in the social realm is warming up as the lunar new year approaches. With the cold traditionally preventing any farm work, the period was associated with even more merriment, feasting, and drinking than the previous solar term. This period usually enjoys many auspicious days for marriage, so the air rings with the sound of gongs and fireworks, accompanying marathon banqueting every few days.[2]

Pentads

Wild geese return north (雁北鄉)
Magpies start building nests (鵲始巢)
Pheasants crow (雉始雊)

As the ethers of yang rise, wild geese start moving back to their homes in the north to avoid the heat just starting to build in the south. It was believed larger, older geese -- the parental generation -- sensed the changes first and therefore departed first. Younger geese -- their offspring -- would follow later.[3] [4]

Magpies start making preparations to lay eggs, endeavoring to have everything ready before the approaching spring. The magpie, symbolizing happiness,[5] also gives comfort that the harshness of winter will give way to a green spring.

Pheasants are of fire, like other active animals such as horses,[6] and therefore are sensitive to the sprouting ethers of yang, welcoming it with their calls.[7] According to the *Book of Rites*, certain animals embody one of the five phases: chickens are wood (木畜), goats are fire (火畜), cows are earth (土畜), dogs are metal (金畜), and pigs are water (水畜).[8]

Agriculture

As with the previous solar term there is less farming activity owing to the weather. Most activities are consumed with winterizing. High mountain tea farms cover their plants with straw, pulled weeds, or plastic film to protect the delicate, valuable leaves. Orchardists prune the limbs of their fruit trees so that branches don't fall off and destroy the fruit. It is a good time to add extra manure for winter wheat. Root cellar doors need to be sealed tight to ensure optimal temperatures around 13°C (55°F), and any stored vegetables and fruit are regularly turned to keep them aired.[9] [10]

Farmers hope for snow on this day as well as the first day of the next solar term, Heavy Snow. If none falls, it means there will be drought during Little Heat and Great Heat of the following year (小寒大寒不下雪，小暑大暑田乾裂).[11]

Health

Cold is a near-malefic phenomenon in Chinese medicine, not to mention the dark yin ethers running rampant across the land. Meanwhile, the body is drained after the travails of the changes of spring, summer, and fall. It is important to fortify the blood to prevent illness. Blood must be kept warm so that it effectively circulates, winter being the time when the blood is said to thicken, presenting great risk to those with heart issues and high blood pressure. Exercise is recommended, but not at the cost of exposing oneself to too much cold.[12] [13]

Customs

COUNTING NINES

The Winter Solstice kicks off the time of "counting nines" (數九), which are nine sets of nine days, totaling 81 days until spring. This period is called "Entering the Nines" (進九). The "third nine" happens right around Little Cold, and is considered the coldest time of the year, just as the sanfu (三伏) were the hottest in the summer (冷在三九, 熱在三伏).[14]

During this time of year, when many are trapped in the house as the cold winds blow and snow continues to pile up, it is a long break for those with a full pantry. For the less fortunate, exposed to the vicissitudes of nature and who lack the necessary amount of fuel and food, it can be a time of anxiety. To offset boredom and distract from fear, there was a tradition of filling in "Cold-Dispelling Pictures" (九九消寒圖).[15] The word xiaohan (消寒), which means to dispel cold, is also a homonym with Little Cold (小寒) if disregarding tones. These would be composed of 81 shapes that needed to be colored in, one for each day until the height of spring around the Spring Equinox, similar to the countdown of the Western advent calendar running up to Christmas.

There were many types of such pictures over the course of history. During the Yuan dynasty, people placed a piece of paper on the window and painted the branches and leaves of a plum tree. As each day passed, one of the nine petals of one of the nine flowers was colored in with red ink. Over the course of time the family would watch as the plum tree changed from a ghostly white to a blazing red, just as spring reached its peak.

During the Ming, such pictures became more commercialized with mass-printing. They showed calendars displaying each period of nine days with descriptions of natural phenomena taking place during that time. By the Qing, each day contained four quadrants, and were colored in according to the weather: upper half for cloudy skies, lower half for clear skies, left for wind, right for rain, and the center for snow.

There were also Counting Nine Pictures with phrases of nine Chinese characters, each with nine strokes. One stroke was painted in per day. One typical phrase was 亭前垂柳珍重待春風, which translates as the "the weeping willow in front of the pavilion preciously waits for the spring wind." [16]

In this way, as the charms of winter began to recede each marked petal or calligraphy stroke foretold the eventual arrival of spring, and an escape from the inevitable cabin fever that set in after days trapped in the home. Those more fortunate to live in larger towns, like the capital, could enjoy "Dispelling Cold Gatherings" (消寒會),[17] held every 9 days, ideally with 9 friends eating and drinking wine encircling a kiln of warm coal.[18]

FLOWER MAKE-UP

Wintersweet flowers (臘梅) are the earlier flowers to bloom in the run up to spring, and often bloom during Little Cold. [19] The yellow wintersweet flowers don't look like the plum flower (梅花) which are not of the same genus. The flower has been an object of admiration among the literati for centuries, and was loved by young women as a form of make-up.

This first came about in the Southern Song dynasty, when the daughter of the Emperor Wu of Song (宋武帝), Princess Shouyang (壽陽) accidentally discovered the beauty of using flowers as a form of make-up.

One day when she was sleeping in the palace, a light breeze blew a few wintersweet petals into the room. As the petals swirled about, a few landed on her forehead. She didn't notice them upon waking, and walked around the palace. Some of her ladies in attendance saw the petals, and giggling, removed them, but they left yellow petal-shaped marks on her forehead. Everybody thought the marks looked pretty, and it soon became fashionable among all the palace ladies to affix petals to their foreheads.

However, wintersweet only bloomed for a short time during Little Cold, so the women of the palace developed a yellow rouge from the flower to use all year round, called *huahuang* (花黄). Some even used yellow paper shaped like various flowers and affixed the petals to their foreheads or cheeks and called it plum flower make-up (梅花妝). [20] [21]

The practice eventually spread to the common folk, and can be seen in the *Ballad of Mulan* (木蘭詩), when she puts on flower make-up and reveals her gender to her fellow soldiers.

Ballad of Mulan
Northern Dynasties Folksong
5th Century

Beside the window combing my wispy hair,
 I face the mirror affixing yellow flower petals.
Exiting the door to see my troopmates,
 they are all astonished:
Serving together for twelve years,
 not knowing Mulan was a woman.
The male hare has large paws,
 the female hare's eyes are squinty;

As the pair of them run side-by-side,
  Who can tell which is male or female?

木蘭詩 ｜ 南北朝
當窗理雲鬢，對鏡貼花黃。
出門看火伴，火伴皆驚惶：
同行十二年，不知木蘭是女郎。
雄兔腳撲朔，雌兔眼迷離；
兩兔傍地走，安能辨我是雄雌？

Plum flower makeup was the height of fashion in its era, and as with cosmetics in many cultures nowadays, people felt women looked naked without it. It was a key marker of young femininity, so much so that the phrase Yellow Flower Maiden (黃花閨女) was equivalent to saying a women was unmarried,[22] as once a woman was married, she stopped applying it. As fashions changed many colors and shapes were used: greens, pinks, reds; butterflies, birds, fish. Women not only used crushed flowers and the petals as well as paper, but also gold leaf, fish scales, and even the translucent wings of grasshoppers.[23] [24]

Festivals

LABA FESTIVAL

The Laba (臘八) Festival falls on the 8th day of the 12th lunar month, the final month of the lunar year. The word *la* (臘) is an ancient word meaning the exchange of old with the new (接).[25] Observance of this festival was already common in the Qin dynasty, and in fact another interpretation of the use of the word "la" is that the character is similar to the character for hunting (獵),[26] the only difference is a moon radical (月) instead of the canine radical (犭). Hunting was closely associated with this holiday in the Qin dynasty, the earliest period of time of known observance. This was a time when the festival was a massive affair, with ringing gongs to invite the arrival of spring and thank the gods and ancestors for fruitful hunts and harvests.[27]

Most of all it was a time to enjoy well-deserved rest, and for many dynasties everybody rested, from farmers to merchants to officials and on up to the emperor. The day of observance moved around between dynasties. During the Han, Cao Wei, and Eastern and Western Jin it took place a number of days after the Winter Solstice.[28] The *Record of Jingchu* (荊楚歲時記) notes that by the Northern and Southern Dynasties the date was finally fixed to the 8th day of the 12th lunar month.[29]

With the rise of Buddhism in China during the Song dynasty, the festival was combined with the celebration of the Buddha's enlightenment.[30] The common tale was that on the day Siddhartha became enlightened, he had reached a state of extreme starvation after years of asceticism. He was close to giving up on his spiritual pursuit when a young girl offered him some congee.[31] After partaking of it, he felt rejuvenated. He then sat under the Bodhi Tree to meditate. Powered by the compassionate gift from the young woman, he achieved enlightenment.[32] In honor of this gift, laba congee (臘八粥) is cooked on this day, especially at temples, and given to all who are hungry.[33]

Soon the tradition evolved so that not only temples, but the entire populace made congee, whether in the most opulent halls of the imperial palace to the lowliest hovel. The oldest recipe was simply red beans and glutinous rice, but many different varieties developed across the country, each locale deeming its version the best.[34] *Old Stories of Wulin* (武林舊事) describes a recipe of walnuts, pine nuts, mushrooms, persimmons, and chestnuts.[35] *Record of the Season in Yanjing* (燕京歲時記) describes brown rice, glutinous rice, white rice, millet, chestnuts, water chestnuts, red beans, and skinned jujubes, all boiled, followed by the addition of red-dyed walnuts, almonds, melon seeds, peanuts, hazelnuts, pine nuts, white sugar, brown sugar, and grapes.[36]

In Lanzhou, the traditional recipe was rice, beans, jujubes, ginkgo nuts, lotus seeds, raisins, dried apricot, dried melon, walnut, white sugar, and diced meat. Families in Henan prefer millet, meng beans, red beans, barley, peanuts, jujube, corn, brown sugar, and walnuts. In Jiangsu, the practices were roughly the same, with the addition of savory elements like green vegetables and oil. In Suzhou, the congee contains mushrooms, water chestnuts, walnuts, pine nuts, euryale seed, jujubes, chestnuts, black fungus, green vegetables, and enoki mushrooms. Clearly there is no set rule, and the dish reflects the rich variety of different food cultures of each region. Regardless of the ingredients, in many homes the congee would be offered to the Door Gods, the Hearth God, the Land God, and the Wealth God, asking for their protection and blessings. [37]

In the Pre-Qin period the observances were richer, and involved a larger pantheon of deities, joining the other rites directed at ancestors, natural features like mountains and streams, and the four seasons. During Little Cold the observance of La (祭臘) is oriented toward the ancestors and eight agricultural deities: 1) God of Agriculture (神農大帝, 先嗇神), the highest level god honored, 2) God of Millet (司嗇神, 後稷神), 3) God of the Field (農神), 4) God of the Field Hut (郵表畷神), 5) Cat Tiger God (貓虎神), a god who helped subdue the population of rats, 6) God of Embankments (坊神), who helped control floods and irrigation, 7) God of the Moat (水庸神), who has become the City God (城隍) of urban centers, likely due to the ubiquity of his presence through the networks of city waterways, and finally, 8) God of Insects (昆蟲神), to help reduce the population of crop-predating pests. Worshipers would send their gratitude for the previous year and the blessings for the next to these eight gods. Each of these gods have origin stories. Two are included below. [38] [39]

Folklore

GOD OF AGRICULTURE

The God of Agriculture (神農大帝), looms large in Chinese folklore. In charge of the growth of crops and the "Five Grains," he also controls medicinal herbs and is therefore the God of Medicine (藥王,

藥仙, 藥王大帝). The historical person on which the deity is based was born in Shaanxi and is considered the ancestor of the Jiang (姜) clan. He invented farming tools and instructed people in the arts of farming, planting, animal husbandry, pottery, textiles, medicinal herbs, and the use of fire. It is for this final talent that he is sometimes considered the Flame Emperor in the South (炎帝).[40]

The Records of the White Tiger Hall Conference (白虎通義) describes his gifts to the world. In ancient times the people lived off hunting and gathering, and as people multiplied and the number of animals declined, food became increasingly meager. After receiving gifts of grain seeds from a mythical bird, the God of Agriculture scattered them on the earth, and taught people how to set up fields and produce crops.[41] [42]

The *Basic Annals of the Three Sovereigns* (三皇本紀) describes his unusual appearance: severely emaciated, and -- excepting his head and four limbs -- totally transparent, his organs visible. This allows him to see the effect of the new medicinal herbs he tastes as he collects them when venturing deep into the mountains and bodies of water. If his organs turned black, the herb was deemed poisonous. As the toxins gradually accumulated, he eventually died. Temples were built in his honor and he was deified. His statue in temples depicts him with short horns, tree leaves as a shawl on his shoulders, and five grains in his hands.[43] [44]

GOD OF MILLET

According to the *Records of the Grand Historian* (史記) in its explanation of the *Classic of Poetry* (詩經), the God of Millet (後稷神) was an ancestor of the Zhou (周) clan. His mother was walking through the southern suburbs of the city when she happened across the footprints of a giant. Repeating a common theme across many myths, she walks across the footprint and become pregnant.[45] [46]

* * *

Months after walking across the giant footprint the mother gave birth to a solid ball of meat. The mother was deeply disturbed by giving birth to such a thing, and seeing it as a bad omen, left it in an alley. After she set it down and started walking away, a herd of cows and a flock of sheep started walking into the alley. She watched, waiting for them to crush the ball of meat. Strangely, they all stepped around it, as if taking care not to harm the sphere of flesh. Some of the cows and sheep would often stop, and nurse it.

Realizing that this would just continue to some uncertain outcome, she took the ball out to a frozen lake, and left it on the ice. As she walked away a number of birds descended on the ball and covered it with feathers to keep it warm. To her surprise cracks appeared in the meat. It broke open and a healthy boy rolled out, crying in a loud, powerful voice. She decided to keep the baby, and raised him to adulthood. She named him "Abandoned."(棄).

As Abandoned grew older he was curious about everything, especially the properties of seeds. He would spend his time walking around the forest, collecting seeds from various plants: soy, gourds, and fruits. He planted them, and they all turned out bigger and tastier than anything that would grow in the wild. He went on to invent farm tools, saving everybody effort and time. He was a patient and helpful teacher, and many came to receive his teachings. Soon farms filled the land.

When Emperor Yao heard, he promoted Abandoned to Master of Agriculture, responsible for all farming. The Emperor named him Hou Ji (后稷), and he was deified as the God of Millet. He represents the earth aspect of the phrase "huangtian houtu" (皇天后土), which describes the divinity of heaven and earth. This is to show he is as equally worshipful as the Heavenly Emperor (Huangtian, 皇天). [47] [48]

* * *

While modern notions of the Laba holiday are centered on Buddhist legends and bowls of congee, for the ancients it was a time of lean and great hope for the coming year, for which they appealed to the many gods who would protect their future harvests. And just like other cultures during this time of year -- Christians with Christmas, Jews with Hanukkah, and many other ancient traditions after the solstice, for Chinese society it was a time of rest, merriment, and a point of light in the darkness just like the hearths they gathered around: a reminder of spring's rebirth.

CHAPTER 24: GREAT COLD 大寒

大寒 / 대한 / だいかん / Đại hàn
Pinyin: dàhán
Literal Meaning: "Big Cold"
Alternative names: Most Frigid, Severe Cold
Period: January 19 or 20 ~ February 3 or 4
Sun's Ecliptic Longitude: 300°

Going out the West Gate of Jiangling on Great Cold
Lu You
Song Dynasty

At dawn I lead my horse out the west gate,
  the weak sun and winter clouds continue their struggle.
When drunk it's easy to be startled awake by a cold gust,
  hands hiding in a heavy coat grasping at fading warmth.
One after another foxes and rabbits seek refuge in dense grass,
  here and there oxen and goats disperse to far villages.
Do not heave dramatic sighs for great mountains and rivers,
  this poor aged traveler is overcome with homesickness.

大寒出江陵西門 | 宋 | 陸游
平明贏馬出西門， 淡日寒雲久吐吞。
醉面衝風驚易醒， 重裘藏手取微溫。
紛紛狐兔投深莽， 點點牛羊散遠村。
不為山川多感慨， 歲窮遊子自消魂。

Great Cold, in addition to signaling even lower temperatures than the previous solar term, represents the very extreme of cold for the year. Yet just as the world reaches the greatest depths of icy weather and the visage of the land is cold and severe, a warmth burns from the distant sun and a flame grows deep within the breast of the earth.

It is the last gasp of winter -- a farewell party where wind howling in the cold nights will soon be calmed by the rising ethers of yang. There are signs a new cycle of seasons will begin, if not from the landscape itself, then certainly from the buzz of humanity as it prepares for a new year. It is a time to discard the old and bring in the new, and call forth good fortune and renewal in the next leg of an ongoing cycle.

Pentads

Hens incubate their young (雞始乳)
Birds of prey fly high and fast (征鳥厲疾)

Rivers and lakes are frozen thick (水澤腹堅)

Hens, as creatures of the wood phase, sense the acceleration in the rise of yang, stimulating the growth of their eggs.[1] Hens also symbolize maternal love and protection, and the unity of family more generally, a fitting symbol of the Lunar New Year for which the whole family will soon be preparing.[2] Their growing eggs also reflect new life that will emerge from a protective shell of earth in spring.

An earlier pentad referred to birds of prey and the murderous energy they represent. Despite the approach of spring, cold still reigns, and the hunting powers of birds of prey , are at their height, [3] as is their desperation while they hunt the warm flesh of the lean animals which serve as their main defense against the cold.

The third pentad refers to the ice on rivers and lakes, which become thickest during this point of the year. The energies of yang are still too young and the warming winds of the east have not yet arrived.[4]

Agriculture

A saying goes "During Little Cold and Great Cold, ice everything enfolds" (小寒大寒，凍成一團).[5] In the north it is still a time staying indoors, drinking, feasting, and getting ready for the New Year.[6]

Any time spent out on the farm is focused on protecting livestock, or perhaps making plans for spring planting. Southern farmers are managing their winter wheat fields. Rainfall is typically at its lowest. Southern China gets less than 5mm to 10mm (0.2 inches – 0.4 inches), while in Northwest China it is as low as 1mm to 5mm (0.04 inches -0.2 inches). Crops planted at this time of year are generally of the less thirsty variety, although some crops like wheat benefit from a little extra watering.[7]

As with Little Cold, farmers want to see heavy snow, and a number of sayings express this sentiment: "Three snowfalls in Great Cold set a plentiful year" (大寒三白定豐年),[8] "three snowfalls in Great Cold and farmers will have plenty to eat and wear" (大寒見三白，農人衣食足),[9] and "do not resent the cold, for it brings next year's wheat" (苦寒勿怨天雨雪,雪來遺我明年麥), a line from a poem by Lu You.[10] The reasons are the same as previously explained: frequent heavy snows and blizzards kill the eggs of the many insects who would threaten the crops in the next year.

Health

Because the ethers of yang are rising yet still weak, it is best to get to bed early and rise early. With exercise and work, overextending oneself can compromise one's vital essence. Emotions need to be regulated as well. As *Master Lü's Spring and Autumn Annals* (呂氏春秋) advises, the sage needs to know the rhythms of the seasons in order to facilitate life (聖人察陰陽之宜，辨萬物之利以便生).[11] One aspect of this is the concept of "nurturing yang in spring and summer, nurturing yin in fall and winter" (春夏養陽，秋冬養陰).[12] This is mainly a principle of avoidance, resisting the temptation of drinking ice-cold drinks in the swelter of summer, and eating overly spicy food in the cold depths of winter, as both compromise yang and yin energies during these times of the year.[13]

During the Great Cold, some Chinese medicine traditions advise defending against the encroaching cold by drinking wine with ginseng and Mongolian milkvetch (黃耆) in the morning, and in the evening, pills made of goqi berries (枸杞) and *rehmannia glutinosa* (地黃).[14]

Customs

Great Cold is usually the time to have Eight Treasures Rice (八寶飯). Glutinous rice is said to nourish qi, regulate the liver, and fortify the stomach, and is a good way to fight off the cold. The dish is made with steamed glutinous rice mixed with sugar, lard, and sweet osmanthus and then layered with different fruits or other sweetened ingredients like jujubes, adlay millet, lotus seeds, and dried longans.[15]

Festivals

WEIYA

Starting from the Land God's birthday on the 2nd day of the 2nd lunar month, also called *Touya* (頭牙), the Land God is celebrated throughout the year during every new and full moon cycle in a practice called *Zuoya* (做牙). This twice a month activity -- on the 2nd and 16th days of the lunar month -- culminates in the last observance of the year called *Weiya* (尾牙) on final 16th day of the 12th lunar month. [16] A saying goes "not observing touya brings a winter of waning, and failure to observe *weiya* brings a lifetime of misfortune" (頭牙無拜衰一冬, 尾牙無拜衰一世人[17]), so it is a significant event on the annual calendar, especially in Taiwan.

The word *ya* (牙) evolved from the word for trading in ancient Chinese: *hu* (互). The similar-looking characters caused the word *ya* to take on the meaning of trading in the Tang dynasty. [18] For this reason Weiya is one of the most important observances on the calendar for businesses, who hold large banquets for their employees. These events have become ever more ostentatious over the years, with giant stages, light shows, and the participation of major pop stars.

LITTLE NEW YEAR

Little New Year (小年) occurs on the 23rd or 24th of the twelfth lunar month -- the date varies by region. [19] In modern times it is associated with cleaning and all the other preparations for the Lunar New Year. The practice of cleaning can be traced back over 3,000 years according to the *Record of Heretofore Lost Works* (拾遺記)[20], when cleaning was used to drive away plague ghosts and ensure security and health. The word for dust in Chinese, chen (塵,) is a homonym with the word chen (陳), which takes the ideas of "old" or "stale" as one of its many meanings. By sweeping away the dust, one is sweeping away the old, and with it any bad memories or lingering misfortunes. [21] In keeping with Chinese metaphysical concepts where the universe is in a constant state of flux, casting out the old and bringing in the new can change one's luck. Even in circumstances where life is going well, it is best to keep the ethers stirring to ensure the renewal of good fortune.

Food is also a major focus. People in Tianjin make Steamed Twelth-Month Rice (蒸臘米). The rice is washed thoroughly, steamed, then set out on a reed mat to completely dry out in the cold. It is then stored in a ceramic pot, where it can last for decades. The rice is said to be good for the sick and elderly, and treats ailments of the spleen as well as diarrhea. [22][23]

Snow is collected in the 12th lunar month and stored in ceramic pots and put in a cool place. The following summer, using this melted snow water to cook is said to keep mosquitos and flies away. Oil pressed at this time is also stored until the following spring. When burned it keeps pests away from silkworms, and can be used for keeping hair shiny and preventing lice.[24]

Some other local specialties at this time of year include a number of different dishes. In Jiangsu, chicken soup is a favorite dish, but in order to have the fortifying qualities necessary for Great Cold it must be an old hen, which is stewed with ginseng, goqi berries, and black fungus. There is a tradition of having one every nine days for each set of nine days starting from the solstice. Those in Nanjing prefer pickled vegetables with pig's feet, involving a process started in Little Cold to ensure the dish achieves the perfect balance of bone to flesh and fat to lean. Nanjing is also well known for their thick soup, which sits somewhere between the heavier version in the north and the lighter version in the south. The dish is also popular because of the flexibility of ingredients, which can be as simple or complex or as frugal or rich as the family wants. Common ingredients include minced meat, tofu, yam, fungus, taro, pickled vegetables and a garnish of parsley and white pepper. Glutinous rice has traditionally been popular in the south, as it is packed with calories and good for fighting off the cold. [25]

Another traditional way to prepare for the New Year was paper-cutting, often forming them into animals symbolic of certain wishes. Three lambs (羊) represented the generative force of three yangs (陽), captured in the phrase "Three lambs bring peace" (三羊開泰). Five bats

(五蝠) sounds like "five fortunes" (五福). Fish (魚) are often depicted because they are a homonym with "surplus" (餘). [26]

With all the food, cleaning, and the arrangement of decor, this solar term is a busy one. A song in Shanxi lists all that needs to be done on each successive day leading up to the end of the term: sweeping and cleaning the house, making flour animals, preparing meat, polishing the tin, and then the final tidying up.[27]

But the very first step, the one that kicks off all this activity, is sending off the Hearth God.

Folklore

THE HEARTH GOD

The Hearth God (灶神) goes by a number of names: the Kitchen God, the Hearth Lord (灶君), the Hearth Prince (灶王爺), the Hearth Duke (灶公), and Lord of the Eastern Kitchen (東廚司命). [28] References to the god first appeared in the Spring and Autumn Period 2,500 years ago in *The Analects of Confucius* (論語), which mentions the god (與其媚於奧，寧媚於竈，何謂也？).[29] The *Book of Rites* mentions the establishment of seven altars of worship, one of which is the hearth,[30] so the god has been revered since ancient times.

During the Qin and Han dynasties a few explanations about the god's origins emerged. According to the *Huainanzi* (淮南子) the god was a merging of the Hearth God and Flame Emperor (炎帝).[31] As some mythologies describe the God of Agriculture (神農) as the Flame Emperor (炎帝) of the southern quarter, commentaries say that the Agricultural God ascended to heaven on a column of flame, and after his death, became the God of the Hearth.[32] In either interpretation, the hearth and fire gods are one and the same, indicating that any modest hearth of the home was considered part of something vast and powerful.

Another origin story is that the god was the first to use fire to cook food. The *Book of Rites* indicates that the Hearth God is feminine, and is referred to as the "Old Woman" (老婦).[33] Some say the god is not an old woman, but a beautiful maiden clad in red (灶神著赤衣，狀如美女).[34] But after the Han dynasty, most records refer to the Hearth God as male[35] with a wife and six daughters. Most modern folk depictions show dual gods, a husband and wife, or one man and two women sitting together, which derives from one of the god's origin tales.[36] In yet another, he is portrayed as a handsome young man, which is why there is also a saying in some areas: "men don't pray to the moon, women don't worship the hearth" (男不拜月，女不祭灶).[37]

The timing of the god's worship is also varied, taking place in different months throughout history, but over time it was simplified to the 23rd of the last lunar month.[38] Great care was taken with the god's worship, as the deity was not only responsible for food and drink for the household, but held an even more important role: observing the family's behavior and reporting their deeds to the Jade Emperor, both good and bad, so that the Jade Emperor can mete out blessings or punishment accordingly. Images of the god could be purchased, and during the ceremony members of the household would put sugar on the Hearth God's lips to sweeten his words when he reports on the family.

Family members would set up a table with wine and incense, as well as candy, water, beans, and hay for the horses drawing his carriage so that he was whisked quickly up to heaven. Hay was spread on the floor from the stove to the door of the kitchen to ensure the horses found their way out.[39]

Some households in Suzhou tie together bundles of kindling as a gift to the god containing the wood of pine, photinia, and holly. People in Zhejiang make gold ingots out of sugar and rice flour, given the deity's connection to the family fortune. After the burning of incense, offerings, and kowtowing, his image would be burned to send him up to heaven, often containing the words "Head of the Home" (一家之主) and the couplets "Ascend to Heaven to speak good words, Return to the world to keep us safe" (上天言好事，下界保平安).[40]

After the Hearth God is sent off, he is considered on holiday, and humans of the world are freer to carry on without the meddling of gods. For this reason there are fewer prohibitions and fewer inauspicious days between his ascent on the 23rd or 24th and his return on the 4th of the first lunar month. Wedding banquets are held nearly every day, as young couples do not need to worry about interference from the gods.[41]

Of all the gods discussed in this book, the Hearth God is the closest to humanity, not only familiar with the daily triumphs and failures of the household, but also familiar with failure himself. In many myths, he is often transformed into a god as a result of his greed, which is also the reason why he is susceptible to bribes when delivering reports to the Jade Emperor.

A REPENTING GOD

Thousands of years ago a man named Zhang Sheng (張生) and his wife, Clove Guo (郭丁香) lived in Zhongyuan. Clove was not just pretty and kind, she was also a hard worker, getting up at the crack of dawn and going to bed late to tackle all of the chores of their household. She grew cotton and made textiles out of the harvest, and grew silkworms for silk. She ate sparingly, and was thrifty. After years of her dedicated hard work, the Zhang household rose in prosperity.

The character of her husband did not rise in pace with their accumulation of wealth, however, and instead of expressing gratitude and honoring his wife, he took a younger wife. The young wife, threatened by Clove's beauty and work ethic, asked Zhang to kick her out. Zhang had always been keen on anything new, and with no appreciation of what he had in Clove, did as he was asked and promptly drove her out of the house.

Clove, penniless, moved out into the wild edge-lands. Through the strength of her own two hands, she once again became prosperous. Meanwhile, Zhang managed to destroy his family fortunes in just a couple years, frittering away any savings and leaving all income-producing activities languishing after the departure of clove. Their situation became so bad eventually they lost their home, and he and his second wife turned to begging to survive.

Through the network of other beggars Zhang heard there was a kindly rich woman on the edge of town. Taking his second wife in tow, he called on the rich woman. After the servants let him and his wife in, he was shocked to see the famous woman was his own first wife. Zhang was consumed in shame, and threw himself into the stove, burning himself to death. Despite his disloyalty, Clove buried him in a grand tomb, and she herself died not too long after.

The Jade Emperor, upon hearing of the story of Clove, transformed her into a Goddess of the Hearth. Zhang was made God of the Hearth, in part for finally feeling a sense of shame for what he had done and killing himself, and in part to serve out his punishment by living in the human world and carefully cataloging the activities of every family.[42] [43] [44]

* * *

Over time, the God of the Hearth was not believed to be as muddle-headed as the man in the old tale, and he grew to intimately know the sufferings of humanity. One could say of all the gods, the hearth deity is the most human due to his flaws, and so was worshiped with great reverence on the 23rd or 24th day of the 12th lunar month, and welcomed back into the home on the 4th day of the first lunar month.

***

With the end of Great Cold and the arrival of Spring Begins, along with the Lunar New Year, we come to the rebirth of the year -- a turning point between cold and warmth, decline and growth. The coming arrival of spring and the cyclic rhythms of nature tell us not only of when to farm or what to wear or the rituals to celebrate, but also speak to the interior rhythms of our own lives.

The inevitable winters of existence, with their helplessness, sorrow, pain, darkness, isolation, and poverty, will all eventually yield. The heavens disallow any aspect of the myriad things to continue into perpetuity, and while that also includes joy and even the length of our own lives, it also includes our sorrows.

And in the constant play of yin against yang, sorrow is the sensation that gives birth to joy, just as cold inexorably gives way to a greening, reborn world set aflame with thunder and flowers.

Lessons of the Solar Terms

Major Teachings of Each Solar Term - A Summary

The 24 solar terms -- set so tightly together as they are, one after another and each only comprising two weeks -- can be indistinguishable when it comes to observing changes in the natural world. Yet each term boasts its unique character, helped not only by the metaphysical cosmologies and myths the ancients used to sketch the incomprehensible contours of the universe, but also by the festivals to honor and celebrate points of the ever-spinning wheel of the year. For these reasons the solar terms are more than just a farmer's almanac, suggesting when to plant this or harvest that. They are also more than a dusty curiosity describing customs, and even more than a cultural asset specific to a single ethnicity or region, as valuable as the calendar is in that respect. Each solar term has much more to say: nested within the each of the solar terms are lessons on topics as wide-ranging as the power of nature, the passage of time, and the richness of life.

Spring Begins is the term of hidden growth, a reawakened world stirring beneath a blanket of snow and ice. It represents rebirth, and a movement from quiet stillness to the start of noisy activity -- literally in the case of Lunar New Year with its fireworks. Equivalent to the Western holiday of Christmas in terms its cultural importance, and similar in terms its emphasis on family union, it contains a key difference that perhaps was once the spirit of the Christmas season in earlier times: the importance of extended rest. Another unique feature of the time, in addition to its emphasis on noise, is the embrace of joining temple crowds for the exchange of luck, and sharing through the giving of red envelopes. There is a call to go out into the world and maintain a larger social web -- a counter to tendencies to hoard and self-isolate. Finally, there is the color of the five phase system which sets off the season of spring: azure -- a color laughing at humanity's attempts to so carefully define and categorize the natural world.

Rain Water is the time of melting and moistening, and with the Lantern Festival a night filled with protective light and fire to hold the angry, destructive powers of the heavens at bay. We also see the generous and kind nature that characterizes the spring season with the myth of Nüwa, protecting the world from natural disasters and the folktale of the Dongfang Shuo, the Jester Extraordinary, arranging a family reunion for a distraught woman of humble station. Yet as much as these tales show deities or people of extraordinary gifts giving aid, there are clear messages that human salvation comes from one's own acts rather than pleading to a distant god for help.

Insects Awaken brings the creative energy of thunder, startling awake all the sleeping beasts. Rain carries aspects of destruction and creation, bringing calamity with the tale of the Water God, Gong Gong, but also healing the formerly cold and dry earth. A certain gentleness takes over as the murderous energy of hawks becomes dovish in the natural realm, and leniency prevails in the human realm of ancient China. The tale of Fuxi and the Builderwood, like so many of the world's myths -- from Europe to Asia to North America -- takes the growing tree as the emblem of connection between the material and spiritual planes.

At the **Spring Equinox** day and night attain balance. Yet the story of the sun and moon goddesses -- one overjoyed and one necessarily distraught as they move in and out of the court of the Eastern God -- speaks of temporary satiation and the gnaw of unmet desire, and the inevitability of cycling between the two over the course of life. The tale of the lychee grove demonstrates a fortuitous accident which damages the tree but results in sweeter fruit, yet only after expressing appreciation of the gifts given by the trees.

During **Clear Bright** sadness contends with joy. Sadness as the Tomb Sweeping Festival calls for revisiting memories of those who are gone; joy as people emerge into a world of unrestrained growth, carrying willow branches as a symbol of rebirth, or sowing a better world for future generations with the planting of trees. Amidst all the activity traditions also mandate pause and gratitude for the bounty of the earth by letting the home fires rest.

The **Grain Rain** is a time to praise water of all types: water falling from the sky and the water that flows in rivers and oceans. Water taken from pools on the Double Third (Shangsi) Festival was said to be especially powerful. This solar term not only acknowledges the power of nature, but also the value of humanity's civilizing tendencies. The tale of Changjie tells of heavenly gifts of five grains given as a reward for creating the written word, as if implying that human beings, with our obsessive and constant innovation, are not some depraved parasitic species or simply part of the natural world but active authors of its regeneration. The myth of the Yellow Emperor at war, allied with animals against dark otherworldly forces, complements this theme, while at the same time acknowledging our capacity create strife and destruction.

Summer Begins is a time of rapid growth and demands the effort which propels our success into autumn and winter. In older times farmers favored the ox, and gave the animal special respect and privileges, not just for it's importance on the farm but for its status as living manifestation of divine favor and fortune. And the legend of the Azure Bull which carried Laozi hints at spiritual potentials even broader than working the land. Cicadas grow noisy at this time of year, and as symbols of purity of rebirth arise in texts from Confucius and Zhuangzi to illustrate the power of the will and our link to ecological cycles.

Little Fullness is the only solar term without a twin to match it on the other side of the year. There is no "Great Fullness," an acknowledgement that more is not necessarily better and the gifts of nature, however modest, should be accepted with grace rather than greed. But this is a different sentiment than the hardscrabble poverty praised in so many organized religions, often born of a distinct preference for the spiritual over the material. For this is also the term of the silkworm, a modest baby moth that helped build the wealth of families, towns, and empires. And the silkworm is fed by the leaves of the mulberry tree, the same species of the mythical sacred tree birthing the sun and moon in the east, as if emphasize that the material is not adversarial to the divine but integral to its expression.

By **Grain Ripens** the plant and animal life continue to flourish, but we also see the first inklings of the death and decline which will advance throughout the rest of the year. The yellow plum rains bring destructive mold, flowers are withering away, and on a particularly "wicked day" the Dragon Boat Festival is held to bring protection against decline. The pentads refer to the merciless shrike, which impales its victims before ripping them apart. Yet the pentads also refer to the praying mantis, a symbol of bravery even in the face of futility, and the admiration and mercy that inspires greater forces.

At the **Summer Solstice** we reach longest day and shortest night. In earlier times it was a period where activity was curtailed, recognizing the need for rest and the unbalancing quality of constant, upward growth. While there are rituals throughout the year to protect against the forces of decline, there is also an acknowledgement of the necessity of quiet so that those inevitable forces are allowed to take hold. But this decay also breeds new life, as embodied by the lotus which matures at this time, reaching toward the sun out of fetid mud. There is also a curious tale where earth thrives when ignored by the gods, an outcome inviting a number of possible interpretations. One is the often destructive effect of intervention when none is actually needed. Another is a parable about solving matters in the here and now rather than reflexively appealing to higher forces.

During **Little Heat** the flowers wither away. The signs of decline intensify and turn into the first sparks of "murderous energy." In the past people maintained a general state of quiet, avoiding the undertaking of major affairs, both to let declining energies collect but also to not disturb the growth that continues throughout the summer. On the Double Sixth Festival the gates of heaven are said to open, rays of light amid the darkness slowly growing as the year spins on, giving people a chance to send requests to spirit realm. In the material realm books and clothes are set out in the sun to fight off the advancing mold, with folktales promoting the value of knowledge over material possessions.

With **Great Heat** comes the extreme high temperatures of the year and the middle of the 24 solar term calendar. Unlike the winter, when heavy clothes and modest fires help people escape the cold, heat can be inescapable. One must lean on stillness of the mind to endure what cannot be changed. For those not working in the oppressive sun themselves, it is a time to be grateful for those who toil to bring us our food. Yet no matter the occupation, most have their own toils, and this is a period to continue the effort that leads to future rewards.

Autumn Begins is a nod to the temporary divergence between experienced reality and the unseen forces at work in broader natural systems. The pentads speak of cold winds arriving while the weather feels anything but. In acknowledgement of the waning heat old traditions call for savoring the peaches of the season, while saving a peach pit to be burned for good fortune at the coming turn of the lunar new year. Myths around this solar term tell of love, loss, and brief annual reunion of a cowherd and a goddess, an allegory of humanity's unceasing effort to connect with the greater cosmos. Another tale of the autumn god Rushou tells of a superstitious Duke who chooses to ignore bad omens, serving as a warning for those who would engage in wishful thinking, procrastinating, or ignoring the obvious signs of growing problems. The autumn is ruled by the Queen Mother of the West, emblem of the immortal life energy that passes through the harvest of one being's necessary demise to sustain another.

The **Heat Departs** pentads speak of murderous energies and with that harvest of ripe grain. In ancient times it was a time for executions and war. Ancient traditions that carry over into modern times include the Ghost Festival, a time to turn to deities and the departed to give thanks for the harvest but also secure protection. Yet it is not just a time for compassion and respect to those who came before. It is also a reminder of the necessity to apply compassion to the world of the living.

In face of the rising severity of the landscape, in ancient times **White Dew** was the time for exacting measurement and care -- a heightened awareness to form and avoidance of carelessness. It is perhaps a recognition of earlier myths, like that of Yu the Great, imposing a sense of order on a chaotic world. But the stories of Yu the Great have other lessons, such as adapting to the moods of nature and learning to channel its destructive aspects, or working to fix the mistakes of those that came before.

Autumn Equinox once again brings daytime and nighttime into alignment before the steady decline of living things during the rest of the year. Many folktales during this time of the year bring attention to the moon, which glows its brightest during these months, so much so that in ancient times emperors chose this period to worship its light. The Equinox Flower matures at this time, representing the death of the sun with the withering of its petals and its future rebirth with the growth of its leaves.

As chilling airs collect, **Cold Dew** is the time of exertion to gather the harvest from the "acres of God" and carrying their produce up into the "granary of the spirit," hinting that the mundane action of feeding ourselves and others is to be appreciated in a grander scheme of growth and sustenance beyond the physical. This term is characterized by a recognition of graceful aging, encouraging the elderly to ascend to high places during the Double Ninth Festival as well as the drinking of chrysanthemum wine, fermented with a flower symbolizing the contradictory ideas of death and longevity. The message is that despite the inevitability of death and decline, there are methods to forestall its arrival in ways that are enjoyable as they are effective.

Frost Fall is the expression of cold, desolate ethers congealing on the surfaces of the land, transforming dew into frost. While the change has its damaging qualities, ice also encases and protects life as plants and animals withdraw and await the warmer airs of spring. Trees blaze in the gloom with red leaves, their transient beauty demanding pause. Persimmons also reach their peak of color. Symbol of joy and longevity, the fruit is feature in one of the most renowned Zen paintings, and described as "passion congealed into stupendous calm," a fitting description of the world at this time as the vibrant life of summer prepares to retire. It is also a time of hunting and war, an acceleration of the death aspects in the air. Yamo of the Zhuang people -- associated with the ubiquitous ox -- goes off to fight and returns victorious, refusing imperial honors and simply asking for time to cultivate her fields. As much as it is a tale admiring those who stay humble, it also recognizes the importance of war as a necessity for protection rather than glory.

A growing quiet enwraps the air of **Winter Begins**. Productive earthly energies draw in, as do animals into their dens and borrows. Harvested fields return to a more wild state. The pentads speak of birds like the partridge retreating into shells deep in the ocean, mirroring this general withdrawal. And the ethereal mollusks resulting from this transformation are mentioned by the poet Su Shi, representing powerful otherworldly forces that are far from the affairs of the world, but which lift the veil for humanity for a short moment, not to inspire awe but out of pity. Again, there is a message of moderating expectations about divine intervention or fate or luck. Ancient traditions called for great care with the remaining bounty of the land and rivers, lest their abuse lead to a cascade of disastrous consequences spreading from the natural to the civil realm. The Black Emperor was traditionally worshiped at this time, with a folktale describing the god's own difficulty in cultivating an inner life even during times of rest and isolation high up in the mountains.

Little Snow builds on this theme of rest. Heaven and earth separate to build and re-energize, like an inhalation -- an antipode to constant advance and progress threatening a dangerous imbalance. The legend of the Azure Lady points to this necessity of winter, and the need for rest and purification of the world with freezing ice. Just as there are times for unbridled increase, there are times for control and reserve. It is as much the case with outward action as it is in the realm of emotion, especially during this dark time of year, when grim moods can take hold as the novelty of the cold has long departed, and nature's full winter beauty has yet to unfold.

Great Snow is a time for more quiet waiting. Yet even before the shortest days of the year the forces of rebirth are starting to move, with pentads speaking of pairing tigers and sprouting milky iris. The hinge of the year of the solstice turning from winter to spring has yet to arrive. Yet nature is already stirring in advance -- sometimes seen, mostly unseen -- a reminder of the mystery of nature and its eventual predictability over longer time yet refusing to match tight human grids of understanding and perception. As brutal as the cold may be to the world outside, a spark glows in the fires of the home, and slow-motion activities like brewing signal faith in the bright tastes and sensations to come in the coming months.

The shortest day and longest night arrive with the **Winter Solstice**. Temperatures will continue to drop but the lengthening days confirm the ascent of yang. It is therefore an auspicious day -- a day to change one's fortune and to maintain an elevated mood as the sun makes its return. Folktales tell of enmity between rats and men, a parable of the blowback from the natural world where humanity's implicit responsibilities are not kept. Another tells of coal, which is featured as a divine gift rather than a source of modern ills, implying a question about how humanity has chosen to use the gifts of the earth.

Temperatures continue their descent during **Little Cold**, but the atmosphere heats up in anticipation of the Lunar New Year. It is a time to eat warm Laba congee, when sharing a simple gruel with family recalls lessons of modest acts of compassion sparking the Buddha's grand spiritual enlightenment. In ancient times it was a period of rest, a period of lean as winter stores were drawn down but also a time of great hope as a point of light of future festivities broke through the dark chill.

The very extreme of low temperatures for the year arrives at **Great Cold**. It is the last gasp of winter as the hidden flame in the depths of the earth begins rising up to meet the approaching sun. It is time to sweep out the old and bring in the new, casting away accumulated dust and its attendant misfortunes -- a reminder to forge one's future rather than to remain ruled by the past. The God of the Hearth -- a deity who was once a flawed man and is member of the pantheon most intimate with the travails of humanity, departs to the heavens to report on what he has seen over the course of the year. Families are inspired to reflect on what has passed since the last lunar year, and prepare for the upcoming festival to welcome the arrival of spring with food, family, and fireworks.

* * *

Broader Themes and Lessons

Individually each of the 24 solar terms roil with the movements of the natural world, colorful festivals, artistic inspiration, and rich folklore, all of which offer varying observations and lessons regardless of era. But taken together broader themes emerge which say much about living in the modern world we have inherited. Earlier in this book, the overview section ended with a brief mention of at least three of these ideas: acknowledging and accepting the mystery and power of the forces operating around us, the importance of ritual in a world characterized with change and uncertainty, and the need for observation and a certain alertness to movements of nature. This section will take some time to go into these ideas in more detail.

A THOUSAND SECRET OPERATIONS

As mentioned in the overview section of this book, humanity has for centuries equated rural settings with purity and urban areas with corruption. There are problems with this conception, which incorrectly places human systems outside of natural ones. Yet at the same time it is a convenient metaphor to capture a larger problem that has grown with industrialization: humankind's perceived separation from the natural world.

As the world has moved from mostly rural to mostly urban, we've come to occupy what ancient Chinese philosophers called "the branch" as opposed to "the root." "The root" refers to agriculture and "the branch" to commerce and exchange. Another way of putting it is the "root" is concerned with direct products of the earth, and "the branch" with ancillary activities based on that initial production.

What is interesting is that this same idea was also put forth by modern Western writers. E.F. Schumacher, author of *Small is Beautiful*, had much to say about the problem with modern economics and its lack of acknowledgment of humanity's dependence on the natural world. As he puts it, there are "primary goods, which man has to win from nature, and secondary goods, which presuppose the existence of primary goods and are manufactured from them."

The word "presuppose" here is key, because as activity focuses on secondary goods, the primary products of the Earth are taken as a given. Decades if not centuries of this thinking has led to exponential advance of industry. While this has brought unprecedented abundance, the tools of economics continue to perpetuate the illusion this state of abundance is normal and sustainable, just as the limited resources of the natural world move in the opposite direction. Expanding on Schumacher's ideas, John Michael Greer in the *Wealth of Nature*, writes "In an age after abundance, the most deeply rooted of our superstitions -- the belief that Nature can be ignored with impunity -- is also the most dangerous."

Greer discusses in great detail how this danger comes about.[1] To summarize in very simple terms, human societies tend to use all the available resources to a point where the productivity of their environment can no longer support that society. The societies then decline until they eventually reach a new, stable equilibrium. The downward fall is not usually one of wild panic and orgies of blood, but one which plays out over centuries, rocking between relative abundance to relative paucity and between widespread misery and joy. The Roman and Mayan empires, as well as Tang and Ming dynasties in China, are textbook examples of this process.[2]

As replete as human history is with examples of abundance and scarcity, one can see this process taking place in the natural world on any scale one can imagine. The process can be as small as a bunch of fruit flies trapped in a petri-dish, bacchanally propagating on a mound sugar. Or it can be as large as the astronomical forces which wiped out house-sized dinosaurs, who yielded their spot to more diminutive species. As sudden and tragic as the turn of events might appear in the bullet points of a lab report or in a geologic timeline, to the fruit fly and the dinosaur, events unfold slowly, imperceptibly, inexorably over generations.

At the risk of being blunt, "flies in the petri-dish" metaphor is not too far from humankind's current situation as we rapidly burn through the finite resources of the earth. The comparison to fruit flies is not a derogatory estimation of humanity, but to illustrate a simple fact that limits exist. Many of the peak oil writers, of which above-mentioned Greer is one, have spent decades building on the conclusions of The

Limits to Growth report published in 1972. [3] The report presented computer simulations of what happens when exponential economic and population growth continually gobbles down the earth's supply of finite resources, most of all the limited fossil fuels that have powered our economies. The simulations up to now have proven prescient, and show a major future decline in industrial output, food production, and population given the fewer resources available.

So what do we do about it? Greer makes an important distinction between a "problem" and a "predicament." [4] A problem calls for a solution; hence, it is solvable. A predicament, however, has no solution. One can respond to a predicament, but responses do not make the predicament go away in the same way that a solution eliminates a problem. The issue is that there is a human tendency to turn predicaments into problems in order to avoid dealing with the predicament. These problems then create new problems which exacerbate the original predicament. This neatly describes the approach civilization took when awareness of this challenge emerged in the 1970s.

The reality of our future resource depletion is talked about much more than it was just a few years ago, but perhaps not with the urgency or starkness it deserves. Techno-futurists have speaking fees to generate and government subsidies to earn. Politicians have to keep their policies economically palatable. Professional environmentalists offer ideas that fit comfortably into the same systems which already draw so many resources. And what many of these pundits offer are solutions, not responses to a predicament.

Even with the lack of mainstream discussion, the understanding of a tough predicament has clearly taken hold in the collective imagination. Only a few short years ago the above projections were often dismissed as the apocalyptic ravings of a radical fringe. But in recent years there is a sense among many that something is "off." Some focus on the political, some the financial, some the metrological, some the social, and some the epidemiological. Many observe all these aspects together coalescing into a nasty ball of current and future suffering. There is a grand realization of sorts that things are "not going well," which is has led to unprecedented levels of anxiety.

Despite the pain, this is an important initial step: recognizing our future as far less certain and predictable than the comforts of modern life had allowed us to assume. To frame the situation in terms of the seasons, one could say we are in the late summer or early autumn of modern industrial society. That brings to mind both inevitability -- you can't stop the arrival of winter -- as well as recognition that while we cannot "solve" winter, we can only respond to it.

Except there is an extra wrinkle to this predicament of declining resources. As opposed to the seasons, which arrive with some predictability, what we are facing is far more mysterious. Just how exactly natural and human systems will handle sharply declining resources, and when, is a far more complex question. No doubt the myriad interactions of trillions of systems will result in something far more surprising than what anybody can imagine.

At the tail-end of the industrial revolution -- a time when there was just as much concern about human society's relationship with the natural world -- a Scottish minister named Henry Duncan wrote prolifically of the seasons. He spoke of their mystery, and the sense of hidden power feverishly at work:

> *"Winter is not the death of Nature, neither is it merely the season of Nature's sleep after the labors of the vegetable world are finished. A thousand secret operations are in progress, by which seeds, buds, and roots, of future plants and flowers, are not only preserved but elaborated, that, when the prolific months of Spring arrive, they may burst into life in all the freshness and vigor of a new birth."*[5]

What is curious about the quote and its mention of "a thousand secret operations" -- especially coming from a Christian reverend who founded the world's first savings bank -- is that it sounds eerily similar to a quote from an ancient Taoist text. It points to a certain universality of the need to acknowledge the unseen in the natural world, and that it moves with a certain inevitability and cyclicality. To give this sentiment a more Chinese context:

388

"The aligned stars trace their revolutions, sun and moon trade their glow, the four seasons follow each other, yin and yang greatly fluctuate, wind and rain give much, the myriad things benefit from this harmony and are born, each receiving nourishment for growth. These matters go unseen, while their results are visible. This is what we call the Divine."[6]

The Xunzi, Discussion of Heaven

列星隨旋, 日月遞炤, 四時代御, 陰陽大化, 風雨博施,
萬物各得其和以生, 各得其養以成, 不見其事, 而見其功,
夫是之謂神

荀子 - 天論

We are now increasingly seeing the visible results of large, unseen forces in our own lives -- in this case the cascade of collective human choices -- transforming our ecologies, economies, and politics, cascading right on down to our social relations and even where we focus our minds. In the passage above Xunzi refers to the unseen as an aspect as the divine. The unseen might as well be divine for the individual sense of gape-mouthed helplessness people feel as massive forces rip through our societies.

Since our hope for managing these forces is limited, the greater priority is managing our individual reaction and response as we begin to understand the point on the historical curve we now occupy, burdened as it is by the weight of exponential industrial expansion. In this sense, as much as the 24 solar terms act as a metaphor for observing subtle changes over the course of year, it also serves as a metaphor for building awareness of what is really happening around us, suggesting that we need to acknowledge and accept the potential of the unseen rather than waiting for its overwhelming manifestation to catch us by surprise. Much like the farmer who steps out the door and sees a unwelcome sun on the first day of Great Cold, it is clear something is "off," and something needs to be done.

THROUGH RITES, HEAVEN AND EARTH JOIN IN HARMONY

The second broader theme of the 24 solar terms connects to the idea of action, in this case the example the calendrical system provides of regular and frequent seasonal observances and rituals. This brings us back to *The Xunzi* mentioned above, which notes "heaven has seasons, earth has riches, humanity has management; humanity forms a triad with the other two. (天有其時，地有其財，人有其治，夫是之謂能參).[7]

The translation of the word "治" as "management" could be controversial because it sounds so anachronistic and annoyingly modern. Some translate the word as "government." Others as "control." But the word "government" is too specific given Xunzi's wider interest in a sense of general order, and the English word "control" implies the vain hope that humanity can control something as powerful as nature. The word "治", while encompassing both of these meanings, has stronger sense of attempting - doing one's best in an impossible situation -- rather than describing the certainty accomplishing a particular goal. Much as the term is used with the earlier myth of Yu in his control of the Great Flood (大禹治水). He makes great strides in harnessing the waters, but it is more an act of management since he never quite fully realizes his goal, and idea of a human -- even a sage king like Yu -- fully controlling the forces of nature is impossible and never-ending.

In this sense the word "management" is a far cry from modern visuals of tie-wearing men with slicked hair, skulking around cubicles, looking to assert dominance with mandates of overtime. It is closer in meaning to the idea of creating some semblance of order out chaos. Maybe even "damage control." Perhaps responding appropriately, rather than solving.

In Xunzi's view, there is order provided by the cosmos, wealth produced by the earth, while humanity is responsible for managing its way through the results of these twin forces. Key to this goal is his advocacy of self-management -- an imposition of limits to avoid spinning off into behaviors which have destructive consequences for wider society. As a species, human self-regulation to align with what the planet can provide is a ship that has long sailed. But within this process of self-regulation, Xunzi is a strong advocate of ritual.

When people hear the word "ritual" there are often a number of dramatic responses. For those who practice rituals in the context of religion, there might be reverence when thinking of their own rituals, and fear or disapproval when thinking of the spooky or ineffectual incantations of others. For those who are not religious, reactions can range from derision to pity: derision at the goofy woo-woo of primitives, or pity at those who have simply added extra ornamentation to self-delusion as a form of self-soothing.

Although Xunzi had much to say about casting judgment on the rituals of others, his thoughts on ritual were more pertinent to the discussion of calendrical ritual:

> "Through rites Heaven and Earth join in harmony, the sun and moon shine, the four seasons proceed in order, the stars and constellations march, the rivers flow, and all things flourish; men's likes and dislikes are regulated and their joys and hates made appropriate. Those below are obedient, those above are enlightened; all things change but do not become disordered; only he who turns his back upon rite will be destroyed." [8]

The Xunzi, Section 19
Translated by Burton Watson[9]

天地以合，日月以明，四時以序，星辰以行，江河以流，
萬物以昌，好惡以節，喜怒以當，以為下則順，以為上則
明，萬變不亂，貳之則喪也。

荀子 - 天論

A modern surface reading might assume that Xunzi was delusional to think that ritual can impact the turning of the stars and seasons, but that is not what he was proposing. His point was that humanity needs to consider their place in the broader cosmos and within a constantly changing system. And this is not about using ritual to bend the universe to one's will, or to praise a deity. In fact of all the Chinese philosophers Xunzi is the most striking in his lack of interest in discussing metaphysical topics. His advocacy of ritual was not in and of itself a promotion of religiosity, but because he felt ritual delivered results.

Now granted, Xunzi occupies the more misanthropic end of spectrum of Chinese philosophers, His running assumption was that ritual was required because, at base, humanity were a bunch of nasty little devils requiring the imposition of order. (Our planet might agree). But the key lesson for a modern reader is the ability for ritual -- in the process of focusing on form and timing -- to enhance one's focus and self-mastery.

Confucius (孔子) had much to say about ritual, and was a major proponent -- perhaps a surprising point of view from a man who was agnostic and avoided discussions of the spiritual world. "The Master does not speak of weird matters, feats of strength, disorder, nor the matters of the spirit." (子不語: 怪、力、亂、神。).

For Confucius, ritual embodied more than what we associate with spiritual practices, and one of the most famous examples was his sense of order and forms in daily life: "if his mat was not straight, he did not sit on it." (席不正，不坐。) Adjusting his mat was not a celebration of obsessive compulsive tics, nor an encouragement of undue focus on process over results, but rather to emphasize what we are capable of affecting in our lives, and to take action. In Confucian thought, small rituals repeated over time build character, influencing not just our imprint on the world, but how that world resonates back to us.

Those who are unfamiliar with ritual -- maybe those who grew up in nonreligious households -- might find the idea of ritual repellent. Perhaps those who grew up in religious households even more so. As an irreligious philosopher, Confucius addressed this himself. In the Book of Rites, it states "Confucius said, 'In dealing with the dead, if we treat them as if they were entirely dead, that would show a lack of affection, and should not be done; or, if we treat them as if they were entirely alive, that would show a lack of wisdom, and should not be done." (孔子曰： 「之死而致死之，不仁而不可為也；之死而致生

之, 不知而不可為也。) Encapsulated within this statement is the ambiguous quality of the reasons for ritual -- that nagging, self-conscious inner voice screaming "this is ridiculous" -- as well as an acknowledgment of the aid it still provides when dealing with a world of uncertainties.

In the modern world most of us inhabit there is a dogmatic focus on the rational. The problem is that we are emotional beings, and often those emotional needs can be satisfied in weird, non-rational ways. Sometimes this takes the form of unconscious, unhealthy behaviors. The point of ritual is to kick us out of these patterns and bring the rational and the emotional in sync. The steps of ritual and the decisions to do it are conscious acts, but the result is subconscious emotional satisfaction, even if it is not immediately perceptible.

Much ink has been spilt on exploring the value of ritual. Tom Driver, in *The Magic of Ritual*[10], makes a convincing case that ritual is as fundamental to humanity as language, and in fact language could be described as a ritual form. He also notes that ritual was killed off -- at least in the West -- by scientific rationalism, leaving most people outside of certain religions or ethnicities a thin to non-existent schedule of observances. With detailed examples he also promotes ritual's ability to engender gifts of order, community, and transformation, outcomes with which Xunzi would likely agree.

Over the course of several books Matt J. Rassano has discussed the role of ritual in human evolution, and in *Mortal Rituals* discusses[11] how the Andes plane-crash survivors (depicted in the movie Alive) employed ritual as a matter of survival. On the opposite end of the spectrum is the Casper ter Kuile's *The Power of Ritual*[12], which hints at the emergence of the modern "bridezilla," casting about wildly and expensively for meaning when there are infinite choices and no clear rites of passage or shared ritual traditions.

The aspect of shared traditions and community can be oversold in societies promoting religious and cultural plurality -- many nations no longer have the luxury or burden of a shared seasonal calendar. So we turn back to Xunzi's focus on self cultivation, and the idea of crafting one's own seasonal calendar and associated rituals.

For most of humanity's time on this earth the cycle of the year provided many opportunities for ritual, and clear acknowledgment of the forces of nature as they arrived and departed, as well as looking closely at ourselves and our communities in the midst of constant seasonal change. Nowadays, the connection of nature to a seasonal calendar is broken. For the non-religious, the year is punctuated by national and commercially inspired holidays, often with a bottleneck of celebrations near the winter. For those who follow Western mainline religions, calendars bring a frenetic bout of activity around winter and spring, or in their daily liturgical forms are more focused on spiritual aspects than the material world which surrounds us. For those who are not necessarily religious, but who have spiritual experiences when out in nature, a more regular calendar tied to passage of time can enhance one's understanding and appreciation of nature's moods. And for those who are religious, other traditions can provide inspiration to enhance their own observance.

It would be naive to suggest that anybody follow the traditions outlined in this book in cases where they are culturally unfamiliar. But the 24 solar terms and the 72 pentads provide an excellent template to catalyze observance and understanding of nature throughout the year. Concerns about cultural appropriation do not apply, because no culture holds a monopoly on the movements of the sun. Not to mention the system has been adopted and adapted by other ethnicities as well, like Japan, Korea, and Vietnam. Moreover, the 24 solar terms, rather than copied wholesale, are more powerful as an inspiration to periodically and regularly observe the natural world around you.

Concerns about religious incompatibility are also not an issue: while the 24 solar terms and 72 pentads have deep roots in Chinese metaphysical philosophy, and are not viewed as religious in the originating culture. If the timing is overly frequent, the 8 stations of the year originally observed in the calendar's earliest version might be more palatable. That sequence would be Spring Begins, Spring Equinox, Summer Begins, Summer Solstice, Autumn Begins, Autumnal Equinox, Winter Begins, Winter Solstice. Interestingly, this timing matches the Western 8-station Wheel of the Year inspired by ancient European practices.

When it comes to ritual, there are many options, often the simplest being the most powerful. One could do what the Chinese do, and just eat a delicious representative food of the season. Although what is interesting is that -- with the exceptions of the Lunar New Year -- these are not orgiastic gorge-fests as is the case with some American holidays, but rather relate to holistic ideas of food intake which promotes physical health. Whatever the choice, what is most important is the idea of a pause. A moment of significance, where one lifts one's head and achieves a separation from the mire of work and responsibility and overstimulating entertainments. The moment could be one of inner reflection -- a ritualized pause to note the passage of life through the year. Or it could be outward, walking the landscape to note what has changed.

Catherine Bell, author of *Ritual: Perspectives and Dimensions* states calendrical rites impose cultural schemes onto nature. [13] Perhaps this is true for most calendrical rites in many traditions, but through a close, sensitive understanding of the natural world around us and attention to her quiet and sometimes unseen changes, we can develop calendrical rites that reflect nature rather than impose our ideas onto it.

Looking at the 24 solar terms readers can consider how those natural changes might be revealed where they live. Residents of North America and the UK can use *Appendix B: North American and British Pentads*, which draws from local US and UK almanacs and maps onto the 24 solar terms and 72 pentads. The tables are simply one example of how to adapt the system to one's local ecology.

The 24 solar terms are not the only way to follow the seasons: there are also phases of the moon, the eight-point Wheel of the Year of alternative spiritual traditions, or the four-season ember days of older Catholic tradition. Liturgical calendars of traditional religions can also be mapped to changes in the national world with some creative thought.

Ritual does not have to be elaborate. Even simply making sure to look up in the sky on certain days, or observing any changes in plants or the behavior of squirrels or birds. Taking a moment to stop and notice the world around you, and thinking about it occasionally throughout the day, will do wonders for poking through unhealthy routines or the haze of obsessive rumination. For some, it might be a productivity hack-- a way to keep trudging along with the tasks we need to complete to get our paychecks. For example, simply being near plants has been shown to lower blood pressure. But more importantly, building a stronger sense of the world around us -- outside of our electronic devices and social stresses -- will do much for our well-being and ultimately for the planet as we begin to rethink our connection with it.

RECLAIMING OUR TIME AND OUR FUTURE

There is another lesson in a greater awareness of the physical world around us. The act of consumption and the use of resources is an inevitable law of existence. Whatever personal effort we might employ to counter ecological impact on the world, there are powerful forces whose reason-for-being is to encourage us to spend and consume as much as possible. But this encouragement to consume does not only take place in the meatspace of door-to-door deliveries and car dealerships but also in the realm of attention.

The attention economy is one of the most lucrative drivers of corporate wealth. The five biggest US tech companies at the time of this writing (Google, Amazon, Apple, Meta, and Microsoft), whose businesses center on capturing human attention, have a combined market capitalization in excess of the annual GDP of Japan. For Europeans, that would be the total GDP of UK, Germany, and France. These companies spend vast resources and unimaginable effort to continue growing on the back of consumers' constant attention. And if the world's largest companies value attention this much, the rest of us should value where we place our attention even more.

Naturalist Aldo Leopold wrote, "the outstanding characteristic of perception is that it entails no consumption and no dilution of any resource."[14] The context of this quote is perception of nature, and in a way he is correct. You can go outside and observe whatever is happening, free of charge. Some might say that this is an almost a revolutionary act, to pull your attention away from the powers of monetization and toward another world which demands no payment.

But in a larger sense the sentence is inaccurate, because it discounts the consumption of the most valuable resource of existence: time.

And again, this is where the 24 solar terms excel, as a map of the passage not just of the natural world, but of the moments of one's own life. As term after term goes by, one can review where attention is directed, and if it is directed in desired ways. The solar terms are a regular reminder, and bi-weekly prompt of our limited time on this earth and the care we must take to ensure we make the most of it. So as the reader goes through, reading about a culture or festivals that might be unfamiliar, they hopefully kindle ideas about one's own relationship with nature, cycles of change, and the preciousness of time.

One might question whether an almanac describing the timing of natural changes is even valid anymore, as climate change brings a steady stream of unwelcome surprises and chronic unpredictability. But that is exactly why paying attention to environmental changes is so important. A certain disregard for the world around us is one of the main drivers of our current predicament. And as the land and skies change it is critical to note how they are changing and what that means for the future. In some areas it is a matter of inconvenience. In others a matter of survival.

Even in places relatively untouched there can also be an overwhelming sense of hopelessness as and endless phantasmagoria of disaster porn shows land consumed in flames and floods and oceans choked with garbage and gasoline. For those sufficiently motivated there is a desire to do something about it. Some turn to collective action, which has its place, assuming it can survive the usual clashing egos and mission creep. There is also the danger of turning a predicament into the illusion of a solvable problem. It is often more productive to first adjust and enhance one's own relationship with nature -- perhaps a more controllable hedge against the random outcomes and energy drain of large groups.

People often underestimate the power of individual action. One of the more reassuring suggestions comes from Dana O'Driscoll's *Sacred Actions: Living the Wheel of the Year Through Earth-Centered Sustainable Practices.* [15] A human-created climate crisis is not the first wave of devastation the earth has experienced. The geologically recent

Ice Age made life exceedingly difficult for much of the planet. But nested within certain glaciers formed what are called glacial refugia: pockets of rich biodiversity that host and protect life in a barren world gripped by bitter cold.[16] The animals and plants in our modern world are experiencing similar conditions, although instead the ground is covered with cement, tended lawns, and monocrop fields instead of snow and ice. There is latitude, even on a small scale, to build one's own refugia, from a small flowerbox in a city apartment to a whole suburban backyard. You cannot save all life, but you can save some of the life that shares the world around you. This is but one of many examples of action that reside in the within the scope of one's own control.

There is another aspect to this pervasive hopelessness and anxiety to which nature provides a possible antidote, which is the process of experiencing nature itself. Richard Louv coined the name of a very modern problem suffered many people in urban environments: nature-deficit disorder. [17] His conjecture is that this separation creates problems with sensory abilities, attention span, and physical and emotional illness. Although not a medical diagnosis, the scientific literature on the positive effect of natural settings on physical and mental health have been well-documented.[18]

One can also cut off the problems of hopelessness and anxiety at the source: by lowering the ubiquitous media feeds engineered to monetize our rapt attention. Of course media isn't the only source of hopeless and anxiety -- and of course there are many. But like the spurious "hot takes" by the aggressively uninformed or surgical headlines crafted to induce outrage, the original goal of consuming news to heighten awareness can have the counter-effect of warping perspective and mediating one's focus through someone else's agenda. And when it comes stories of grand ecological catastrophe or poor judgment taking place hundreds of miles away, one's attention is better spent looking at what can be done in the realm close to home.

A valid criticism of the use of the word "nature" throughout this book is that it sets nature as something separate from human beings. For most of humanity's existence, the world was just "the world." Modern lives have become so mediated by complex systems and abstractions that we even created a special, heavy abstraction called "nature" to describe "that bunch of trees out there." But the physical world is our basic unit of life. What the 24 solar terms suggest is that life is not just on your phone, or in your house or office, or even in your head: its out there and within the self, and changing and cycling in a constant dance. And just as the moods of nature are continually changing and the living world adapts in response, the appropriate action for each person at each time is similarly unique.

So for all the discussion of grand unseen forces, rituals of the year, and ecological action, all anybody has do is very simple. It is contained within the ancient quote in the *I Ching* that kicked off this book, and is repeated here as an ode to the cyclic quality of the seasons:

"Look up to witness the stars,
stoop down to observe the earth,
and know the causes of the hidden and the visible."

仰以觀於天文，
俯以察於地理，
是故知幽明之故。

APPENDICES

Appendix A: Chinese and Japanese Pentads

Although Japan retained the names of the 24 solar terms originally used in China, over time the 72 pentads were adjusted to better suit the climate of Japan during the Edo period. The names currently in use were set in the Japanese calendar in 1874. [1] They serve as a living historical example of how the pentads have been adopted and adapted into another culture. Some pentads were retained unchanged, which are left blank in the table below. Some were switched to other times of the year to match Japan's different climate and ecology, which are marked in italics. In some cases completely new phenomena were tracked, and are marked in bold.

Term	No.	China	Japan
1 Spring Begins	1	East winds thaw the earth	
	2	Hibernating insects stir	*Orioles sing*
	3	Fish swim through receding ice	
2 Rain Water	4	Otters sacrifice fish.	**Rain moistens the soil**
	5	Wild geese head north	**Rose clouds appear**
	6	Grass and trees bud	
3 Insects Awaken	7	Peach trees begin to blossom	*Hibernating insects stir*
	8	Orioles sing	*Peach trees begin to blossom*
	9	Hawks are transformed into doves	**Insects become butterflies**
4 Spring Equinox	10	Swallows arrive	**Sparrows make nests**
	11	Thunder utters its voice	*Cherry blossoms bloom*
	12	Lightning begins	
5 Clear Bright	13	Vernicia begins to flower	*Swallows arrive*
	14	Voles transform into quails	*Wild geese head north*
	15	Rainbows begin to appear	
	16	Duckweed begins to grow	**First reeds sprout**
	17	Turtledoves clap their wings.	**Frost stops, rice grows**

6 Grain Rain	18	Hoopoe birds alight on mulberry trees	*Peonies bloom*
7 Summer Begins	19	Frogs croak	
	20	Earth-worms surface	
	21	King snakegourds grow	**Bamboo sprouts**
8 Little Fullness	22	Sowthistle is in seed	**Silkworms eat mulberry**
	23	Delicate herbs die	**Red flowers thrive**
	24	Winter wheat is harvested	
9 Grain Ripens	25	Mantises are born	
	26	Shrikes begin to sing	*Decaying grass transforms into fireflies*
	27	Mockingbirds cease their calls	**Plums turn yellow**
10 Summer Solstice	28	Deer shed their antlers	**Heal-All plants wither**
	29	Cicadas begin to chirp	**Sweet flag flourishes**
	30	Crow-dipper herb grows	
11 Little Heat	31	Warm winds arrive	
	32	Crickets live in the walls	**Lotus starts to bloom**
	33	Young hawks learn to hunt	
12 Great Heat	34	Decaying grass transforms into fireflies	*Vernicia begins to flower*
	35	Ground is wet and air is humid	
	36	Heavy rains are frequent	
13 Autumn Begins	37	Cool winds arrive	
	38	White dew descends	*Cold cicadas chirp*
	39	Cold cicadas chirp	*White dew descends*
14 Heat Departs	40	Hawks sacrifice birds	**Cotton bolls ripen**
	41	Heaven and Earth become severe	
	42	Grains become ripe	
15 White Dew	43	Wild geese go south	**Grass whitens with dew**
	44	Swallows return north	**Wagtails call**
	45	Flocking birds store up provisions	*Swallows return north*

16 Autumnal Equinox	46	Thunder restrains its voice	
	47	Hibernating insects block burrow entrances	
	48	Waters begin to dry up	
17 Cold Dew	49	The last wild geese fly south	
	50	Sparrows enter the sea and become clams	
	51	Chrysanthemums display yellow flowers	*Crickets live in the walls.*
18 Frost Fall	52	Mountain wolves sacrifice prey	**Frost begins to fall**
	53	Grass and plants yellow and fall	**Light rains patter**
	54	All insects bow in hibernation	**Leaves turn color**
19 Winter Begins	55	Water begins to freeze	**Camellia blooms**
	56	Ground begins to harden	
	57	Pheasants enter the water and become mollusks	**Marigold is fragrant**
20 Little Snow	58	Rainbows hide and are unseen	
	59	Heaven's ether ascends, Earth's ether descends.	**North winds scatter leaves**
	60	All is closed up and winter is fully formed	**Mandarins ripen**
21 Great Snow	61	Flying squirrels are silent	*All is closed up and winter is fully formed*
	62	Tigers begin to pair	**Bears and insects retreat to dens**
	63	Milky iris sprouts	**Salmon swim upstream**
22 Winter Solstice	64	Earth-worms coil together	**Heal-All plants sprout**
	65	Milu deer shed their antlers	
	66	Springs begin to flow	**Wheat sprouts from snow**
23 Little Cold	67	Wild geese return north	**Celery flourishes**
	68	Magpies start building nests	*Springs begin to flow*
	69	Pheasants crow	
	70	Hens gestate their young	**Butterbur thrives**

24 Great Cold	71	Birds of prey fly high and fast	*Rivers and lakes are frozen thick*
	72	Rivers and lakes are frozen thick	*Hens gestate their young*

Appendix B: North American and British Pentads

Although both North America and the U.K. have never delineated the year into 72 five-day segments, there are plenty of almanacs which can be used to form an approximate sequence of seasonal phenomena. For the U.S., the *Old Farmer's Almanac* is riddled with phrases that sound strikingly similar to those in China's seasonal calendar. The U.K., also has its share of almanacs; the below references *The Book of the Seasons; or the Calendar of Nature* by William Howitt, published in 1831. These books are not a perfect match for the varied ecosystems of these countries, but the below represents an example of how a local calendar of pentads can be constructed.

Term	No.	North America	United Kingdom
1 Spring Begins	1	Pussy-willows begin to bud	Snow-drops bloom
	2	Owls lay eggs	Moles build hillocks
	3	Winter's back breaks	Hazel catkins flourish
2 Rain Water	4	Salmon swim upstream	Damp and foggy air permeates
	5	Skunks pair together	Dace collect among riverweeds
	6	Gnats stay hidden	Sap stirs
3 Insects Awaken	7	Hummingbirds fly north	Rooks collect dirt
	8	Bees skim treetops	Earth dries
	9	Snakes awaken	Trout rise
4 Spring Equinox	10	Salamanders mass their eggs	Green herbs sprout
	11	Chipmunks awaken	Bees take flight
	12	Crows watch from nests	Reptiles awake
5 Clear Bright	13	Trees are full of leaves	Birch begins to leaf
	14	Robins are settled in nests	Lapwings nest on fallow earth
	15	Azure butterflies flutter through woods	Elms become green
6 Grain Rain	16	Grouse drum in the underbrush	Oaks become full
	17	Ants secure hills from rain	Hawks nest on high
	18	Poplars begin to leaf	Blackthorn flowers gleam

7 Summer Begins	19	Black clouds bring clear weather	Primrose petals scatter
	20	Frost prepares fertile soil	Dragonflies light on banks
	21	Does rear fawns	Nightingales call
8 Little Fullness	22	Tent caterpillars adorn apple trees	Rye is in ear
	23	Catfish guard their young	Perch swim swift rivers
	24	Morels thrive in wooded shadows	Gorse covers heaths
9 Grain Ripens	25	Insects hordes reach their peak	Insects fill the air
	26	Daisy fields bloom	Rhododendron abound
	27	Water births mayfly swarms	Black clouds assemble
10 Summer Solstice	28	Frogs chant	Corn shoots emerge
	29	Young robins take flight	Bream tread still streams
	30	The Dog Star creates swelter	Full willows sway
11 Little Heat	31	Black-eyed Susan's bloom	Grayling leap
	32	Clear days bring rainy nights	Bluebells wave
	33	Cornscateous air permeates	Cranberries mature
12 Great Heat	34	Sedge pollen fills the air	Birds grow quiet
	35	Aged monarchs return\	Streams shrink
	36	Gray squirrels produce second litter	Corn ripens
13 Autumn Begins	37	The Dog Star relents	Young grouse mature
	38	Ragweed blooms	Reeds stretch high
	39	Cats hunt in the night	Hedge-fruit ruddies
14 Heat Departs	40	Birds molt and grow silent	Rains bring mushrooms
	41	Hummingbirds retreat south	White fogs trace valley floors
	42	Fog brings fair weather	Hares congregate
15 White Dew	43	Crickets sing in the night	Green oaks turn yellow
	44	Muskrats build thatch dens	Wood-owls hoot
	45	First snows dust mountains	Hazel turns gold
16 Autumn	46	Woodchucks slumber	Young thrushes first sing
	47	Banded wooly bear caterpillars thrive	Orchards grow heavy

al Equinox	48	Milkweed floats on the winds	Autumnal crocus spring up
17 Cold Dew	49	Little brown bats hibernate	Fogs envelop coasts
	50	Birds carry witch-hazel to new lands	Trees drop leaves
	51	Traveling robins fill gray skies	Ivy covers rocks
18 Frost Fall	52	Trees bear their autumn colors	Teal arrive at lakes
	53	Crisp air descends	Seeds scatter
	54	Reptiles retreat to the earth	Gray mists rest on hills
19 Winter Begins	55	Buck deer compete	Ferns turn red
	56	Black bears retreat to dens	Frogs retreat to mud
	57	Warm winds blow their last	Frost covers puddles
20 Little Snow	58	Crab apples ripen	Leaves whirl on wind
	59	Trees display naked limbs	Salmon ascend rivers
	60	Dead weeds feed hungry birds	Grey plovers depart
21 Great Snow	61	Winterberry show their fruit	Deer withdraw to dales
	62	Kingfishers charm the wind and waves	Ferns wither
	63	Pogonip fills the air	Winds hiss
22 Winter Solstice	64	Stars shine in the night sky	All flowers depart
	65	Crayfish mate under the ice	Laughing goose arrive
	66	Mourningcloaks alight on snow	Frost bites the earth
23 Little Cold	67	Codfish spawn	North-east winds carry snow
	68	Tumbleweeds roam	Larks go hungry
	69	Bears birth cubs	Hoar Frost feathers all
24 Great Cold	70	The first thaw arrives	Thrushes hunt snails
	71	Raccoons couple	Seeds hide in earth
	72	Groundhogs emerge from burrows	Wrens await in spruce

Appendix C: Weather Portents

Spring Begins
- Rain: good harvest
- Thunder: poor livestock yields
- Morning fog: clear skies

Rain Water
- Rain: good harvest
- Cold weather: plenty of water
- Rain on Lantern Festival: scarce rain before Clear Bright

Insects Awaken
- Thunder: good harvest
- Thunder before Insects Awaken: 49 days of constant rain

Spring Equinox
- Rain: will rain until after Clear Bright; also means fewer illnesses and a bigger harvest
- Eastern wind: warm, wet weather, and a good harvest
- Western wind: early arrival of warm weather, poor harvest

Clear Bright
- Rain: more beneficial rains, and clear skies during Grain Rain
- Clear skies: forthcoming drought

Grain Rain
- Timing: early in the lunar month foretells a plague
- Eastern wind: plenty of rain
- No harvesting tea three days before or after Grain Rain

Summer Begins
- Rain: good harvest
- Timing: However, if rain occurs on the first or second of the lunar month, fruits and grains will not grow
- Timing: If Clear Bright does not fall in the third lunar month, and Summer Begins does not fall in the fourth lunar month, harvests will be poor
- Northern wind: drought
- Southeast wind: good fortune
- Northwest wind: misfortune

Little Fullness
- Rain: good harvest

Grain Ripens
- Rain: Fourth month showers mean more rain in fifth month, and fiery heat in the sixth month
- Thunder: good harvest
- Northwest wind: drought

Summer Solstice
- Thunder in Hunan province: drought in the sixth lunar month
- Rain in Hunan province: Sanfu period will be extremely hot
- Timing in Henan province: Solstice at the beginning of the fifth lunar month means a good harvest; at the end of the month, harvests will be poor

Little Heat
- Eastern wind: typhoons
- No thunder: typhoons
- Thunder on the first of the sixth month: no typhoons
- Any thunder during the term: plum rains will return
- Rain on the sixth day of the sixth month: frost in 100 days
- Southwest winds in Jiangsu province: poor harvest

Great Heat
- Odd day: abundance
- Even Day: rat infestation
- Cooler weather: floods and typhoons, poor harvests
- Red sunset: typhoons

Autumn Begins
- No rain: poor harvest
- Rain in Hebei province: flooding
- Thunder in Hubei, Henan, Zhejiang provinces: poor harvest
- Rainbows in Shandong, Jiangxi, and Jiansu provinces: poor harvest
- Thunder: taiphoons
- Timing: If Autumn Begins falls in the sixth lunar month, the fishing season will end early; if in the seventh, the fishing season will end later

Heat Departs
- Rain in Jiangsu province: good harvest
- Rain in Henan province: poor harvest
- Red dawn: typhoons

White Dew
- Morning dew: good harvest
- Rain: poor harvest
- Timing: rain on the eighth day of the eighth month means rain all month

Autumnal Equinox
- Clear skies and fluffy clouds: good harvest
- Thunder: poor harvest
- Rain in Anhui and Jiangsu provinces: good harvest
- Eastern wind: drought
- Timing: Mid-Autumn festival before Autumnal Equinox means a poor harvest; after the equinox, harvest will be good

Cold Dew

- Typhoons if it previously rained during White Dew

Frost Fall

- Morning frost: good harvest
- Frost before Frost Fall: poor harvest

Winter Begins

- Southeast wind in Hebei and Shandong provinces: poor harvest
- Clear skies in Hunan, Zhejiang, and Jiangxi: clear winter
- Rain in Sichuan province: Clear skies during Winter

Light Snow

- Snowfall: good harvest
- Thunder in the tenth month means livestock will suffer disease

Heavy Snow

- Snowfall: good harvest
- Dark clouds at dawn in the south: heavy wind and rain

Winter Solstice

- Rain in Southern China: clear weather after the New Year
- Clear skies in the south: good harvest
- Rain in Hubei province: drought

Little Cold

- Cold weather: good harvest
- No snow: drought
- Heavy snowfall on the first of the twelfth month: drought
- Thunder in the twelfth month: swine suffer disease

Great Cold

- Cold weather: good harvest

- Heavy snowfall: good harvest

Appendix D: Chinese Dynasties

Xia	2070–1600 BC
Shang	1600–1046 BC
Western Zhou	1046–771 BC
Eastern Zhou	770–256 BC
Qin	221–207 BC
Western Han	202 BC–AD
Xin	9–23
Eastern Han	25–220
Three Kingdoms	220–280
Western Jin	266–316
Eastern Jin	317–420
Sixteen Kingdoms	304–439
Northern dynasties	386–581
Southern dynasties	420–589
Sui	581–619
Tang	618–690
Wu Zhou	690–705
Five Dynasties	907–960
Ten Kingdoms	907–979
Liao	916–1125
Western Liao	1124–1218
Northern Song	960–1127
Southern Song	1127–1279
Western Xia	1038–1227
Jin	1115–1234
Yuan	1271–1368
Northern Yuan	1368–1635
Ming	1368–1644
Southern Ming	1644–1662
Later Jin	1616–1636
Qing	1636–1912

REFERENCE LIST

Introduction

[1] Murray, G. (1912). Sallustius: On the Gods and the World. IV. That the species of Myth are five, with examples of each. In Four Stages of Greek Religion (p. 192). Columbia University Press.

[2] Nichols, R., & Greer, J. M. (2011). An Examination of Creative Myth (from The Cosmic Shape, 1946). In The Druid Revival Reader (p. 216). Starseed Publications.

[3] Nichols, R., & Greer, J. M. (2011). An Examination of Creative Myth (from The Cosmic Shape, 1946). In The Druid Revival Reader (p. 212). Starseed Publications.

[4] Sullivan, M.; Murphy, F. D. (1996). In Art and Artists of Twentieth-Century China (p. 150). University of California Press.

[5] Tse-tung, M. (2004). Criticize Han chauvinism. Selected Works of Mao Tse-tung. Retrieved January 11, 2023, from https://www.marxists.org/reference/archive/mao/selected-works/volume-5/mswv5_25.htm

Overview

[1] Huang, S. (1991), Chinese Traditional Festivals. The Journal of Popular Culture, 25: 163-180. https://doi.org/10.1111/j.0022-3840.1991.1633111.x

[2] Lin, Q., & Wang , K. (2016, December 1). UNESCO inscribes China's '24 solar terms' on Intangible Cultural Heritage List. The State Council of the People's Republic of China. Retrieved January 12, 2023, from http://english.www.gov.cn/news/top_news/2016/12/01/content_281475504974635.htm

[3] 國家教育研究院. (2021). 節. 教育部《國語辭典簡編本》. Retrieved January 12, 2023, from https://dict.concised.moe.edu.tw/dictView.jsp?ID=22133&la=0&powerMode=0

[4] 國家教育研究院. (2021). 氣. 教育部《國語辭典簡編本》. Retrieved January 12, 2023, from https://dict.concised.moe.edu.tw/dictView.jsp?ID=22133&la=0&powerMode=0

[5] 張超 (2014). 第一章---二十四節氣與曆法--智慧與勤勞的象徵(p. 27). In 二十四節氣常識一本通. 龍圖騰文化有限公司

[6] Date and Time of the 24 Solar Terms. (n.d.). https://www.hko.gov.hk/en/gts/astronomy/Solar_Term.htm

[7] 張超 (2014). 第一章---二十四節氣與曆法--智慧與勤勞的象徵(p. 23). In 二十四節氣常識一本通. 龍圖騰文化有限公司

[8] Woodhead, L., Partridge, C., & Kawanami, H. (2016). Chapter 5, Chinese Religions, Human Agency and the Cosmos. In Religions in the Modern World: Traditions and Transformations (3rd ed., p. 150). Routledge.

[9] 周易, 象傳, 復

[10] 道德經, 40

[11] Fung, Y.-L., & Bodde, D. (1948). Chapter 2: The Background of Chinese Philosophy, Reversal is the Movement of the Tao. In A Short History Of Chinese Philosophy (p. 19). The Macmillan Company.

[12] 漢書, 志, 律曆志, 律曆志上, 16

[13] 五行四季旺衰. 每日頭條. (2018, January 22). Retrieved January 12, 2023, from https://kknews.cc/zh-tw/news/nvjn5q5.html

[14] 漢書, 志, 律曆志, 16

[15] Bodde, D. (1981). The Chinese cosmic magic known as watching for the ethers (1959). In Essays on Chinese Civilization (pp. 351–372). Princeton University Press.

[16] Yi-Long, H., & Chih-ch'eng, C. (1996). The Evolution and Decline of the Ancient Chinese Practice of Watching for the Ethers. Chinese Science, 13, 82–106. http://www.jstor.org/stable/43290381

[17] 行政院農業委員會. (n.d.). 有關節氣. Retrieved January 12, 2023, from https://www.coa.gov.tw/ws.php?id=2507769

[18] Weather Spark. (n.d.). Huanghe Climate, Weather By Month, Average Temperature (China). Retrieved January 12, 2023, from https://weatherspark.com/y/112852/Average-Weather-in-Huanghe-China-Year-Round#Figures-PrecipitationProbability

[19] Hocken, V. (n.d.). The Chinese calendar. Time and Date AS. Retrieved January 12, 2023, from https://www.timeanddate.com/calendar/about-chinese.html

[20] 三立新聞網. (2019, October 28). 寶島神很大／拜拜請問我　初一、十五要拜什麼？ ｜. Retrieved January 12, 2023, from https://travel.setn.com/News/625885

Wisdom Ancient and Modern

[1] Kammen, M. G. (2004). Chapter 1: From Antiquity to the Eighteenth Century in Europe. In A Time to Every Purpose: The Four Seasons in American Culture (p. 37). University of North Carolina Press.

[2] Kammen, M. G. (2004). Chapter 5: Nature Writers, Reader Response, and the Ambivalence of Urban America. In A Time to Every Purpose: The Four Seasons in American Culture (p. 201). University of North Carolina Press.

[3] Trans: Johnson, K., (2009). Book II. In The Georgics: A Poem of the Land by Virgil (Lines 458–540). Penguin Classics.

[4] Frodsham, J. D. (1960). The Origins of Nature Poetry. (pp. 74-75) Asia Major: A British Journal of Far Eastern Studies. Percy Lund, Humphries & Company. https://www2.ihp.sinica.edu.tw/file/1621JrZcUMV.pdf

[5] Kammen, M. G. (2004). Introduction: Seasonal Cycles and Sequences. In A Time to Every Purpose: The Four Seasons in American Culture (p. 27). University of North Carolina Press.

Chapter 1: Spring Begins

[1] 張超 (2014). 第二章---春天伊始的節氣, 立春時民間風俗 (p. 40). In 二十四節氣常識一本通. 龍圖騰文化有限公司

[2] 漢語網. (n.d.). 春季養生諺語. 春季養生諺語. Retrieved November 15, 2022, from https://www.chinesewords.org/sentence/3200-16.html

[3] 張超 (2014). 第二章---春天伊始的節氣, 立春時民間風俗 (p. 66). In 二十四節氣常識一本通. 龍圖騰文化有限公司

[4] 禮記, 月令, 1-9

[5] 張超 (2014). 第二章---春天伊始的節氣, 立春時民間風俗 (p. 43). In 二十四節氣常識一本通. 龍圖騰文化有限公司

[6] Grainger, A. (1921). Chinese Festivals. In Studies in Chinese Life (pp. 49–49). Canadian Methodist Mission Pr.

[7] 隋書, 卷七志第二, 禮儀二, 12

[8] 殷登國 (1983). 立春. In 中國的花神與節氣 (pp. 107-112). 民生報業書

[9] 殷登國 (1983). 立春. In 中國的花神與節氣 (p. 112). 民生報業書

[10] 殷登國 (1983). 立春. In 中國的花神與節氣 (p. 112-113). 民生報業書

[11] 殷登國 (1983). 立春. In 中國的花神與節氣 (p. 113). 民生報業書

[12] 張超 (2014). 第二章---春天伊始的節氣, 立春時民間風俗 (p. 45). In 二十四節氣常識一本通. 龍圖騰文化有限公司

[13] JY International Cultural Communications Co., Ltd. (n.d.). Explainer: Why is Chinese New Year Called "Spring Festival"? That's Online. https://www.thatsmags.com/china/post/8389/explainer-why-is-chinese-new-year-called-spring-festival

[14] 黄昏国学网. (2014, June 22). 鴻鈞老祖是誰? 解析《封神演義》中鴻鈞老祖. 黄昏國學網. https://web.archive.org/web/20190703173037/http://guoxue.huanghun.com/shenhua/91.html

[15] 山海經, 海內經 17.

[16] 神異經, 41

[17] 宋岳雪 (2014). 春到人間草木知--立春 (p. 20). In 歲月之二十四節氣裡的眾神節慶與傳說. 貓咪予花兒

[18] 百科知識. (n.d.). 句芒[中國古代神話中的木神、春神]:句（gōu）芒，中國古代民間神話中的 -百科知識中文網. https://www.jendow.com.tw/wiki/句芒[中國古代神話中的木神、春神]

[19] 宋岳雪 (2014). 春到人間草木知--立春 (pp. 20-21). In 歲月之二十四節氣裡的眾神節慶與傳說. 貓咪予花兒

[20] 墨子, 卷八, 明鬼下, 5

[21] 山海經, 海外東經, 16

[22] Yang, D., An, D., & Turner, J. A. (2005). Handbook of Chinese Mythology (pp 126-127). ABC-CLIO.

[23] Yang, D., An, D., & Turner, J. A. (2005). Handbook of Chinese Mythology (p. 211). ABC-CLIO.

[24] 宋岳雪 (2014). 春到人間草木知--立春 (p. 22). In 歲月之二十四節氣裡的眾神節慶與傳說. 貓咪予花兒

[25] 顧氏求古錄, 宋真宗廣生帝君讀, 2 [宋真宗登泰山時, 加封青帝為廣生帝君, 並撰刻碑記, 讚頌青帝"節彼俗宗, 莫茲東土, 生育之地, 靈仙之府]

[26] Wikipedia contributors. (2022, October 28). 青色. 維基百科, 自由的百科全書. https://zh.m.wikipedia.org/zh-tw/青色

[27] Wang, J. & Guan, C. (2022). The tenacity of culture as represented by the Chinese color term Qing. Language and Semiotic Studies. https://doi.org/10.1515/lass-2022-0002

[28] 說文解字, 艸部, 282

[29] 宋岳雪 (2014). 春到人間草木知--立春 (pp. 23). In 歲月之二十四節氣裡的眾神節慶與傳說. 貓咪予花兒

[30] Yang, D., An, D., & Turner, J. A. (2005). Handbook of Chinese Mythology (p. 148). ABC-CLIO.

Chapter 2: Rain Water

[1] 古今類傳, 古今類傳卷之一, 45

[2] 逸周書, 時訓解, 1

[3] 殷登國 (1983). 雨水. In 中國的花神與節氣 (p. 116). 民生報業書

[4] 張超 (2014). 第三章---雨水--天氣回暖, 降雨量增多的節氣 (p. 77). In 二十四節氣常識一本通. 龍圖騰文化有限公司

[5] 張超 (2014). 第三章--雨水--天氣回暖, 降雨量增多的節氣 (p. 88). In 二十四節氣常識一本通. 龍圖騰文化有限公司

[6] 中華人民共和國中央人民政府. (n.d.). 24 節氣: "雨水"養生篇. http://big5.www.gov.cn/gate/big5/www.gov.cn/fwxx/jk/2007-10/11/content_773950.htm

[7] 張超 (2014). 第三章---雨水--天氣回暖, 降雨量增多的節氣 (p. 79). In 二十四節氣常識一本通. 龍圖騰文化有限公司

[8] 四川日报. (February 10, 2012). 寻味民俗, 四川省人民政府网站. https://web.archive.org/web/20120425053136/https://www.sc.gov.cn/10462/10464/10756/2012/2/10/10198310.shtml

[9] 史記, 書, 樂書, 6

[10] 尹晓龙 (2019), 西汉太一神祭祀与元宵节起源——唐代崇道思想下的政治附会; 中国民俗学网, https://www.chinafolklore.org/web/index.php?NewsID=19013

[11] 宋岳雪 (2014). 天街小雨潤如酥--雨水 (p. 25). In 歲月之二十四節氣裡的眾神節慶與傳說. 貓咪予花兒

[12] 宋岳雪 (2014). 天街小雨潤如酥--雨水 (p. 25). In 歲月之二十四節氣裡的眾神節慶與傳說. 貓咪予花兒

[13] 文化部文化資產局--國家文化資產網. (n.d.). 鹽水蜂炮. https://nchdb.boch.gov.tw/assets/advanceSearch/folklore/20080627000004

[14] 宋岳雪 (2014). 天街小雨潤如酥--雨水 (p. 25-26). In 歲月之二十四節氣裡的眾神節慶與傳說. 貓咪予花兒

[15] 御定淵鑑類函, 卷十三, 8

[16] 宋岳雪 (2014). 天街小雨潤如酥--雨水 (p. 26). In 歲月之二十四節氣裡的眾神節慶與傳說. 貓咪予花兒

[17] 新北市客家民俗信仰館. (n.d.). 元宵節. Retrieved November 19, 2022, from https://www.hakka-beliefs.ntpc.gov.tw/files/15-1001-2516,c215-5.php

[18] 百山探索. (2016, February 21). 史上最全元宵節的傳說故事. Retrieved December 25, 2022, from https://read01.com/zh-tw/Jyz24z.html#.Y3huF-RByF4

[19] Britannica, T. Editors of Encyclopaedia. (Aug 04, 2023) Lantern Festival. Encyclopedia Britannica. https://www.britannica.com/topic/Lantern-Festival

[20] 宋岳雪 (2014). 天街小雨潤如酥--雨水 (pp. 26-27). In 歲月之二十四節氣裡的眾神節慶與傳說. 貓咪予花兒

[21] Legends of Lantern Festival. (n.d.). Retrieved November 19, 2022, from https://english.visitbeijing.com.cn/article/47OO1XJ9ild

[22] 金門日報全球資訊網. (n.d.). 元宵節. Retrieved November 19, 2022, from https://www.kmdn.gov.tw/1117/1271/1277/325090/

[23] 宋岳雪 (2014). 天街小雨潤如酥--雨水 (pp. 27-28). In 歲月之二十四節氣裡的眾神節慶與傳說. 貓咪予花兒

[24] Pregadio, F. (2008). Dongfang Shuo. In Encyclopedia of Taoism (pp. 366–367). Routledge.

[25] Ban, G.; Watson, B. (1974). Han Shu 65. In Courtier and commoner in ancient China: Selections from the "history of the former Han" by Pan Ku (pp. 79–80). Columbia University Press.

[26] Vervoorn, A. (1990). Chapter Four: Eremitism at Court. In Men of the cliffs and caves: The development of the Chinese eremitic tradition to the end of the han dynasty (pp. 204–204). Chinese University Press.

[27] Declercq, D. (1998). Chapter One - Poisoned Panegyric: On Dongfang Shuo, Yan Xiong, and the Birth of a Literary Model. In Writing against the state: Political rhetorics in third and fourth century China (pp. 23–23). Brill.

[28] Pregadio, F. (2008). Dongfang Shuo. In Encyclopedia of Taoism (pp. 366–367). Routledge.

Chapter 3: Insects Awaken

[1] 夢梁錄, 卷六, 1[十月孟冬...月中雨, 謂之「液雨」, 百蟲飲此水而藏蟄; 至來春驚蟄, 雷始發聲之時, 百蟲方出蟄]

[2] 羅東鎮農會. (n.d.). 驚哲. 24 節氣. Retrieved December 26, 2022, from http://www.24solar.tw/24solar-3.htm

[3] Dikotter, F., & Sautman, B. (1997). Myths of Descent, Racial Nationalism and Ethnic Minorities in the People's Republic of China. In The Construction of Racial Identities in China and Japan: Historical and Contemporary Perspectives (pp. 76–78). University of Hawai'i Press.

[4] 宋岳雪 (2014). 凍雷驚笋欲抽芽--驚蟄 (p. 29). In 歲月之二十四節氣裡的眾神節慶與傳說. 貓咪予花兒

[5] 行政院農業委員會農業試驗所. (n.d.). 驚蟄之介紹及民俗諺語 - 驚蟄 Insects Awaken. 農作物災害預警平台. Retrieved November 20, 2022, from https://disaster.tari.gov.tw/ARI/solarterm/web_new/Solar_term_3.html

[6] 黃帝內經, 素問, 四氣調神大論, 1

[7] Ni, M. (2011). Chapter 2: The Art of Life through the Four Seasons. In The Yellow Emperor's Classic of Medicine. Shambhala.

[8] 禮記, 月令, 10-19

[9] Karlgren, Bernhard. (1930). Some fecundity symbols in ancient China. Stockholm : A.B. Hasse

[10] 殷登國 (1983). 驚蟄. In 中國的花神與節氣 (p. 127). 民生報業書

[11] 張超 (2014). 第四章---驚蟄--春雷震響,冬眠動物復生的節氣 (p. 98). In 二十四節氣常識一本通. 龍圖騰文化有限公司

[12] 張超 (2014). 第四章---驚蟄--春雷震響,冬眠動物復生的節氣 (p. 99-100). In 二十四節氣常識一本通. 龍圖騰文化有限公司

[13] 吉成名. (1998). 龍抬頭節研究. 民俗研究, (48), 28－34. https://www.chinafolklore.org/upload/news/Attach-20120223184559.pdf

[14] Yao Lan. (2014, March 3). Dragon Head Raising Day: it's haircut time. Ecns.cn (China News Service - CNS). http://www.ecns.cn/learning-Chinese/2014/03-03/103136.shtml

[15] Promotional Centre of Beijing Municipal Bureau of Culture and Tourism (Beijing Tourism Operations Monitoring Centre). (2017, February 27). Dragon Heads-Raising Day. Beijing Tourism. Retrieved November 20, 2022, from https://english.visitbeijing.com.cn/article/47ONlLAief8

[16] 宋岳雪 (2014). 凍雷驚筍欲抽芽--驚蟄 (p. 31). In 歲月之二十四節氣裡的眾神節慶與傳說. 貓咪予花兒

[17] Cai, Y. (2022, July 5). Spring Series: Flower Fairies Festival — The. Chinese Street Market. https://www.chinesestreetmarket.com/foodculture/flower-fairies-festival

[18] 宋岳雪 (2014). 凍雷驚筍欲抽芽--驚蟄 (pp. 31-32). In 歲月之二十四節氣裡的眾神節慶與傳說. 貓咪予花兒

[19] Britannica, T. Editors of Encyclopaedia. (Aug 13, 2012). Shangqing. Encyclopedia Britannica. https://www.britannica.com/topic/Shangqing

[20] 淮南子, 天文訓, 14

[21] 呂洪年. (2010, June 5). 杭州"花朝節"憶舊. 聯誼報. Retrieved November 20, 2022, from https://baike.baidu.hk/reference/7610542/117557GW02dDG4G_gIg8KMJ5conxYqmPdrp-6uF7_t7naCj2UZR4LqVlvgE6GAmP0GOw95fOMDCFa7kyC_VTh8aZMlax8pF7uroUgq811c5dqLnWG7yJFs-i3K6LCHJjzdeZ_dVLFYPJ7zxtWNZCoGKboDsdKfiAFAgBgKhtsl8

[22] People's Daily Online. (2013, March 22). Paying homage to the flower god. Paying homage to the Flower God - People's Daily Online. Retrieved November 20, 2022, from http://en.people.cn/90782/8178535.html

[23] Ma, Z. (2014). On The Folk Customs of Huazhao Festival Which Is a Kind Of Intangible Cultural Heritage and its Modern Value. Conservation Science in Cultural Heritage, 14(2), 155–174. https://doi.org/10.6092/issn.1973-9494/5450

[24] Yao Lan. (2018, November 20). Wind showers bring March Flowers. China News Service Website . Retrieved November 20, 2022, from http://www.ecns.cn/learning-chinese/2018-11-20/detail-ifyzwcft9470778.shtml

[25] 宋岳雪 (2014). 凍雷驚筍欲抽芽--驚蟄 (p. 32). In 歲月之二十四節氣裡的眾神節慶與傳說. 貓咪予花兒

[26]Yang, D., An, D., & Turner, J. A. (2008). Handbook of Chinese Mythology. In Linglun (pp. 169–136). Oxford University Press.

[27]Allan, T. (1999). A Bureaucracy of Gods. In Land of the Dragon: Chinese Myth (p. 105). Metro Books.

[28] Werner, E. T. C. (1986). Chapter VI: Myths of Thunder, Lightning, Wind and Rain. In Ancient Tales & Folklore of China (p. 203). B. Mitchell.

[29] Timeless Myths. (2022, March 21). Leizi: Chinese lightning goddess. Retrieved November 20, 2022, from https://www.timelessmyths.com/gods/chinese/leizi/

[30] 宋岳雪 (2014). 凍雷驚筍欲抽芽--驚蟄 (p. 33). In 歲月之二十四節氣裡的眾神節慶與傳說. 貓咪予花兒

[31] Allan, T., Phillips, C., & Chinnery, J. D. (2005). The Great Flood. In Land of the Dragon: Chinese Myth (pp. 42–42). Barnes & Noble.

[32] Liu, S. T. T. (1983). Gods from the Dawn of Time. In Dragons, Gods & Spirits from Chinese Mythology (p. 17). Schocken Books.

[33] Allan, T., Phillips, C., & Chinnery, J. D. (2005). Mother of the World. In Land of the Dragon: Chinese myth (pp. 40–41). Barnes & Noble.

[34] Liu, S. T. T. (1983). Yu Controls the Flood. In Dragons, Gods & Spirits from Chinese Mythology (p. 33). Schocken Books.

[35] Liu, S. T. T. (1983). Yu Controls the Flood. In Dragons, Gods & Spirits from Chinese Mythology (p. 33). Schocken Books.

[36] Cheng, M. (1995). Local God of the Land. In The Origin of Chinese Deities (p. 226). Foreign Languages Press.

[37] West, S. H., & Idema, W. L. (2015). The Bamboo-Leaf Boat. In The Orphan of Zhao and Other Yuan Plays: The Earliest Known Versions (p. 216). Columbia University Press.

[38] Allan, T., Phillips, C., & Chinnery, J. D. (2005). Fuxi Scales the Heavenly Ladder. In Land of the Dragon: Chinese myth (p. 43). Barnes & Noble.

[39] 淮南子, 墬形訓,7

[40] 山海經, 海內經, 12

[41] 山海經, 海內南經, 14

[42] Werner, E. T. C. (1922). Myths of Thunder, Lightning, Wind and Rain - Lei Kung in the Tree . In Myths and Legends of China (pp. 200–201). George G. Harrap & Co. Ltd.

[43] Liu, S. T. T. (1983). Gods and Superstiions. In Dragons, Gods & Spirits from Chinese Mythology (pp. 121-124). story, Schocken Books.

[44] Newfields. (n.d.). Fisherman and Woodcutter on a Riverbank. Indianapolis Museum of Art Online Collection. Retrieved November 20, 2022, from http://collection.imamuseum.org/artwork/75686/

[45] Stryk, L., & Takayama, T. (1973). Notes. In T. Ikemoto (Ed.), Zen Poems of China and Japan: The Crane's Bill (p. 109). Anchor Books.

Chapter 4: Spring Equinox

[1] 宋岳雪 (2014). 綠柳才黃半未均--春分 (p. 34). In 歲月之二十四節氣裡的眾神節慶與傳說. 貓咪予花兒

[2] Wang, X., & He, J. (2011). Mythology of Lightning in Ancient China. (p. 840) 2011 7th Asia-Pacific International Conference on Lightning. doi:10.1109/apl.2011.6110244

[3] 行政院農業委員會農業試驗所. (n.d.). 春分之介紹及民俗諺語 - 春分 Vernal Equinox. 農作物災害預警平台. Retrieved November 20, 2022, from https://disaster.tari.gov.tw/ARI/solarterm/web_new/Solar_term_4.html

⁴ 張超 (2014). 第五章---春分--畫夜等長的節氣 (p. 113-114). In 二十四節氣常識一本通. 龍圖騰文化有限公司

⁵ 張超 (2014). 第五章---春分--畫夜等長的節氣 (p. 119-120). In 二十四節氣常識一本通. 龍圖騰文化有限公司

⁶ Ni, M. (2011). Chapter 74: Essentials of Disease and Therapy. In The Yellow Emperor's Classic of Medicine. Shambhala.

⁷ 黃帝內經,素問, 至真要大論, 2

⁸ 荊楚歲時記, 第一部寶顏堂秘笈本, 39

⁹ 殷登國 (1983). 春分. In 中國的花神與節氣 (p. 129). 民生報業書

¹⁰ 遵生八箋, 四時調攝箋, 203

¹¹ DaoText.org. (n.d.). 上清八道秘言圖. 道藏典籍全文數據庫. Retrieved November 21, 2022, from http://www.daotext.org/toc4.php?docid=483

¹² 宋岳雪 (2014). 綠柳才黃半未均--春分 (p. 35). In 歲月之二十四節氣裡的眾神節慶與傳說. 貓咪予花兒

¹³ 說文解字, 卷二, 示部, 64

¹⁴ Aijmer, G. (2010). Cold Food, Fire and Ancestral Production: Mid-spring Celebrations in Central China. Journal of the Royal Asiatic Society, 20(3), 322, 330. doi:10.1017/s1356186310000064

¹⁵ 東京夢華錄, 第八卷, 秋社, 1

¹⁶ 宋岳雪 (2014). 綠柳才黃半未均--春分 (p. 36). In 歲月之二十四節氣裡的眾神節慶與傳說. 貓咪予花兒

¹⁷ 宋岳雪 (2014). 綠柳才黃半未均--春分 (p. 36-37). In 歲月之二十四節氣裡的眾神節慶與傳說. 貓咪予花兒

¹⁸ Cheng, M. (1995). Local God of the Land. In The Origin of Chinese Deities (p. 228). Foreign Languages Press.

¹⁹ Cheng, M. (1995). Local God of the Land. In The Origin of Chinese Deities (p. 226). Foreign Languages Press.

²⁰ Hassan , M. K., &; bin Basri, G. (2005). In The Encyclopedia of Malaysia. Archipelago Press.

²¹ Cheng, M. (1995). Local God of the Land. In The Origin of Chinese Deities (p. 137). Foreign Languages Press.

²² Cheng, M. (1995). Local God of the Land. In The Origin of Chinese Deities (p. 136). Foreign Languages Press.

²³ 宋岳雪 (2014). 綠柳才黃半未均--春分 (pp. 37-39). In 歲月之二十四節氣裡的眾神節慶與傳說. 貓咪予花兒

²⁴ 天龍. (2023, June 24). 春分拜荔園的傳說（故事）. 美文苑 Retrieved December 4, 2023, from https://www.meiweny.cn/gushi/cqgs/65465.html

²⁵ 山海經, 大荒南經, 27

²⁶ 山海經, 大荒西經, 30

²⁷ 9900 歷史文物頻道. (2020, May 26). 帝俊、常羲、羲和，這三大神的愛恨情仇，竟影響了地球的陰晴圓缺. Retrieved November 21, 2022, from https://www.9900.com.tw/talk/BBSShowV2.aspx?jid=81a1bf3e5254004ff947

[28] 宋岳雪 (2014). 綠柳才黃半未均--春分 (pp. 39-40). In 歲月之二十四節氣裡的眾神節慶與傳說. 貓咪予花兒

[29] Yang, D., An, D., & Turner, J. A. (2005). Handbook of Chinese Mythology (p. 97). ABC-CLIO.

[30] 山海經,大荒東經, 28

[31] Yang, D., An, D., & Turner, J. A. (2005). Handbook of Chinese Mythology (p. 97). ABC-CLIO.

Chapter 5: Clear Bright

[1] 殷登國 (1983). 清明. In 中國的花神與節氣 (p. 133). 民生報業書

[2] 新竹縣教育研究發展暨網路中心. (n.d.). 客家代表花. Retrieved December 4, 2022, from https://web.archive.org/web/20200726233445/http://web2.ctsh.hcc.edu.tw/stu98/s9811126/public_html/r07.html

[3] 翼城縣廣播電視台. (2021, June 21). 物候：清明二候--田鼠化為鴽_百科 TA 說. 百科. Retrieved December 4, 2022, from https://baike.baidu.com/tashuo/browse/content?id=ab7fe12603c822ec10029397

[4] 大戴禮記, 夏小正, 3.13

[5] 好問答網 . (2021, March 3). 田鼠化為鴽是什麼意思. Retrieved December 4, 2022, from https://www.betermondo.com/a/202101/1231.html

[6] 周公解夢, 25, 夢見田鼠

[7] Chinasage. (2021, January 23). Bird symbolism in Chinese Art 鸟 niǎo. Birds in Chinese Symbolism. Retrieved December 4, 2022, from https://www.chinasage.info/symbols/birds.htm#XLXLSymQuail

[8] Eberhard, W. (2006). R, Rain. In A Dictionary of Chinese Symbols: Hidden Symbols in Chinese Life and Thought (p. 302). Routledge.

[9] 張超 (2014). 第六章---清明--天氣晴朗,草木返的節氣 (pp. 126-127). In 二十四節氣常識一本通. 龍圖騰文化有限公司

[10] 行政院農業委員會農業試驗所. (n.d.). 清明之介紹及民俗諺語 - 清明 Clear and Bright. 農作物災害預警平台. Retrieved November 20, 2022, from https://disaster.tari.gov.tw/ARI/solarterm/web_new/Solar_term_5.html

[11] 張超 (2014). 第六章---清明--天氣晴朗,草木返的節氣 (pp. 133-134). In 二十四節氣常識一本通. 龍圖騰文化有限公司

[12] 花蓮慈濟醫學中心營養師團隊與中醫團隊. (2018, April 3). 清明肝氣最旺！中醫：宜吃菠菜疏肝、木瓜養胃:早安健康. https://www.edh.tw/. Retrieved December 4, 2022, from https://www.edh.tw/article/18525

[13] 宋岳雪 (2014). 春城何處不飛花 -- 清明 (p. 45). In 歲月之二十四節氣裡的眾神節慶與傳說. 貓咪予花兒

[14] 殷登國 (1983). 清明. In 中國的花神與節氣 (p. 134). 民生報業書

[15] Wu, D. (2010). Pure Brightness and Cold Food Day. In A Panoramic View of Chinese Culture (p. 126). Simon & Schuster.

[16] 禮記, 月令, 20-30

[17] Cartwright, M. (2017, October 17). Ancestor Worship in Ancient China. World History Encyclopedia. Retrieved from https://www.worldhistory.org/article/1132/ancestor-worship-in-ancient-china/

[18] Vanderbilt University. (1970, April 19). Qingming Festival. Vanderbilt University. Retrieved December 6, 2022, from https://www.vanderbilt.edu/diversity/qingming-festival/

[19] 張超 (2014). 第六章---清明--天氣晴朗,草木返的節氣 (p. 126). In 二十四節氣常識一本通. 龍圖騰文化有限公司

[20] 宋岳雪 (2014). 春城何處不飛花 -- 清明 (p. 43). In 歲月之二十四節氣裡的眾神節慶與傳說. 貓咪予花兒

[21] 帝京景物略, 卷二, 71

[22] 張超 (2014). 第六章---清明--天氣晴朗,草木返的節氣 (pp. 128-130). In 二十四節氣常識一本通. 龍圖騰文化有限公司

[23] 五雜俎, 卷二 · 天部二, 26

[24] Xu Lin. (2019, April 5). Families come together to honor, cherish and remember ancestors. English.Gov.cn. Retrieved December 6, 2022, from http://english.www.gov.cn/news/top_news/2019/04/05/content_281476595282272.htm

[25] 宋岳雪 (2014). 春城何處不飛花 -- 清明 (p. 43). In 歲月之二十四節氣裡的眾神節慶與傳說. 貓咪予花兒

[26] 張超 (2014). 第六章---清明--天氣晴朗,草木返的節氣 (p. 128). In 二十四節氣常識一本通. 龍圖騰文化有限公司

[27] 殷登國 (1983). 清明. In 中國的花神與節氣 (p. 136). 民生報業書

[28] 中華民俗藝術基金會. (n.d.). 清明節俗一斷鷂放災. Folk.org.tw. Retrieved December 6, 2022, from http://folk.org.tw/dictionary/page03.htm

[29] 禮記, 月令, 4, 盛德在木

[30] 山海經, 海外北經, 10

[31] Campany, R. F., & Ge, H. (2002). Dong Feng. In To live as long as heaven and earth: A translation and study of Ge Hong's traditions of divine transcendents (pp. 141–146). University of California Press.

[32] Aijmer, G. (2010). Cold Food, Fire and Ancestral Production: Mid-spring Celebrations in Central China. Journal of the Royal Asiatic Society, 20(3), 322. doi:10.1017/s1356186310000064

[33] 荊楚歲時記, 第一部寶顏堂秘笈本, 42

[34] 周禮, 天官冢宰, 85

[35] 新論, 26

[36] Holzman, D. (1986). The Cold Food Festival in early medieval China. Harvard Journal of Asiatic Studies, 46(1), 56–60. https://doi.org/10.2307/2719075

[37] China.org.cn. (n.d.). Cold Food Festival -- time to feast on Cold foods. Retrieved December 9, 2022, from http://www.china.org.cn/culture/2008-04/07/content_14407806.htm

[38] Aijmer, G. (2010). Cold Food, Fire and Ancestral Production: Mid-spring Celebrations in Central China. Journal of the Royal Asiatic Society, 20(3), pp. 323-324. doi:10.1017/s1356186310000064

[39] Holzman, D. (1986). The Cold Food Festival in early medieval China. Harvard Journal of Asiatic Studies, 46(1), 62 63. https://doi.org/10.2307/2719075

[40] Aijmer, G. (2010). Cold Food, Fire and Ancestral Production: Mid-spring Celebrations in Central China. Journal of the Royal Asiatic Society, 20(3), 338. doi:10.1017/s1356186310000064

[41] Eberhard, W. (2006). W, Willow. In A Dictionary of Chinese Symbols: Hidden Symbols in Chinese Life and Thought (p. 392-393).entry, Routledge.

[42] Silbergeld, J. (1980). Kung Hsien's self-portrait in Willows, with notes on the Willow in Chinese painting and literature. Artibus Asiae, 42(1), 12. https://doi.org/10.2307/3250007

[43] 白振有. (2004). "柳" 的國俗語義. 廣西社會科學, (6). https://doi.org/http://www.cqvip.com/qk/82725x/2004006/9814596.html

[44] 齊民要術, 齊民要術卷三~卷五, 種槐、柳、楸、梓、梧、柞第五十, 6

[45] 台大獅子吼佛學專站. (n.d.). 鬼怖木. 丁福保佛學大辭典. Retrieved December 9, 2022, http://buddhaspace.org/dict/dfb/data/%25E9%25AC%25BC%25E6%2580%2596%25E6%259C%25A8.html

[46] 殷登國 (1983). 清明. In 中國的花神與節氣 (p. 140). 民生報業書

[47] Wu, D. (2010). Pure Brightness and Cold Food Day. In A Panoramic View of Chinese Culture (p. 126). Simon & Schuster.

[48] Holzman, D. (1986). The Cold Food Festival in early medieval China. Harvard Journal of Asiatic Studies, 46(1), 52-54. https://doi.org/10.2307/2719075

[49] Aijmer, G. (2010). Cold Food, Fire and Ancestral Production: Mid-spring Celebrations in Central China. Journal of the Royal Asiatic Society, 20(3), 331-332. doi:10.1017/s1356186310000064

[50] 宋岳雪 (2014). 春城何處不飛花 -- 清明 (p. 45-46) . In 歲月之二十四節氣裡的眾神節慶與傳說. 貓咪予花兒

[51] Lü Buwei, Knoblock, J., & Riegel, J. K. (2000). Part I, The Almanacs, Book 12. In The Annals of Lü Buwei-Lüshi Chunqiu (pp. 263–264). Stanford Univ. Press.

[52] Sima, Q., Nienhauser, W. H., & Cheng, T. F. (2006). Chin, Hereditary House. In The Grand Scribe's Records. The Hereditary Houses of Pre-Han China (Vol. 1, pp. 332–333). Indiana University Press.

[53] Legge, J. (1872). The Ch-hun Tsew, with the Tso Chuen, XXIV. In The Chinese Classics (Vol. 5, pp. 191–192). Lane, Crawford & Co.

[54] 韓非子, 外儲說左上第三十二

[55] Holzman, D. (1986). The Cold Food Festival in Early Medieval China. Harvard Journal of Asiatic Studies, 46(1), 51. https://doi.org/10.2307/2719075

Chapter 6: Grain Rain

[1] Xiong, Z. (2006). 台灣客家節氣諺語及其文化意涵研究 - Hakka culture relates to Taiwan Hakka proverbs of the twenty-four solar terms (thesis). 國立雲林科技大學漢學資料整理研究所碩士, Douliou, Yunlin, Taiwan, R.O.C.

[2] 宋岳雪 (2014). 一夕輕雷落萬絲 -- 穀雨 (p. 49) . In 歲月之二十四節氣裡的眾神節慶與傳說. 貓咪予花兒

[3] Barbieri-Low, A. J. (2015). Translation Notes. In Law, State, and Society in Early Imperial China (p. 852). Brill.

[4] Chinese Art Auction Administration. (n.d.). A pale green jade turtledove. Bonhams. Retrieved December 10, 2022, from https://www.bonhams.com/auctions/23423/lot/29/

[5] 搜狗百科. (n.d.). 鹅鸠 Baike.sogou.com. Retrieved December 1, 2023, from https://baike.sogou.com/v72286651.htm

[6] Lai, C. M. (1998). Messenger of Spring and Morality: Cuckoo Lore in Chinese Sources. Journal of the American Oriental Society, 118(4), 530–542. https://doi.org/10.2307/604785

[7] 山海經, 西山經, 49

[8] 殷登國 (1983). 穀雨. In 中國的花神與節氣 (p. 142). 民生報叢書

[9] 二十四節氣 -- 穀雨 - 努力小農. (n.d.). Retrieved December 10, 2022, from https://mihumisang.org/web/news_detail.php?ID=0qrua11afr2i2wom

[10] 行政院農業委員會. (n.d.). 穀雨（國曆 4 月 19 或 20 或 21 日）. Retrieved December 10, 2022, from https://www.coa.gov.tw/ws.php?id=2507778

[11] 張超 (2014). 第七章---穀雨--降水明顯增多,有利穀物生長的節氣 (pp, 146-147). In 二十四節氣常識一本通. 龍圖騰文化有限公司

[12] 黃慧玫. (2022, April 19). 「穀雨」節氣總是虛累累? 中醫籲: 5 方法顧脾護胃、袪除濕氣就能除百病. Heho 健康. Retrieved December 10, 2022, from https://heho.com.tw/archives/215565

[13] 臺中市大雅區衛生所. (n.d.). 四季養生藥膳之製作. Retrieved December 10, 2022, from https://www.dayaphc.taichung.gov.tw/1809298/post

[14] 張超 (2014). 第七章---穀雨--降水明顯增多,有利穀物生長的節氣 (pp, 153-154). In 二十四節氣常識一本通. 龍圖騰文化有限公司

[15] 月令粹編, 月令粹編, 163

[16] 楊玉君. (2009, November 11). 驅邪. 文化部國家文化資料庫. Retrieved December 10, 2022, from https://nrch.culture.tw/twpedia.aspx?id=2036

[17] 殷登國 (1983). 穀雨. In 中國的花神與節氣 (pp. 145-148). 民生報叢書

[18] 王雨蒙、文一. (n.d.). 貼符除毒蟲. ChinaCulture.org. Retrieved December 10, 2022, from http://en.chinaculture.org/gb/gb/2010guyu/2010-04/19/content_376833.htm

[19] 自由時報 (2021, December 27). 謠言終結站》壁虎尿液毒性大務必驅趕? 查核中心: 錯誤 - 即時新聞 - 自由健康網. 自由時報電子報. Retrieved December 10, 2022, from https://health.ltn.com.tw/article/breakingnews/3781928

[20] IMEDIA. (n.d.). Are geckos really poisonous? Can gecko urine cause deafness? Geckos are misunderstood. Retrieved December 10, 2022, from https://min.news/en/news/1c2013e2b946098b87f3b71afa8bbf9b.html

[21] Kotangale JP. Food poisoning and house gecko: myth or reality? J Environ Sci Eng. 2011 Apr;53(2):227-30. PMID: 23033707.

[22] 丁曼真. (2009, September 9). 穀雨. 文化部國家文化資料庫. Retrieved December 10, 2022, from https://nrch.culture.tw/twpedia.aspx?id=11749

[23] 三度漢語網. (n.d.). 風俗走穀雨是什麼樣子的 . 3DU.TW. Retrieved December 10, 2022, from https://www.3du.tw/content/OHBrNmc=.htm

[24] 張超 (2014). 第七章---穀雨--降水明顯增多,有利穀物生長的節氣 (pp, 149-150). In 二十四節氣常識一本通. 龍圖騰文化有限公司

[25] Baidu. (2022, October 27). 高禖. 百度百科. Retrieved December 10, 2022, from https://baike.baidu.hk/item/%E9%AB%98%E7%A6%96/5510998

26 高禖. (n.d.). 華人百科. Retrieved October 5, 2021, from https://www.itsfun.com.tw/高禖/wiki-9260641-7171831

27 李亨利. (1998, March 22). 上巳節 求良緣. etaoist. Retrieved December 10, 2022, from http://www.etaoist.org/taoist/index.php/2011-08-07-02-10-49/2011-08-07-04-53-23/1044-2011-09-29-13-17-58

28 宋岳雪 (2014). 一夕輕雷落萬絲 -- 穀雨 (pp. 49-50) . In 歲月之二十四節氣裡的眾神節慶與傳說. 貓咪予花兒

29 張超 (2014). 第七章---穀雨--降水明顯增多,有利穀物生長的節氣 (pp, 150-151). In 二十四節氣常識一本通. 龍圖騰文化有限公司

30 宋岳雪 (2014). 一夕輕雷落萬絲 -- 穀雨 (pp. 50-51) . In 歲月之二十四節氣裡的眾神節慶與傳說. 貓咪予花兒

31 張超 (2014). 第七章---穀雨--降水明顯增多,有利穀物生長的節氣 (pp, 149-150). In 二十四節氣常識一本通. 龍圖騰文化有限公司

32 DY, A. C. (2014). The Virgin Mary as Mazu or Guanyin: The Syncretic Nature of Chinese Religion in the Philippines. Philippine Sociological Review, 62, 41–63. http://www.jstor.org/stable/43486492

33 Pregadio, F. (2008). Mazu. In Encyclopedia of Taoism (Vol. II, pp. 741–744). Routledge.

34 周濯街 (2001). 媽祖. 國家出版社.

35 Yuan, H. (2006). Mazu, Mother Goddess of the Sea. In The Magic Lotus Lantern and Other Tales from the Han Chinese (pp. 122–124). Libraries Unlimited.

36 农民的小帮手. (n.d.). 穀雨有"講究"? 今日穀雨，牢記"吃 3 樣做 3 事忌 2 事"，平安迎夏. 知乎專欄. Retrieved December 10, 2022, from https://zhuanlan.zhihu.com/p/501933985

37 張超 (2014). 第七章---穀雨--降水明顯增多,有利穀物生長的節氣 (p, 151). In 二十四節氣常識一本通. 龍圖騰文化有限公司

38 張樹棟, 龐多益, & 鄭如斯. (1999). 第三章 信息載體——文字的產生發展和規範. In 中華印刷通史. 印刷業出版社.

39 宋岳雪 (2014). 一夕輕雷落萬絲 -- 穀雨 (pp. 51-52) . In 歲月之二十四節氣裡的眾神節慶與傳說. 貓咪予花兒

40 淮南子, 本經訓, 4

41 Wen, B. (2016). The History of Fu Craft. In The Tao of Craft: Fu talismans and casting sigils in the Eastern Esoteric Tradition. North Atlantic Books.

42 Giddens, S., & Giddens, O. (2006). Introduction. In Chinese Mythology (p. 4). Rosen Publishing Group.

43 Allan, T., Phillips, C., & Chinnery, J. D. (2005). Gifts of the Gods. In Chinese Myth (pp. 51-53). Barnes & Noble.

44 Yang, D., An, D., & Turner, J. A. (2005). Huang Di. In Handbook of Chinese Mythology (pp 138-144). ABC-CLIO.

45 iNews. (n.d.)., Folklore "going to rain", why did the big girl and the little wife go for a stroll in the wild? So there is a story here. Retrieved December 10, 2022, from https://inf.news/en/culture/133f86d0f4af7de02162885a7b73b44d.html

[46] 信息中心. (2012, March 26). 牡丹故事：灑脫紅花仙 不俗黑牡丹. 中華人民共和國文化和旅遊部. Retrieved December 10, 2022, from https://www.mct.gov.cn/preview/special/3578/3587/201204/t20120411_236821.html

[47] 宋岳雪 (2014). 一夕輕雷落萬絲 -- 穀雨 (pp. 52-53) . In 歲月之二十四節氣裡的眾神節慶與傳說. 貓咪予花兒

Chapter 7: Summer Begins

[1] Olcott, W. T. (1914). Ancient Ideas of the Sun and Moon. In Sun Lore of All Ages: A Collection of Myths and Legends Concerning the Sun and Its Worship (p. 36). G. P. Putnam's and Sons.

[2] Hawkes, J. (1963). Sun Father and Earth Mother. In Man and the Sun (p. 59). The Cresset Press.

[3] 行政院農業委員會. (n.d.). 節氣時光. 食農教育資訊整合平臺. Retrieved December 11, 2022, from https://fae.coa.gov.tw/theme_data.php?theme=kids_edu_topics&id=6

[4] 國家教育研究院. (2021). 辭典檢視 [螻蟈] . 教育部《重編國語辭典修訂本》2021. Retrieved December 11, 2022, from https://dict.revised.moe.edu.tw/dictView.jsp?ID=60703&la=0&powerMode=0

[5] 光山縣人民政府辦公室. (2017, May 5). 今日立夏. 光山縣人民政府. Retrieved December 11, 2022, from http://www.guangshan.gov.cn/news/tpxw/2017-05-05/47036.html

[6] 七修類稿, 卷三天地類, 18

[7] 月令七十二候集解, 月令七十二候集解, 63

[8] 本草綱目, 蟲之四 （濕生類二十三種，附錄七種）,蚯蚓, 5

[9] 莊溪. (n.d.). 王瓜. 認識植物 - 植物面面觀. Retrieved December 11, 2022, from http://kplant.biodiv.tw/%E7%8E%8B%E7%93%9C/%E7%8E%8B%E7%93%9C.htm

[10] 星火綠農. (2020, May 5). 螻蟈鳴，蚯蚓出，王瓜生. 今天頭條. Retrieved December 11, 2022, from https://twgreatdaily.com/Jbkh43EBfGB4SiUwYGnL.html

[11] 遵生八牋, 卷四, 60

[12] 中華人民共和國中央人民政府. (2007, October 11). Gov.cn. Retrieved December 11, 2022, from http://big5.www.gov.cn/gate/big5/www.gov.cn/fwxx/content_774022.htm

[13] 中華人民共和國中央人民政府. (2007, October 11). Gov.cn. Retrieved December 11, 2022, from http://big5.www.gov.cn/gate/big5/www.gov.cn/fwxx/content_774022.htm

[14] 行政院農業委員會. (n.d.). 立夏（國曆 5 月 5 或 6 或 7 日） . Retrieved December 10, 2022, from https://www.coa.gov.tw/ws.php?id=2507779

[15] 國學堂. (2014, March 9). 立夏時民間禁忌. 國易堂-中國周易、易經算命文化傳播網. Retrieved December 11, 2022, from https://www.guoyi360.com/24jieqi/lixia/6734.html

[16] 張超 (2014). 第八章---立夏-夏季開始的節氣 (pp. 163-164). In 二十四節氣常識一本通. 龍圖騰文化有限公司

[17] 王彤. (2010). 第二篇夏季養生法. In 黃帝內經二十四節氣養生法. 捷徑文化. (http://www.book853.com/wap.aspx?nid=2498&p=25&cid=173)

[18] 張超 (2014). 第八章---立夏-夏季開始的節氣 (p. 170). In 二十四節氣常識一本通. 龍圖騰文化有限公司

[19] 禮記, 月令, 31-40

[20] 帝京景物略, 卷二, 72

[21] 殷登國 (1983). 穀雨. In 中國的花神與節氣 (p. 150). 民生報業書

[22] 殷登國 (1983). 穀雨. In 中國的花神與節氣 (p. 152). 民生報業書

[23] 張超 (2014). 第八章---立夏-夏季開始的節氣 (pp. 164-165). In 二十四節氣常識一本通. 龍圖騰文化有限公司

[24] 殷登國 (1983). 穀雨. In 中國的花神與節氣 (p. 154). 民生報業書

[25] 采風教室 . (n.d.). 門檻=戶凳 ～慕人. Retrieved December 11, 2022, from http://lugang.tomio.idv.tw/cdwc1d.htm

[26] 東森新聞. (2021, May 5). 「立夏」2 大禁忌一次看 坐門檻小心衰整年. Yahoo! Sports. Retrieved December 11, 2022, from https://tw.sports.yahoo.com/news/%E7%AB%8B%E5%A4%8F-2%E5%A4%A7%E7%A6%81%E5%BF%8C-%E6%AC%A1%E7%9C%8B-%E5%9D%90%E9%96%80%E6%AA%BB%E5%B0%8F%E5%BF%83%E8%A1%B0%E6%95%B4%E5%B9%B4-035600345.html

[27] 張超 (2014). 第八章---立夏-夏季開始的節氣 (p. 167). In 二十四節氣常識一本通. 龍圖騰文化有限公司

[28] 殷登國 (1983). 穀雨. In 中國的花神與節氣 (p. 154). 民生報業書

[29] 殷登國 (1983). 穀雨. In 中國的花神與節氣 (pp. 154-155). 民生報業書

[30] 張超 (2014). 第八章---立夏-夏季開始的節氣 (pp. 165-166). In 二十四節氣常識一本通. 龍圖騰文化有限公司

[31] 中國天氣網. (2010, May 4). 立夏各地風俗. Gov.cn. Retrieved December 11, 2022, from http://big5.www.gov.cn/gate/big5/www.gov.cn/fwxx/wy/2010-05/04/content_1598858.htm

[32] 張超 (2014). 第八章---立夏-夏季開始的節氣 (pp. 166-167). In 二十四節氣常識一本通. 龍圖騰文化有限公司

[33] Bathing the buddha arches. Buddha's Day & Multicultural Festival. (2022, May 10). Retrieved December 11, 2022, from https://buddhaday.org.au/events/bathing-the-buddha-arches/

[34] Dharma Drum Mountain Global. (2021). Dharma Drum Mountain Branches Worldwide Celebrate the Buddha's Birthday. DDM Global News. Retrieved December 11, 2022, from https://www.dharmadrum.org/portal_b1_cnt_page.php?cnt_id=968&folder_id=23

[35] Chang , C. C. (n.d.). The origin of bathing the buddha. Dharma Drum Mountain. Retrieved December 11, 2022, from http://ddm.dharmadrum.org/content/printpage.aspx?type=news&sn=1594

[36] Puti Meditation College Ltd. (2020, April 21). Cloud Buddha Bathing. 浴佛. Retrieved December 11, 2022, from https://www.putizen.org/sheji/cloud-buddha-bathing/

[37] Baidu. (2020, July 10). 牛王誕. 百度百科. Retrieved December 11, 2022, from https://baike.baidu.hk/item/%E7%89%9B%E7%8E%8B%E8%AA%95/6542889

[38] 宋岳雪 (2014). 殘紅一片無綠處 -- 立夏 (pp. 57-58) . In 歲月之二十四節氣裡的眾神節慶與傳說. 貓咪予花兒

[39] Pliny the Elder, P. G., & Jones, W. H. S. (1980). LCL 370. In Natural history (p. 551). Harvard Univ. Press.

[40] Claude de, W., & Auroville, I. (n.d.). Cretan bull - interpretation - greek mythology. Mythologie Grecque. https://www.greekmyths-interpretation.com/en/final-labours-heracles-interpretation-greek-mythology/cretan-bull-interpretation/

[41] Sohu. (2021, February 12). 中国人为什么如此"牛": 中华民族基因中"牛"最特殊_野牛. Retrieved December 11, 2022, from https://www.sohu.com/a/450548680_260616

[42] 宋岳雪 (2014). 殘紅一片無綠處 -- 立夏 (pp. 58-59). In 歲月之二十四節氣裡的眾神節慶與傳說. 貓咪予花兒

[43] 列異傳, 5-6

[44] 列異傳, 52

[45] 列仙傳, 老子, 1

[46] 西遊記, 心猿空用千般計　水火無功難煉魔

[47] 封神演義, 三姑計擺黃河陣 (16), 老子一氣化三清 (9), 三教大會萬仙陣 (7)

[48] 東遊記, 戲放青牛亂宮

Chapter 8: Little Fullness

[1] 殷登國 (1983). 小滿. In 中國的花神與節氣 (p. 156). 民生報業書

[2] 埤雅, 卷三十二, 15

[3] 康熙字典, 非部, 十一, 1

[4] 莊溪. (n.d.). 王瓜. 認識植物 - 植物面面觀. Retrieved December 11, 2022, from http://kplant.biodiv.tw/%E5%B1%B1%E8%8A%A5%E8%8F%9C/%E5%B1%B1%E8%8A%A5%E8%8F%9C.htm

[5] 行政院農業委員會. (n.d.). 小滿. 農業知識入口網. Retrieved December 12, 2022, from https://kmweb.coa.gov.tw/theme_data.php?theme=solar_terms&id=313

[6] Gujin Tushu Jicheng, Volume 682 (1700-1725).djvu/5（June 2, 2020）. Wikisource. Retrieved December 12, 2022 from https://zh.wikisource.org/w/index.php?title=Page:Gujin_Tushu_Jicheng,_Volume_682_(1700-1725).djvu/5&oldid=1841804

[7] 清嘉錄, 3, 小滿動二車

[8] Baidu. (2022, August 25). 小滿動三車. 百度百科. Retrieved December 12, 2022, from https://baike.baidu.hk/item/%E5%B0%8F%E6%BB%BF%E5%8B%95%E4%B8%89%E8%BB%8A/53627612

[9] 張超 (2014). 第九章---小滿-麥類作物籽粒始飽滿的節氣 (pp. 181-182). In 二十四節氣常識一本通. 龍圖騰文化有限公司

[10] 自由時報 (2022, May 21). 「小滿」節氣防暑濕! 中醫: 清淡飲食 戒怒戒躁. 健康網 - 樂活飲食. Retrieved December 12, 2022, from https://health.ltn.com.tw/article/breakingnews/3934284

[11] 行政院農業委員會農業試驗所. (n.d.). 小滿之介紹及民俗諺語 - 小滿 Grain buds. 農作物災害預警平台. Retrieved December 12, 2022, from https://disaster.tari.gov.tw/ARI/solarterm/web_new/Solar_term_8.html

[12] 行政院農業委員會農業試驗所. (n.d.). 廿四節氣農諺歌. Retrieved December 12, 2022, from https://disaster.tari.gov.tw/ARI/solarterm/web_new/Solar_term_taiwan_4.html

[13] UNESCO. (n.d.). Sericulture and silk craftsmanship of china. Silk Roads Programme. Retrieved December 12, 2022, from https://en.unesco.org/silkroad/silk-road-themes/intangible-cultural-heritage/sericulture-and-silk-craftsmanship-china

[14] Baidu. (n.d.). 祈蠶節. 百度百科. Retrieved December 12, 2022, from https://baike.baidu.com/item/%E7%A5%88%E8%9A%95%E8%8A%82/61091263

[15] 中國天氣網. (2010, May 19). 小滿節氣的習俗. Retrieved December 12, 2022, from http://big5.www.gov.cn/gate/big5/www.gov.cn/fwxx/wy/2010-05/19/content_1609151.htm

[16] Baidu. (2022, July 19). 白族繞三靈. 百度百科. Retrieved December 12, 2022, from https://baike.baidu.hk/item/%E7%99%BD%E6%97%8F%E7%B9%9E%E4%B8%89%E9%9D%88/3439025

[17] 張超 (2014). 第九章---小滿-麥類作物籽粒始飽滿的節氣 (p. 180). In 二十四節氣常識一本通. 龍圖騰文化有限公司

[18] 農書, 卷六, 5

[19] UNESCO. (n.d.). Sericulture and Silk Craftsmanship of China. Intangible Cultural Heritage. Retrieved December 12, 2022, from https://ich.unesco.org/en/RL/sericulture-and-silk-craftsmanship-of-china-00197

[20] 史記, 本紀, 五帝本紀, 5

[21] 宋岳雪 (2014). 麥穗初齊稚子嬌--小滿 (p. 68). In 歲月之二十四節氣裡的眾神節慶與傳說. 貓咪予花兒

[22] 宋岳雪 (2014). 麥穗初齊稚子嬌--小滿 (p. 68-69). In 歲月之二十四節氣裡的眾神節慶與傳說. 貓咪予花兒

[23] 童心. (n.d.). 螺祖的传说. BJtextile. Retrieved December 12, 2022, from http://www.bjtextile.com/information/history/301.htm

[24] Liu, S. T. T. (1983). The Silkworm. In Dragons, Gods & Spirits from Chinese Mythology (p. 45). Schocken Books.

[25] 搜神記, 第十四卷

[26] 太平廣記, 昆蟲七, 蠶女

[27] Liu, S. T. T. (1983). The Silkworm. In Dragons, Gods & Spirits from Chinese Mythology (p. 45). Schocken Books.

[28] Liu, S. T. T. (1983). The Silkworm. In Dragons, Gods & Spirits from Chinese Mythology (p. 46). Schocken Books.

[29] Martens, F. H. (1921). XXI - The Girls with the Horse's Head or The Silkworm Goddess. In R. Wilhelm (Ed.), The Chinese Fairy Book (pp. 56–57). Frederick A, Stokes Company.

[30] 宋岳雪 (2014). 麥穗初齊稚子嬌--小滿 (p. 69-70). In 歲月之二十四節氣裡的眾神節慶與傳說. 貓咪予花兒

[31] Liu, S. T. T. (1983). The Silkworm. In Dragons, Gods & Spirits from Chinese Mythology (p. 46). Schocken Books.

[32] Baidu. (2021, December 4). 青衣神. 百度百科. Retrieved December 12, 2022, from https://baike.baidu.hk/item/%E9%9D%92%E8%A1%A3%E7%A5%9E/2455071

[33] 宋岳雪 (2014). 麥穗初齊稚子嬌--小滿 (pp. 70-71). In 歲月之二十四節氣裡的眾神節慶與傳說. 貓咪予花兒

[34] XinMedia. (2016, May 10). [四川]老子傳道的聖地成都青羊宮. 欣傳媒. Retrieved December 12, 2022, from https://blog.xinmedia.com/album/71032

Chapter 9: Grain Ripens

[1] 中文數位化技術推廣基金會. (2021). 芒. 國語辭典簡編本. Retrieved December 13, 2022, from https://dict.concised.moe.edu.tw/dictView.jsp?ID=4283&la=0&powerMode=0

[2] 國家林業和草原局. (2022, June 7). 二十四節氣｜村村逐芒種 播谷滿蒥田. 防城港市林業局. Retrieved December 13, 2022, from http://www.fcgs.gov.cn/lyj/dtxx/202206/t20220607_254323.html

[3] Laufer, Berthold (1913) "The Praying Mantis in Chinese Folklore (Illustrated).," The Open Court: Vol. 1913 : Iss. 1 , Article 6. https://opensiuc.lib.siu.edu/ocj/vol1913/iss1/6

[4] 莊子, 外篇, 山木, 8.1

[5] 莊子, 內篇, 人間世, 4

[6] 世界針灸學會聯合會. (n.d.). 二十四節氣文化專題- 芒種. -World Federation of acupuncture-moxibustion societies. Retrieved December 13, 2022, from http://en.wfas.org.cn/news/daodu-detail.html?nid=733&cid=41

[7] Brewster, W. (1894). Note on the Habits of the Northern Shrike (Lanius borealis). The Auk, 11(4), 329–330. https://doi.org/10.2307/4068622

[8] Knickelbine, J. (2020, February 8). Meet the 'butcher bird,' which impales its victims on thorns and Barbed Wire. Herald Times Reporter. Retrieved December 13, 2022, from https://www.htrnews.com/story/life/2020/02/08/butcher-bird-shrikes-impale-bodies-victims-thorns-barbed-wire-wisconsin/4682445002/

[9] Blanchan, N. (1907). The Butcher Birds or Shrikes. In Birds Every Child Should Know (p. 79). Grosset and Dunlap.

[10] Forshaw, J. M. (1991). In Encyclopedia of Animals: Birds (p. 180). Merehurst Limited.

[11] 詩經, 國風, 豳風, 七月, 3.1

[12] 殷登國 (1983). 芒種. In 中國的花神與節氣 (p. 160). 民生報業書

[13] 台北時報. (1999, September 8). Bird Poacher Busted in National Park. Taipei Times. Retrieved December 13, 2022, from https://www.taipeitimes.com/News/local/archives/1999/09/09/0000001440

[14] 伯勞鳥生態環境展示館. 楓港社區文化共享平台. (n.d.). Retrieved December 13, 2022, from http://fun.aeweb.com.tw/Web/notice-detail.php?doc=9_%E4%BC%AF%E5%8B%9E%E9%B3%A5%E7%94%9F%E6%85%8B%E7%92%B0%E5%A2%83%E5%B1%95%E7%A4%BA%E9%A4%A8

[15] 御定淵鑑類函, 卷四百二十八, 75

[16] 殷登國 (1983). 芒種. In 中國的花神與節氣 (pp. 160-162). 民生報業書

[17] 新華社. (2008, June 5). 5 日芒種: "三夏"大忙時節防汛抗災工作不容放鬆. 中央政府門戶網站. Retrieved December 13, 2022, from http://big5.www.gov.cn/gate/big5/www.gov.cn/fwxx/kp/2008-06/05/content_1006245.htm

[18] 張超 (2014). 第十章---芒種-夏收種繁忙的節氣 (p. 193). In 二十四節氣常識一本通. 龍圖騰文化有限公司

[19] 一天網. (2022, June 12). 芒種至, 俗語"芒種刮北風, 旱斷青苗根", 啥意思? . Retrieved December 13, 2022, from https://onday.cc/zh-tw/article/490402.html

[20] 張超 (2014). 第十章---芒種-夏收種繁忙的節氣 (pp. 191-192). In 二十四節氣常識一本通. 龍圖騰文化有限公司

[21] 張超 (2014). 第十章---芒種-夏收種繁忙的節氣 (p. 197). In 二十四節氣常識一本通. 龍圖騰文化有限公司

[22] Yahoo! (2022, June 7). 節氣芒種濕熱煩躁 喝這個最好! 一味茶飲生津止渴 精油怡情防蚊. Yahoo! News. Retrieved December 13, 2022, from https://tw.news.yahoo.com 節氣芒種濕熱煩躁-喝這個最好-味茶飲生津止渴-精油怡情防蚊-000000998.html

[23] Liu, S. T. T. (1983). Yu Controls the Flood. In Dragons, Gods & Spirits from Chinese Mythology (p. 33). Schocken Books.

[24] 禮記, 月令, 41-48

[25] 齊民要術, 卷三, 14

[26] 清嘉錄, 三, 黃梅天

[27] 曹雪芹, 紅樓夢, 第二十七回

[28] Gujin Tushu Jicheng, Volume 555 (1700-1725).djvu/30. (June 10, 2020). Wikisource. Retrieved December 13, 2022 from https://zh.wikisource.org/w/index.php?title=Page:Gujin_Tushu_Jicheng,_Volume_555_(1700-1725).djvu/30&oldid=1909174

[29] 西京雜記, 第五, 6

[30] 宋岳雪 (2014). 年年披絮插秋寒(p. 74-75). In 歲月之二十四節氣裡的眾神節慶與傳說. 貓咪予花兒

[31] 棗樹開甲. 鄭州航空港區天澤苗木種植專業合作社. (n.d.). Retrieved December 13, 2022, from http://www.huizaojiesui.com/aspcms/news/2014-12-9/209.html

[32] TIMEART. (n.d.). 芒種, 五月節. 謂有芒之種穀可稼種矣. Retrieved December 13, 2022, from https://timeart.co/corn-on-ear/

[33] Baidu. (2022, June 3). 端午的"端"和"午"是啥意思? 端午最初並不是為紀念屈原的. 到百科. Retrieved December 13, 2022, from https://baike.baidu.com/tashuo/browse/content?id=eca9aca4e86b594ed52788c0

[34] 宋岳雪 (2014). 麥穗初齊稚子嬌--小滿 (p. 60). In 歲月之二十四節氣裡的眾神節慶與傳說. 貓咪予花兒

[35] 穆天子傳 -> 卷五 -> 1

[36] 百科知識中文網. 龍舟賽. (n.d.). Retrieved December 13, 2022, from https://www.jendow.com.tw/wiki/%E9%BE%8D%E8%88%9F%E8%B3%BD

[37] 文民設計部. (2022, March 7). 這地方端午不一樣: 全台唯一媽祖端午出巡「祭江洗港」劃分陰陽保安寧. 台灣文民. Retrieved December 13, 2022, from https://www.taiwanfolk.com/blog/detail/21

[38] 太平御覽, 時序部十六, 五月五日, 5

[39] 百科知識中文網. (n.d.). 惡日:古時迷信稱農曆五月五日為惡日. Retrieved December 13, 2022, from https://www.jendow.com.tw/wiki/%E6%83%A1%E6%97%A5

[40] 史記, 列傳, 孟嘗君列傳

[41] Sima, Qian (1995). The Grand Scribe's Records, vol. VII. Bloomington, Indiana: Indiana University Press. pp. 189

[42] MPA Media. (n.d.). Mugwort Leaf (ai ye). Acupuncture Today. Retrieved December 13, 2022, from https://acupuncturetoday.com/herbcentral/mugwort_leaf.php

[43] Angier, Bradford (1974). Field Guide to Edible Wild Plants. Harrisburg, PA: Stackpole Books. p. 224. ISBN 0-8117-0616-8. OCLC 799792.

[44] Rajput, S. B., Tonge, M. B., & Karuppayil, S. M. (2014). An overview on traditional uses and pharmacological profile of Acorus calamus Linn. (Sweet flag) and other Acorus species. Phytomedicine : international journal of phytotherapy and phytopharmacology, 21(3), 268–276. https://doi.org/10.1016/j.phymed.2013.09.020

[45] 中華民國文化部. (2010, June 7). 五月五慶端午. 鬥陣看社區民俗活動拼活力!. 台灣社區通. Retrieved December 26, 2022, from

https://communitytaiwan.moc.gov.tw/Item/Detail/五月五慶端午. 鬥陣看社區民俗活動拼活力!

[46] 荊楚歲時記, 第一部寶顏堂秘笈本, 59

[47] 宋岳雪 (2014). 麥穗初齊稚子嬌--小滿 (p. 61-62). In 歲月之二十四節氣裡的眾神節慶與傳說. 貓咪予花兒

[48] 孫次舟 (1944), 屈原是文學弄臣的發疑, 中央日報

[49] Storm Media Group . (2020, June 22). 不是中國人不能過端午節? 他揭超驚人歷史真相: 端午節其實源自越南! -. 風傳媒. Retrieved December 13, 2022, from https://www.storm.mg/lifestyle/1378687?page=1

[50] Nam quốc văn. (2019, June 10). 【越南想想】蛤! ? 端午節源頭來自越南. Thinking Taiwan. Retrieved December 13, 2022, from https://www.thinkingtaiwan.com/content/7658

[51] 宋岳雪 (2014). 麥穗初齊稚子嬌--小滿 (p. 62-63). In 歲月之二十四節氣裡的眾神節慶與傳說. 貓咪予花兒

[52] Baidu. (2022, June 10). 曹娥. 百度百科. Retrieved December 13, 2022, from https://baike.baidu.hk/item/%E6%9B%B9%E5%A8%A5/4231775

[53] Baidu. (2022, March 28). 迎濤神. 百度百科. Retrieved December 13, 2022, from https://baike.baidu.hk/item/%E8%BF%8E%E6%BF%A4%E7%A5%9E/15796465

[54] 宋岳雪 (2014). 麥穗初齊稚子嬌--小滿 (p. 65-67). In 歲月之二十四節氣裡的眾神節慶與傳說. 貓咪予花兒

Chapter 10: Summer Solstice

[1] 周冰. (2022, June 21). 24 solar terms: 6 things you may not know about summer solstice. Chinadaily.com.cn. Retrieved December 14, 2022, from https://www.chinadaily.com.cn/a/202206/21/WS5d0c0ff0a3103dbf14329653_3.html

[2] 殷登國 (1983). 夏至. In 中國的花神與節氣 (p. 169). 民生報業書

[3] 中央社即時新聞. (2011, June 21). 夏至 古時候放假一天. Retrieved December 14, 2022, from https://web.archive.org/web/20111117104401/http://www2.cna.com.tw/ShowNews/Detail.aspx?pNewsID=201106210244&pType0=aCN&pTypeSel=0

[4] 漢書, 傳, 薛宣朱博傳, 8

[5] 完顏紹元. (2015, October 20). 古代公務員的休假制度. Retrieved December 14, 2022, from https://www.ylib.com/sango/newplace/newplace051020.asp

[6] Steven HCF, Sum TS (2017) Transformations of Cultural Heritage of Dragon Boat Racings in Hong Kong Context. Anthropol 5: 194. p.2, doi:10.4172/2332-0915

[7] 本草綱目, 獸之二, (獸類三十八種), 鹿, 23

[8] 類經圖翼, 卷一, 運氣, 卷一: 運氣上, 五行生成數解, 57

[9] KKNews. (2015, May 5) 南極仙翁為何選鹿作為他的坐騎? 每日頭條. . Retrieved December 14, 2022, from https://kknews.cc/zh-tw/history/3j9be6g.html

[10] Arthur, S. (2009). Eating Your Way to Immortality: Early Daoist Self-Cultivation Diets. Journal of Daoist Studies, 2(1), p.35. doi:10.1353/dao.2009.0001

[11] 殷登國 (1983). 夏至. In 中國的花神與節氣 (p. 167). 民生報業書

[12] Stuart, J. (2020, March 25). The cicada in China. Smithsonian's National Museum of Asian Art. Retrieved December 14, 2022, from https://asia.si.edu/cicadas/

[13] 莊子, 外篇, 山木, 8.1

[14] 殷登國 (1983). 夏至. In 中國的花神與節氣 (p. 167). 民生報業書

[15] Liao, M. (2022, February 8). Summer solstice marks shorter days and Yin's rising. www.theepochtimes.com. Retrieved December 14, 2022, from https://www.theepochtimes.com/summer-solstice-marks-shorter-days-and-yins-rising_2554510.html

[16] 中華人民共和國中央人民政府. (2019, June 21). 夏至的由來. 中國政府網. Retrieved December 14, 2022, from http://big5.www.gov.cn/gate/big5/www.gov.cn/fwxx/wy/2010-06/21/content_1632282.htm

[17] 荊楚歲時記 -> 第一部寶顏堂秘笈本, 三三, 67

[18] 張超 (2014). 第十一章---夏至-炎熱將至, 日最長, 夜最短的節氣 (pp. 205-206). In 二十四節氣常識一本通. 龍圖騰文化有限公司

[19] Staying healthy in summer according to Chinese medicine. American College of Traditional Chinese Medicine. (2018, June 19). Retrieved December 14, 2022, from https://www.actcm.edu/blog/featured/summer

[20] 張超 (2014). 第十一章---夏至-炎熱將至, 日最長, 夜最短的節氣 (pp. 209-210). In 二十四節氣常識一本通. 龍圖騰文化有限公司

[21] 張鈺鑫醫師. (2022, August 16). 臺中榮民總醫院-taichung veterans general Hospital--「古法今用」中榮中醫今夏推出-"溫肺定喘天灸法". 全球資訊網. Retrieved December 14, 2022, from https://www.vghtc.gov.tw/UnitPage/RowViewDetail?WebRowsID=9e24573d-5591-4cfb-b775-a1636b85fabc&UnitID=268349df-a784-4ed4-8b9f-92cceb6f449f&CompanyID=e8e0488e-54a0-44bf-b10c-d029c423f6e7&UnitDefaultTemplate=6

[22] Zhou, F., Yan, L. J., Yang, G. Y., & Liu, J. P. (2015). Acupoint herbal patching for allergic rhinitis: a systematic review and meta-analysis of randomised controlled trials. Clinical Otolaryngology, 40(6), 551–568. https://doi.org/10.1111/coa.12410

[23] Wen, C. Y. Z., Liu, Y. F., Zhou, L., Zhang, H. X., & Tu, S. H. (2015). A Systematic and Narrative Review of Acupuncture Point Application Therapies in the Treatment of Allergic Rhinitis and Asthma during Dog Days. Evidence-Based Complementary and Alternative Medicine, 2015, 1–10. https://doi.org/10.1155/2015/846851

[24] 欽定授時通考, 卷四十六, 94

[25] 史記, 書, 封禪書, 4

[26] KKNews. (2019, June 21). 今日夏至, 這天山東各地普遍要吃涼麵條, 老風俗看看啦 每日頭條. 美食. Retrieved December 14, 2022, from https://kknews.cc/food/kvql93r.html

[27] 台灣大紀元. (2015, June 23). 夏至陽氣至極 帝王祭地祈求風調雨順. Retrieved December 14, 2022, from https://www.epochtimes.com.tw/夏至陽氣至極-帝王祭地祈求風調雨順.html

[28] 易奇八字. (2017, April 24). 夏至"忌雨"和"防"疰夏""習俗-夏至-养生-夏至. 易奇八字. Retrieved December 14, 2022, from https://www.yiqibazi.com/jq/50/81/5298.html

[29] 潯州府O鑫森淼焱垚. (2021, May 9). 广西玉林: 吃狗肉之风源自秦国德公, 盛于玉林, 可是你知道怎么挑选狗肉吗? _手机网易网. 狗肉|玉林|羊肉|黑狗. https://m.163.com/dy/article/G9IHFLN10543HBSA.html

[30] 張超 (2014). 第十一章---夏至-炎熱將至, 日最長, 夜最短的節氣 (p. 207). In 二十四節氣常識一本通. 龍圖騰文化有限公司

[31] Linshi, J. (2021, April 28). Yulin Festival: China dog meat eating event sparks backlash. Time. Retrieved December 14, 2022, from https://time.com/2891222/yullin-festival-dog-meat-china/

[32] 清嘉錄 三, 囯帝生日磨刀雨, 7

[33] 天氣萬年曆. (2018, May 17). 2018. Retrieved December 14, 2022, from https://wannianli.tianqi.com/news/220198.html

[34] 農曆五月二十三夏至，為啥說夏至在月末不好？老祖宗的忠告. Toutiao.com. (2022, June 19). Retrieved December 14, 2022, from https://www.toutiao.com/article/7110862000909681152/?wid=1671006792658

[35] 壹讀. (2015, June 22). 山東郯城夏至習俗: 牛喝參湯過夏至. read01. Retrieved December 14, 2022, from https://read01.com/zh-hk/y65joQ.html

[36] 酉陽雜俎, 續集卷八‧支動, 35

[37] 張超 (2014). 第十一章---夏至-炎熱將至, 日最長,夜最短的節氣 (p. 207). In 二十四節氣常識一本通. 龍圖騰文化有限公司

[38] Baidu. 觀荷節. 百度百科. (n.d.). Retrieved December 14, 2022, from https://baike.baidu.com/item/观荷节/7436472

[39] Li, Z (2008). "Nutrient value and processing of lotus seed". Acad Period Agric Prod Process. 2008: 42–43.

[40] 張超 (2014). 第十一章---夏至-炎熱將至, 日最長,夜最短的節氣 (p. 209). In 二十四節氣常識一本通. 龍圖騰文化有限公司

[41] Liu, Z., & Shu, Y. (2008b). Reflections on Dream of the Red Chamber. Cambria Press.

[42] 岳雪 (2014). 綠蔭幽草勝花時--夏至 (pp. 79-80). In 歲月之二十四節氣裡的眾神節慶與傳說. 貓咪予花兒

[43] KKNews. (2018, July 12). 唐代女詩人晁采與文茂青梅竹馬，終成眷屬. 每日頭條. Retrieved December 14, 2022, from https://kknews.cc/zh-tw/culture/e3genan.html

[44] Baidu. (2021, December 5). 晁採. 百度百科. Retrieved December 14, 2022, from https://baike.baidu.hk/item/晁採//7431791

[45] Syro-Malabar Catholic Church or Church of Malabar Syrian Catholics. (2017, June 24). Feast of St. John the Baptist and Summer Solstice. St. Alphonsa SyroMalabar Church Baltimore. Retrieved December 14, 2022, from https://stalphonsachurch.org/feast-of-st-john-the-baptist-and-summer-solstice/

[46] Baidu. (2022, June 20). 星迴節. 百度百科. Retrieved December 14, 2022, from https://baike.baidu.hk/item/星迴節/8358646

[47] 岳雪 (2014). 綠蔭幽草勝花時--夏至 (pp. 78-79). In 歲月之二十四節氣裡的眾神節慶與傳說. 貓咪予花兒

[48] 火把节 (彝族火把节). 百度百科. (n.d.). Retrieved December 14, 2022, from https://baike.baidu.com/item/火把节 (彝族火把节)/49849756?fromtitle=彝族火把节&fromid=10771285

[49] 岳雪 (2014). 綠蔭幽草勝花時--夏至 (p. 82). In 歲月之二十四節氣裡的眾神節慶與傳說. 貓咪予花兒

[50] 央視國際. (2003, July 22). 火把節的民俗文化內涵. 清境火把節〈活動官網〉. Retrieved December 14, 2022, from https://torch.cja.org.tw/index.php/studies/233-2010-07-23-21-25-42.html

[51] Minahan, James B. (2014). Ethnic Groups of North, East, and Central Asia: An Encyclopedia. ABD-CLIO. p. 316. ISBN 9781610690188.

[52] 岳雪 (2014). 綠蔭幽草勝花時--夏至 (p. 87). In 歲月之二十四節氣裡的眾神節慶與傳說. 貓咪予花兒

[53] 中華人民共和國中央人民政府. (2007, November 9). 彝族. 中國政府網. Retrieved December 14, 2022, from http://big5.www.gov.cn/gate/big5/www.gov.cn/node_13949/content_800942.htm

[54] 南詔野史, 41(皮邏閣)

[55] 岳雪 (2014). 綠蔭幽草勝花時--夏至 (p. 83). In 歲月之二十四節氣裡的眾神節慶與傳說. 貓咪予花兒

[56] Newton. (n.d.). 白潔夫人. 中文百科全書. Retrieved December 14, 2022, from https://www.newton.com.tw/wiki/白潔夫人

[57] 林錦婷. (2007). 《南詔野史》「火燒松明樓」故事研究——歷史與傳說的演變. 有鳳初鳴年刊, 3, 91–102.

[58] Tabulation on the 2010 Population Census of the People's Republic of China. 國家統計局. (n.d.). Retrieved December 14, 2022, from http://www.stats.gov.cn/tjsj/pcsj/rkpc/6rp/indexch.htm

[59] Skutsch, C., & Ryle, J. M. (2005). Bai. In Encyclopedia of the World's Minorities (pp. 175–176). Routledge.

[60] 岳雪 (2014). 綠蔭幽草勝花時--夏至 (p. 84). In 歲月之二十四節氣裡的眾神節慶與傳說. 貓咪予花兒

[61] KKNews. (2018, October 25). 關於火的神話故事，關於火的神話傳說. 每日頭條. Retrieved December 14, 2022, from https://kknews.cc/zh-tw/news/za6yvop.html

Chapter 11: Little Heat

[1] 客都寶. (2018, July 7). 「小暑一聲雷，倒轉做黃梅」什麼意思？ 明天小暑，農民朋友注意啦 原文網址：https://kknews.cc/agriculture/9omyngq.html. 每日頭條. Retrieved December 16, 2022, from https://kknews.cc/zh-tw/agriculture/9omyngq.html

[2] New Tang Dynasty Television. (2020, July 5). 小暑：倏忽溫風至 因循小暑來. Retrieved December 16, 2022, from https://www.ntdtv.com/b5/2020/07/05/a102886557.html

[3] 詩經, 國風, 唐風, 蟋蟀

[4] 七修類稿, 卷三天地類, 22

[5] Chinatravel.com. (n.d.). Chinese Cricket Culture. Retrieved December 16, 2022, from https://web.archive.org/web/20210228201747/https://www.chinatravel.com/facts/chinese-cricket-culture.htm

[6] Teal, C. (2022, May 14). What is the symbolism of the cricket in China? The Classroom | Empowering Students in Their College Journey. Retrieved December 16, 2022, from https://www.theclassroom.com/what-is-the-symbolism-of-the-cricket-in-china-12081068.html

[7] Feng, E. (2021, October 23). Inside the jaw-clenching world of cricket fighting in China. NPR. Retrieved December 16, 2022, from https://www.npr.org/2021/10/23/1045988512/china-cricket-fighting

[8] 月令七十二候集解, 84

[9] Eberhard, W. (2006). R, Rain. In A Dictionary of Chinese Symbols: Hidden Symbols in Chinese Life and Thought (p. 105). Routledge.

[10] 殷登國 (1983). 小暑. In 中國的花神與節氣 (pp. 176-177). 民生報業書

[11] 網信浙江. (2017, July 7). 今日小暑! 民間吃「三寶」你知道是哪「三寶」嗎？. READ01.COM . Retrieved December 17, 2022, from https://read01.com/xDD66x5.html#.Y51wtxVByF4

[12] 行政院農業委員會 . (n.d.). 小暑（國曆 7 月 6 或 7 或 8 日）. Retrieved December 17, 2022, from https://www.coa.gov.tw/ws.php?id=2507783

[13] 張超 (2014). 第十二章---小暑-天氣開始炎熱的節氣 (p. 219). In 二十四節氣常識一本通. 龍圖騰文化有限公司

[14] 黃帝內經, 靈樞經, 百病始生, 1

[15] 食農教育資訊整合平臺. (n.d.). 節氣時光. Retrieved December 16, 2022, from https://fae.coa.gov.tw/theme_data.php?theme=kids_edu_topics&id=17

[16] 禮記, 月令, 49-56

[17] 中國首都網 - 千龍網. (2018, June 29). 吃暑羊、食新、封齋 盤點小暑節氣的習俗-千龍網·. Retrieved December 17, 2022, from http://culture.qianlong.com/2018/0629/2665826.shtml

[18] 中國天氣網. (2010, July 5). 小暑節氣的習俗. Gov.cn. Retrieved December 17, 2022, from http://big5.www.gov.cn/gate/big5/www.gov.cn/fwxx/wy/2010-07/05/content_1645592.htm

[19] 中國新聞網. (2020, July 6). 小暑習俗知多少？民間流行"食新"、吃藕. 人民網. Retrieved December 17, 2022, from http://js.people.com.cn/BIG5/n2/2020/0706/c360306-34136736.html

[20] 中國孔子網綜合. (2019, July 4). 小暑諺語. 中國孔子網. Retrieved December 17, 2022, from http://www.chinakongzi.org/zt/4080/xswh/201907/t20190704_197663.htm

[21] 張超 (2014). 第十二章---小暑-天氣開始炎熱的節氣 (p. 220). In 二十四節氣常識一本通. 龍圖騰文化有限公司

[22] 苗族飲食在苗年的時候苗族人都習慣吃些啥. 中國傳統文化 - 老資料網. (n.d.). Retrieved December 17, 2022, from https://www.laoziliao.net/doc/1635503590080645

[23] 林慧文. (1993). 惠州古城的传统风俗. Guang dong ren min chu ban she. ISBN 7218012450. OCLC 299466452.

[24] 求真百科. (2020, November 24). 蟲王節檢視原始碼討論檢視歷史. 蟲王節 Retrieved December 17, 2022, from https://www.factpedia.org/index.php?title 虫王节&variant=zh-hant

[25] CN 職場指南 白族的傳統節日. (2022, July 27). Retrieved December 17, 2022, from http://www.cnrencai.com/others/jieri/595060.html

[26] Baidu. (2022, August 3). 花兒會. 百度百科. Retrieved December 17, 2022, from https://baike.baidu.hk/item/花兒會 /3880495

[27] 中國新聞網—人民政協報. (2011, July 10). "六月六"少数民族节日习俗. 民俗學博客-Folklore Blogs. Retrieved December 17, 2022, from https://www.chinesefolklore.org.cn/blog/?action-viewnews-itemid-24032

[28] 百科知識中文網. (n.d.). 姑姑節:姑姑節，農曆六月初六，又稱"回娘家節". Retrieved December 18, 2022, from https://www.jendow.com.tw/wiki/姑姑節

[29] Baidu. (2022, November 16). 天貺節. 百度百科. Retrieved December 17, 2022, from https://baike.baidu.hk/item/天貺節 /1100545

30 郭庚儒. (2022, July 4). 「天貺節」玉皇大帝出巡民間! 「開天門」必備 4 供品 求財、求壽、補運、補財庫. TVBS. Retrieved December 17, 2022, from https://health.tvbs.com.tw/life/333672

31 張超 (2014). 第十二章---小暑-天氣開始炎熱的節氣 (pp. 221-222). In 二十四節氣常識一本通. 龍圖騰文化有限公司

32 岳雪 (2014). 青草池塘處處蛙--小暑 (p. 90). In 歲月之二十四節氣裡的眾神節慶與傳說. 貓咪予花兒

33 岳雪 (2014). 青草池塘處處蛙--小暑 (p. 90). In 歲月之二十四節氣裡的眾神節慶與傳說. 貓咪予花兒

34 晉書, 列傳第十九 阮籍 嵇康 向秀 劉伶 謝鯤 胡毋輔之 畢卓 王尼 羊曼 光逸, 11

35 世說新語, 排調, 31

36 岳雪 (2014). 青草池塘處處蛙--小暑 (p. 91). In 歲月之二十四節氣裡的眾神節慶與傳說. 貓咪予花兒

37 KKNews. (2017, September 2). 《世說新語》品讀: 滿腹詩書何所為. 每日頭條. Retrieved December 18, 2022, from https://kknews.cc/zh-hk/essay/m2ajl3z.html

38 貓苑, 貓苑卷下, 316

39 岳雪 (2014). 青草池塘處處蛙--小暑 (p. 91). In 歲月之二十四節氣裡的眾神節慶與傳說. 貓咪予花兒

40 中國食品科技網. (2015, July 21). 農曆六月六習俗: 伏季節令洗晾曬 哈碾筋逮包子 原文網址: https://read01.com/zO86gO.html. 壹讀 READ01.COM. Retrieved December 18, 2022, from https://read01.com/zO86gO.html#.Y56gPBVByF4

41 Kemp, J. (2022, September 12). Tribute Elephants at the Qing Court. David Leffman. Retrieved December 18, 2022, from https://www.davidleffman.com/elephants-and-tribute-at-the-qing-court/

42 Aldrich, M. A. (2008). The Western Tartar City. In The Search for a Vanishing Beijing: A Guide to China's Capital Through the Ages (pp. 216–219). Hong Kong University Press.

43 Baidu. (2022, October 4). 躲山_百度百科. 百度百科. Retrieved December 18, 2022, from https://baike.baidu.hk/item/躲山/4692876

44 中國政府網綜合. (2007, November 9). 布依族. Retrieved December 18, 2022, from http://big5.www.gov.cn/gate/big5/www.gov.cn/node_13949/content_800920.htm

45 張超 (2014). 第十二章---小暑-天氣開始炎熱的節氣 (pp. 222-223). In 二十四節氣常識一本通. 龍圖騰文化有限公司

46 Allan, T., Phillips, C., & Chinnery, J. D. (2005). From the Vapors of Chaos. In Land of the Dragon: Chinese Myth (p. 30). Barnes & Noble.

47 Allan, T., Phillips, C., & Chinnery, J. D. (2005). From the Vapors of Chaos. In Land of the Dragon: Chinese Myth (pp. 31-33). Barnes & Noble.

48 Yang, L., An, D., & Turner, J. A. (2008). Handbook of Chinese Mythology (Handbooks of World Mythology). (pp. 176-181). Oxford University Press.

49 Werner, E. T. C. (1986). Chapter III: Costmogony--P'an Ku and the Creation Myth. In Ancient Tales & Folklore of China (p. 78). B. Mitchell.

50 Werner, E. T. C. (1986). Chapter III: Costmogony--P'an Ku and the Creation Myth. In Ancient Tales & Folklore of China (p. 76). B. Mitchell.

51 Yang, L., An, D., & Turner, J. A. (2008). Handbook of Chinese Mythology (Handbooks of World Mythology). (p. 178). Oxford University Press.

[52] Yang, L., An, D., & Turner, J. A. (2008). Handbook of Chinese Mythology (Handbooks of World Mythology). (pp. 177-178). Oxford University Press.

[53] Yang, L., An, D., & Turner, J. A. (2008). Handbook of Chinese Mythology (Handbooks of World Mythology). (p. 179). Oxford University Press.

[54] Yang, L., An, D., & Turner, J. A. (2008). Handbook of Chinese Mythology (Handbooks of World Mythology). (p. 178). Oxford University Press.

[55] Yang, L., An, D., & Turner, J. A. (2008). Handbook of Chinese Mythology (Handbooks of World Mythology). (p. 180-181). Oxford University Press.

[56] Werner, E. T. C. (1986). Chapter III: Costmogony--P'an Ku and the Creation Myth. In Ancient Tales & Folklore of China (p. 78-79). B. Mitchell.

[57] 姑姑節:姑姑節，農曆六月初六，又稱"回娘家節. 百科知識中文網. (n.d.). Retrieved December 18, 2022, from https://www.jendow.com.tw/wiki/姑姑節

[58] 張超 (2014). 第十二章---小暑-天氣開始炎熱的節氣 (p. 222). In 二十四節氣常識一本通. 龍圖騰文化有限公司

[59] Sima Qian (2006), Nienhauser, William H. Jr.; et al. (eds.), The Grand Scribe's Records, Vol. V: The Hereditary Houses of Pre-Han China, Pt. 1, (pp. 331-331). Bloomington: Indiana University Press.

[60] 董凱. (2022, May 27). 回娘家. 网易公司. Retrieved December 18, 2022, from https://www.163.com/dy/article/H8DFL1JD0521DPVG.html

[61] 岳雪 (2014). 青草池塘處處蛙--小暑 (p. 93-94) . In 歲月之二十四節氣裡的眾神節慶與傳說. 貓咪予花兒

[62] 岳雪 (2014). 青草池塘處處蛙--小暑 (p. 94-95) . In 歲月之二十四節氣裡的眾神節慶與傳說. 貓咪予花兒

[63] 廣西民族報. (2018, October 19). 神秘的西林唱婭王. 每日頭條. Retrieved December 18, 2022, from https://kknews.cc/news/3bky828.html

Chapter 12: Great Heat

[1] 文海披沙, 三, 人情難易

[2] 道德經, 45

[3] Baidu. (2022, January 14). 腐草為螢. 百度百科. Retrieved December 20, 2022, from https://baike.baidu.hk/item/腐草為螢/10814619

[4] 七修類稿, 卷三天地類, 23

[5] National Palace Museum. (n.d.). 宋李迪風雨歸牧 軸, K2A000087N000000000PAA, Open Government Data License, version 1.0

[6] 中華人民共和國中央人民政府. (2007, October 11). 大暑. 中國政府網. Retrieved December 20, 2022, from http://big5.www.gov.cn/gate/big5/www.gov.cn/fwxx/content_774032.htm

[7] 湖南省气象局. (2009, July 23). 大暑. 湖南省气象服务中心. Retrieved December 20, 2022, from http://hn.cma.gov.cn/qxkp/qxzs/200907/t20090723_636931.html

[8] 中國天氣網. (2009, July 23). 大暑節氣的由來. Retrieved December 20, 2022, from http://big5.www.gov.cn/gate/big5/www.gov.cn/fwxx/wy/2009-07/23/content_1372468.htm

[9] 張超 (2014). 第十三章---大暑--一年中最熱的節氣 (pp. 231-232). In 二十四節氣常識一本通. 龍圖騰文化有限公司

[10] 王学思. (2015, July 22). 二十四节气: 大暑. 中國民俗學網. Retrieved December 20, 2022, from https://www.chinafolklore.org/web/index.php?NewsID=15252

[11] Green Bay, WI Weather Forecast Office. (2021, June 10). Heat safety. NOAA's National Weather Service. Retrieved December 20, 2022, from https://www.weather.gov/grb/heat

[12] 張超 (2014). 第十三章---大暑--一年中最熱的節氣 (p. 234). In 二十四節氣常識一本通. 龍圖騰文化有限公司

[13] 商業周刊. (2013, July 15). 夏天如何避免得冷氣病? 商業周刊 1286 期. 良醫健康網. Retrieved December 20, 2022, from https://health.businessweekly.com.tw/AArticle.aspx?id=ARTL000001712

[14] 禮記, 月令, 57

[15] 中華民國文化部. (2011, July 15). 穀仔弦說唱半年節. 基隆市 仁愛區 基隆市原鄉文化協進會. Retrieved December 20, 2022, from https://sixstar.moc.gov.tw/blog/junjon/myArticleAction.do?method=doViewArticleNewDetail&articleId=27857

[16] Baidu. (n.d.). 半年节 -. 快懂百科. Retrieved December 20, 2022, from https://www.baike.com/wikiid/5741024560314360151?view_id=2e016ztl99b94w

[17] 行政院農業委員會. (n.d.). 趣味鄉土諺語. 農業兒童網. Retrieved December 20, 2022, from https://kids.coa.gov.tw/view.php?func=solar&id=14& print=1

[18] 右台仙館筆記, 28 (臨海縣民比年癘疾, 過大暑不瘳...)

[19] 封神演義, 姜子牙歸國封神, 99

[20] Baidu. (2022, July 4). 黑虎玄壇. 百度百科. Retrieved December 20, 2022, from https://baike.baidu.hk/item/黑虎玄壇/15719960

Chapter 13: Autumn Begins

[1] 國語辭典. (n.d.). 秋老虎. Retrieved December 21, 2022, from https://dictionary.chienwen.net/word/ae/c7/796e9e-秋老虎.html

[2] 張超 (2014). 第十四章---立秋--秋季開始的節氣 (pp. 242-243). In 二十四節氣常識一本通. 龍圖騰文化有限公司

[3] 七修類稿, 卷三天地類, 24

[4] 國語, 周語中, 21.2

[5] 月令七十二候集解, 94

[6] 中華人民共和國中央人民政府. (2009, August 6). 二十四節氣-立秋. 中國政府網. Retrieved December 21, 2022, from http://big5.www.gov.cn/gate/big5/www.gov.cn/fwxx/content_1385019.htm

[7] 張超 (2014). 第十四章---立秋--秋季開始的節氣 (pp. 243-244). In 二十四節氣常識一本通. 龍圖騰文化有限公司

[8] 張超 (2014). 第十四章---立秋--秋季開始的節氣 (p. 250). In 二十四節氣常識一本通. 龍圖騰文化有限公司

[9] 中國醫藥大學附設醫院. (2022, August 5). 立秋養生法: 醫療新聞. Retrieved December 21, 2022, from https://www.cmuh.cmu.edu.tw/NewsInfo/NewsArticle?no=8017

[10] 禮記, 月令, 59-66

[11] 東京夢華錄, 第八卷, 立秋

[12] 夢梁錄, 卷四, 七月（立秋附）

[13] 帝京景物略, 卷二, 75

[14] 酌中志, 卷二十飲食好尚紀略, 5

[15] 殷登國 (1983). 立秋. In 中國的花神與節氣 (p. 190). 民生報業書

[16] Baidu. (2022, October 13). 貼秋膘. 百度百科. Retrieved December 21, 2022, from https://baike.baidu.hk/item/貼秋膘/7304941

[17] 快樂羊倌兒. (2021, June 16). 二十四節氣之立秋. 百科 TA 说. Retrieved December 21, 2022, from https://baike.baidu.com/tashuo/browse/content?id=9ecbf4e3df17c3d59ec0e152

[18] Baidu. (2022, August 5). 咬秋. 百度百科. Retrieved December 21, 2022, from https://baike.baidu.hk/item/咬秋/6245521

[19] 殷登國 (1983). 立秋. In 中國的花神與節氣 (p. 191). 民生報業書

[20] 張超 (2014). 第十四章---立秋--秋季開始的節氣 (p. 246). In 二十四節氣常識一本通. 龍圖騰文化有限公司

[21] Baidu. (2022, August 12). 七夕節. 百度百科. Retrieved December 21, 2022, from https://baike.baidu.hk/item/七夕節/226647

[22] 詩經, 小雅, 小旻之什, 大東, 5

[23] 搜狐教育頻道. (2006, January 16). 讲给孩子——中国四大民间故事. Sohu.com. Retrieved December 21, 2022, from https://web.archive.org/web/20200527184105/https://learning.sohu.com/20060116/n241419607.shtml

[24] 中國人民共和國中央人民政府. (2009, August 26). 牛郎織女的故事. 中國政府網. Retrieved December 21, 2022, from http://big5.www.gov.cn/gate/big5/www.gov.cn/fwxx/wy/2009-08/26/content_1401844.htm

[25] 張超 (2014). 第十四章---立秋--秋季開始的節氣 (p. 248). In 二十四節氣常識一本通. 龍圖騰文化有限公司

[26] 潤芳. (2019, July 30). 七夕，有用鳳仙花給小姑娘染指甲的習俗. 每日頭條. Retrieved December 21, 2022, from https://kknews.cc/culture/amaqabg.html

[27] 雨燕江南. (2017, August 21). 七夕葡萄架，偷听悄悄话. 简书. Retrieved December 21, 2022, from https://www.jianshu.com/p/a2772a77b22f

[28] 張超 (2014). 第十四章---立秋--秋季開始的節氣 (p. 249). In 二十四節氣常識一本通. 龍圖騰文化有限公司

[29] 張超 (2014). 第十四章---立秋--秋季開始的節氣 (p. 249). In 二十四節氣常識一本通. 龍圖騰文化有限公司

[30] 養生之道網. (2015, July 31). 七夕習俗：喜蛛應巧預兆好姻緣. 壹讀. Retrieved December 21, 2022, from https://read01.com/zh-tw/jz07jE.html#.Y6KgWRVByF4

[31] 張超 (2014). 第十四章---立秋--秋季開始的節氣 (p. 248). In 二十四節氣常識一本通. 龍圖騰文化有限公司

[32] 張超 (2014). 第十四章---立秋--秋季開始的節氣 (p. 248). In 二十四節氣常識一本通. 龍圖騰文化有限公司

[33] ENORTH NETNEWS Co.,LTD. (2012, August 21). 七夕節的十大開運習慣. 北方網情監測及服務. Retrieved December 21, 2022, from https://baike.baidu.com/reference/226647/f7e7u1jO9aR7aLWLMG-PhdGf69LAWZhFFigTmM9Kzqcm_rfYj5WXzwJs0Pw0T52qd-47vAfOVYMBu5yTH9h4nuwFzhYeYVRWvJF6A3Tjh8rr_g4_KhA_yg

[34] 國立臺灣歷史博物館. (n.d.). 轉大人─臺灣民間信仰中的七娘媽廟. 台灣女人. Retrieved December 21, 2022, from https://women.nmth.gov.tw/?p=1934

[35] 初一十五科技有限公司. (n.d.). 拜床母床公〉嬰幼孩童補運平安金紙 | 初一十五. Retrieved December 21, 2022, from https://www.blessingday.me/products/motherofthebed

[36] 秀美派. (2021, August 29). 移床要看日子嗎 - 奢華品質. Retrieved December 21, 2022, from https://www.xiumeipai.com/zh-tw/dapei/shehuapinzhi/675388.html

[37] Baidu. (2022, August 19). 秋社. 百度百科. Retrieved December 21, 2022, from https://baike.baidu.hk/item/秋社/19728863

[38] 岳雪 (2014). 滿街梧桐月明中--立秋 (p. 103). In 歲月之二十四節氣裡的眾神節慶與傳說. 貓咪予花兒

[39] 岳雪 (2014). 滿街梧桐月明中--立秋 (pp. 104-106). In 歲月之二十四節氣裡的眾神節慶與傳說. 貓咪予花兒

[40] 今日頭條. (2022, May 30). 山海經之蓐收. Toutiao.com. Retrieved December 21, 2022, from https://www.toutiao.com/article/7103318999953310240/

[41] Baidu. (2021, November 28). 蓐收. 百度百科. Retrieved December 21, 2022, from https://baike.baidu.hk/item/蓐收/8551761

[42] 淮南子, 天文訓, 6

[43] 山海經, 海外西經, 23

[44] 詩經, 小雅, 祈父之什, 斯干, 7.1

[45] 岳雪 (2014). 滿街梧桐月明中--立秋 (p. 106). In 歲月之二十四節氣裡的眾神節慶與傳說. 貓咪予花兒

[46] Baidu. (2021, December 9). 皇娥. 百度百科. Retrieved December 21, 2022, from https://baike.baidu.hk/item/皇娥/4181868

[47] Cahill, S. E. (1995). The Most Honored One. In Transcendence & Divine Passion: The Queen Mother of the West in Medieval China (pp. 12–13). Stanford Univ. Press.

[48] Cheng, M. (1995). The Queen Mother of the West. In The Origin of Chinese Deities (p. 226). Foreign Languages Press.

[49] Yang, D., An, D., & Turner, J. A. (2005). Handbook of Chinese Mythology (pp 221). ABC-CLIO.

[50] 中華維德文化協會. (2018, May 18). 西王母. Retrieved December 21, 2022, from https://www.weide.org.tw/2018-05-18.html

[51] 山海經, 西山經, 49

[52] 山海經, 海內北經, 3

[53] Theobald, U. (2010, August 13). Xiwangmu 西王母, the queen mother of the west. www.chinaknowledge.de. Retrieved December 21, 2022, from http://www.chinaknowledge.de/Literature/Religion/personsxiwangmu.html

[54] Monaghan, P., & Dashu, M. (2011). Xi Wangmu: The Great Goddess of China. In Goddesses in World Culture (p. 143). Praeger.

[55] Dashu, M. (n.d.). Xi Wangmu: Shamanic Great Goddess of China. Suppressed Histories. Retrieved December 21, 2022, from https://www.suppressedhistories.net/goddess/xiwangmu.html

[56] Yang, D., An, D., & Turner, J. A. (2005). Handbook of Chinese Mythology (p. 219). ABC-CLIO.

[57] Cahill, S. E. (1995). The Most Honored One. In Transcendence & Divine Passion: The Queen Mother of the West in Medieval China (pp. 12–13). Stanford Univ. Press.

[58] Cheng, M. (1995). Local God of the Land. In The Origin of Chinese Deities (p. 145). Foreign Languages Press.

[59] Yang, D., An, D., & Turner, J. A. (2005). Handbook of Chinese Mythology (p. 219). ABC-CLIO.

[60] Yang, D., An, D., & Turner, J. A. (2005). Handbook of Chinese Mythology (p. 161). ABC-CLIO.

[61] Allan, T., & Phillips, C. (2012). The Square Earth. In Ancient China's Myths and Beliefs (p. 37). Rosen Publishing.

[62] Allan, T., & Phillips, C. (2012). The Square Earth. In Ancient China's Myths and Beliefs (p. 37). Rosen Publishing.

[63] Yang, D., An, D., & Turner, J. A. (2005). Handbook of Chinese Mythology (p. 222). ABC-CLIO.

[64] Yang, D., An, D., & Turner, J. A. (2005). Handbook of Chinese Mythology (p. 221). ABC-CLIO.

[65] Cheng, M. (1995). Local God of the Land. In The Origin of Chinese Deities (p. 143). Foreign Languages Press.

[66] Yang, D., An, D., & Turner, J. A. (2005). Handbook of Chinese Mythology (p. 222). ABC-CLIO.

[67] Yang, D., An, D., & Turner, J. A. (2005). Handbook of Chinese Mythology (p. 220). ABC-CLIO.

[68] Werner, E. T. C. (1986). IV. The Gods of China. In Ancient Tales and Folklore of China (pp. 136–137). B. Mitchell.

Chapter 14: Heat Departs

[1] 七修類稿, 卷三天地類, 25

[2] 陳喬宣. (2009, September 9). 處暑. 台灣大百科全書. Retrieved December 23, 2022, from https://nrch.culture.tw/twpedia.aspx?id=11757

[3] 行政院農業委員會. (n.d.). 趣味鄉土諺語 - 處暑(國曆 8 月 22 日或 23 日或 24 日). 農業兒童網. Retrieved December 23, 2022, from https://kids.coa.gov.tw/view.php?func=solar&id=16

[4] 全球趣味資訊. (2020, August 21). 「處暑」七月半，可有人陪你看曇花一現？. iFuun. Retrieved December 23, 2022, from http://www.ifuun.com/a2020082226453502/

[5] 岳雪 (2014). 漠漠輕寒上小樓--處暑 (p. 109). In 歲月之二十四節氣裡的眾神節慶與傳說. 貓咪予花兒

[6] 中國天氣網. (2010, August 23). 處暑節氣的習俗與活動. 中國政府網. Retrieved December 23, 2022, from http://big5.www.gov.cn/gate/big5/www.gov.cn/fwxx/wy/2010-08/23/content_1685995.htm

[7] 詩經, 國風, 豳風, 七月

[8] OurSci.org. (2008, October 12). 七月流火. Wayback Machine. Retrieved December 23, 2022, from https://web.archive.org/web/20061113182400/http://www.oursci.org/magazine/200208/020831.htm

[9] 岳雪 (2014). 漢漠輕寒上小樓--處暑 (p. 109). In 歲月之二十四節氣裡的眾神節慶與傳說. 貓咪予花兒

[10] KKNews. (2021, August 24). 七月流火，九月授衣，處暑已到，秋天還會遠嗎? 紫牛新聞. 每日頭條. Retrieved December 23, 2022, from https://kknews.cc/zh-mo/culture/o4ge2jo.html

[11] 月令七十二候集解, 處暑

[12] 七修類稿, 卷三天地類, 氣候集解,處暑

[13] 殷登國 (1983). 處暑. In 中國的花神與節氣 (p. 193). 民生報業書

[14] 行政院農業委員會. (n.d.). 霜降（國曆 10 月 23 或 24 日）（農委會）. 行政院農業委會農業全球資訊網. Retrieved December 23, 2022, from 2

[15] 中華人民共和國中央人民政府. (2007, October 11). 處暑. 中國政府網. Retrieved December 23, 2022, from http://big5.www.gov.cn/gate/big5/www.gov.cn/fwxx/content_774063.htm

[16] 清嘉錄, 五, 秋興

[17] 行政院農業委員會. (n.d.). 趣味鄉土諺語 - 處暑(國曆 8 月 22 日或 23 日或 24 日). 農業兒童網. Retrieved December 23, 2022, from https://kids.coa.gov.tw/view.php?func=solar&id=16

[18] 張超 (2014). 第十五章---處暑--炎熱即將過去的節氣 (p. 261). In 二十四節氣常識一本通. 龍圖騰文化有限公司

[19] 葉明憲. (2015, June 23). 夏季中醫養生之道. 農業知識入口網. Retrieved December 23, 2022, from https://kmweb.coa.gov.tw/theme_data.php?theme=news&sub_theme=agri_life&id=54273

[20] 北京處暑吃鴨習俗的介紹 - 三度漢語網. 三度漢語網 3DU.TW. (n.d.). Retrieved December 23, 2022, from https://www.3du.tw/knowledge/NjE0NHU=.html

[21] 張超 (2014). 第十五章---處暑--炎熱即將過去的節氣 (pp. 265-266). In 二十四節氣常識一本通. 龍圖騰文化有限公司

[22] GetIt01. (n.d.). 七月半（中元節）的習俗是如何來的？ Retrieved December 23, 2022, from https://www.getit01.com/p20171216111682/

[23] 張超 (2014). 第十五章---處暑--炎熱即將過去的節氣 (p. 264). In 二十四節氣常識一本通. 龍圖騰文化有限公司

[24] Baidu. (2022, November 18). 寶蓮燈. 百度百科. Retrieved December 23, 2022, from https://baike.baidu.hk/item/寶蓮燈/44926

[25] Yuan, H. (2006). The Magic Lotus Lantern. In The Magic Lotus Lantern and Other Tales from the Han Chinese (pp. 83–85). Libraries Unlimited.

[26] 自陳鳳麗. (2021, August 8). 農曆七月鬼門開 民俗專家：這個月勿說「鬼」字 - 生活. The Liberty Times. Retrieved December 23, 2022, from https://news.ltn.com.tw/news/life/breakingnews/3631318

[27] Allan, T. (1999). A Bureaucracy of Gods. In Land of the Dragon: Chinese Myth (p. 107). Metro Books.

[28] 三立新聞網. (2019, July 29). 鬼月必知 10 大禁忌! 「靠牆走...」小心撞到好兄弟: 生活: 三立新聞網. 生活中心, setn.com . Retrieved December 23, 2022, from https://www.setn.com/News.aspx?NewsID=577741

[29] Khor, S. (n.d.). 30 Things That Are Believed To Be Totally Taboo During The Hungry Ghost Festival. AEON Says. Retrieved December 23, 2022, from https://says.com/my/lifestyle/things-you-should-not-do-on-hungry-ghost-festival

[30] Focus Taiwan - CNA English News. (2015, August 13). Top 10 taboos to avoid during Ghost Month in Taiwan. Focus Taiwan. Retrieved December 23, 2022, from https://focustaiwan.tw/culture/201508130025

[31] 普渡公怎麼拜?普渡公由來. 民間習俗. (n.d.). Retrieved December 23, 2022, from https://sim.org.tw/festival151.html

[32] 李宇涵. (2022, July 25). 中元節普渡供品怎麼準備? 中. https://www.edh.tw/. Retrieved December 23, 2022, from https://www.edh.tw/article/25095

[33] 張超 (2014). 第十五章---處暑--炎熱即將過去的節氣 (p. 263). In 二十四節氣常識一本通. 龍圖騰文化有限公司

[34] Tseng, J. (2022, August 12). 【中元普渡攻略】拜拜時間、供品、禁忌事項懶人包！. Klook 客路部落格. Retrieved December 23, 2022, from https://www.klook.com/zh-TW/blog/things-you-should-know-about-chungyuan-festival/

[35] Tseng, J. (2022, August 12). 【中元普渡攻略】拜拜時間、供品、禁忌事項懶人包！. Klook 客路部落格. Retrieved December 23, 2022, from https://www.klook.com/zh-TW/blog/things-you-should-know-about-chungyuan-festival/

[36] 張超 (2014). 第十五章---處暑--炎熱即將過去的節氣 (p. 261-265). In 二十四節氣常識一本通. 龍圖騰文化有限公司

[37] 懷荏荏. (2019, December 18). 說中元目犍連神通第一 蓋不過亡母業力. www.epochtimes.com. Retrieved December 23, 2022, from https://www.epochtimes.com/b5/17/7/30/n9478840.htm

[38] Grant, B., & Idema, W. L. (2012). Escape from Blood Pond Hell: The tales of Mulian and Woman Huang. University of Washington Press.

[39] 岳雪 (2014). 漢漢輕寒上小樓--處暑 (p. 111) . In 歲月之二十四節氣裡的眾神節慶與傳說. 貓咪予花兒

Chapter 15: White Dew

[1] 七修類稿, 卷三天地類, 白露

[2] 行政院農業委員會. (2018, September 1). 9 月金柑健康管理作業. 金柑主題館. Retrieved December 24, 2022, from https://kmweb.coa.gov.tw/subject/subject.php?id=34596&print=Y

[3] 國立教育廣播電台. (2018, September 9). 24 節氣之白露. Channel+. Retrieved December 24, 2022, from https://channelplus.ner.gov.tw/channel-folks/修課專區/中臺科大通識課程(107 年第 2 學期)/多元文化/program/48964

[4] Eberhard, W. (2006). G, Goose. In A Dictionary of Chinese Symbols: Hidden Symbols in Chinese Life and Thought (p. 156). Routledge.

[5] 殷登國 (1983). 白露. In 中國的花神與節氣 (p. 200). 民生報業書

[6] Williams, C. A. S. (1974). Swallow. In Chinese Symbolism and Art Motifs (p. 380). Tuttle.

[7] Eberhard, W. (2006). C, Crane. In A Dictionary of Chinese Symbols: Hidden Symbols in Chinese Life and Thought (pp 86-87). Routledge.

[8] Williams, C. A. S. (1974). Swallow. In Chinese Symbolism and Art Motifs (pp. 101-102). Tuttle.

[9] Eberhard, W. (2006). H, Heron. In A Dictionary of Chinese Symbols: Hidden Symbols in Chinese Life and Thought (p. 175). Routledge.

[10] White Heron and Lotus. Philadelphia Museum of Art. (n.d.). Retrieved December 24, 2022, from https://philamuseum.org/collection/object/197858

[11] KKNews. (2017, August 8). 古代的愛鶴與養鶴之人. 每日頭條. Retrieved December 24, 2022, from https://kknews.cc/zh-tw/history/l6jvv3g.html

[12] 殷登國 (1983). 白露. In 中國的花神與節氣 (p. 201). 民生報業書

[13] 七修續稿, 卷三義理類, 29

[14] 國立教育廣播電台. (2018, September 9). 24 節氣之白露. Channel+. Retrieved December 24, 2022, from https://channelplus.ner.gov.tw/channel-folks/修課專區/中臺科大通識課程(107 年第 2 學期)/多元文化/program/48964

[15] KKNews. (2019, September 4). 農諺:「白露日落雨，到一處壞一處」，白露節氣下雨有何說法. 每日頭條. Retrieved December 25, 2022, from https://kknews.cc/zh-tw/culture/4jj5n82.html

[16] 白露前是雨，白露后是鬼. 百度百科. (n.d.). Retrieved December 25, 2022, from https://baike.baidu.com/item/白露前是雨，白露后是鬼/22918646

[17] KKNews. (2019, September 2). 俗話說:「處暑雨甜，白露雨苦」，白露下雨有何說法 原文網址: https://kknews.cc/culture/bmp3xro.html. 每日頭條. Retrieved December 25, 2022, from https://kknews.cc/zh-tw/culture/bmp3xro.html

[18] Baidu. (2022, October 21). 春捂秋凍. 百度百科. Retrieved December 25, 2022, from https://baike.baidu.hk/item/春捂秋凍/737903

[19] 黃慧玫. (2021, September 7). 「白露」養生怎麼做? 中醫師提醒: 把握 4 關鍵，調養不生病的好體質. Heho 健康. Retrieved December 25, 2022, from https://heho.com.tw/archives/188835

[20] 中國新聞網. (2020, September 7). 白露節氣到! 為何要飲"白露茶"、吃龍眼?. 人民網. Retrieved December 25, 2022, from http://yn.people.com.cn/health/BIG5/n2/2020/0907/c228588-34275561.html

[21] 張超 (2014). 第十六章---白露--天氣轉涼,出現露水的節氣 (p. 278). In 二十四節氣常識一本通. 龍圖騰文化有限公司

[22] 容乃加. (2016, September 7).【文史】露從今夜白 「白露」節氣到了. 大紀元時報 香港｜獨立敢言的良心媒體. Retrieved December 25, 2022, from http://hk.epochtimes.com/news/2016-09-07/文史-露從今夜白-白露-節氣到了-5844135

[23] 禮記, 月令, 67-75

[24] White Dew Tea: The first cup of tea in Autumn. CGTN. (2021, September 7). Retrieved December 25, 2022, from https://news.cgtn.com/news/2021-09-07/White-dew-tea-the-first-cup-of-tea-in-autumn-13mP6goZKUw/index.html

[25] 方志委. (2022, September 7). 白露: 正是秋意漸濃時. 民俗风情. Retrieved December 25, 2022, from http://www.fuzhou.gov.cn/zgfzzt/zjrc/mdfc/msfq/202210/t20221026_4457403.htm

[26] 張超 (2014). 第十六章---白露--天氣轉涼,出現露水的節氣 (p. 277). In 二十四節氣常識一本通. 龍圖騰文化有限公司

[27] 四川日報. (2021, September 7). 白露：露凝而白，大雁南飛. 人民網. Retrieved December 25, 2022, from https://epaper.scdaily.cn/shtml/scrb/20210907/261304.shtml

[28] 尚書,夏書,禹貢

[29] 中華人民共和國中央人民政府. (2010, September 7). 白露：民間有"吃龍眼""祭禹王"等習俗. 中國政府網. Retrieved December 25, 2022, from http://big5.www.gov.cn/gate/big5/www.gov.cn/fwxx/wy/2010-09/07/content_1697626.htm

[30] 廣東省國學會. (2021, June 17). 白露 | 露凝而白，清明疏凈. 百科 TA 说. Retrieved December 25, 2022, from https://baike.baidu.com/tashuo/browse/content?id=ab5d18ced740cd85fb13669f

[31] 張超 (2014). 第十六章---白露--天氣轉涼,出現露水的節氣 (p. 276). In 二十四節氣常識一本通. 龍圖騰文化有限公司

[32] Allan, T. (1999). The Sage Kings. In Land of the Dragon: Chinese Myth (p. 84). Metro Books.

[33] Liu, S. T. T. (1983). Yu Controls the Flood. In Dragons, Gods & Spirits from Chinese Mythology (p. 33). Schocken Books.

[34] Allan, T. (1999). The Sage Kings. In Land of the Dragon: Chinese Myth (p. 84). Metro Books.

[35] Lewis, M. E. (2006). The Flood Myths of Early China. State University of New York Press.

[36] Yang, D., An, D., & Turner, J. A. (2005). Handbook of Chinese Mythology (pp 136-141). ABC-CLIO.

[37] Liu, S. T. T. (1983). Yu Controls the Flood. In Dragons, Gods & Spirits from Chinese Mythology (p. 32-33). Schocken Books.

[38] Allan, T. (1999). The Sage Kings. In Land of the Dragon: Chinese Myth (pp. 84). Metro Books.

[39] Yang, D., An, D., & Turner, J. A. (2005). Handbook of Chinese Mythology (pp 238-239). ABC-CLIO.

[40] Allan, T. (1999). The Sage Kings. In Land of the Dragon: Chinese Myth (pp. 92-94). Metro Books.

[41] Yang, D., An, D., & Turner, J. A. (2005). Handbook of Chinese Mythology (p 241). ABC-CLIO.

[42] Lewis, M. E. (2006). Introduction. In The Flood Myths of Early China. (p. 16) Amsterdam University Press.

[43] Lewis, M. E. (2006). Chapter 1: Flood and Cosmogony. In The Flood Myths of Early China. (p. 34) Amsterdam University Press.

[44] 本草綱目,水部,水之一 天水類一十三種,露水, 4

[45] 岳雪 (2014). 草木摇落路為霜--白露 (pp. 114-115) . In 歲月之二十四節氣裡的眾神節慶與傳說. 貓咪予花兒

Chapter 16: Autumnal Equinox

[1] 漢典. (n.d.). 分字的解釋. Retrieved December 26, 2022, from https://www.zdic.net/hant/分

[2] 春秋繁露 -> 陰陽出入上下

[3] 張超 (2014). 第十七章---秋分--晝夜等長的節氣 (pp. 286-287). In 二十四節氣常識一本通. 龍圖騰文化有限公司

[4] 蔡容英. (2006, October 14). 奇異張狂的在地花卉---紅花石蒜. 金門日報. Retrieved December 26, 2022, from https://www.kmdn.gov.tw/1117/1271/1274/42031

[5] 羅慧珍. (n.d.). 曼珠沙華－重生. 臺中市港區藝術中心. Retrieved December 26, 2022, from https://www.art.tcsac.gov.tw/works/Details.aspx?Parser=99%2C6%2C33%2C%2C%2C%2C238

[6] 唔科學. (2021, September 1). 彼岸花:開一千年,落一千年,花葉永不相見. 人人焦點. Retrieved December 26, 2022, from https://ppfocus.com/0/cu4953dbb.html

[7] 羅東鎮農會. (n.d.). 驚哲. 24 節氣. Retrieved December 26, 2022, from http://www.24solar.tw/24solar-3.htm

[8] 殷登國 (1983). 秋分. In 中國的花神與節氣 (p. 205). 民生報業書

[9] 行政院農業委員會. (n.d.). 白露、秋分. 臺灣農業故事館. Retrieved December 26, 2022, from https://theme.coa.gov.tw/100/view.php?issue=24032&id=24059

[10] 廣韻, 入聲, 屑, 玦, 13

[11] 經濟日報. (2022, October 2). "三秋"生產順利 秋糧豐收在望. 新華網. Retrieved December 26, 2022, from http://big5.news.cn/gate/big5/www.news.cn/fortune/2022-10/02/c_1129047632.htm

[12] 中國天氣網. (2009, September 22). 秋分節氣期間的氣候特點. 中國政府網. Retrieved December 26, 2022, from http://big5.www.gov.cn/gate/big5/www.gov.cn/fwxx/wy/2009-09/22/content_1423332.htm

[13] 中國天氣網. (2009, September 22). 秋分節氣各地流行的諺語. 中國政府網. Retrieved December 26, 2022, from http://big5.www.gov.cn/gate/big5/www.gov.cn/fwxx/wy/2009-09/22/content_1423337.htm

[14] 張超 (2014). 第十七章---秋分--晝夜等長的節氣 (p. 287). In 二十四節氣常識一本通. 龍圖騰文化有限公司

[15] 黃帝內經‧素問, 四氣調神大論篇第二, 秋三月

[16] 仁傳醫療文教基金會. (n.d.). 秋分 | 二十四節氣. 仁心聯醫. Retrieved December 26, 2022, from https://zenheart.com.tw/Solar_terms16.php

[17] 張超 (2014). 第十七章---秋分--晝夜等長的節氣 (pp. 293-294). In 二十四節氣常識一本通. 龍圖騰文化有限公司

[18] 馬慧娟. (2016, August 5). 「秋分到.蛋兒俏」原來秋分也能立蛋!? Retrieved December 26, 2022, from https://news.cts.com.tw/cts/general/201509/201509241663641.html

[19] 淮南子 -> 繆稱訓, 22

[20] 禮記註疏 -> 卷四十七考證, 4

[21] 宋史, 志第五十六, 禮六吉禮六

[22] 殷登國 (1983). 秋分. In 中國的花神與節氣 (p. 206). 民生報業書

[23] 史記, 書, 天官書, 18

[24] 中國天氣網. (2009, September 22). 秋分節氣各種習俗. 中國政府網. Retrieved December 26, 2022, from http://big5.www.gov.cn/gate/big5/www.gov.cn/fwxx/wy/2009-09/22/content_1423325.htm

[25] 大紀元. (2017, November 28). 夏至陽氣至極 帝王祭地祈求風調雨順. www.epochtimes.com. https://www.epochtimes.com/b5/15/6/21/n4462671.htm

[26] 張超 (2014). 第十七章---秋分--晝夜等長的節氣 (p. 289). In 二十四節氣常識一本通. 龍圖騰文化有限公司

[27] 三度漢語網. (2019, September 14). 中秋節會做哪些事情. 三度漢語網 3DU.TW. Retrieved December 26, 2022, from https://www.3du.tw/knowledge/NjRzd2E=.html

[28] 老資料網. (n.d.). 什麼是樹中秋? 老廣州們家中還會必備哪樣東西? . 文史知識. Retrieved December 26, 2022, from https://www.laoziliao.net/doc/1635303192966751

[29] 幸福时光旅行箱. (2020, October 1). 中秋節故事: 月亮上的動物除了玉兔還有蟾蜍, 你知道它的來歷嗎? . 今天頭條. Retrieved December 26, 2022, from https://twgreatdaily.com/axpN5HQBd8y1i3sJmDWQ.html

[30] Baidu. (2022, September 10). 月餅. 百度百科. Retrieved December 26, 2022, from https://baike.baidu.hk/item/月餅/248376

[31] 何丙仲. (2014, August 18). 中秋博餅習俗管窺. 金門日報. Retrieved December 26, 2022, from https://www.kmdn.gov.tw/1117/1271/1274/242651

[32] 張超 (2014). 第十七章---秋分--晝夜等長的節氣 (p. 292-293). In 二十四節氣常識一本通. 龍圖騰文化有限公司

[33] 歷史小廚. (2019, September 10). 逼迫嫦娥奔月, 殺死后羿的逢蒙, 也讓孟子的觀點受到爭議! . 每日頭條. Retrieved December 26, 2022, from https://kknews.cc/zh-tw/n/vl56yvq.html

[34] Yang, D., An, D., & Turner, J. A. (2005). Handbook of Chinese Mythology (p. 90). ABC-CLIO.

[35] 百度百科. (2018, September 24). 藏在古籍里的真相: 嫦娥是誰? Xinhuanet. Retrieved December 26, 2022, from https://baike.baidu.hk/reference/68389/aad8EVPcl0wwVfenqRLQ-w4KR7YxAJMn87Gsg6SjUnJWxEdYrh-HvdAxDOfSEb5TQzVMxBih25sVisgBEHF8Oby1Eo3Qse9KKWaN8GF05wLd2dzbtw

[36] 雜家, 淮南子, 覽冥訓

[37] Yang, D., An, D., & Turner, J. A. (2005). Handbook of Chinese Mythology (p. 88). ABC-CLIO.

[38] Yang, D., An, D., & Turner, J. A. (2005). Handbook of Chinese Mythology (p. 89). ABC-CLIO.

[39] Yang, D., An, D., & Turner, J. A. (2005). Handbook of Chinese Mythology (p. 86). ABC-CLIO.

[40] 岳雪 (2014). 風清露秋期半--秋分 (p. 120). In 歲月之二十四節氣裡的眾神節慶與傳說. 貓咪予花兒

[41] 山海經, 大荒東經, 33

[42] 岳雪 (2014). 風清露秋期半--秋分 (p. 119). In 歲月之二十四節氣裡的眾神節慶與傳說. 貓咪予花兒

Chapter 17: Cold Dew

[1] 月令七十二候集解, 寒露

[2] 李商隱詩選, 李商隱詩選

3 張超 (2014). 第十八章---天氣轉涼漸冷的節氣 (p. 302). In 二十四節氣常識一本通. 龍圖騰文化有限公司

4 百度百科. (2020, November 10). 寒露: 秋声乍起，芰荷为衣. 百科 TA 说. Retrieved December 27, 2022, from https://baike.baidu.com/tashuo/browse/content?id=eba29de2bbd99ac00214e029

5 殷登國 (1983). 寒露. In 中國的花神與節氣 (p. 213). 民生報業書

6 史書, 國語, 晉語九

7 五雜俎, 卷二‧天部二, 56

8 竹窗隨筆, 蛇成龍

9 藝誠科技. (2014, August 1). 我國古代的物候知識 - 科學月刊 science Monthly. 科學月刊 Science Monthly. Retrieved December 27, 2022, from https://www.scimonth.com.tw/archives/4702

10 吉林鄉村廣播. (2019, October 8). 今日寒露｜鴻雁來賓，崔入水為蛤，菊有黃華. 今天頭條. Retrieved December 27, 2022, from https://twgreatdaily.com/FldTr20BMH2_cNUgLCLv.html

11 壹讀 (2016, June 23). 菊花有什麼象徵意義？菊花代表什麼？. Retrieved December 27, 2022, from https://read01.com/zh-tw/yLL5de.html

12 張超 (2014). 第十八章---天氣轉涼漸冷的節氣 (p. 303). In 二十四節氣常識一本通. 龍圖騰文化有限公司

13 中華人民共和國中央人民政府. (2007, October 11). 寒露. 中國政府網. Retrieved December 25, 2022, from http://big5.www.gov.cn/gate/big5/www.gov.cn/fwxx/content_774066.htm

14 飛資得資訊股份有限公司. (n.d.). &;台灣客家語常用詞辭典. 臺灣客家語常用詞辭典. Retrieved December 25, 2022, from https://hakkadict.moe.edu.tw/cgi-bin/gs32/gsweb.cgi?o=dalldb&s=id&searchmode=basic&checknoback=1

15 中華人民共和國中央人民政府. (2009, October 8). 白露身不露 寒露腳不露. 中國政府網. Retrieved December 25, 2022, from http://big5.www.gov.cn/gate/big5/www.gov.cn/fwxx/jk/2009-10/08/content_1433822.htm

16 三度漢語網 (n.d.). 為什麼寒露不能露腳的由來. Retrieved December 25, 2022, from https://www.3du.tw/knowledge/YzF1aGs=.html

17 禮記, 月令, 76-85

18 上海黃浦. (2022, October 8). 寒露習俗之一 流行鬥蟋蟀. 寒露習俗之一 流行斗蟋蟀_上观新闻. Retrieved December 27, 2022, from https://www.jfdaily.com/sgh/detail?id=874445

19 歲時節氣｜寒露：吃螃蟹的這些講究，你知道幾個？. 今天頭條. (2020, October 9). Retrieved December 27, 2022, from https://twgreatdaily.com/A-1xC3UBURTf-Dn5GM69.html

20 陳熙遠. (2009, November 9). 重陽. 文化部國家文化資料庫. Retrieved December 27, 2022, from https://nrch.culture.tw/twpedia.aspx?id=2043

21 呂氏春秋, 季秋紀, 九月紀, 2

22 岳雪 (2014). 最是橙黃橘綠時--寒露 (p. 123). In 歲月之二十四節氣裡的眾神節慶與傳說. 貓咪予花兒

23 搜狐. (2022, September 26). 重阳寒露前，必定是灾年，为啥？今年重阳节在寒露之前吗？火星-阳气-九月. Retrieved December 27, 2022, from https://www.sohu.com/a/587076433_581550

[24] 西京雜記,第三, 15

[25] 藝文類聚, 卷四, 歲時中, 九月九日

[26] 百菊集譜, 卷四, 13

[27] 岳雪 (2014). 最是橙黄橘綠時--寒露 (p. 123). In 歲月之二十四節氣裡的眾神節慶 與傳說. 貓咪予花兒

[28] 夢梁錄, 卷五, 九月 (重九附)

[29] 中華人民共和國中央人民政府. (2010, October 14). 民俗專家: 重陽節吃重陽糕寓 意步步登高. 中國政府網. Retrieved December 27, 2022, from http://big5.www.gov.cn/gate/big5/www.gov.cn/fwxx/wy/2010-10/14/content_1722795.htm

[30] Baidu. (2022, June 20). 五色重陽糕. 百度百科. Retrieved December 27, 2022, from https://baike.baidu.hk/item/五色重陽糕/6810228

[31] Baidu. (2022, May 26). 重陽糕. 百度百科. Retrieved December 27, 2022, from https://baike.baidu.hk/item/重陽糕/4515978

[32] 張超 (2014). 第十八章---天氣轉涼漸冷的節氣 (p. 307). In 二十四節氣常識一本通. 龍圖騰文化有限公司

[33] 風土記

[34] 張超 (2014). 第十八章---天氣轉涼漸冷的節氣 (p. 306). In 二十四節氣常識一本通. 龍圖騰文化有限公司

[35] Virgil, & Mandelbaum, A. (1971). Book III, 35. In The Aeneid of Virgil (p. 58). Bookman Books.

[36] Protheroe, A. (2021, October 11). Easter and the legend of the dogwood tree. Plant Me Green. Retrieved December 27, 2022, from https://www.plantmegreen.com/blogs/news/easter-and-the-legend-of-the-dogwood-tree

[37] Wauters, L. (2021, October 8). Dogwood – Stealth. Tree Spirit Wisdom. Retrieved December 27, 2022, from https://treespiritwisdom.com/tree-spirit-wisdom/dogwood-tree-symbolism/

[38] McLeod, J. (2022, April 11). Weather folklore: What is a dogwood winter? Farmers' Almanac. Retrieved December 27, 2022, from https://www.farmersalmanac.com/what-is-dogwood-winter-12086

[39] 西京雜記, 第三, 15

[40] 以菊花 夢梁錄, 卷五, 九月 (重九附)

[41] 張超 (2014). 第十八章---天氣轉涼漸冷的節氣 (pp. 306-307). In 二十四節氣常識一 本通. 龍圖騰文化有限公司

[42] 王勉. (2017, November 21). 陶淵明與菊之緣. 希望之聲. Retrieved December 27, 2022, from https://www.soundofhope.org/post/244280?lang=b5

[43] Watson, B. (1971). The Poetry of Reclusion. In Chinese lyricism: Shih poetry from the second to the twelfth century (p. 79). Columbia University Press.

[44] Cheung, K.-K. (2015). Affinity of mindscape and landscape in Tao Qian and Emerson. US-China Foreign Language, 13(4), 1. https://doi.org/10.17265/1539-8080/2015.04.007

[45] Hinton, D. (2010). T'ao Ch'ien. In Classical Chinese Poetry: An anthology. Farrar Straus and Giroux.

[46] Chang, K.-i S., & Owen, S. (2010). From the Eastern Jin through the early Tang (317-649). In The Cambridge History of Chinese Literature (pp. 210–222). Cambridge University Press.

[47] 翁敏華. (2020, December 15). 重陽節與陶淵明. 人人焦點. Retrieved December 27, 2022, from https://ppfocus.com/0/tr5af1517.html

[48] 續齊諧記, 續齊諧記, 9

[49] Baidu. (2021, December 12). 費長房. 百度百科. Retrieved December 27, 2022, from https://baike.baidu.hk/item/費長房/33906

[50] 岳雪 (2014). 最是橙黃橘綠時--寒露 (p. 124-125). In 歲月之二十四節氣裡的眾神節慶與傳說. 貓咪予花兒

Chapter 18: Frost Fall

[1] 月令七十二候集解, 霜降

[2] 中華人民共和國中央人民政府 (n.d.). 霜降的氣候特徵. 中國政府網. Retrieved December 28, 2022, from http://big5.www.gov.cn/gate/big5/www.gov.cn/fwxx/wy/2009-10/22/content_1446213.htm

[3] 張蕃. (2019, October 24). 為何說"霜降殺百草"? . 光明網. Retrieved December 28, 2022, from https://kepu.gmw.cn/2019-10/24/content_33262247.htm

[4] 張超 (2014). 第十九章---露水凝結成霜的節氣 (p. 316-317). In 二十四節氣常識一本通. 龍圖騰文化有限公司

[5] Lydekker, R. (1907). The Dhole, or Wild Dog. In The Game Animals of India, Burma, Malaya, and Tibet (pp. 362–363). Rowland Ward Ltd.

[6] Cohen, J. A. (1978). Cuon alpinus. Mammalian Species, (100), 1–3. https://doi.org/10.2307/3503800

[7] Geptner, V. G., & Hoffmann, R. S. (1998). Red Wolf Cuon alpinus Pallas, Part 1A: Sirenia and Carnivora (Sea Cows, Wolves, and Bears). In Mammals of the Soviet Union (pp. 568–571). Smithsonian Institution Libraries and the National Science Foundation.

[8] Fox, M. W. (1984). The Whistling Hunters: Field Studies of the Asiatic Wild Dog (Cuon alpinus). State University of New York Press.

[9] Baidu. (2021, June 8). 大道知行知行堂. 霜降 | 秋天最後一道絕美風景. 百科 TA 说. Retrieved December 28, 2022, from https://baike.baidu.com/tashuo/browse/content?id=5c986f701ba23cfeacc8f0e5

[10] 殷登國 (1983). 霜降. In 中國的花神與節氣 (p. 217). 民生報業書

[11] 中國氣象報. (2013, October 23). 23 日"重陽"逢"霜降" 登高賞景需防寒. 中國政府網. Retrieved December 28, 2022, from http://big5.www.gov.cn/gate/big5/www.gov.cn/fwxx/sh/2012-10/23/content_2248999.htm

[12] 國家教育研究院. (2021). 三秋. 教育部《重編國語辭典修訂本》 2021. Retrieved December 28, 2022, from https://dict.revised.moe.edu.tw/dictView.jsp?ID=144658&la=0&powerMode=0

[13] 中國氣象報. (2013, October 23). 23 日"重陽"逢"霜降" 登高賞景需防寒. 中國政府網. Retrieved December 28, 2022, from http://big5.www.gov.cn/gate/big5/www.gov.cn/fwxx/sh/2012-10/23/content_2248999.htm

[14] 張超 (2014). 第十九章---露水凝結成霜的節氣 (p. 317-318). In 二十四節氣常識一本通. 龍圖騰文化有限公司

[15] 中華人民共和國中央人民政府. (2007, October 11). 24 節氣: "霜降"養生篇. 中國政府網. Retrieved December 28, 2022, from http://big5.www.gov.cn/gate/big5/www.gov.cn/fwxx/jk/2007-10/11/content_774114.htm

[16] 蘇州地方志. (2016, June 2). 蘇州方言的俚詞俗語. 蘇州地情網. Retrieved December 28, 2022, from http://dfzb.suzhou.gov.cn/dfzb/fstc/201606/1a34dcf4699847e2b65ee2f0000a2c38.shtml

[17] 張超 (2014). 第十九章---露水凝結成霜的節氣 (p. 317-318). In 二十四節氣常識一本通. 龍圖騰文化有限公司

[18] 康涵菁中醫師. (n.d.). 一年補透透，不如補霜降！「霜降養生」吃對解秋燥，改善過敏、喉嚨痛: 健康遠見 - 對身體好！. Retrieved December 28, 2022, from https://health.gvm.com.tw/article/95386

[19] 廖德修、鄭郁萋. (2017, October 24). 秋寒•空汙 變天要人命. Yahoo! News. Retrieved December 28, 2022, from https://tw.news.yahoo.com/秋寒-空汙-變天要人命-215005951.html

[20] 張超 (2014). 第十九章---露水凝結成霜的節氣 (p. 319-320). In 二十四節氣常識一本通. 龍圖騰文化有限公司

[21] 殷登國 (1983). 霜降. In 中國的花神與節氣 (pp. 217-218). 民生報業書

[22] 楊萬里的《秋山》賞讀: 老烏柏，小紅楓，共醉秋光. 每日頭條. (2019, November 7). Retrieved December 28, 2022, from https://kknews.cc/zh-tw/culture/rn6nbyv.html

[23] 殷登國 (1983). 霜降. In 中國的花神與節氣 (pp. 218-219). 民生報業書

[24] 張超 (2014). 第十九章---露水凝結成霜的節氣 (p. 318). In 二十四節氣常識一本通. 龍圖騰文化有限公司

[25] 欣傳媒 Xinmedia. (2016, October 19). 秋季最後一個節氣　霜降五大習俗. 欣傳媒. Retrieved December 28, 2022, from https://www.xinmedia.com/article/64673

[26] Williams, C. A. S. (1974). Persimmon. In Chinese Symbolism and Art Motifs (pp. 321-322). Tuttle.

[27] Eberhard, W. (2006). P, Persimmon. In A Dictionary of Chinese Symbols: Hidden Symbols in Chinese Life and Thought (p. 286). Routledge.

[28] 人人焦點. (2020, December 22). 「紅」運當頭,柿柿如意. 人人焦點. Retrieved December 28, 2022, from https://ppfocus.com/0/fo5d0d1ab.html

[29] Ruyi Scepter with Eight Buddhist Treasures. The Lizzadro Museum of Lapidary Art. (2020, April 9). Retrieved December 28, 2022, from https://lizzadromuseum.org/ruyi-scepter-with-eight-buddhist-treasures/

[30] 爾雅翼, 卷十, 柿

[31] 新唐書, 列傳第一百二十七, 文藝中, 69

[32] 柿葉學書. 字典網. (n.d.). Retrieved December 28, 2022, from https://www.70thvictory.com.tw/lishi/diangu/5/34455na.htm

[33] Waley, A. (1958). Chapter XVII - Zen Buddhism - the Dragon. In An Introduction To The Study Of Chinese Painting (p. 231). Grove Press Inc.

[34] Levine, G. P., & Nelson, J. (2012). Zen Art: Pure Gesture, Nationalist Aesthetic, or Nothing at All? In I. Prohl (Ed.), Handbook of Contemporary Japanese Religions (p. 537). Brill.

[35] Lee, S. E. (1982). Chinese Painting and Ceramics of the Song Dynasty. In A History of Far Eastern Art (p. 362). Prentice-Hall, Inc and Harry N. Abrams, Inc.

[36] 隨息居飲食譜, 24

[37] Migo. (2015, November 10). 柿子營養價值原來這麼多！但你可知道柿子食用禁忌有哪些嗎？. 無毒農. Retrieved December 28, 2022, from https://greenbox.tw/Blog/BlogPostNew/6622/persimmon-nutrition

[38] KKNews. (2017, October 16). 當心！秋冬柿子又甜又好吃，這些食用禁忌務必要知道！ 每日頭條. Retrieved December 28, 2022, from https://kknews.cc/zh-tw/health/26jmlrr.html

[39] 岳雪 (2014). 萬頹霜天競自由--霜降 (p. 127-128). In 歲月之二十四節氣裡的眾神節慶與傳說. 貓咪予花兒

[40] Baidu. (2021, April 4). 農曆二十四節氣（壯族霜降節）. 百度百科. Retrieved December 28, 2022, from https://baike.baidu.hk/item/農曆二十四節氣（壯族霜降節）/56170090

[41] 岳雪 (2014). 萬頹霜天競自由--霜降 (p. 129). In 歲月之二十四節氣裡的眾神節慶與傳說. 貓咪予花兒

[42] Baidu. (n.d.). 壯族霜降節. 快懂百科. Retrieved December 28, 2022, from https://www.baike.com/wikiid/492664074245707743?view_id=401prb1rejmoe8

Chapter 19: Winter Begins

[1] 魏水明. (2009, September 9). 立冬. 文化部國家文化資料庫. Retrieved December 30, 2022, from https://nrch.culture.tw/twpedia.aspx?id=11762

[2] 岳雪 (2014). 晴窗早覺愛朝曦--立冬 (p. 130-131). In 歲月之二十四節氣裡的眾神節慶與傳說. 貓咪予花兒

[3] 殷登國 (1983). 立冬. In 中國的花神與節氣 (p. 222). 民生報業書

[4] 國家教育研究院. (2021). 屠. 《重編國語辭典修訂本》2021. Retrieved December 30, 2022, from https://dict.revised.moe.edu.tw/dictView.jsp?ID=9024&la=0&powerMode=0

[5] 臺北市華藏實驗教育機構. (n.d.). 立冬. Retrieved December 30, 2022, from https://hwadzan.tp.edu.tw/web/study/study_in.jsp?cp_id=CP1667272940096

[6] 國家教育研究院. (2021, November 4). 海市蜃樓. 教育部成語典. Retrieved December 30, 2022, from https://dict.idioms.moe.edu.tw/idiomView.jsp?ID=289&webMd=2&la=1

[7] Schafer, E. H. (1989). Fusang and Beyond: The Haunted Seas to Japan. Journal of the American Oriental Society, 109(3). https://doi.org/10.2307/604140

[8] Young , A. T. (n.d.). An introduction to mirages. Mirages and Green Flashes. Retrieved December 30, 2022, from https://web.archive.org/web/20071010083709/https://mintaka.sdsu.edu/GF/mirages/mirintro.html

[9] O'Meara, S. J. (2014, May 26). The Bewitching Fata Morgana. Astronomy.com. Retrieved December 30, 2022, from https://astronomy.com/magazine/stephen-omeara/2014/05/the-bewitching-fata-morgana

[10] Herrad, I. R. (n.d.). Vanishing Tricks of a Goddess. Magnetic North Writers. Retrieved from https://web.archive.org/web/20090810091923/http://geocities.com/magnorth_writing/ournonfictionimogen.html

[11] Watson, B. (1965). Part 4: Return: 1084 to 1093, 64: Mirage at Sea. In Su Tung-p'o: Selections from a Sung Dynasty Poet (p. 104). Columbia University Press.

[12] Zhang, C. (2017). Learning to Write Naturally: the Problem of Southern Song Poetry in the Late Twelfth Century (thesis). http://nrs.harvard.edu/urn-3:HUL.InstRepos:40046571

[13] 中華民國福建省連江縣政府. (2022, November 15). 圖與文／十月小陽春 - 馬祖日報. 馬祖日報. Retrieved December 30, 2022, from https://w3.matsu-news.gov.tw/news/article/205040

[14] Sintz, K. (2017, December 29). Freeze warnings?: Tips for Protecting Your Yard. Vista Landscaping. Retrieved December 30, 2022, from https://www.vlnola.com/blog/2017/12/8/tips-for-protecting-plants-from-cold-weather

[15] 蘇州工業園區管理委員會. (2021, February 3). 第五編（居民）第三章（風俗）. Retrieved December 30, 2022, from http://www.sipac.gov.cn/szdaglzx/yqfzktzz/202102/f4d1b082b0484772abed5129130b0c34.shtml

[16] 湖南省氣象局. (2008, September 18). 節氣諺語- 立冬. Retrieved December 30, 2022, from http://hn.cma.gov.cn/qxkp/ctyy/200809/t20080918_637006.html

[17] 張超 (2014). 第二十章---立冬---冬季開始的節氣 (p. 329). In 二十四節氣常識一本通. 龍圖騰文化有限公司

[18] KKNews. (2017, October 7). 關於立冬節氣的一些民間習俗和禁忌. 每日頭條. Retrieved December 30, 2022, from https://kknews.cc/zh-tw/news/gz8r2o9.html

[19] 吳明珠中醫師. (2019, November 7). 中醫吳明珠：立冬日，補腎日！補腎養陽一招勝參湯: 早安健康. https://www.edh.tw/. Retrieved December 30, 2022, from https://www.edh.tw/article/23009

[20] 黃慧玫. (2022, November 4). 「立冬」來了！中醫師教你正確進補，補冬不上火. Heho 健康. Retrieved December 30, 2022, from https://heho.com.tw/archives/248975

[21] 楊晴雯. (2019, November 8). 立冬進補大啖薑母鴨、四物雞！醫警告「8種人」吃了恐傷身: 三立新聞網. Retrieved December 30, 2022, from https://www.setn.com/news.aspx?newsid=631931

[22] KKNews. (2018, February 20). 閩南人千百年的民間習俗文化！. 每日頭條. Retrieved December 30, 2022, from https://kknews.cc/zh-tw/psychology/9333v55.html

[23] 張超 (2014). 第二十章---立冬---冬季開始的節氣 (pp. 330-331). In 二十四節氣常識一本通. 龍圖騰文化有限公司

[24]KKNews. (2016, November 7)（立冬在潮汕地區，立冬進補，你知道吃什麼嗎？ - 每日頭條. 每日頭條. Retrieved December 30, 2022, from https://kknews.cc/health/bxokgro.html

[25] 禮記, 月令, 86-95

[26] 殷登國 (1983). 立冬. In 中國的花神與節氣 (p. 224). 民生報業書

[27] 元氣網. (2019, November 8). 立冬進補要滋補也需顧健康 營養師推薦一菜一湯. Retrieved December 30, 2022, from https://health.udn.com/health/story/6037/4152322

[28] 張超 (2014). 第二十章---立冬---冬季開始的節氣 (p. 330). In 二十四節氣常識一本通. 龍圖騰文化有限公司

[29] 殷登國 (1983). 立冬. In 中國的花神與節氣 (p. 225). 民生報業書

[30] 國家教育研究院. (2021). 玄. 《重編國語辭典修訂本》2021. Retrieved December 30, 2022, from https://dict.revised.moe.edu.tw/dictView.jsp?ID=7387&la=0&powerMode=0

[31] Cheng, M. (1995). Local God of the Land. In The Origin of Chinese Deities (p. 148). Foreign Languages Press.

[32] Medhurst, W. H. (1847). In A Dissertation on the Theology of the Chinese: with a view to the elucidation of the most appropriate term for expressing the Diety in the Chinese language (p. 260). Mission Press.

[33] Cheng, M. (1995). Local God of the Land. In The Origin of Chinese Deities (p. 151). Foreign Languages Press.

[34] Baidu. (2022, July 22). 顓頊. 百度百科. Retrieved December 30, 2022, from https://baike.baidu.hk/item/顓頊/7226038

[35] 山海經, 海內經, 5

[36] Cheng, M. (1995). Local God of the Land. In The Origin of Chinese Deities (p. 150). Foreign Languages Press.

[37] Yang, D., An, D., & Turner, J. A. (2005). Handbook of Chinese Mythology (p. 245). ABC-CLIO.

[38] Yang, D., An, D., & Turner, J. A. (2005). Handbook of Chinese Mythology (p. 245). ABC-CLIO.

[39] Cheng, M. (1995). Local God of the Land. In The Origin of Chinese Deities (p. 148). Foreign Languages Press.

[40] Cheng, M. (1995). Local God of the Land. In The Origin of Chinese Deities (p. 155). Foreign Languages Press.

[41] 搜神記, 第十六卷, 1

[42] Baidu. (2020, September 26). 項冥. 百度百科. Retrieved December 30, 2022, from https://baike.baidu.hk/item/項冥/7875838

[43] 山海經, 卷八, 15

[44] Yang, D., An, D., & Turner, J. A. (2005). Handbook of Chinese Mythology (p. 245). ABC-CLIO.

Chapter 20: Light Snow

[1] 張超 (2014). 第二十一章---小雪---降水形式由雨變為雪的節氣 (pp. 340-341). In 二十四節氣常識一本通. 龍圖騰文化有限公司

[2] National Palace Museum. (n.d.). 明呂紀寒雪山雞圖　軸, K2A000455N000000000PAA, Open Government Data License, version 1.0

[3] 釋名, 釋天, 虹

[4] Eberhard, W. (2006). R, Rain. In A Dictionary of Chinese Symbols: Hidden Symbols in Chinese Life and Thought (p. 302). Routledge.

[5] 中國天氣網. (2009, November 20). 小雪節氣的諺語與民謠. 中國政府網. Retrieved January 2, 2023, from http://big5.www.gov.cn/gate/big5/www.gov.cn/fwxx/wy/2009-11/20/content_1469042.htm

[6] 張超 (2014). 第二十一章---小雪---降水形式由雨變為雪的節氣 (p. 341). In 二十四節氣常識一本通. 龍圖騰文化有限公司

[7] 青海省氣象局. (November 22, 2022). 小雪節氣習俗知多少？民間流行吃這些美味. Retrieved January 2, 2023, from http://qh.cma.gov.cn/qxfw/qxkp/202211/t20221122_5191893.html

[8] 張超 (2014). 第二十一章---小雪---降水形式由雨變為雪的節氣 (p. 341). In 二十四節氣常識一本通. 龍圖騰文化有限公司

[9] Hospital Authority/醫院管理局 (n.d.). 醫院管理局. 小雪. . Retrieved January 2, 2023, from https://cmk.ha.org.hk/zh-cht/information-index/news/solar_terms/小雪

[10] 張超 (2014). 第二十一章---小雪---降水形式由雨變為雪的節氣 (pp. 342-343). In 二十四節氣常識一本通.龍圖騰文化有限公司

[11] 呱呱資訊. (n.d.). 明天小雪，民間傳統要醃"寒菜 5 寶"，老傳統別忘，酸爽咸香過冬. Retrieved January 2, 2023, from https://web.archive.org/web/20211206115859/https://www.guaguazixun.com/complex/68035.html

[12] 殷登國 (1983). 小雪. In 中國的花神與節氣 (p. 230). 民生報業書

[13] 張超 (2014). 第二十一章---小雪---降水形式由雨變為雪的節氣 (pp. 342). In 二十四節氣常識一本通.龍圖騰文化有限公司

[14] 殷登國 (1983). 小雪. In 中國的花神與節氣 (p. 232). 民生報業書

[15] Baidu. (2022, February 26). 三白酒. 百度百科. Retrieved January 2, 2023, from https://baike.baidu.hk/item/三白酒 2/2969236

[16] Baidu. (n.d.). 地官大帝. 百度百科. Retrieved January 2, 2023, from https://baike.baidu.com/item/地官大帝

[17] 三立新聞網. (2019, October 16). 掌管天下禍福　賜福、赦罪、解厄的三官大帝:. 三立新聞網. Retrieved January 2, 2023, from https://www.setn.com/news.aspx?newsid=618757

[18] 搜狗百科. (n.d.). 水官. Retrieved January 2, 2023, from https://baike.sogou.com/v72294476.htm#!

[19] Baidu. (n.d.). 地官大帝. 百度百科. Retrieved January 2, 2023, from https://baike.baidu.com/item/地官大帝

[20]Baidu. (2022, October 16). 下元節. 百度百科. Retrieved January 4, 2023, from https://baike.baidu.hk/item/下元節/9163346

[21] 夢梁錄, 卷六, 立冬

[22] 岳雪 (2014). 座看青竹變瓊枝--小雪 (p. 135-136) . In 歲月之二十四節氣裡的眾神節慶與傳說. 貓咪予花兒

[23] 淮南子, 天文訓, 14

[24] 全唐詩, 卷五百三十九, 霜月

[25] 春秋左傳, 襄公, 襄公四年, 2

[26] 山海經, 中山經, 28

[27] 人人焦點. (2021, February 6). 霜降: 青女武羅傳說. Retrieved January 4, 2023, from https://ppfocus.com/0/cucb8d039.html

[28] Baidu. (n.d.). 青女. 快懂百科. Retrieved January 4, 2023, from https://www.baike.com/wikiid/7471259539041647098?view_id=5h44r1kutjyjuo

[29] Baidu. (n.d.). 青女. 搜狗百科.Retrieved January 4, 2023, from https://baike.sogou.com/m/fullLemma?lid=180912626

[30] 岳雪 (2014). 座看青竹變瓊枝--小雪 (p. 136-137) . In 歲月之二十四節氣裡的眾神節慶與傳說. 貓咪予花兒

Chapter 21: Heavy Snow

[1] KKNews. (2015, December 7). 雪花飄，雪花飄，老天下的殺人刀. 每日頭條. Retrieved January 4, 2023, from https://kknews.cc/zh-tw/culture/kxol3bb.html

[2] 馬麟（年代不詳）。[名畫集真 冊 宋馬麟暮雪寒禽]。《數位典藏與數位學習聯合目錄》。http://catalog.digitalarchives.tw/item/00/11/0e/11.html （2022/10/31 瀏覽）。

[3] 武林舊事, 卷三, 賞雪

[4] 國家教育研究院. (2021). 鶡旦. 教育部《重編國語辭典修訂本》2021. Retrieved January 4, 2023, from https://dict.revised.moe.edu.tw/dictView.jsp?ID=79866&la=0&powerMode=0

[5] KKNews. (2016, December 7). 大雪話三候——鶡旦不鳴, 虎始交, 荔挺生. 每日頭條. Retrieved January 4, 2023, from https://kknews.cc/zh-tw/news/kx25eop.html

[6] 類經圖翼, 卷一, 運氣, 十一月, 大雪

[7] 類經圖翼, 卷一, 運氣, 十一月, 大雪

[8] Legge, J. (1885). Khu Li or Summary of the Rules of Propriety, Book I, The Yueh Ling or Proceedings of Government in the Different Months, Sect. IV, Pt. II. In F. M. Muller (Ed.), The Sacred Books of the east (Vol. XXVII, p. 305). Oxford.

[9] KKNews. (2016, December 7). 大雪話三候——鶡旦不鳴, 虎始交, 荔挺生. 每日頭條. Retrieved January 4, 2023, from https://kknews.cc/zh-tw/news/kx25eop.html

[10] 顏氏家訓, 書證, 5

[11] 中國氣象報社. (1990, January 29). 冬季降雪有哪些好處. 中國氣象局官方網站. Retrieved January 4, 2023, from https://www.cma.gov.cn/kppd/kppdqxyr/kppdshqx/201212/t20121215_196999.html

[12] 中國天氣網. (2009, December 7). 大雪節氣的趣味諺語. 中國政府網. Retrieved January 4, 2023, from http://big5.www.gov.cn/gate/big5/www.gov.cn/fwxx/wy/2009-12/07/content_1481533.htm

[13] Sweetser, R. (2021, December 20). The beauty and benefits of snow in the garden. Almanac.com. Retrieved January 4, 2023, from https://www.almanac.com/beauty-and-benefits-snow-garden

[14] 張超 (2014). 第二十二章---大雪---千里冰封, 萬里飄雪的節氣 (pp. 348-349). In 二十四節氣常識一本通. 龍圖騰文化有限公司

[15] 張超 (2014). 第二十二章---大雪---千里冰封, 萬里飄雪的節氣 (pp. 348-349). In 二十四節氣常識一本通. 龍圖騰文化有限公司

[16] 行政院農業委員會. (n.d.). 大雪 (國曆 12 月 6 或 7 或 8 日). Retrieved January 4, 2023, from https://www.coa.gov.tw/ws.php?id=2507793

[17] 張超 (2014). 第二十二章---大雪---千里冰封, 萬里飄雪的節氣 (p. 351). In 二十四節氣常識一本通. 龍圖騰文化有限公司

[18] 自由時報 (2021, December 7). 健康網》「大雪」注意養心保暖 中醫分享 4 關鍵. 自由時報電子報. Retrieved January 4, 2023, from https://health.ltn.com.tw/article/breakingnews/3760243

[19] KKNews. (2018, July 24). 痘疹娘娘, 到底是誰？. 每日頭條. Retrieved January 4, 2023, from https://kknews.cc/zh-tw/history/3ob8pj3.html

[20] 行政院農業委員會. (n.d.). 大雪 (國曆 12 月 6 或 7 或 8 日). Retrieved January 4, 2023, from https://www.coa.gov.tw/ws.php?id=2507793

[21] 禮記, 月令, 96-103

[22] "綠色青浦微信公众号 (2022, December 14). 小雪醃菜, 大雪醃肉青浦菜場內咸貨飄香. 上海市青浦區人民政府. Retrieved January 4, 2023, from https://www.shqp.gov.cn/shqp/shms/20221214/1063528.html

[23] 張超 (2014). 第二十二章---大雪---千里冰封, 萬里飄雪的節氣 (pp. 349-350). In 二十四節氣常識一本通. 龍圖騰文化有限公司

[24] 建丹節. 快懂百科. (2022, November 15). Retrieved January 6, 2023, from https://www.baike.com/wikiid/1121256973182673742?view_id=3llipmh0m8q5ts

[25] 搜狗指南. (2019, August 15). 民族知識小科普, 鄂倫春族米特爾節是什麼樣的. Retrieved January 6, 2023, from https://zhinan.sogou.com/guide/d316514126934.htm?ch=zn.xqy.related.pc

[26] 張超 (2014). 第二十二章---大雪---千里冰封, 萬里飄雪的節氣 (p. 350). In 二十四節氣常識一本通. 龍圖騰文化有限公司

[27] 岳雪 (2014). 天地無私玉萬家--大雪 (p. 140). In 歲月之二十四節氣裡的眾神節慶與傳說. 貓咪予花兒

[28] Baidu. (2020, June 27). 侗年. 百度百科. Retrieved January 6, 2023, from https://baike.baidu.hk/item/侗年/1137786

[29] 岳雪 (2014). 天地無私玉萬家--大雪 (pp. 140-141). In 歲月之二十四節氣裡的眾神節慶與傳說. 貓咪予花兒

[30] 中文天下分支機構 朗朗中文. (n.d.). 彝族太陽會 - 傳統節日. 朗朗中文 yes! Chinese. Retrieved January 6, 2023, from http://www.langlangchinese.com/v2010/culture/traFestiv/festivalInfo.do?id=2&id1=105

[31] 岳雪 (2014). 天地無私玉萬家--大雪 (pp. 141-142). In 歲月之二十四節氣裡的眾神節慶與傳說. 貓咪予花兒

[32] 中文天下分支機構 朗朗中文. (n.d.). 彝族太陽會 - 傳統節日. 朗朗中文 yes! Chinese. Retrieved January 6, 2023, from http://www.langlangchinese.com/v2010/culture/traFestiv/festivalInfo.do?id=2&id1=105

[33] Baidu. (2022, September 19). 三女找太阳. 百度百科. Retrieved January 6, 2023, from https://baike.baidu.com/item/三女找太阳/6401059

[34] 岳雪 (2014). 天地無私玉萬家--大雪 (pp. 141-142). In 歲月之二十四節氣裡的眾神節慶與傳說. 貓咪予花兒

Chapter 22: Winter Solstice

[1] Almanac Publishing Co. (2023, January 3). The first day of Winter: Winter Solstice 2023 - when and what is it? Farmers' Almanac. Retrieved January 6, 2023, from https://www.farmersalmanac.com/winter-solstice-first-day-winter

[2] 杨贵名, 唐守顺 & 张永. (2012, December 19). 冬至. 中國氣象局政府門戶網站. Retrieved January 6, 2023, from https://www.cma.gov.cn/2011xzt/essjqzt/20121218/202111/t20211105_4210466.html

[3] 殷登國 (1983). 冬至. In 中國的花神與節氣 (p. 240). 民生報業書

[4] 壹讀. 楚塵文化. (2016, December 20). 冬至 | 蚯蚓結, 麋角解, 水泉動. Retrieved January 6, 2023, from https://read01.com/aMPRdD.html#.Y7eHtxVByF4

[5] 類經圖翼, 卷一, 運氣, 十一月, 冬至

[6] 國家教育研究院. (n.d.). 四不像 (大衛鹿). 樂詞網. Retrieved January 6, 2023, from https://terms.naer.edu.tw/detail/8d4d2f3f54f90e68b2d4667c36a0e35b/?seq=3

[7] 殷登國 (1983). 冬-至. In 中國的花神與節氣 (p. 240). 民生報業書

[8] 富平縣人民政府. (2012, August 3). 冬至禁忌 - 民俗風情. Retrieved January 6, 2023, from http://www.fuping.gov.cn/Home/Article/detail/id/16397.html

[9] 張超 (2014). 第二十三章---冬至---寒冬到來,日最短的節氣 (p. 361). In 二十四節氣常識一本通. 龍圖騰文化有限公司

[10] 張超 (2014). 第二十三章---冬至---寒冬到來,日最短的節氣 (p. 365). In 二十四節氣常識一本通. 龍圖騰文化有限公司

[11] Yahoo! (2019, December 21). 冬至養生首重養腎、補氣血! 吳明珠中醫師: 別錯過 5 大好食. Yahoo! News. Retrieved January 6, 2023, from https://tw.news.yahoo.com/冬至養生首重養腎-補氣血-吳明珠中醫師-別錯過 5 大好食-000000356.html

[12] 仁心堂中醫診所. (n.d.). 冬至: 二十四節氣. Retrieved January 6, 2023, from https://zenheart.com.tw/Solar_terms22.php

[13] 今天頭條. (2019, October 17). 冬至也有一些禁忌. Retrieved January 6, 2023, from https://twgreatdaily.com/dKOB2G0BMH2_cNUgrp3N.html

[14] 張超 (2014). 第二十三章---冬至---寒冬到來,日最短的節氣 (p. 364). In 二十四節氣常識一本通. 龍圖騰文化有限公司

[15] 張超 (2014). 第二十三章---冬至---寒冬到來,日最短的節氣 (p. 365). In 二十四節氣常識一本通. 龍圖騰文化有限公司

[16] 北京日報. (2012, December 12). 二十四節氣是公歷產物 最早制定出冬至. 中國報協網. Retrieved January 7, 2023, from http://culture.people.com.cn/BIG5/n/2012/1221/c172318-19973018.html

[17] 岳雪 (2014). 天地無私玉萬家--大雪 (p. 144). In 歲月之二十四節氣裡的眾神節慶與傳說. 貓咪予花兒

[18] 岳雪 (2014). 天地無私玉萬家--大雪 (p. 145). In 歲月之二十四節氣裡的眾神節慶與傳說. 貓咪予花兒

[19] 北京日報. (2012, December 12). 二十四節氣是公歷產物 最早制定出冬至. 中國報協網. Retrieved January 7, 2023, from http://culture.people.com.cn/BIG5/n/2012/1221/c172318-19973018.html

[20] 岳雪 (2014). 天地無私玉萬家--大雪 (p. 145). In 歲月之二十四節氣裡的眾神節慶與傳說. 貓咪予花兒

[21] 東森新聞. (2018, December 22). 真假?! 冬至 5 大「禁忌、習俗」曝光 想發大財這樣做. Yahoo! News. Retrieved January 7, 2023, from https://tw.news.yahoo.com/真假-冬至 5 大-禁忌-習俗-曝光-084000229.html

[22] 岳雪 (2014). 天地無私玉萬家--大雪 (p. 145). In 歲月之二十四節氣裡的眾神節慶與傳說. 貓咪予花兒

[23] 殷登國 (1983). 冬至. In 中國的花神與節氣 (p. 244). 民生報業書

[24] 契丹國志, 契丹國志卷之二十七, 28

[25] 殷登國 (1983). 冬至. In 中國的花神與節氣 (p. 245). 民生報業書

[26] 帝京景物略 -> 卷二, 79

[27] 清稗類鈔, 時令類, 冬至郊天

[28] 燕京歲時記, 冬至

[29] 殷登國 (1983). 冬至. In 中國的花神與節氣 (p. 245-246). 民生報業書

[30] 張超 (2014), 第二十三章---冬至---寒冬到來,日最短的節氣 (p. 362). In 二十四節氣常識一本通. 龍圖騰文化有限公司

[31] KKNews. (2017, December 21). 湯圓餃子臘肉九層糕，冬至你家吃什麼？最後的省份深得我心. 每日頭條. Retrieved January 7, 2023, from https://kknews.cc/zh-tw/history/3en6qao.html

[32] 台視新聞. (n.d.). 吃的順序也講究!「陰陽兩全」紅、白湯圓一起吃. Retrieved January 7, 2023, from https://news.ttv.com.tw/news/11012210037100N/amp

[33] Buy123.com.tw. (2020, December 21). 冬至習俗知多少？生活市集部落格｜生活好事集. Retrieved January 7, 2023, from https://blog.buy123.com.tw/life/archives/6963/

[34] 黃富祺, 陳耿閎. (2021, December 12). 吃的順序也講究!「陰陽兩全」紅、白湯圓一起吃. Yahoo! News. Retrieved January 7, 2023, from https://tw.news.yahoo.com/吃的順序也講究-陰陽兩全-紅-白湯圓一起吃-131614363.html

[35] 張超 (2014). 第二十三章---冬至---寒冬到來,日最短的節氣 (p. 363). In 二十四節氣常識一本通.龍圖騰文化有限公司

[36] Baidu. (2021, November 23). 祛寒嬌耳湯. 百度百科. Retrieved January 7, 2023, from https://baike.baidu.hk/item/祛寒嬌耳湯/8771784

[37] 人人焦點. (2020, November 27). 爲什麼冬至不吃餃子會「凍掉耳朵」 Retrieved January 6, 2023, from https://ppfocus.com/0/cu5575460.html

[38] 大紀元 (2018, December 23). 為什麼冬至不吃餃子會「凍掉耳朵」 Retrieved January 6, 2023, from https://www.epochtimes.com/b5/18/12/22/n10925820.htm

[39] 張超 (2014). 第二十三章---冬至---寒冬到來,日最短的節氣 (p. 363-364). In 二十四節氣常識一本通.龍圖騰文化有限公司

[40] 新商報. (2013, December 23)._中国各地冬至饮食风俗：从饺子到麻糍.搜狐. Retrieved January 7, 2023, from http://news.sohu.com/20131223/n392209996.shtml

[41] 張超 (2014). 第二十三章---冬至---寒冬到來,日最短的節氣 (p. 364). In 二十四節氣常識一本通.龍圖騰文化有限公司

[42] 範文資料庫. (n.d.). 冬至吃湯圓的傳說故事. Retrieved January 7, 2023, from https://www.mingyanjiaju.org/fanwen/dongzhi/4122675.html

[43] 岳雪 (2014). 天地無私玉萬家--大雪 (p. 145-146). In 歲月之二十四節氣裡的眾神節慶與傳說. 貓咪予花兒

[44] 岳雪 (2014). 天地無私玉萬家--大雪 (p. 146-147). In 歲月之二十四節氣裡的眾神節慶與傳說. 貓咪予花兒

[45] Baidu. (2021, December 20). 竈神. 百度百科. Retrieved January 7, 2023, from https://baike.baidu.hk/item/竈神/16860

[46] 岳雪 (2014). 天地無私玉萬家--大雪 (p. 146-147). In 歲月之二十四節氣裡的眾神節慶與傳說. 貓咪予花兒

[47] KKNews. (2016, July 18). 竈神是個什麼神仙，屬害不. 每日頭條. Retrieved January 7, 2023, from https://kknews.cc/zh-tw/culture/a4ml6j.html

Chapter 23: Little Cold

[1] 張超 (2014). 第二十四章---小寒---天氣開始寒冷,且愈來愈冷的節氣 (p. 374). In 二十四節氣常識一本通.龍圖騰文化有限公司

[2] 岳雪 (2014). 侵凌雪色還萱草--小寒 (p. 149). In 歲月之二十四節氣裡的眾神節慶與傳說. 貓咪予花兒

3 殷登國 (1983). 小寒. In 中國的花神與節氣 (p. 249). 民生報業書

4 類經圖翼, 卷一, 運氣, 小寒

5 Eberhard, W. (2006). M, Magpie. In A Dictionary of Chinese Symbols: Hidden Symbols in Chinese Life and Thought (p. 211-212). Routledge.

6 Liu, S. T. T. (1983). Yu Controls the Flood. In Dragons, Gods & Spirits from Chinese Mythology (p. 33). Schocken Books.

7 類經圖翼, 卷一, 運氣, 小寒

8 禮記正義, 卷十四月令第六, 16

9 張超 (2014). 第二十四章---小寒---天氣開始寒冷, 且愈來愈冷的節氣 (p. 375). In 二十四節氣常識一本通. 龍圖騰文化有限公司

10 中國政府網. (2010, January 4). 小寒節氣農業生產活動. Retrieved January 8, 2023, from http://big5.www.gov.cn/gate/big5/www.gov.cn/fwxx/wy/2010-01/04/content_1502561.htm

11 Sohu. (2023, January 4). 俗語"小寒大寒不下雪，小暑大暑田乾裂", 今年小寒下雪嗎？. 搜狐. Retrieved January 8, 2023, from https://www.sohu.com/a/624908979_227742

12 自由時報. (2023, January 5). 健康網》小寒怎麼補？ 中醫：防寒補腎為主. 自由時報電子報. Retrieved January 8, 2023, from https://health.ltn.com.tw/article/breakingnews/4175959

13 張超 (2014). 第二十四章---小寒---天氣開始寒冷, 且愈來愈冷的節氣 (pp. 378-379). In 二十四節氣常識一本通. 龍圖騰文化有限公司

14 Baidu. (2022, October 26). 數九. 百度百科. Retrieved January 8, 2023, from https://baike.baidu.hk/item/數九/113816

15 海上. (2005). 冬九九. In 中國人的歲時文化 (pp. 161－162). 岳麓書社.

16 殷登國 (1983). 小寒. In 中國的花神與節氣 (p. 252-255). 民生報業書

17 國家研究院. (2021). 消寒會. 重編國語辭典修訂本. Retrieved January 8, 2023, from https://dict.revised.moe.edu.tw/dictView.jsp?ID=106369&la=0&powerMode=0

18 殷登國 (1983). 小寒. In 中國的花神與節氣 (p. 255). 民生報業書

19 容乃加. (2021, June 3). 節氣花信風臘梅香濃勝小寒. 大紀元. Retrieved January 8, 2023, from https://www.epochtimes.com/b5/17/1/11/n8690971.htm

20 岳雪 (2014). 侵凌雪色還萱草--小寒 (pp. 150-151). In 歲月之二十四節氣裡的眾神節慶與傳說. 貓咪予花兒

21 林念慈. (2022, January 12). 【心靈補給站】卻將香蠟吐成花. 青年日報. Retrieved January 8, 2023, from https://www.ydn.com.tw/news/newsInsidePage?chapterID=1474967&type=undefined

22 教育部. (2020) 黃花閨女. 成語檢視 - 教育部《成語典》 [進階版]. (2020). Retrieved January 8, 2023, from https://dict.idioms.moe.edu.tw/idiomView.jsp?ID=12106&webMd=2&la=0

23 Baidu. (2022, December 31). 梅花妝. 百度百科. Retrieved January 8, 2023, from https://baike.baidu.hk/item/梅花妝/10758732

24 岳雪 (2014). 侵凌雪色還萱草--小寒 (pp. 150-151). In 歲月之二十四節氣裡的眾神節慶與傳說. 貓咪予花兒

25 康熙字典, 肉部, 十五, 臘

465

[26] KKNews. (2018, January 25). 臘月並不一定是陰曆十二月！「臘」和「蠟」「獵」是什麼關係？每日頭條.Retrieved January 8, 2023, from https://kknews.cc/zh-tw/culture/z2vz6ql.html

[27] 張超 (2014). 第二十四章---小寒---天氣開始寒冷,且愈來愈冷的節氣 (p. 377). In 二十四節氣常識一本通. 龍圖騰文化有限公司

[28] 岳雪 (2014). 侵凌雪色還萱草--小寒 (p. 150). In 歲月之二十四節氣裡的眾神節慶與傳說. 貓咪予花兒

[29] 荊楚歲時記, 第一部寶顏堂秘笈本. 89

[30] 荊楚歲時記, 第一部寶顏堂秘笈本. 89

[31] Laba Festival. 中國網. (n.d.). Retrieved January 8, 2023, from http://www.china.org.cn/living_in_china/spring-festival-2009/2009-01/07/content_17070617.htm

[32] Buddha Dharma Education Asssociation Inc. (n.d.). Buddhist studies: Primary level unit 3. under the Bodhi Tree. BuddhaNet. Retrieved January 8, 2023, from http://www.buddhanet.net/e-learning/buddhism/pbs2_unit03.htm

[33] Laba Festival. Chinaculture.org. (n.d.). Retrieved January 8, 2023, from http://en.chinaculture.org/library/2008-01/28/content_28554.htm

[34] 張超 (2014). 第二十四章---小寒---天氣開始寒冷,且愈來愈冷的節氣 (p. 377). In 二十四節氣常識一本通. 龍圖騰文化有限公司

[35] 武林舊事, 卷三, 歲晚節物

[36] 燕京歲時記, 臘八粥

[37] 張超 (2014). 第二十四章---小寒---天氣開始寒冷,且愈來愈冷的節氣 (p. 378). In 二十四節氣常識一本通. 龍圖騰文化有限公司

[38] 岳雪 (2014). 侵凌雪色還萱草--小寒 (p. 151). In 歲月之二十四節氣裡的眾神節慶與傳說. 貓咪予花兒

[39] Baidu. (n.d.). 臘八節. 快懂百科. Retrieved January 8, 2023, from https://www.baike.com/wikiid/3164955743230204680

[40] 百科知識中文網. (n.d.). 神農大帝[中國上古部落首領]. Retrieved January 8, 2023, from https://www.jendow.com.tw/wiki/神農大帝

[41] 白虎通德論, 卷一, 號

[42] 白虎通義, 卷一

[43] 岳雪 (2014). 侵凌雪色還萱草--小寒 (pp. 152-153). In 歲月之二十四節氣裡的眾神節慶與傳說. 貓咪予花兒

[44] KKNews. (2019, March 22). 快速讀懂史記—《三皇本紀》. 每日頭條. Retrieved January 8, 2023, from https://kknews.cc/zh-tw/culture/j9yp4py.html

[45] 史記, 表, 三代世表

[46] 史記, 本紀, 周本紀

[47] 岳雪 (2014). 侵凌雪色還萱草--小寒 (pp. 153-154). In 歲月之二十四節氣裡的眾神節慶與傳說. 貓咪予花兒

[48] 中文百科. (n.d.). 后稷. Retrieved January 8, 2023, from http://m.zwbk.org/lemma/114320

Chapter 24: Great Cold

[1] 類經圖翼, 卷一, 運氣, 大寒

[2] KKNews. (2017, January 18). 古人筆下的「難」，竟有這麼多含義！. 每日頭條. Retrieved January 8, 2023, from https://kknews.cc/zh-tw/culture/e92kzbq.html

[3] 類經圖翼, 卷一, 運氣, 大寒

[4] 類經圖翼, 卷一, 運氣, 大寒

[5] 馬祖日報. (2023, Jan 8). 年味漸濃　節氣進入「小寒」，保暖工作要做好. Retrieved January 9, 2023, from https://www.matsu-news.gov.tw/news/article/206713

[6] 行政院農業委員會. (n.d.). 大寒（國曆 1 月 19 或 20 或 21 日）. Retrieved January 9, 2023, from https://www.coa.gov.tw/ws.php?id=2507772

[7] 張超 (2014). 第二十五章---大寒---一年最冷的節氣 (pp. 386-387). In 二十四節氣常識一本通. 龍圖騰文化有限公司

[8] KKNews. (2021, January 19). 俗語說"大寒三白定豐年"，大寒三白到底是什麼？答案來了. 每日頭條. Retrieved January 9, 2023, from https://kknews.cc/zh-tw/n/lg9ej6g.html

[9] 行政院農業委員會農業試驗所. (n.d.). 大寒之介紹及民俗諺語 - 大寒 Great Cold. 農作物災害預警平台. Retrieved January 9, 2023, from https://disaster.tari.gov.tw/ARI/solarterm/web_new/Solar_term_24.html

[10] Baidu. (2020, November 30). 屢雪二麥可望喜而作歌. 百度百科. Retrieved January 9, 2023, from https://baike.baidu.com/item/屢雪二麦可望喜而作歌/14124968

[11] 呂氏春秋, 季春紀, 盡數

[12] 黃帝內經, 素問, 四氣調神大論, 2

[13] 張超 (2014). 第二十五章---大寒---一年最冷的節氣 (pp. 391-392). In 二十四節氣常識一本通. 龍圖騰文化有限公司

[14] 李清風. (2021, January 27). 大寒是吃種子最佳時節！腎虛者別錯過最後機會. 紐約中醫 - 坤德中醫養生軒 | New York Four Seasons Acupuncture PC. Retrieved January 9, 2023, from https://ny-fsa.com/health/大寒是吃種子最佳時節！腎虛者別錯過最後機會/

[15] 食力 foodNEXT. (2022, January 19). 消寒糕是年糕、八寶飯又有哪 8 位寶？大寒這麼吃 為春天暖身. Retrieved January 9, 2023, from https://www.foodnext.net/life/culture/paper/5357669294

[16] 陳益源. (2009, November 9). 尾牙. 文化部國家文化資料庫. Retrieved January 9, 2023, from https://nrch.culture.tw/twpedia.aspx?id=2046

[17] National Center for Traditional Art (Ed.). (2008, June 19). Wei Ya Festival. National Center for Traditional Arts. Retrieved March 26, 2022, from https://web.archive.org/web/20150227001631/http://ttf.ncfta.gov.tw/en-us/Season/Content.aspx?Para=13

[18] 陳益源. (2009, November 9). 尾牙. 文化部國家文化資料庫. Retrieved January 9, 2023, from https://nrch.culture.tw/twpedia.aspx?id=2046

[19] 張超 (2014). 第二十五章---大寒---一年最冷的節氣 (p. 389). In 二十四節氣常識一本通. 龍圖騰文化有限公司

[20] 拾遺記, 拾遺記卷一, 唐堯

[21] 岳雪 (2014). 重裘藏手取微溫--大寒 (p. 157). In 歲月之二十四節氣裡的眾神節慶與傳說. 貓咪予花兒

[22] KKNews. (2021, January 20). 今日大寒遇臘八，這些習俗了解一下. 日頭條. Retrieved January 9, 2023, from https://kknews.cc/zh-hk/culture/v5nrqky.html

[23] 張超 (2014). 第二十五章---大寒---一年最冷的節氣 (p. 388). In 二十四節氣常識一本通. 龍圖騰文化有限公司

[24] 殷登國 (1983). 大寒. In 中國的花神與節氣 (p. 257). 民生報業書

[25] 張超 (2014). 第二十五章---大寒---一年最冷的節氣 (pp. 387-388). In 二十四節氣常識一本通. 龍圖騰文化有限公司

[26] 張超 (2014). 第二十五章---大寒---一年最冷的節氣 (p. 391). In 二十四節氣常識一本通. 龍圖騰文化有限公司

[27] 張超 (2014). 第二十五章---大寒---一年最冷的節氣 (p. 390). In 二十四節氣常識一本通. 龍圖騰文化有限公司

[28] 國史館臺灣文獻館. (2016, December 28). 典藏品介紹：司命真君（灶神）. Retrieved January 9, 2023, from https://www.th.gov.tw/epaper/site/page/153/2256

[29] 論語, 八佾, 13

[30] 禮記, 祭法, 6

[31] 淮南子, 氾論訓, 24

[32] 呂氏春秋, 卷第四, 4

[33] 禮記, 禮器, 17

[34] 蕭放. (2009, January 21). 灶神：形象‧傳說‧祭祀. 中國民俗學網. Retrieved January 9, 2023, from https://www.chinafolklore.org/web/index.php?NewsID=3802

[35] Cheng, M. (1995). The Truth About the Kitchen God. In The Origin of Chinese Deities (p. 29). Foreign Languages Press.

[36] 蕭放. (2009, January 21). 灶神：形象‧傳說‧祭祀. 中國民俗學網. Retrieved January 9, 2023, from https://www.chinafolklore.org/web/index.php?NewsID=3802

[37] 張超 (2014). 第二十五章---大寒---一年最冷的節氣 (p. 390). In 二十四節氣常識一本通. 龍圖騰文化有限公司

[38] 岳雪 (2014). 重裘藏手取微溫--大寒 (p. 157). In 歲月之二十四節氣裡的眾神節慶與傳說. 貓咪予花兒

[39] 張超 (2014). 第二十五章---大寒---一年最冷的節氣 (p. 389-390). In 二十四節氣常識一本通. 龍圖騰文化有限公司

[40] KKNews. (2018, February 8). 上天言好事，下界保平安. 每日頭條. Retrieved January 9, 2023, from https://kknews.cc/zh-tw/psychology/kmxnqpp.html

[41] 岳雪 (2014). 重裘藏手取微溫--大寒 (p. 157). In 歲月之二十四節氣裡的眾神節慶與傳說. 貓咪予花兒

[42] 岳雪 (2014). 重裘藏手取微溫--大寒 (pp. 158-159). In 歲月之二十四節氣裡的眾神節慶與傳說. 貓咪予花兒

[43] 笑看浮華蒼生 PLUS. (2021, December 18). 民間故事：關於灶王爺的傳說. 網易首頁. Retrieved January 9, 2023, from https://www.163.com/dy/article/GRGND3E205524H5G.html

[44] Welch, P. B.. (2014, December 29). "the Chinese kitchen god". Academia.edu. Retrieved January 9, 2023, from https://www.academia.edu/9947714/_The_Chinese_Kitchen_God

Lessons of the Solar Terms

[1] Greer, J. M. (2005). How Civilizations Fall: A Theory of Catabolic Collapse. Ecosophia. Retrieved January 13, 2023, from https://www.ecosophia.net/civilizations-fall-theory-catabolic-collapse/

[2] Dry spells spelled trouble in ancient China. (2008, November). NSF - National Science Foundation. Retrieved April 18, 2024, from https://www.nsf.gov/news/news_summ.jsp?cntn_id=112585

[3] Meadows, D. H. (1982). The Limits to Growth: A Report for the Club of Rome's Project on the Predicament of Mankind. Universe Books.

[4] Greer, J. M. (2008). The Long Descent: A User's Guide to the End of the Industrial Age. (p. 22). New Society Publishers.

[5] Duncan, H. D. (1836). Preface. In Sacred Philosophy of the Seasons: The Perfections of God in the Phenomena of the Year (Vol. Winter, p. iv). William Oliphant and Son.

[6] 荀子, 天論, 3

[7] 荀子, 天論

[8] 荀子, 禮論, 13

[9] Watson, B. (1963). A Discussion of Rites. In Hsün Tzu: Basic Writings (p. 94). Columbia University Press.

[10] Driver, T. F. (1991). Chapter 2: Ritualizing: The Animals Do It and So Do We. In The Magic of Ritual: Our Need for Liberating Rites that Transform Our Lives & Our Communities (p. 12). HarperSanFrancisco.

[11] Rossano, M. J. (2013). Mortal Rituals: What the Story of the Andes Survivors Tells us about Human Evolution. Columbia University Press.

[12] Kuile, C. T. (2020). Section 5.37. In Power of Ritual: Turning Everyday Activities into Soulful Practices. HarperOne.

[13] Bell, C. (1997). Part II Rites: The Spectrum of Ritual Activites, Calendrical Rites 1997. In Ritual: Perspectives and Dimensions (p. 103). Oxford University Press.

[14] Leopold, Aldo. (1949). Conservation Esthetic. In Sand County Almanac: Sketches of Here and There (p. 173). Oxford University Press.

[15] O'Driscoll, D., (2021). Sacred Actions: Living the Wheel of the Year Through Earth-Centered Sustainable Practices. Red Feather Mind, Body, Spirit.

[16] Damh the Bard (Host). (2021, June 18). DruidCast - A Druid Podcast (171) [Audio podcast episode]. In Druidcast. The Order of Bards, Ovates, & Druids. https://druidcast.libsyn.com/druidcast-a-druid-podcast-episode-171

[17] Louv, R. (2011). The Nature Principle: Human Restoration and the End of Nature-Deficit Disorder. Algonquin Books of Chapel Hill.

[18] Bratman, G. N., Hamilton, J. P., Hahn, K. S., Daily, G. C., & Gross, J. J. (2015). Nature experience reduces rumination and subgenual prefrontal cortex activation. Proceedings of the National Academy of Sciences, 112(28), 8567–8572. https://doi.org/10.1073/pnas.1510459112

Appendicies

[1] To, C. (2003, August 30). 二十四節気をさらに三分割し、物語性を付け加えたもの. Wikipedia.org; ウイキメデイア財団. https://ja.wikipedia.org/wiki/%E4%B8%83%E5%8D%81%E4%BA%8C%E5%80%99#cite_ref-1

Index

The index is organized in the following categories: Animal Symbolism, Books & Documents, Deities, Dynasties, Ethnicities, Festivals, Food, Historical Figures, Music, Mythological Figures, Paintings, Philosophy, Places, Plants & Herbs, and Poets

ABOUT THE AUTHOR

James W. Murphy spent his childhood near the tide pools and harbors of Los Angeles, his adolescence in the forests and valleys of Oregon, and most of his adulthood in the cozy alleys of Taipei and dusty boulevards of Beijing. He's been a teacher, a translator, a technology industry analyst, and an editorial director of research books and journals with a major scientific publisher. He graduated Magna cum Laude from the University of Oregon with a B.A. and departmental honors in Chinese Language and Literature, and holds a Masters of Business Administration from the University of Southern California. He currently lives in the misty hills of southern Taipei with his wife, Monica.